Readings on
Microsoft® Windows® and WOSA

Microsoft Press

PUBLISHED BY
Microsoft Press
A Division of Microsoft Corporation
One Microsoft Way
Redmond, Washington 98052-6399

Copyright © 1995 by Microsoft Corporation

Library of Congress Cataloging-in-Publication Data pending.

Printed and bound in the United States of America.

1 2 3 4 5 6 7 8 9 MLML 0 9 8 7 6 5

Distributed to the book trade in Canada by Macmillan of Canada, a division of Canada Publishing Corporation.

A CIP catalogue record for this book is available from the British Library.

Microsoft Press books are available through booksellers and distributors worldwide. For further information about international editions, contact your local Microsoft Corporation office. Or contact Microsoft Press International directly at fax (206) 936-7329.

Intel is a registered trademark of Intel Corporation. IBM is a registered trademark of International Business Machines Corporation. Lotus is a registered trademark of Lotus Development Corporation. CodeView, Microsoft, MS, MS-DOS, QuickC, and XENIX are registered trademarks of Microsoft Corporation. Tandy is a registered trademark of Tandy Corporation.

Contents

INTRODUCTION

Welcome to the self-study guide for the Microsoft® Windows® Operating Systems and Services Architecture examinations I and II. This guide contains almost all of the information you need to know in order to pass those two examinations. Its contents have been carefully selected from the best resources at Microsoft—product documentation, resource kits, current Microsoft Press books, the *Microsoft Systems Journal*, and the *Microsoft Developer Network News*, to name a few. Much of this material has been written by people well-known for their expertise in Microsoft products.

Each article has been selected for its timeliness and comprehensive coverage. In all cases we have tried to include articles that combine architectural constructs and implementation details. After reading this book, you will see how Microsoft operating systems and services work together. You will also understand how to exploit the advantages of the architecture through object-oriented technology.

How to Use This Guide

This guide was designed with exam preparation in mind. We assume that readers come to this book with varying skill levels and backgrounds, but that all of you have two things in common. First, almost all of you have extensive experience with Windows, both as users and developers of Windows applications. Second, you all share the same goal: to become a Microsoft Certified Solution Developer.

This book is designed to provide quick access to the technical data you need without you having to scan through introductory chapters or background data. You can start at any point in the book that suits your background or knowledge level.

How This Guide is Organized

This guide is divided into 14 sections, beginning with the big picture and moving into the details that make up that big picture. Topics move from a discussion of operating systems, to some of the details of the user interface, to OLE, to Open Database Connectivity, and finally to other services available in Windows. In outline form, this book covers:

- Introduction to the Windows operating systems
- User interface design
- Windows operating system architecture
- OLE
- Open Database Connectivity (ODBC)
- Messaging Application Program Interface (MAPI)
- Windows Telephony API (TAPI)
- License Service API (LSAPI)

- Windows SNA API and Windows Sockets
- Windows Open Services Architecture (WOSA) Extensions for Financial Services and for Real-Time Market Data

Chapter Overviews

Chapter 1 reviews the features and benefits of Microsoft Windows 95, Microsoft Windows NT™ Workstation, and Microsoft Windows NT Server.

Chapter 2 introduces the user interface enhancements in Windows 95 and Windows NT.

Chapters 3 and 4 review the key architectural features of Windows. Chapter 3 reviews the details of event-driven programming, preemptive and non-preemptive multitasking, threads and processes as well as the benefits of symmetric versus asymmetric multiprocessing. Chapter 4 describes how memory is managed in Windows, details methods for sharing data and memory, describes techniques for error and exception handling, and reviews of how objects are used in Windows.

Chapters 5 through 8 cover all the details of OLE. Chapter 5 reviews the features and benefits of OLE for users and programmers, including coverage of component software and the registration database. Chapter 6 reviews the primary mechanisms for building OLE documents—object linking and embedding. Chapter 7 explores the details of OLE automation with a discussion of controller applications, object-server applications, and the contents of type libraries. Chapter 8 rounds out the discussion of OLE with articles on the differences between Visual Basic custom controls and OLE controls, and a review of OLE controls functionality.

Chapters 9 and 10 contain articles covering fundamentals and advanced topics of ODBC. Chapter 9 reviews key concepts in ODBC—drivers, the Driver Manager, data sources, cursors, bookmarks, and the cursor library. Chapter 10 reviews ODBC API and SQL conformance levels, single- and multiple-tier drivers, and the performance implications of prepared versus direct execution.

Chapters 11 and 12 review fundamental and advanced MAPI. Articles in Chapter 11 review the MAPI services available to developers and discuss the roles of the server messaging system, address books, message store, message spooler, transport provider, and profile provider. Chapter 12 topics include the differences among Simple MAPI, Common Messaging Calls, and extended MAPI; unified log-ons; and the store-and-forward functionality.

Chapters 13 and 14 contain articles on the rest of the Windows Open Services Architecture (WOSA)—Telephony API (TAPI), License services API (LSAPI), Windows SNA API, Windows Sockets API, and extensions to the Windows Open Services Architecture for financial services and for real-time markets.

Where to Get More Information

This topical approach also acknowledges that you will have further questions about topics and will want to know more about specific topics and issues. To help you find more data, we have provided full bibliographic citations to the origin of the selected reading. You can refer to the original source for further details, or you can access the same data, in context, on the January 1995 release of the Microsoft Developer Network Development Library.

Disclaimer

Reviewing all the articles in this book will give you a comprehensive view of the architecture for both Windows operating systems and their related services. However, merely reading about these products is not enough. You need hands-on experience to become a Microsoft Certified Solution Developer.

C H A P T E R   1

Features and Benefits of Windows NT Server, Windows NT Workstation, and Windows 95

Topic

Compare and Contrast Windows NT Server, Windows NT Workstation and Windows 95.

Content

Why Have Two Desktop Operating Systems?[1]

It is important to understand that there are two distinct design points for Microsoft's family of operating systems—one centered on the mainstream system (in 1994), and another centered on the leading-edge system. It is not currently possible to have one operating system implementation that fully exploits the broad range of hardware available at any point in time. For mainstream systems (currently represented by products such as subnotebook and entry-level desktop machines), the Windows "Windows 95" design goal is to deliver responsive performance for a broad range of applications while conserving the amount of system resources used. On the leading-edge system (for example, a dual-processor workstation or multi-processor RISC server), Windows NT was designed to fully exploit the capabilities of the hardware and provide the most advanced services for the most demanding applications.

As a result of the requirements placed on the new enterprise solutions, all major operating system developers have recognized the necessity of moving to a micro-kernel architecture for their leading-edge operating systems. This includes

---

[1] This material is also available on the Microsoft Developer Network Development Library under Technical Articles, Windows (32-bit) Articles, Development Environment Articles. Copyright 1994. Used with permission. All rights reserved.

Microsoft, IBM®, Sun® (and most UNIX® vendors), and Novell®. Only Microsoft made this commitment over 5 years ago and began shipping Windows NT to developers in July 1992 with general availability in July 1993. This architecture allows vendors to enhance systems to respond to the rapidly changing requirements of the business solutions being developed, while maintaining flexibility to exploit new hardware and peripherals.

Both Windows "Windows 95" and Windows NT Workstation provide a common base of functionality that is required by all customers, including ease of use, power, connectivity, and manageability. Microsoft is committed to and will deliver parity in basic functionality (such as the user interface)to each platform as quickly as possible. The further differences between the two platforms are a result of their different design goals. Windows "Windows 95" is focused on making computing easier for anyone using a wide range of personal and business applications on desktop and portable computers. To protect their current investment, these users require the highest level of compatibility with today's applications and device drivers.

Windows NT Workstation is focused on providing the most powerful desktop operating system for solving complex business needs. For developers; technical, engineering, and financial users; and business operations application users, it delivers the highest level of performance to support the most demanding business applications. It also provides the highest levels of reliability, protection, and security for those applications that you can't afford to have fail while exploiting the latest hardware innovations such as RISC processors and multi-processor configurations. This focus on solving business needs is also reflected in the emphasis on maintenance and regular system updates.

Over time, as mainstream machines become more powerful, technologies implemented first on the leading-edge Windows operating system product will migrate to the mainstream product. Sometimes technical innovations will appear first on the mainstream product, due to timing of releases or because some features are focused on ease of use for general endusers. The guiding principle for product planning is for the leading-edge product to provide a superset of the functionality in the mainstream product.

For application developers Microsoft has just one Windows programming platform, defined by Win32®—the 32-bit Windows application programming interface and OLE. By following a few simple guidelines, developers can write a single application that runs across the Windows operating system product family. If they wish, developers can target specific operating system products because the functionality they provide is important to their particular application, but that is not a requirement.

Usage Scenarios

The decision about which platform to deploy should be based on what tasks people are trying to accomplish. The two platforms provide a very complementary set of capabilities that can accommodate a broad range of use scenarios. Consider the following examples.

Most office environments require people to perform a variety of general tasks such as word processing, database queries, or spreadsheet analysis, using productivity applications like the Microsoft Office suite. They may also be using applications that are specific to their particular business. Most companies have an installed base of personal computers, peripheral devices and applications and want to maximize their investment in that computing infrastructure. For them, Windows "Windows 95" is the best choice.

Many companies have employees who spend a high fraction of their working hours away from their office, whether they're at a customer site, in a hotel, or out in the field, and rely on personal computers to help them perform their jobs. These mobile computer users have similar requirements for application and device compatibility but also need an operating system which places lower demands on the hardware, including amount of memory, battery power, and use of disk space. For these customers, Windows "Windows 95" is also the best choice.

Engineers, scientific researchers, statisticians, and other technical users often need the capability to use processing-intensive applications for data analysis and large design activities. Windows NT Workstation, with its support for symmetric multiprocessing (SMP) and its portability to different high-performance platforms like those based on Pentium™, Alpha, or MIPS® CPUs, can provide the performance of a leading-edge workstation or minicomputer at a fraction of the cost. Moreover, Windows NT Workstation still runs personal productivity applications on the same machine.

In industries that need to protect sensitive data or application files, such as banking and defense, Windows NT Workstation is the right choice for the secure desktop. The NTFS file system, combined with appropriate security procedures, helps prevent unauthorized access to systems and data. Moreover, the security model in Windows NT Workstation is designed to be compliant with C2-level certification. With these features, a Windows NT system can even be shared by multiple users and still maintain security for all files on the system.

Many users require very high levels of availability and performance and cannot afford downtime, regardless of the application that they are running. Very often these types of systems are being "right-sized" from mini and mainframe systems. For example, many manufacturing systems today use 16-bit applications to manage their company's production line. Windows NT Workstation supports running these Win16 applications in separate address space (often referred to as separate virtual machines). For users, this means that even if one of these applications fails, all of the other applications continue to run. Windows NT Workstation also provides complete protection for 32-bit applications and the ability to automatically recover (reboot if necessary) if the system goes down.

Similarities

Benefit/Feature	Windows 95	Windows NT Workstation
Ease of Use		
Auto-detection of hardware during installation and configuration		
Next-generation Windows User Interface (re-designed usability)	Yes	Yes
Plug and Play technology that lets you add hardware without reconfiguring your computer	Yes	Next Release
Auto-detection of hardware during installation and configuration	Yes	Next Release
Next-generation Windows User Interface (redesigned usability).		
Power		
32-bit, pre-emptive multitasking design provides responsiveness between applications that you need to work more efficiently. No more waiting.	Yes	Yes
Win32 API for application development, OLE for linking data across apps	Yes	Yes
Connectivity		
LAN connectivity and peer-to-peer networking, with all popular protocols including TCP/IP, IPX/SPX, and NetBeui	Yes	Yes
Open networking architecture provides choice of clients, transports and drivers and extensibility for support of third-party networking applications	Yes	Yes
Remote access services built into give you remote access to your workstation	Yes	Yes
Manageability		
Open system management architecture provides infrastructure for third party system management solutions	Yes	Yes
Supports existing and emerging system management standards (SNMP, DMI)	Yes	Yes
Desktop user profiles (can be modified by anyone on the system) and monitoring tools	Yes	Yes

Benefit/Feature	Windows 95	Windows NT Workstation
Application Support	Yes	Yes
Runs Win16 applications	Yes	Yes
Runs Win32 and OLE applications	Yes	Yes
System and peripheral support	Yes	Yes
Fully exploits 386DX, 486, and Pentium platforms	Yes	Yes
Protection and Security		
Complete crash-protection between Win16 applications by running Win16 applications in separate address spaces	No	Yes
Offers C-2 certifiable user-level security over access to a standalone workstation. Files, folders, and applications on both desktop and server can be made "invisible" to specific users	No	Yes
Secure user profiles to control access to desktop, applications, and system configuration files.	No	Yes
Data protection through transacted file system	No	Yes
Has automatic recovery from a system failure	No	Yes
Application Support		
Runs MS-DOS® applications	Complete support	Most
Supports multiple file systems beyond MS-DOS's FAT file system—HPFS, NTFS	No	Yes
Uses Open GL graphics library to enable advanced 3-D graphics.	Next release	Yes
Runs IBM Presentation Manager(through 1.3) & POSIX 1003.2 applications	No	Yes
System and Peripheral Support		
Runs MS-DOS device drivers	Yes	No
Runs Win16 device drivers	Yes	No
Supports disk compression	Yes	Yes
Runs on PowerPC™, MIPS, and DEC™ Alpha-based RISC systems	No	Yes
Supports multiprocessor configurations for scaleable performance without changing operating system or applications	No	Yes

Benefit/Feature	Windows 95	Windows NT Workstation
Support and Service		
Quick Fix Engineering teams to solve problems in critical sites (issues which block business systems usage or deployment)	No	Yes
Monthly maintenance releases posted to electronic services (e.g., CompuServe®, Internet)	No	Yes
Quarterly Service Pack Releases: Distribution vehicle (CD-ROM and floppy) for maintenance releases	No	Yes

Content

Writing Great 32-Bit Applications for Windows[2]

Creating Applications That Exploit Windows 95 and Also Run on Windows NT and Windows 3.1 (with Win32s)

In 1994, 5 key characteristics will identify a "great" Microsoft Windows-based application. At a high level, these are:

1. Use of the Win32 Application Programming Interface (API).
2. Inclusion of OLE functionality.
3. Adherence to the new User Interface Design Guide for Windows 95 (this book will be available in a future release of the Microsoft Development Library).
4. Plug and Play event awareness.
5. Shell support.

In this article, you will find a detailed table that provides specific features for you to add into your product. The table can be used to determine what happens on Microsoft Windows NT and Windows version 3.1 (with Win32s) when you take advantage of Win32 features. The table also shows the enhancements that the next version of Microsoft Windows (called Windows 95) brings to the Windows platform.

The table is divided into three sections, organized by the platforms you wish to target and the time frame within which you plan to release your product. All of the functionality listed in this table will be available in the next major release of Windows NT (code-named Cairo).

---

[2] This material is also available on the Microsoft Developer Network Development Library under Backgrounders and White Papers, Operating Systems. Copyright 1994. Used with permission. All rights reserved.

Section 1 describes the features you can and should use in your Win32-based applications that you ship today, before Windows 95 ships.

Section 2 describes additional features you can take advantage of in the applications that you ship with Windows 95. Your application will also run on Windows NT and Windows 3.1 (with Win32s). A few features initially available in Windows 95 will not be available in Windows NT until Cairo.

Section 3 lists some of the features and functionality provided by Windows NT today that will not be available in Windows 95.

Italic text indicates features which the platform offers rather than API functionality.

Note Windows 95 is a code name for a future release of the Windows operating system. Windows NT Windows NT™ 3.5 and Windows NT Cairo are code names for future releases of the Windows NT operating system. It is our intention to provide the most accurate and up-to-date information in this document. This information is subject to change without notice and does not represent a commitment on the part of Microsoft Corporation.

Section 1: What You Can Use and Ship in Your Application Today

Recommended Features and Platform Functionality	Windows 95	Windows NT	Windows 3.1 with Win32s	Comments
OLE 32-bit functionality	Yes	Yes*	Yes*	*32-bit OLE will ship with next version of Windows NT (code-named Windows NT™ 3.5) and Win32s 1.2 in Q2 1994.
Visual editing	Yes	Yes	Yes	Consistent way to create compound documents
OLE drag and drop	Yes	Yes	Yes	Streamlines existing clipboard operation, enables drag and drop with Windows 95 shell
Automation	Yes	Yes	Yes	Enables cross-application programmability
Populate OLE compound files	Yes	Yes	Yes	Populate the summary stream in compound files
Associate documents with application	Yes	Yes	Yes	Use OLE class ID to associate documents with applications
Register icons	Yes	Yes	Yes	Register small and large icons for Windows 95 integration
Register verbs	Yes	Yes	Yes	Register for drag-and-drop open or other verbs for context-sensitive menus

Recommended Features and Platform Functionality	Windows 95	Windows NT	Windows 3.1 with Win32s	Comments
Support Print-to	Yes	Yes	Yes	Print-to in registry for drag-and-drop printing
Windows Sockets/NetBIOS	Yes	Yes	Yes	Defines network programming interface
Memory-mapped files	Yes	Yes	Yes	Copy a file's contents into virtual memory. Good for sharing data.
Common dialogs	Yes	Yes	Yes	Common dialogs have 3-D look in Windows 95
Find	Yes	Yes	Yes	
Replace	Yes	Yes	Yes	
Print	Yes	Yes	Yes	
Print Setup	Yes	Yes	Yes	
Color	Yes	Yes	Yes	
Structured exception handling	Yes	Yes	Yes	Use structured exception handling for more robust applications.
Configuration/Setup	Yes	Yes	Yes	Support express install; minimal install; uninstall. Use registry, not WIN.INI.
National Language Support (NLS)	Yes	Yes	No	
32-bit flat memory model	Yes	Yes	Yes	
Separate address space	Yes	Yes	No	
Asynchronous input model	Yes	Yes	No	
Preemptive multitasking	Yes	Yes	No	Win32s runs on Windows 3.1 and provides non-preemptive multitasking.
User and GDI system resources	Expanded	Unlimited	Win3.1 limits	Windows 95 has 32-bit heaps for User and GDI, expanded list box limits.
3-D Look	Yes	2-D	2-D	Applications running on Windows NT and Win32s can code own 3-D look.
Property sheets exposed by shell	Yes	Won't appear	Won't appear	Windows 95 shell will display property sheets for objects
Context menu on button 2	Yes	Yes	Yes	User interface guideline
Long filenames (LFN)	Yes	Yes	Won't appear	Win32 API handles this; make sure buffers are large enough.

Recommended Features and Platform Functionality	Windows 95	Windows NT	Windows 3.1 with Win32s	Comments
Universal naming convention (UNC)	Yes	Yes	Yes*	For example, \\server\share. *Win32s supports this on Windows for Workgroups.
Focus on documents	Yes	Yes	Yes	User interface guideline; write document-centric applications.
Simple MAPI/CMC	Yes	Yes	Universal thunk	Can code own Simple MAPI/CMC support on Win32s with the universal thunk.
Network API	Yes	Yes	Universal thunk	Can code own WNet API support on Win32s using the universal thunk.
Named pipes	Yes (client)	Yes	No*(Stubs)	Windows 95 will support client side named pipes; Windows NT has both server and client side support. * Can code own client side named pipes using Win32s universal thunk.
Remote procedure calls (RPC)	Yes	Yes	No*	Client and server OSF DCE compliant RPC. *Can code own client side RPC using Win32s universal thunk.
Threads	Yes	Yes	No (Stubs)	Threads optimize the use of hardware and application performance.
Paths/beziers	Yes	Yes	No (Stubs)	In Windows 95, only MoveTo, LineTo, PolyBezierTo are recorded in a path.
Win32 COMM API	Yes	Yes	No (Stubs)	Win32 interface to communications functions.
Console support	Yes*	Yes	No (Stubs)	Win32 interface that provides consoles that manage I/O for character-mode applications. *Windows 95 supports all console API except the code page APIs.
Print APIs	Yes (No forms)	Yes	No (Stubs)	Win32 API available for print spooler.
Multimedia API	Yes	Yes	Windows 3.1 level	Win32s supports most Windows 3.1 multimedia API.
Remote access services	Yes	Yes	No	
Enhanced metafiles	Yes	Yes	No	Device-independent resolution and pictures

Section 2: Additional Win32 Features You Can Use and Ship When Windows 95 Ships

Recommended Features and Platform Functionality	Windows 95	Windows NT™ 3.5 (Windows NT 3.5)	Windows 3.1 with Win32s 1.2	Comments
Common controls	Yes	Yes	Yes	Available for Win32s and Windows NT via redistributable DLLs when Windows 95 ships.
Tabs	Yes	Yes	Yes	Used for property sheets
Drag list boxes	Yes	Yes	Yes	Allows you to drag list box items around in the list box.
Toolbar	Yes	Yes	Yes	
Status bar	Yes	Yes	Yes	
Column heading	Yes	Yes	Yes	Sizable, sortable button headers for columns
Spin buttons	Yes	Yes	Yes	Up/down arrow buttons for increasing/decreasing contents.
Slider	Yes	Yes	Yes	Movable slider control
Scrolling button indicator	Yes	Yes	Yes	For scrolling toolbar buttons.
Rich text object	Yes	Yes	Yes	Rich text control expands limits, allows different font sizes and types.
Progress indicator	Yes	Yes	Yes	Gas gauge.
Tree View	Yes	Yes	Yes	Used by Explorer mode (+/-) to expand/contract directories.
List View	Yes	Yes	Yes	Small and large icon views, used in Windows 95 shell
New common dialogs	Yes	Yes	Yes	Available for Win32s and Windows NT via redistributable DLLs when Windows 95 ships.
Open	Yes	Yes	Yes	New common dialogs support tree and details views. Also supports long filenames and UNC names (as Windows NT dialogs do today).
Save as	Yes	Yes	Yes	
Plug and Play event awareness	Yes	Won't get events	Won't get events	Monitor events to accommodate resources coming and going.
Viewers	Yes	Not used	Not used	Provide viewers for your data types
Windows 95 style help	Yes	Won't appear	Won't appear	New help features.
Context menu help	Yes	Won't appear	Won't appear	

Recommended Features and Platform Functionality	Windows 95	Windows NT™ 3.5 (Windows NT 3.5)	Windows 3.1 with Win32s 1.2	Comments
New authorable buttons	Yes	Write own code	Write own code	
MAPI 1.0	Yes	Yes	No	MAPI 1.0 will be available for Windows NT when Windows 95 ships
More multimedia (ACM/VCR/VfW1.1)	Yes	Yes	No	Multimedia, Compression, Video for Windows
Telephony API 1.0/ Unimodem API	Yes	No*	No voice/data and port contention*	Will be available for Windows NT within 6 months of Windows 95 release.
File merge/reconciliation	Yes	No (Cairo)	No	Add file merge to your applications to enhance mobile computing.
Image color matching API	Yes	No (Cairo)	No	Use for consistent color across devices such as displays, printers, scanners, etc.
Pen	Yes	No (Cairo)	No	The Windows 95 shell will be pen aware applications should also be pen aware.
Windows 95 help cue cards	Yes	No (Cairo)	No	Pop-up context help for objects on screen.
Container name space in Explorer	Yes	No (Cairo)	No	Container in directory hierarchy that contains specific non-ordered objects (for example, mail, control panel, printers).

Section 3: Win32 Features You Can Use and Ship in Windows NT Today

Recommended Features and Platform Functionality	Windows 95	Windows NT	Windows 3.1 with Win32s	Comments
Unicode Win32 API	No (Stubs)	Yes	No (Stubs)	Global character encoding.
Event logging	No (Stubs)	Yes	No (Stubs)	Centralized way for applications to record important events and to view logs of those events.
Service control manager API	No (Stubs)	Yes	No (Stubs)	Manage installed services, logon and security information, etc.
World transforms	Scaling Only	Yes	No (Stubs)	Windows 95 provides scaling, but not shearing or rotation.
Asynchronous file I/O	No	Yes	No (Stubs)	Windows 95 will map these to standard file I/O APIs.
Security API	No (Stubs)	Yes	No (Stubs)	Application interface to security control functions.
32-bit coordinate system	No	Yes	No	
Security (C2 certifiable)	No	Yes	No	
Portable to non-Intel® platforms	No	Yes	No	MIPS, Alpha, PowerPC
Scaleable to symmetric multiprocessors	No	Yes	No	

CHAPTER 2

Windows User Interface Design

Topic

Apply interface design guidelines when incorporating dialog boxes in an application.[1]

Content

Dialog Boxes

A *dialog box* provides an exchange of information or dialog between the user and your software. Use a dialog box to gather additional information from the user—information that may be required to execute a particular command or task. As a result, dialog boxes typically contain only controls.

Because dialog boxes generally appear after choosing a particular menu item or command button, set the title text to be the name of the associated command for the window; for example, for a Print command on the File menu, the title text should be Print, not Print... or File Print.

Layout

Orient controls in dialog boxes in the way people read information. In countries where roman alphabets are used, this means left to right, top to bottom. Locate the primary field with which the user interacts as close to the upper-left corner as possible. The same is true for orienting controls within groups in the dialog box.

---

[1] Complete text for all of the material in this chapter can be found in the *Windows 95 User Interface Design Guide (October 1994 Version)*. All references here to chapter titles and numbers are to that publication. Copyright 1994. Used with permission.

Lay out the major command buttons either stacked along the upper-right border of the dialog box or lined up across the bottom of the dialog box. The most important button — typically the default command — should be the first button in the set. If you use the OK and Cancel buttons, group them together. If you include a Help button, make it the last button in the set. You can use other arrangements if there is a compelling reason, such as a natural mapping relationship. For example, it makes sense to place buttons labeled North, South, East, and West in a compass-like layout.

For more information about layout and spacing, see Chapter 13, "Visual Design."

Shortcuts in Dialog Boxes

Optionally, you can use double-clicking on a single selection control, such as an option button or single selection list, to set or select the option and execute the default button of the dialog box.

Common Dialog Box Interfaces

The system provides prebuilt interfaces for many common operations. Use these interfaces where appropriate. They can save you time while providing a high degree of consistency.

Note These interfaces have been revised from the ones provided in previous releases.

Open Dialog Box

The Open dialog box (shown in Figure 2.1) allows the user to browse the file system, including direct browsing of the network, and includes controls to open a specified file.

Figure 2.1   The Open dialog box.

The dialog box automatically handles the display of long filenames and file links, direct manipulation transfers (for example, drag and drop), and access to an icon's pop-up menus.

If you open a file link, the resulting window is that of the object to which the link refers. In other words, the effect is the same as if the user directly opened the original file. Therefore, display the name of the original file, not the name of the file link. Similarly, when saving the file, the changes are saved back to the original file.

Save Dialog Box

The Save dialog box (shown in Figure 2.2) is designed to save a file using a particular name, location, and format. Display this dialog box when the user chooses the Save command and a filename has not been supplied or confirmed by the user. You use this same dialog box for a Save As command by changing the title bar text to Save As.

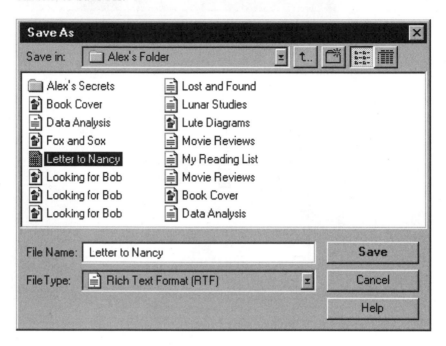

Figure 2.2   The Save dialog box.

This dialog box is similar to the Open dialog box except that the File Type field lists the possible formats for the target file. The File Type field replaces Files of Type—the type filter field. The Open dialog box also provides navigational controls that allow the user to browse the file system.

Find and Replace Dialog Boxes

The Find and Replace dialog boxes provide controls that search for a text string specified by the user and optionally replace it with a second text string specified by the user. These dialog boxes are shown in Figure 2.3.

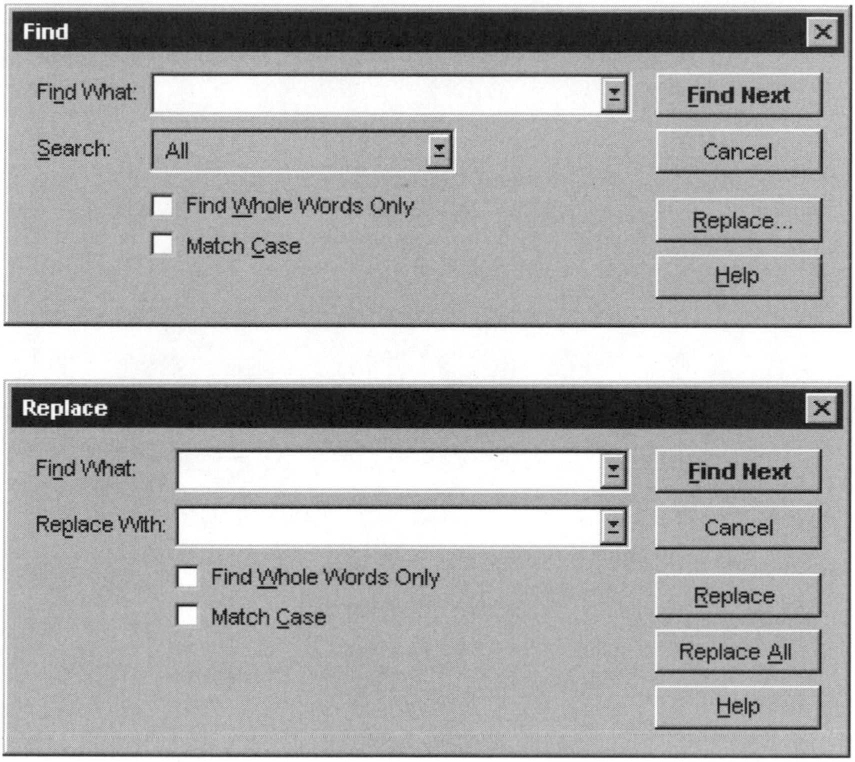

Figure 2.3   The Find and Replace dialog boxes.

Print Dialog Box

The Print dialog box (shown in Figure 2.4) allows the user to select what to print, the number of copies to print, and the collation sequence for printing. It also allows the user to choose a printer and provides a command button that provides shortcut access to that printer's properties.

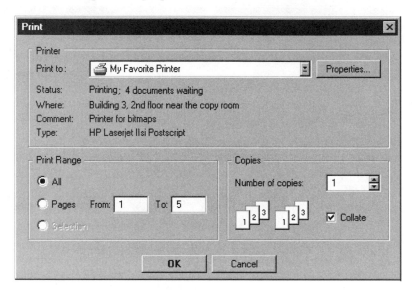

Figure 2.4   The Print dialog box.

Print Setup Dialog Box

The Print Setup dialog box displays the list of available printers and provides controls for selecting a printer as well as setting paper orientation, size, and source, and other printer properties. Figure 2.5 shows this dialog box.

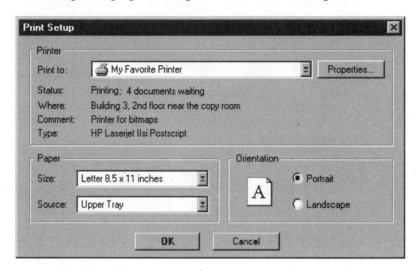

Figure 2.5   The Print Setup dialog box.

Note   This dialog box provides compatibility with applications designed for Windows 3.1. Users access these properties through the property sheet of the appropriate printer, rather than from an application. Therefore, this dialog box is not recommended for applications following the guidelines in this book.

Page Setup Dialog Box

The Page Setup dialog box provides controls for specifying properties about the page elements and layout. You can use it either as a dialog box, as shown in Figure 2.6, or as a property page in a property sheet window.

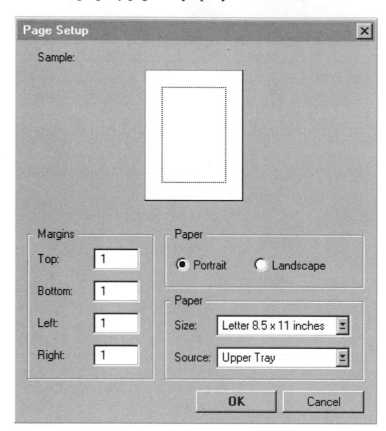

Figure 2.6   Page Setup interface used as a dialog box.

In this context, page orientation refers to the orientation of the page and not to the printer, which may also have these properties. Generally, the page's properties override those set by the printer, but only for the printing of that page (or document).

Font Dialog Box

You can use the Font dialog box to display the font properties of a selection of text. Figure 2.7 shows the Font dialog box.

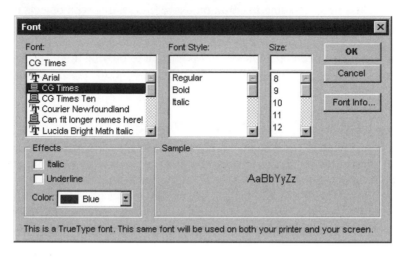

Figure 2.7   The Font dialog box.

Color Dialog Box

The Color dialog box provides controls for selecting the color property of a particular object..

Topic

Apply interface design guidelines when creating and displaying windows.

Content

Windows

Windows are a fundamental part of the Microsoft Windows 95 interface; consistency in window design is particularly important because it enables users to easily transfer their learning skills and focus on their tasks rather than learning new conventions. This chapter describes the common types of windows, as well as recommendations regarding general window appearance and operations.

Common Types of Windows

Windows provide the fundamental way a user views and interacts with data. Because windows provide access to different types of information, they can be classified according to common usage. Interacting with objects typically involves a *primary window* in which most primary viewing and editing activity takes place. In addition, multiple or supplemental *secondary windows* may be included to allow users to specify parameters or options, or to provide more specific details about the objects or actions included in the primary window. For more information about secondary windows, see Chapter 8, "Secondary Windows."

Primary Window Components

A typical primary window consists of a frame (or border) that defines its extent, and a title bar that identifies what is being viewed in the window. If the viewable content of the window exceeds the current size of the window, scroll bars are used. The window can also include other components like menu bars, toolbars, and status bars. For more information about these components, see Chapter 7, "Menus, Controls, and Toolbars" and the section "Scrolling Windows" later in this chapter.

Figure 2.8 shows the common components of a primary window.

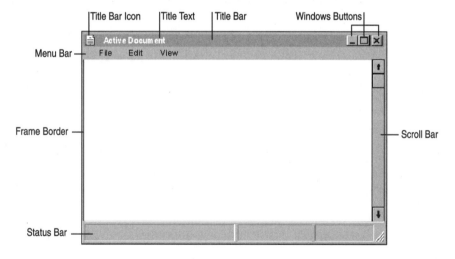

Figure 2.8   Typical primary window.

The Window Frame

Every window has a boundary that defines its shape. A sizable window has a distinct border area that provides a control point for resizing the window using direct manipulation with the mouse. If the window cannot be resized, the border coincides with the edge of the window.

The Title Bar

At the top edge of the window, inside its border, is the *title bar*, which extends across the width of the window. The title bar identifies what the window is viewing, such as a document, spreadsheet, or application. It also serves as a control point for moving the window and gives access to commands that apply to the windows and its associated view. For example, clicking on the title bar with mouse button 2 displays the pop-up menu for the window. For more information about pop-up menus, see Chapter 7, "Menus, Controls, and Toolbars."

The Title Bar Icon

The small version of the icon of the object appears in the upper-left corner of the title bar. The title bar icon provides access (through a pop-up menu) to the operations for that object. For more information about icon design, see Chapter 13, "Visual Design."

If the window represents a "tool" (that is, it does not create, load, and save separate data files), then it uses the small version of the application's icon in its title bar, as shown in Figure 2.9.

Figure 2.9 **"Tool" Object title bar.**

If the application loads and saves documents or data files, then place the icon that represents its document or data type in the title bar, as shown in Figure 2.10.

Figure 2.10 **Document title bar.**

If the application uses the multiple document interface (MDI), then use the application's icon in the parent window's title bar, and use an icon that reflects the application data file type in the child window's title bar, as shown in Figure 2.11.

Figure 2.11 **MDI application and document title bars.**

However, if a user maximizes the child window and hides the title bar, and its title information merges with the parent, then the icon from the child window's title bar is displayed in the menu bar of the parent window. If multiple child windows are open within the MDI parent window, then the icon from the active (topmost) child window's icon is displayed, as shown in Figure 2.12.

Figure 2.12   MDI parent window title bar with a maximized child window.

For more information about MDI, see Chapter 9, "Window Management."

Title Text

The title text is a label that identifies the name of the object being viewed through the window. It should also correspond to the current icon in the title bar; that is, if a document or data file is being viewed, the name of the document appears. The name and icon always represent the outermost container (the object that was opened), even if the user selects an embedded object or navigates down the internal hierarchy of an object.

If the object currently has no user-supplied name, then include a placeholder in the title, such as (untitled), or the short type name, for example Document *n*, Sheet *n*, Chart *n*, where *n* is a number (as in Document 1). Ideally, use this name as the proposed default filename for the object. For more information about short type names, see Chapter 10, "Interacting with the Shell."

When the title is a filename, do not include the full storage (path) name because it is usually not meaningful for most users and may be confusing. Display the text exactly as it is stored in the file system (using both uppercase and lowercase, as appropriate).

The title text can also optionally include the name of the application in use. The name of the document appears first, followed by a hyphen, then the application name, as shown in Figure 2.13. If the application is a tool that has no associated data files, then only the application's name is displayed.

Note The order of the document (or data) filename and application name is a change from Windows 3.1.

Figure 2.13   Title text order: Document Name — Application Name.

If the name of the displayed object in the window changes—for example, when the user edits the name in the object's property sheet—then update the title text to reflect that change. Always maintain the association between the object and its open window.

Avoid having your application drawing directly into the title area or adding other controls. Such added items may make it difficult for the user to read the name in the title, particularly because the size of the title bar varies with the size of the window. In addition, the system uses this area for displaying special controls. For example, in some international versions of Windows 95, the title area provides information or controls associated with the input of certain languages.

Window Buttons

Command buttons appear on the right side of the title bar. They are associated with the commands of the window and act as shortcuts to specific commands. Clicking a title bar button with mouse button 1 invokes the command associated with the button. Clicking a title bar command button with button 2 displays the pop-up menu for the window. For the pen, use tapping and barrel-tapping support (or the menu gesture), respectively. For more information about command buttons in the pop-up menu of a window, see Chapter 7, "Menus, Controls, and Toolbars."

Typically, the following buttons appear in a primary window (provided that the window supports the respective functions).

Command button	Operation
☒	Closes the window.
▬	Minimizes the window
▢	Maximizes the window

Basic Window Operations

There are a number of basic operations for a window. These operations include:

- Activation and deactivation
- Opening and closing
- Moving and sizing
- Scrolling and splitting

The following sections describe these operations.

Activating and Deactivating Windows

While the system supports the display of multiple windows, the user generally works within a single window at a time. This window is called the *active window*. The active window is typically at the top of the window order. It is also visually distinguished by its title bar, which is displayed in the active window title color. All other windows are *inactive* with respect to the user's input; that is, while other windows may have ongoing processes, only the active window receives the user's input. The title bar of an inactive window displays the system inactive window color of the system.

The user activates a window by switching to it; this inactivates any other windows. With the mouse or pen, the user simply clicks or taps on any part of the window, including its interior, to activate it. If the window is minimized, the user clicks (taps) on the button representing the window in the task bar. From the keyboard, the ALT+TAB key combination switches between primary windows. (SHIFT+ALT+TAB also switches between windows, but in reverse order.) The reactivation of a window should not affect any preexisting selection; the selection and focus are restored to the previously active state.

When reactivating a primary window, the window and all its secondary windows come to the top of the window order and maintain their relative positions. If the user activates a secondary window, its primary window comes to the top of the window order along with the primary window's other secondary windows.

When a window becomes inactive, the highlighting of any selection within it is hidden to prevent confusion as to which window is receiving keyboard input. A direct manipulation transfer (OLE drag and drop) is an exception. Here, the selection may be shown if the pointer is over the window during the drag. However, the window is not activated unless you release the mouse button (lift the pen tip) in that window. For more information about selection appearance, see Chapter 13, "Visual Design."

Opening and Closing Windows

When you open a primary window, an entry for it is included on the task bar. If the window has been previously opened, restore the window to its size and position when it was last closed. If possible and appropriate, reinstate the other related view information, such as selection state, scroll position, and type of view. When opening a primary window for the first time, open it to a reasonable default size and position as best defined by the object (or application). Opening the primary window activates that window and places it at the top of the window order. If the user attempts, within the same desktop, to open a primary window that is already open, follow these recommendations:

File type	Action when open is reexecuted
Document or data file.	Activates the window of the object and displays it at the top of the Z-order.
Application file.	Presents a message box indicating the open instance(s) of that application and offers the user the option to switch to a particular open instance or create a new instance. Either choice activates that window and brings it to the top of the Z-order.
Document file that is already open in a multiple document interface (MDI) application.	Activates the window of the object; the MDI parent window comes to the top of the Z-order, and the document appears at the top of its Z-order within the MDI parent window.
Document file that is not already open, but its associated multiple document interface (MDI) application is already running (open).	Opens a new instance of the MDI application (at the top of the Z-order) loaded with the document window.

For more information about MDI, see Chapter 9, "Window Management."

When opening a window, consider the size and orientation of the current screen upon which it will be opened. For example, with some systems the screen may be *landscape* oriented (long dimension along the bottom) and with others it may be *portrait* oriented. The screen resolution may vary as well. In such cases, adjust the size and position of the window from its stored state so that it will appear appropriately on the screen.

A primary window is closed by clicking (for pen, tapping) the Close button in the title bar or choosing the Close command from the window's pop-up menu. In addition, double-clicking (with the pen, double-tapping) on the title bar icon is a shortcut for closing the window and, if appropriate, exiting the application.

After attempting to close a window, if there are any pending transactions, a message is displayed asking the user whether to save any changes, discard any changes, or cancel the close operation. If there are no pending transactions, the window is closed.

Closing the primary window of an object closes any of its dependent secondary windows as well. Whether closing the primary window also ends all the application processes depends on the design of the software. For example, closing the window of a document typically terminates any active code or processes remaining for inputting or formatting text. However, closing the window of a printer has no effect on the jobs in the printer's queue. In both cases, closing the window removes its entry from the task bar.

Moving Windows

A window can be moved either by dragging its title bar (with the mouse or pen) or by using the Move command on the window's pop-up menu. With most systems, an outline representation moves with the pointer during the operation, and the window is redisplayed in the new location after the move is completed. With the keyboard interface, after the user chooses the Move command, arrow keys move the outline and pressing the ENTER key ends the operation — the window is redrawn at the new location. After moving a window, allow the user to reposition it; the window cannot be positioned entirely off the screen, however. For more information about the pop-up menu of a window, see Chapter 7, "Menus, Controls, and Toolbars."

A window need not be active before being moved. The action of moving the window implicitly activates it. Moving a window may result in clipping or revealing information shown in the window, and activation may affect the view state of the window (for example, the current selection can be displayed). In general, however, moving a window does not affect the content being viewed in that window.

Resizing Windows

The size of primary windows can be changed by dragging the sizing border with the mouse or pen at the edge of a window or by using the Size command on the window's menu. With most systems, an outline representation of the window moves with the pointer. After the size operation is completed, the window assumes its new size. With the keyboard, the user can choose the Size command, use the arrow keys, and press the ENTER key to size a window. For more information about the pop-up menu or a window, see Chapter 7, "Menus, Controls, and Toolbars."

A window need not be active before it is sized. The action of sizing the window implicitly makes it active, and it remains active after the sizing operation. Generally, after making a window smaller through resizing, information is clipped. However, there may be situations where the information may need to be displayed differently (rewrapping or scaling) so that it fits within the window. Consider and test such variations carefully because they will not be consistent with the resizing behavior of most windows.

While the size of a primary window varies, based on the user's preference, you can define a window's maximum and minimum size. When defining these sizes, consider the reasonable usage within the window, and the size and orientation of the screen.

Maximizing Windows

Maximizing a window increases the size of the window to its largest, optimum size. While the system default setting for the maximum size is as large as the screen, you can to define the size to be less (or in some cases more) than the screen dimensions. In addition, because screen resolution and orientation vary, your software should not assume a fixed screen size but should adapt to the shape and size defined by the system.

Although the user may be able to resize a window directly to its maximum size, the Maximize command simplifies this operation. The command is available on a window's pop-up menu, or by using the Maximize command button in the title bar of a window.

Minimizing Windows

The user can choose the Minimize command on the window's pop-up menu or the title bar Minimize command button to minimize a window. Minimizing a window means to reduce it to its smallest size. For primary windows, minimizing removes the window from the screen but leaves its entry in the task bar. For information about managing MDI document windows, see Chapter 9, "Window Management."

Note The former Windows 3.1 representation of a minimized window as an icon is no longer appropriate. To reflect some status information about the open but minimized window, use the entry on the task bar. For more information about status notification, see Chapter 10, "Interacting with the Shell."

Restoring Windows

After maximizing or minimizing a window, you can use the Restore command to restore it to its previous size. For maximized windows, this command can be made available from the window's pop-up menu or by using the button which replaces the Maximize button in the title bar of the window. Restore a minimized window to its former size by clicking (for pen, tapping) on the button in the task bar that represents the window or using ALT+TAB (or SHIFT+ALT+TAB). Choosing the Restore command from the pop-up menu or its button in the task bar also restores the window.

Scrolling Windows

When the content viewed in a window exceeds the size of that window, the window should support scrolling. Scrolling enables the user to view portions of the object that are not currently visible in a window. Scrolling is commonly supported with a scroll bar. A *scroll bar* is a rectangular control consisting of *scroll arrows*, a *scroll box*, and the *scroll bar shaft*, as shown in Figure 2.14.

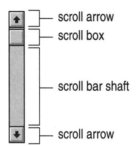

— scroll arrow
— scroll box

— scroll bar shaft

— scroll arrow

Figure 2.14   Scroll bar and its components.

A window can have a vertical scroll bar, a horizontal scroll bar, or both. The scroll bar aligns with the edge of the window for the respective orientation it supports. If the content is never scrollable in a particular direction, do not include a scroll bar for that direction.

Common practice is to display scroll bars if, under any circumstances, the view requires scrolling. If the window becomes inactive or resized, so that its content does not require scrolling, it is recommended that the display of the scroll bars be maintained. While removing the scroll bars potentially allows the display of more information as well as feedback about the state of the window, it also requires the user to explicitly activate the window to scroll. In addition, consistent display of scroll bars provides a more stable environment.

Scroll Arrows

Scroll arrow buttons appear at each end of a scroll bar, pointing in opposite directions away from the center of scroll bar. The scroll arrows point in the direction that the window "moves" over the data. When the user clicks (with pen, taps) a scroll arrow, the data in the window appears to move in the opposite direction to reveal information in the direction of the arrow in increments of the appropriate amount. The granularity of the increment depends on the nature of the content and context. For textual content, this is typically one line of text for vertical scrolling; for spreadsheets, it is one row. In most cases, it is best to maintain the scrolling granularity throughout a window. When a window cannot be scrolled any farther in a particular direction, disable the associated scroll arrow.

The scroll arrow buttons have a special auto-repeat behavior when pressed and held. This action causes the window to continue scrolling in the associated direction as long as the pointer remains over the arrow button. While pressing the mouse button (for pen, while the tip remains down), if the pointer is moved off the arrow button, the auto-repeat behavior stops until the pointer is moved back over to the arrow button.

Scroll Box

The scroll box (sometimes referred to as the elevator, thumb, or slider) moves along the scroll bar to indicate how far the visible portion is from the top (for vertical scroll bars), or from the left edge (for horizontal scroll bars). For example, if the current view is in the middle of a document, the scroll box in the vertical scroll bar is in the middle of the scroll bar.

The size of the scroll box can also vary. This reflects the relationship of what is visible in the window and the entire content of the document, as shown in Figure 2.15.

Note The proportional scroll box was not supported in earlier releases of Windows.

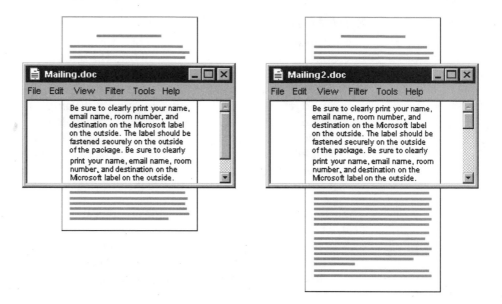

Figure 2.15   Proportional relationship between scroll box and view content.

For example, if the content of the entire document is visible in a window, the scroll box extends the entire length of the scroll bar, and the scroll arrows are disabled. Avoid making the minimum size of the scroll box smaller than the width of a sizing handle, such as a window's sizing border.

The user can also scroll a window by dragging the scroll box. Your software should update the view continuously as the scroll box is moved. However, if you cannot support scrolling at a reasonable speed, scroll the information at the end of the drag operation.

If the user starts dragging the scroll box and then moves outside the scroll bar, the scroll box returns to its original position. The distance the user can move the pointer off the scroll bar before the scroll box snaps back to its original position is proportional to the width of the scroll bar. If dragging ends at this point, you cancel the scroll action (no scrolling occurs). However, if the user moves the pointer back within this scroll sensitivity area, it returns to tracking with the pointer movement. This behavior allows a user to scroll without having to remain within the scroll bar, as well as to cancel selectively the initiation of a drag-scroll operation.

Dragging the scroll box to the end of the scroll bar implies scrolling to the end of that dimension. However, this may not always mean that the area cannot be scrolled farther. If the structure that contains the data is larger than the data itself, then you may interpret dragging the scroll box to the end of its scroll bar as moving to the end of the data rather than to the end of the structure. For example, the structure of a typical spreadsheet exceeds the data in that spreadsheet — that is, the spreadsheet may have 65,000 rows, but there is data in only the first 50. So dragging the scroll box to the bottom of the vertical scroll bar can be implemented so that it scrolls to the last row containing data rather than the last row of the spreadsheet.

Scroll Bar Shaft

The scroll bar shaft not only provides a visual context for the scroll box, it also serves as part of the scrolling interface. Clicking in the scroll bar shaft scrolls the height of the visible area in the direction of the click. For example, in a vertical scroll bar, if the user clicks in the shaft below the scroll box, the view scrolls the height of the view.

When scrolling the view, allow one unit of overlap from the previous view, as shown in Figure 2.16. For example, if the user clicks below the scroll box, the top line of the next screen becomes the line that was at the bottom of the former screen. The same is true of clicking above the scroll box and horizontal scrolling. This helps the user maintain a reference point.

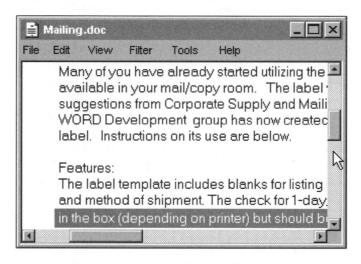

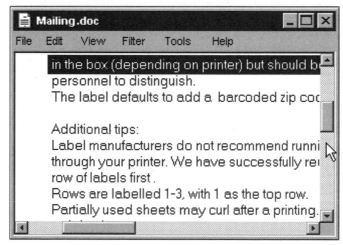

Figure 2.16   Clicking in the scroll bar shafts scrolls by screens.

Pressing and holding mouse button 1 with the pointer in the shaft auto-repeats the scrolling action. If the user moves the pointer outside the scroll bar sensitivity area while holding the mouse button down, the scrolling action stops. The user can resume scrolling by moving the pointer back into the scroll bar area. (This behavior is similar to the effect of dragging the scroll box.)

Automatic Scrolling

The techniques previously summarized describe the explicit ways to scroll. However, the user may also scroll as a secondary result of some situations. This type of scrolling is called *automatic scrolling*. The situations in which automatic scrolling occurs are as follows:

- When the user begins or adjusts a selection and drags past the edge of the scroll bar or window, scroll the area in the direction of the drag.

- When the user drags an object and approaches the edge of a scrollable area, scroll the area if the user pauses at the edge.

- When the user enters text from the keyboard at the edge of a window or moves or copies an object into a location at the edge of a window, the view should scroll to allow the user to focus on the information currently visible. The amount to scroll depends on context. For example, for typing in text vertically, scroll a single line at a time. However, when scrolling horizontally, scroll in units greater than a single character to prevent continuous or uneven scrolling. Similarly, for graphic objects, scroll based on the size of the object rather than individual pixels.

- If an operation results in a selection or moves the cursor, scroll the view to display the new selection. For example, for a Find command that selects a matching object, scroll the object into view, because the user usually wants to focus on that location. In addition, other forms of navigation may cause scrolling. For example, completing an entry of a field in a form may result in navigating to the next field. In this case, if the field is not visible, the form scrolls to display it.

For more information about scrolling, see Chapter 4, "Input Basics."

Keyboard Scrolling

Navigation keys support scrolling with the keyboard. When using a navigation key, the cursor moves to the appropriate location. For example, pressing arrow keys at the edge of a scrollable area scrolls in the corresponding direction in addition to moving the cursor. Similarly, PAGE UP and PAGE DOWN scroll comparably to clicking in the scroll bar shaft, but also move the cursor.

You may optionally use the SCROLL LOCK key to facilitate keyboard scrolling. When the SCROLL LOCK key is toggled on, navigation keys move without affecting the selection.

Adjacent Controls

It is sometimes convenient to locate controls or status bars adjacent to a scroll bar and position the end of the scroll bar to accommodate them. Split box controls are an example of such controls; however, you can also use other types of controls. Take care to avoid cluttering up the scroll bar area; this can make it difficult for users to scroll, particularly if you reduce the scroll bar too much. If you need a large number of controls, a toolbar may be a better approach. For more information about toolbars, see Chapter 7, "Menus, Controls, and Toolbars."

Splitting Windows

A window may be split into two or more separate viewing areas, called *panes*. For example, a split window can allow the user to examine two parts of a spreadsheet at the same time. A split window can also display different yet simultaneous views of the same object (data).

The panes that appear in a window can be implemented either as part of a window's basic design or as a user-configurable option. To support splitting a window, use a *split box*. A split box consists of a special control contained in the scroll bar. The split box should be just large enough for the user to successfully target it with the pointer. (The default size of a size handle, such as the window size border, is a good guideline.) If the window is not split, the split box is typically located at the top of the up arrow button of the vertical scroll bar and to the left of the left arrow button of a horizontal scroll bar.

The user can split a window by dragging the split box to the desired position. Dragging the split box to the end of the scroll bar closes the split. Double-clicking (with the pen, double-tapping) is the optional shortcut for splitting the window, for closing a split, or for splitting a window at some default location, such as in the middle of the window or to the last split location.

When positioning the hotspot of the pointer over a split box, change the pointer's image to provide feedback to the user and help the user target the split box. In addition, a representation of the split box and split bar should move with the pointer while the split box is dragged.

When a window is split, display two parallel lines extending from the split box to the other side of the window. These lines are called the *split bar*. Separate the lines by at least one pixel of blank space.

A Split command is added to the window or view's menu to provide a keyboard interface for splitting the window. The Split command splits the window in the middle or at a context-defined location. Move the split box up or down with arrow keys (or by dragging with the mouse or pen); pressing ENTER sets the split at the current location. Pressing ESC cancels the split mode.

You can also use other commands to create a split window. You can define specialized views that split a window when selected by the user. Similarly, you can remove the split of a window by closing or unselecting that view.

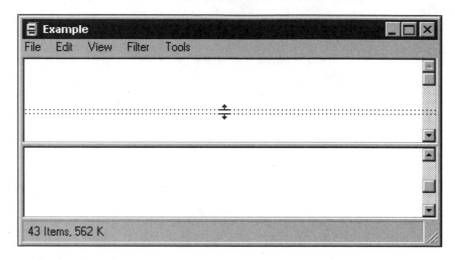

Figure 2.17   Moving the split bar.

When the user splits a window, add scroll bars if the resulting panes require scrolling. The information in panes may need to be scrolled so that the split bar does not obscure the content over which it appeared. The scroll bars usually scroll the view in the panes independently in the direction perpendicular to the split. For example, the vertical scroll bars of a set of panes in a horizontally split window would typically be controlled separately. Use a single scroll bar (at the appropriate side of the window) for a set of panes that scrolls together. If the panes require independent scrolling, a scroll bar should appear in each pane.

When you use split window panes to provide separate views, maintain each one's view properties independently, such as view type and selection state. However, if you want selection state shared across the panes, display a selection in all panes and support selection adjustment across panes.

When a window is closed, save the window's split state (that is, number of splits, where they appear, scrolled position in each split, and the window's selection state) as part of the view state information for that window so that it can be restored the next time the window is opened.

Topic

Apply interface design guidelines when creating menus in an application.

Content

Menus

Menus are a common way of presenting commands in an interface. They permit a user to see the available commands within a context without having to remember the specific names or syntax of those commands.

There are several forms of menus, including drop-down menus, pop-up menus, and cascading menus. The following sections cover these menus in more detail.

The Menu Bar and Drop-down Menus

A menu bar is one of the most common forms of menus. The *menu bar* is a special area displayed across the top of a window directly below the title bar. A menu bar (as shown in Figure 2.18) provides access to *drop-down menus*—collections of menu choices displayed when a user selects a particular entry on the menu bar.

Figure 2.18   A menu bar.

Note   While the use of a menu bar is a common convention for displaying commands, it is not a requirement. The long-term design evolution of menu bars is toward unification with toolbars—specifically, a menu bar can be considered a toolbar configured with "menu" controls. As with toolbars, you can provide an option for a user to display a menu bar. If you design your software to make a menu bar optional, supplement the interface with other interfaces, such as pop-up menus, handles, and toolbars, so that a user can access the functionality normally supplied by the menu bar through other means.

Drop-down Menu Interaction

Choosing a particular menu title displays its associated drop-down menu. To display a drop-down menu with the mouse, the user points to the menu title and presses or clicks mouse button 1. This procedure highlights the menu title and opens the menu. The pen interface for drop-down menus is similar to the mouse interface; tapping with the pen has the same effect as clicking the mouse.

If the user opens a menu by pressing the mouse button while the pointer is over the menu title, the user can drag the pointer over menu items in the menu. As the user drags the pointer, each menu is highlighted, tracking the pointer as it moves through the menu. Releasing the mouse button with the pointer over a menu item chooses the command associated with that menu item and removes the drop-down menu. If the user moves the pointer off the menu and then releases the mouse button, the menu is "canceled" and the drop-down menu is removed. However, if the user moves the pointer back onto the menu (before the mouse button is released), the highlighting returns to tracking the pointer and the user can select a menu item.

If the user opens a menu by clicking on the menu title, the menu title is highlighted and the drop-down menu remains displayed until the mouse is clicked again. If the user clicks a menu item in the drop-down menu (or drags over and releases on a menu item), the command associated with the menu item is executed, and the drop-down menu is no longer displayed.

The keyboard interface for drop-down menus uses the ALT key to activate the menu bar. Pressing an alphanumeric key while holding the ALT key, or after releasing the ALT key, displays any drop-down menu whose access key matches the alphanumeric key (matching is not case sensitive). Pressing a subsequent alphanumeric key chooses the first menu item with the matching access character.

The user can also use arrow keys to access drop-down menus from the keyboard. If the user presses the ALT key but has not yet selected a drop-down menu, LEFT ARROW and RIGHT ARROW keys can select a menu title on the menu bar. At the end of the menu bar, pressing another arrow key in the corresponding direction wraps around to the other end of the menu bar. Pressing the ENTER key displays the drop-down menu associated with the selected menu title. If a drop-down menu is already displayed on that menu bar, then pressing LEFT ARROW or RIGHT ARROW navigates to the next drop-down menu in that direction, unless the drop-down menu has multiple columns, in which case the arrow keys move to the next column in that direction.

Pressing UP ARROW or DOWN ARROW also displays a drop-down menu if none is currently open. In an open drop-down menu, pressing one of these keys moves to the next menu item in that direction, wrapping around at the top or bottom. If the drop-down menu has multiple columns, then pressing the arrow keys wraps around to the next column.

The user can close a drop-down menu by pressing the ALT key whenever the menu bar is active. This not only closes the drop-down menu, it also deactivates the menu bar. Pressing the ESC key also closes a drop-down menu. However, the ESC key closes only the current menu level. For example, if a drop-down menu is open, pressing ESC closes the drop-down menu but leaves its menu title highlighted. Pressing ESC a second time unhighlights the menu title and deactivates the menu bar, returning input focus to the content information in the window.

If the user presses a shortcut key to access a command in a drop-down menu, the command executes immediately; the menu that contains the command can optionally highlight its menu title, but the drop-down menu is not displayed.

Common Drop-down Menus

This section describes the conventions for some common drop-down menus. Although these menus are not required for all applications, apply these guidelines when including these menus in your software interface.

The File Menu

The File menu provides an interface for the primary operations on an object as a whole—that is, a complete file. Include commands such as Open, Save, Send, or Print. These commands usually correspond to those included on the pop-up menu of the icon displayed in the title bar of the window.

If your application supports an Exit command, place this command at the bottom of the File menu. Use the Exit command to close any open windows and files and stop any further processing. If the object remains active even when its window is closed —for example, a folder or printer—then use Close instead of Exit.

The Edit Menu

Include general-purpose commands for editing the objects displayed in the window on the Edit menu. These include the transfer commands—Cut, Copy, Paste, and Paste Link, as well as the following commands (if they are supported):

Command	Function
Undo	Reverses last action.
Repeat	Repeats last action.
Find and Replace	Searches for and substitutes text.
Delete	Removes the current selection.
Duplicate	Creates a copy of the current selection.

Consider including these commands on the pop-up menu of a selected object.

The Edit menu also includes command items for OLE objects. For more information about menus for OLE objects, see Chapter 11, "Working with Embedded and Linked Objects."

The View Menu

The View menu includes commands for changing the user's view of data in the window. Include commands on this menu that affect the view and not the data itself (for example, magnification commands, such as Zoom). Also include commands for controlling the display of particular interface elements in the view (for example, Show Ruler). You can find View menu items on the pop-up menu of a window.

The Window Menu

The Window menu is used in multiple document interface-style (MDI) applications. Include commands for managing the windows within an MDI workspace. You should also include these commands on the pop-up menu of the parent MDI window.

For more information about the design of MDI software, see Chapter 9, "Window Management."

The Help Menu

The Help menu contains commands that provide access to Help information. Include a Help Topics command that provides access to the Help Topics browser, which displays main topics included in your application's Help file. Here you may also include commands that provide access to other forms of user assistance.

For more information about the Help Topics browser and support for user assistance, see Chapter 12, "User Assistance."

If you want to provide access to copyright and version information for your application, you may include an About *<application name>* command on this menu. When the user chooses this command, display a window containing the application's name, version number, copyright information, and any other informational properties of the object. You can include this information in a special dialog box or by displaying a copyright page of the property sheet of the application's main executable (.EXE) file. .

Pop-up Menus

Even if you include a menu bar in your software's interface, you should also incorporate pop-up menus, as shown in Figure 2.19. Pop-up menus provide an efficient way for the user to access the operations of objects. Because pop-up menus are displayed at the pointer's current location, they eliminate the need for the user to move the pointer to the menu bar or a toolbar. Because pop-up menus contain commands that are specific to the context or object, they can reduce the number of commands the user must browse through, and because pop-up menus are displayed only upon demand, they do not take up dedicated screen space.

Figure 2.19   A sample pop-up menu.

The appearance of a pop-up menu is similar to a drop-down menu, except that it does not have a menu title. It is best to keep the size of the pop-up menu as small as possible. Avoid including individual properties or lists of items. Also, avoid creating pop-up menus with only a single menu item.

The menu items in a pop-up menu are contextual to the selected object (or objects); the commands in the menu apply only to that selection or its immediate context. For example, a pop-up menu for a text selection might include the font properties of the text as well as the properties of the paragraph of which the selection is a part; although usually it is best to present these properties in a property sheet the user can display by choosing the Properties command from the menu.

The commands included on a pop-up menu may not always be supplied by the object itself, but rather be a combination of those commands provided by the object and by its current container. For example, the pop-up menu for files in a directory folder includes transfer commands. However, the folder (container) supplies these commands, not the files.

For more information about the integration of commands for OLE objects, see Chapter 11, "Working with Embedded and Linked Objects."

Avoid using a pop-up menu as the exclusive means of access to a particular operation. However, the menu items in a pop-up menu need not be limited only to commands that are included in menu bar drop-down menus.

The following are the general guidelines for ordering menu items in a pop-up menu.

- Place an object's primary commands first (for example, commands such as Open, Play, and Print), transfer commands, other commands supported by the object (whether provided by the object or by its context), and a What's This? command.

- Order the transfer commands as Cut, Copy, Paste, Paste Link.

- Place the Properties command, when present, as the last command on the menu.

For more information about transfer commands, see Chapter 5, "General Interaction Techniques." For more information about the What's This? command, see Chapter 12, "User Assistance." For more information about recommendations for the commands on pop-up menus for icons, see the section "Icon Pop-up Menus," later in this chapter.

Pop-up Menu Interaction

With a mouse, the user displays a pop-up menu by clicking an object with button 2. The down transition of the mouse button identifies the object. The up transition displays the menu, typically to the right and below the hot spot of the pointer (although this is adjusted to avoid having the menu clipped by the edge of the screen).

If the pointer is over an existing selection when the user invokes the menu, the menu applies to that selection. If the menu is outside a selection but within the same selection scope, then the button down point establishes a new selection (usually resetting the current selection in that scope) and displays the menu for the new selection. However, if the user clicks the button a second time within the same selection, the menu is simply removed. Pressing the ESC key also dismisses the menu, as will clicking the selected object again with button 1.

You can support pop-up menus for objects that are implicitly selected or cannot be selected directly. For example, you can provide pop-up menus for controls such as scroll bars through a button 2 click, or for static items in a status area. However, when adding pop-up menus for objects such as controls, include the menu items that relate to commands that the control represents. For example, a scroll bar represents a navigational view of a document, so commands might include Beginning of Document, End of Document, Next Page, and Previous Page. The exception is when the control is treated as an object itself in a forms layout or window design environment.

The pen interface uses an action handle in pen-enabled controls to access the pop-up menu for the selection. Tapping on the action handle displays the pop-up menu, as shown in Figure 2.20.

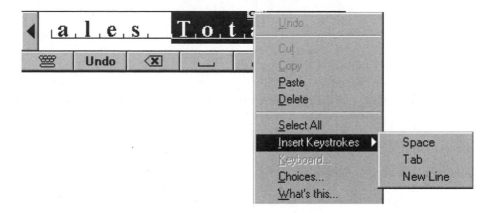

Figure 2.20   The action handle provides access to pop-up menus.

You can also use techniques such as barrel tapping or the pop-up menu gesture to display a pop-up menu. This interaction is equivalent to a mouse button 2 click.

For more information about pen interaction techniques, see Chapter 5, "General Interaction Techniques."

The keyboard interface for displaying a pop-up menu for a selection is SHIFT+F10. In addition, menu access keys, arrow keys, ENTER, and ESC keys all operate in the same fashion in the menu as they do in drop-down menus.

Common Pop-up Menus

The pop-up menus included in any application depend on the objects and context supplied by that application. However, there are some common pop-up menus that you should support.

The Window Pop-up Menu

The window pop-up menu (not to be confused with the Window drop-down menu found in MDI applications) is a pop-up menu associated with the window. It replaces the former Control menu (also known as the System menu). The common commands included on this menu are Close, Restore, Move, Size, Minimize, and Maximize.

You can also include other commands on the window's menu that apply to the window or the view within the window. For example, an application can append a Split command to the menu to facilitate splitting the window into panes. Similarly, you can add commands that affect the view (for example, Outline), commands that add, remove, or filter elements from the view (for example, Show Ruler/Hide Ruler), or commands that open certain subordinate or special views in secondary windows (for example, Show Color Palette).

The user can display a window's pop-up menu by clicking mouse button 2 on any area of the window that is not part of the data viewed in the window. Specifically, this allows access to the window pop-up menu from anywhere in the title bar area, including the title bar buttons, but excluding the title bar icon and any sizable border. You can also access the window pop-up menu by clicking button 1 on the icon in the title bar. For the pen, performing the pop-up menu equivalent (barrel tapping or pop-up menu gesture) on these areas displays the menu. Use ALT+SPACEBAR to access the menu from the keyboard.

Icon Pop-up Menus

Pop-up menus displayed for icons display operations of the objects represented by the icons. Accessing the pop-up menu of an application or document icon follows the standard conventions for pop-up menus (for example, displayed with a mouse button 2 click).

The pop-up menu of an application's icon (for example, the Microsoft Wordpad executable file) typically includes the following commands.

Table 2.1 Application File Icon Pop-up Menu Items

Command	Meaning
Cut	Removes the file to the Clipboard.
Copy	Places a copy of the file on the Clipboard.
Create Link	Creates a link of the file in the same location (directory).
Delete	Deletes the file.
What's This?	Displays contextual Help information for the application.
Properties	Displays the properties for the application file.

For more information about the What's This? command, see Chapter 12, "User Assistance." For more information about the Properties command, see Chapter 8, "Secondary Windows."

If the application creates data or document files that are separate from the application file, then you may include a New command that creates a data file of the type supported by the application. Optionally, the command can display a list of data file types the application can create, from which the user may choose. Typically, the newly created data file is opened.

The icon in the title bar of a window also represents an object. As a result, include a pop-up menu with appropriate commands for the title bar's icon in addition to the icon that appears on the desktop or folders.

When the icon of the application appears in the title bar (that is, an application that does not load or save files, such as the Windows Calculator program), then the commands on the pop-up menu for the title bar icon are the same as the main icon, except that Close replaces the Open command.

For an icon representing a data or document file, the following are the suggested menu items for the pop-up menu for its icon.

Table 2.2 Document (or Data File) Icon Pop-up Menu Items

Command	Meaning
Open	Opens the document's (primary) window.
Print	Prints the document on the current default printer.
Cut	Removes the file to the Clipboard.
Copy	Places a copy of the file on the Clipboard.
Delete	Deletes the document (file).
What's This?	Displays contextual Help information for the document.
Properties	Displays the properties for the document (file).

The pop-up menu for the icon in the title bar of the data or document file's open window has the same commands, with the following exception: replace the Open command with a Close command and add Save if the edits in the document require explicit saving to the document's file.

For MDI-style applications, include the following commands, where appropriate, on the pop-up menu for the application's icon in the title bar of the parent MDI window:

Table 2.3 MDI Application Pop-up Menu Items

Command	Meaning
Close (or Exit)	Closes the MDI workspace.
Save All	Saves all documents open in the MDI workspace (and the state of the MDI window).
Insert New...	Creates a new document or displays a list of documents supported from which the user can choose to create a new one.
Find...	Displays a window that allows the user to specify criteria to locate a document.
What's This?	Displays contextual Help information for the application.
Properties	Displays properties of the MDI workspace.

For more information about the design of MDI-style applications, see Chapter 9, "Window Management."

Cascading Menus

A *cascading menu* (also known as a *hierarchical menu* or child menu) is a submenu of a menu item. The visual cue for a cascading menu is the inclusion of a triangular arrow on the right side of its parent menu item.

You can use cascading menus to provide additional choices rather than taking up additional space in the parent menu. However, they tend to add complexity to the menu interface. The farther a user must navigate to get to a particular choice, the more burdensome the interface. Cascading menus require more coordination to handle the changes in direction necessary to navigate through them. Because of these design tradeoffs, use cascading menus sparingly; when you use them, limit them to a single level. As an alternative, consider making the choices available in a dialog box, particularly when the choices are independent settings; this allows the user to select multiple options in one invocation of the command, or as options on a toolbar.

The user interaction for a cascading menu is similar to that of a drop-down menu from the menu bar, except that a cascading menu displays after a short time-out. This avoids unnecessary flashing of the menu if the user is browsing or navigating to another item in the parent menu. The menu is also removed after a short time-out. This enables the user to drag more directly from the parent menu item into the cascading menu.

Topic

Apply interface design guidelines when incorporating controls in an application.

Content

Controls

Controls are graphic objects that represent the properties or operations of other objects. Some controls display and allow editing of particular values. Other controls initiate an associated command.

Like most elements of the interface, controls provide feedback indicating when they have the input focus and when they are activated. For example, when interacting with controls using a mouse, each control indicates its selection on the down transition of the mouse button, but does not activate until button up (unless the control supports auto-repeat).

Controls are generally interactive only when the pointer (hot spot) or focus is on the control. If the user moves the pointer off the control (or for some controls, such as scroll bars, outside a defined hot zone of the control), the control no longer responds to the input device. However, if the user moves the pointer back onto the control, it once again responds to the input device.

While controls provide specific interfaces for user interaction, you can also include pop-up menus for controls. This can provide an effective way to transfer the value of the control or to provide access to contextual Help information. The interface to pop-up menus for controls follows the standard conventions for pop-up menus, except that it does not affect the state of the control; that is, clicking the control with button 2 does not have the same effect as clicking the control with button 1. The only action is the display of the pop-up menu.

For more information about the access to contextual Help information using a pop-up menu, see Chapter 12, "User Assistance."

A pop-up menu for a control is contextual to what the control represents, rather than the control itself. Therefore, do not include commands, such as Set, Unset, Check, or Uncheck. The exception is in a forms design or window layout context, where the commands on the pop-up menu can apply to the control itself.

When controls are nested or used on a white background, their appearance is different. For more information about presenting controls in this situation, see Chapter 13, "Visual Design."

Buttons

Buttons are controls that initiate actions or change properties. There are three basic types of buttons: command buttons, option buttons, and check boxes.

Command Buttons

A *command button*, also known as a push button, is a control, commonly rectangular in shape, that includes a label (text, graphic, or sometimes both), as shown in Figure 2.21.

Figure 2.21   Command buttons.

Clicking a command button with mouse button 1 (for pens, tapping) executes the command associated with the button. When the user presses the mouse button, the input focus moves to the button, and the button state changes to the pressed appearance. If the user moves the pointer off the command button while the mouse button remains pressed, the button returns to its original state. However, if the user moves the pointer back over the button while the mouse button is pressed, the button returns to the pressed state.

When the user releases the mouse button and the pointer remains on the command button, the command associated with the control is executed. If the pointer is not on the control when the user releases the mouse button, no action occurs.

You can define access keys and shortcut keys for command buttons. In addition, the SPACEBAR activates a command button if the user moves the input focus to the button, for example, in a dialog box.

For more information about navigation and activation of controls, see Chapter 8, "Secondary Windows."

The effect of choosing a button is immediate with respect to its context. For example, in toolbars, clicking a button carries out the associated action. In a secondary window, such as a dialog box, activating a button may initiate a transaction within the window, or apply a transaction and close the window.

The command button's label represents the action the button initiates. In a textual label, the text should follow the same capitalization conventions defined for menus. If the control is unavailable (disabled), the label of the button appears unavailable.

For more information about the appearance of unavailable buttons, see Chapter 13, "Visual Design."

Include an ellipsis (...) as a visual cue for buttons associated with commands that require additional information. Like menu items, the use of ellipses indicates that further information is needed, not simply that a window will appear. Executing some buttons can result in the display of a message box, but this does not imply that the command button's label should include an ellipsis.

You can use command buttons to enlarge a secondary window and display additional options, also known as an *unfold button*. An unfold button is not really a different type of control, but the use of a command button for the specific function. When using a command button for this purpose, include a double chevron (>>) as part of the button's label.

For more information about the use of buttons with ellipses and unfold buttons in secondary windows, see Chapter 8, "Secondary Windows."

In some cases, a command button can represent an object and its default action. For example, the task bar buttons represent an object's window as well as the Restore command. Clicking on the button with mouse button 1 executes the default command of the object. Clicking on the button with mouse button 2 displays a pop-up menu associated with the object.

You can also use command buttons to reflect a mode or property value (similar to the use of option buttons or check boxes). While the typical interaction for a command button is to return to its normal "up" state, if you use it to represent a state, display the button in the option-set appearance, which is a checkerboard pattern in the button's highlight color on the background of the button, as shown in Figure 2.22.

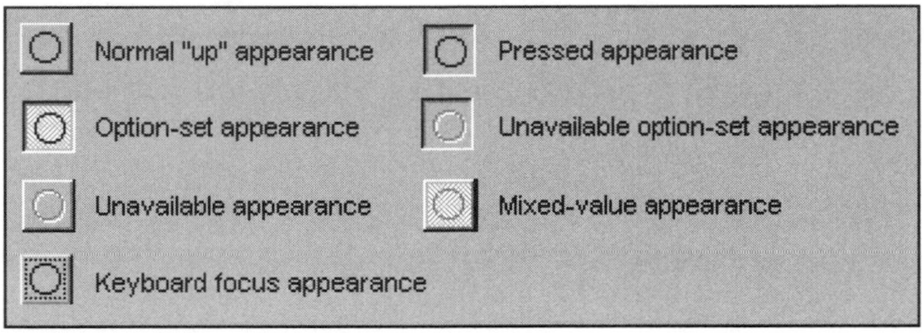

Figure 2.22   Command button appearances.

For more information about the appearance of different states of buttons, see Chapter 13, "Visual Design."

You can also use command buttons to set tool modes—for example, in drawing or forms design programs for drawing out specific shapes or controls. In this case, design the button labels to reflect the tool's use. When the user chooses the tool (that is, when the button is clicked), display the button using the option-set appearance and change the pointer to indicate the change of the mode of interaction.

Menu Buttons

A *menu button* uses a command button to display a pop-up menu. While this is not a specific control provided by the system, you can create this interface using the standard components.

A menu button looks just like a standard command button. However, as a part of its label, it includes a triangular arrow similar to the one found in cascading menu titles.

A menu button supports the same type of interaction as a drop-down menu; the menu is displayed when the button is pressed. This allows the user to drag into the menu from the button and make menu selections, through the use of highlighting, to track the movement of the pointer.

Clicking a command button also displays the menu. Interaction with the menu is the same as with any pop-up menu. For example, clicking a menu item executes the associated command. Clicking outside the menu or on the command button removes the menu.

When pressed, the command button displays the pressed appearance. When the user releases the button and the menu is displayed, the command button displays the option-set appearance, a checkerboard appearance using the button's highlight color on the background of the button. Otherwise, the command button's appearance is the same as that of a typical command button. For example, if the button is unavailable, the button displays the unavailable appearance.

For more information about the appearance of button states, see Chapter 13, "Visual Design."

Option Buttons

An *option button* (also known as a *radio button*) represents a single choice within a limited set of mutually exclusive choices—that is, in any group of option buttons, only one option in the group can be set. Accordingly, always group option buttons in sets of two or more, as shown in Figure 2.23.

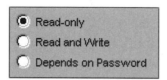

Figure 2.23   A set of option buttons.

Option buttons appear as a set of small circles. When an option button choice is set, a dot appears in the middle of the circle. When the choice is not the current setting, the circle is empty. Avoid using option buttons to initiate an action other than setting a particular option or value represented by the option button. The only exception is that you may support double-clicking the option button as a shortcut for setting the value and executing the default command of the window in which the option buttons appear, if choosing an option button is the default user action for the window.

You can use option buttons to represent a set of choices for a particular property. When the option buttons must reflect a selection with mixed values for that property, then display all the buttons in the group using the mixed-value appearance to indicate that multiple values exist for that property, as shown in Figure 2.24.

Figure 2.24   Option buttons with mixed-value appearance.

If the user chooses any of option buttons with mixed-value appearance, then that value is applied to the property; the dot appears in that button and all the other buttons in the group appear empty.

For more information about mixed-value appearance, see Chapter 13, "Visual Design."

Limit use of option buttons for small sets of options (typically seven or less, but always at least two). If you need more choices, consider using another control, such as a single selection list box or drop-down list box.

Option buttons include a textual label. If you need graphic labels, then consider using command buttons instead. Define the label to best represent the value or effect for that choice. You also use the label to indicate when the choice is unavailable.

For more information about unavailable appearance, see Chapter 13, "Visual Design."

Because option buttons appear as a group, you can use a group box control to visually define the group. The group box can have its own label, which allows you to label option buttons to be relative to the group box's label. For example, a group of option buttons labeled Alignment might have individual labels such as Left, Right, and Center.

As with command buttons, the mouse interface for choosing a button uses a click with mouse button 1 (for pen, tap), either on the button's circle or on the button's label. The input focus moves to the option button when the user presses the mouse button, and the button displays its pressed appearance. If the user moves the pointer off the option button before releasing the mouse button, the option button returns to its former state. The option is not set until the user releases the mouse button while the pointer is over the control. Releasing the mouse button outside of the option button or its label has no effect on the current setting of the option button. In addition, successive mouse clicks on the same option button do not toggle the button's state; the user needs to explicitly select an alternative choice in the group to cancel a choice.

Assign access keys to option button labels to provide a keyboard interface to the buttons. You can also define the TAB or arrow keys to allow the user to navigate and choose a button.

For more information about navigation and interaction with option buttons, see Chapter 8, "Secondary Windows."

Check Boxes

Like option buttons, check boxes support options that are either on or off; however, check boxes differ from option buttons in that you use check boxes for nonexclusive choices. A check box appears as a square box with an accompanying label. When the choice is set, a check mark appears in the box. When the choice is not set, the check box is empty, as shown in Figure 2.25.

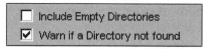

Figure 2.25   A set of check boxes.

As in the case of independent settings in menus, use check boxes only when both states of the choice are clearly opposite and unambiguous. If this is not the case, then consider using option buttons or some other form of single selection choice control instead.

A check box's label is typically textual. Use command buttons when you need a graphical label. Define the label to appropriately express the value or effect of the choice. You can also use the label to indicate when the control is unavailable.

Group related check box choices. Grouping check boxes does not prevent the user from setting the check boxes on or off in any combination. Each check box's setting is typically independent of the others; however, you can use a check box's setting to affect other controls. For example, you can use the state of a check box to filter the content of a list. If you have a large number of choices or if the number of choices may vary, consider using a multiple selection list box instead of check boxes.

Clicking a check box with mouse button 1 (for pen, tap), either on the check box square or on the check box's label, chooses that button and toggles its state. When the user presses the mouse button, the input focus moves to the control and the check box assumes its pressed appearance. Like option buttons and other controls, if the user moves the pointer off the control while holding down the mouse button, the control's appearance returns to its original state. The setting state of the check box does not change until the user releases the mouse button. To change the control's setting, position the pointer over the check box or its label when releasing the mouse button.

Define access keys for check box labels to provide a keyboard interface for navigating to and choosing a check box. In addition, the SPACEBAR toggles a check box when the input focus is on the check box (for example, in a dialog box).

For more information about the guidelines for selecting access keys, see Chapter 4, "Input Basics." For more information about navigation and choosing controls with the keyboard, see Chapter 8, "Secondary Windows."

If you use a check box to display the value for the property of a multiple selection whose values for that property differ (for example, for a text selection that is partly bold), display the check box in its mixed-value appearance that uses a checkerboard pattern inside the box, as shown in Figure 2.26.

Figure 2.26   A Mixed-Value Check Box (Magnified).

For more information about the mixed-value appearance, see Chapter 13, "Visual Design."

Choosing a mixed-value check box sets the associated value by placing a check mark in it. Choosing it again turns off the value. Choosing it a third time toggles the value back to the mixed-value state. This three-state toggling occurs only when the values are mixed.

List Boxes

A *list box* is a convenient preconstructed control for displaying a list of choices to the user. The choices may be text, color, icons, or other graphics. The purpose of a list box is to display a collection of items and, in most cases, support selection of a choice of an item (or items) in the list.

List boxes are best for displaying large numbers of choices that vary in number or content. If a particular choice is not available, omit the choice from the list. For example, if a point size is not available for the currently selected font, do not display that size in the list.

For more information about unavailable appearance, see Chapter 13, "Visual Design."

Order entries in a list that is the most appropriate for the content in the list and to facilitate easy user browsing. For example, alphabetize a list of filenames, but put a list of dates in chronological order. If there is no natural or logical ordering for the content, use alphabetical ordering (ascending; for example, 0-9, A-Z).

List box controls do not include their own labels. However, you may include a label using a static text field; the label enables you to provide a descriptive reference for the control as well as keyboard access to the control. Make certain that your support for keyboard access moves the input focus to the list box and not to the static text field label.

For information about navigation to controls in a secondary window, see Chapter 8, "Secondary Windows." For information about defining access keys for control labels, see Chapter 4, "Input Basics."

When a list box is disabled, display its label using an unavailable appearance. If possible, display all of the entries in the list in unavailable appearance to avoid confusing the user as to whether the control is enabled or not.

For more information about displaying information in unavailable appearance, see Chapter 13, "Visual Design."

The width of the list box should be sufficient to display the average width of an entry in the list. If that is not practical because of space or the variability of what the list may include, consider one or more of the following options:

- Make the list box wide enough to allow the entries in the list to be sufficiently distinguished.

- Use ellipses (...) in the middle or at the end of long text entries to shorten them, while preserving the important characteristics needed to distinguish them. For example for long pathnames, usually the beginning and end of the path are the most critical; you can use ellipses to shorten the entire name: \SAMPLE\...\EXAMPLE.

- Include a horizontal scroll bar. This option reduces some usability, because adding the scroll bar reduces the number of entries you can view at one time. In addition, if most entries in the list box would not need to be horizontally scrolled, including a horizontal scroll bar accommodates the infrequent case.

List boxes can be classified by the way they display a list and by the type of selection they support.

Single Selection List Boxes

A *single selection list box* is designed for the selection of only one item in a list. Therefore, the control provides a mutually exclusive operation similar to a group of option buttons, except that a list box can more efficiently handle a large number of items. Define a single selection list box to be tall enough to show at least three to eight choices (depending on the design constraints of where the list box is used), as shown in Figure 2.27. It should always include a vertical scroll bar. If all the items in the list are visible, then follow the window scroll bar guidelines for disabling the scroll arrows and enlarging the scroll box to fill the scroll bar shaft.

Figure 2.27   A single selection list box.

The currently selected item in a single selection list box is highlighted using selection appearance.

The user can select an entry in a single selection list box by clicking on it with mouse button 1 (for pen, tapping). Because this type of list box supports only single selection, choosing an entry unselects any other item selected in the list. The scroll bar in the list box allows the mouse user to scroll through the list of entries, following the interaction defined for scroll bars. The keyboard interface uses navigation keys, such as the arrow keys, HOME, END, PAGE UP, and PAGE DOWN, as well as alphanumeric keys (for example, pressing M scrolls the entry beginning with M to the top of the list). These keys not only navigate to an entry in the list, but also select it.

For more information about the interaction techniques of scroll bars, see Chapter 6, "Windows."

If the choices in the list box represent values for a property of a selection, then make the current value visible and selected when displaying the list. If the list box reflects mixed values for a multiple selection, then no entry in the list should be selected.

Drop-down List Boxes

Like a single selection list box, a *drop-down list box* provides for the selection of a single item from a list of items; the difference is that the list is displayed upon demand. In its closed state, the control displays the current value for the control. The user opens the list to change the value. Figure 2.28 shows the drop-down list box in its closed and opened state.

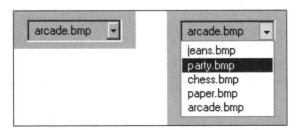

Figure 2.28   Drop-down list box (closed and opened state).

Make the width of a closed drop-down list box a few spaces larger than the average width of the items in its list. The open list component of the control should be tall enough to show three to eight items, following the same conventions as a single selection list box. The width of the list should be wide enough not only to display the choices in the list, but also to allow the user to drag directly into the list.

The interface for drop-down list boxes is similar to that for menus. For example, the user can press the mouse button to display (open) the list. Choosing an item in the list automatically closes the list. Similarly, arrow keys display the list. Using ALT+UP ARROW, ALT+DOWN ARROW, a navigation key, or an access key to move to another control automatically closes the list. When the list is closed, preserve any selection made while the list was open (unless the user presses a Cancel command button).

Drop-down list boxes are an effective way to conserve space and reduce clutter. However, the design tradeoff is that they require more user interaction for browsing and selecting an item than a single selection list box.

If the choices in a drop-down list represent values for the property of a multiple selection and the values for that property are mixed, then display no value in the current setting component of the control.

Extended and Multiple Selection List Boxes

Although most list boxes are single selection lists, some contexts require the user to choose more than one item. *Extended selection list boxes* and *multiple selection list boxes* support this functionality.

Extended and multiple selection list boxes follow the same conventions for height and width as single selection list boxes. Base the width of the box on the average width of the entries in the list. The height should be able to display no less than three items and generally no more than eight, unless the size of the list varies with the size of the window.

Extended selection list boxes support the selection interface for contiguous and disjoint selection. That is, extended selection list boxes are optimized for a single item selection or for a single range, while still providing for disjoint selections.

For more information about contiguous and disjoint selection techniques, see Chapter 5, "General Interaction Techniques."

When you want to support user selection of several entries from a list, but the grouping of the entries does not make extended selection efficient, you can define a multiple selection list box. Whereas extended selection list boxes are optimized for individual item or range selection, multiple selection list boxes are optimized for independent selection.

Use check boxes that precede each item for items in a multiple selection list box, as shown in Figure 2.31. Such an appearance helps the user distinguish the difference in the interface of the list box with a familiar convention. It also serves to differentiate keyboard navigation from the state of a choice.

When using check boxes in a list box, the appearance of the check box differs slightly. For more information about the appearance of controls in a list box, see Chapter 13, "Visual Design."

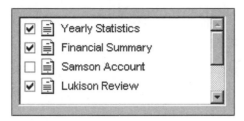

Figure 2.29   A multiple selection list box.

List View Boxes

A *list view* is a special extended selection list box control that displays a set of objects. It supports viewing objects by their large icon, small icon, as a list, or as a table. It is often used with a tree control, which is described in the following section.

Tree Control Boxes

A *tree control* is a special list box control that displays a set of objects as an indented outline based on their logical hierarchical relationship. The control includes buttons that allow the outline to be expanded and collapsed, as shown in Figure 2.30. You can use a tree control to display the relationship between a set of containers or other hierarchical views.

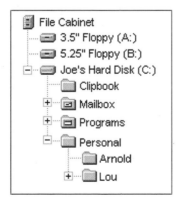

Figure 2.30   A tree control.

Text Fields

Windows 95 includes a number of controls that facilitate the display, entry of text, or editing of a text value. Some of these controls combine a basic text entry field with other types of controls.

Text fields do not include labels as a part of the control. However, you can add one using a static text field. Including a label helps identify the purpose of a text field and provides the means of indicating when the field is disabled. You can also define access keys for the text label to provide keyboard access to the text field. When using a static text label, define keyboard access to move the input focus to the text field with which the label is associated rather than to the static text field itself.

For more information about text fields, see "Static Test Fields" later in this chapter.

When using a text field for input of a restricted set of possible values, for example, a field where only numbers are appropriate, consider validating user input immediately, either by ignoring inappropriate characters or by providing feedback indicating that the value is invalid or both.

For more information about validation of input, see Chapter 8, "Secondary Windows."

You can use text fields to display information that is read-only; that is, they are appropriate for text that cannot be directly edited by a user. Read-only text fields allow the data to be selected but not edited.

For more information about the visual presentation of read-only text fields, see Chapter 13, "Visual Design."

Text Boxes

A *text box* (also known as an edit control) is a rectangular control in which the user enters or edits text, as shown in Figure 2.31. It can be defined to support a single line or multiple lines of text. The outline border of the control is optional, although typically displayed.

Figure 2.31   Standard text box.

The standard text box control provides basic text input and editing support. Editing support includes the insertion or deletion of characters and the option of text wrapping. Individual font or paragraph properties are not supported (although the entire control can support font properties).

A text box supports standard interactive techniques for navigation and contiguous selection. Horizontal scrolling is supported for single-line text boxes, and horizontal and vertical scroll bars are supported for multiple-line text boxes.

For more information about the conventions for selection and editing of text, see Chapter 5, "General Interaction Techniques."

You can limit the number of characters accepted as input for a text box to whatever is appropriate for the context. In addition, text boxes defined for fixed-length input can also support *auto-exit*; that is, as soon as the last character is typed in the text box, the focus moves to the next control. For example, you can define a five-character auto-exit text box to facilitate the entry of zip code, or three two-character auto-exit text boxes to support the entry of date. However, because the automatic focus shift behavior may be unexpected, use auto-exit text boxes sparingly. They are best limited to situations involving extensive data entry.

Rich-text Boxes

A *rich-text box* (as shown in Figure 2.32) offers the same basic text editing support as a standard text box. In addition, a rich-text box supports individual character font and paragraph formatting (properties).

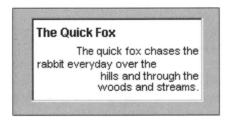

Figure 2.32   A rich-text box.

Combo Boxes

A *combo box* is a control that combines a text box with a list box, as shown in Figure 2.33. This allows the user to type in an entry or choose one from the list.

Figure 2.33   A combo box.

The text box and its associated list box have a dependent relationship. As text is typed into the text box, the list scrolls to the nearest match. In addition, selecting an item in the list box automatically uses that entry to replace the content of the text box.

The interface for the control follows the conventions supported for each component, except that UP ARROW and DOWN ARROW move only in the list box.

Drop-down Combo Boxes

A *drop-down combo box* (as shown in Figure 2.34) combines the characteristics of a text box with a drop-down list box. More compact than a regular combo box, it can be used when space needs to be conserved, trading off the additional interaction as drop-down lists do.

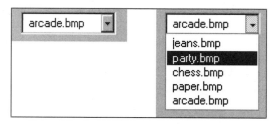

Figure 2.34   Combo box (closed and open).

The closed state of a drop-down combo box is similar to that of a drop-down list, except that the text box is interactive. Clicking the button component of the control opens the list. Clicking the button component a second time, choosing an item in the list, or clicking another control also closes the list. Pressing UP ARROW or DOWN ARROW (or ALT+UP ARROW or ALT+DOWN ARROW) also displays the list.

Pressing a navigation key, such as TAB, or an access key (or ALT+UP ARROW or ALT+DOWN ARROW) will close the list. When the list is closed, preserve any selection made while the list was open (unless a Cancel command button is pressed).

When the list is displayed, the interdependent relationship between the text box and list is the same as it is for standard combo boxes when text is typed into the text box. When the user chooses an item in the list, the interaction is the same as for drop-down lists; the selected item becomes the entry in the text box.

Spin Boxes

Spin boxes are text boxes that accept a limited set of discrete ordered input values. A spin box is a combination of a text box and a pair of buttons, as shown in Figure 2.35. The buttons on the control allow the user to increment or decrement values in the text box.

Figure 2.35   A spin box.

The user can type a text value directly into the control or use the buttons to change the value. Pressing UP ARROW or DOWN ARROW also changes the value.

You can use a single set of spin box buttons to edit a sequence of related text boxes, for example, time as expressed in hours, minutes, and seconds. The buttons affect only the text box that currently has the input focus.

Static Text Fields

You can use static text fields to present read-only textual information. However, an application can still alter read-only text, if appropriate, to reflect a change in state. For example, you can use static text to display the current directory path or the status information such as page number, key states, or time and date. Figure 2.36 demonstrates a static text field.

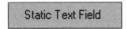

Figure 2.36   A Static Text Field.

You can also use static text fields to provide labels or descriptive information for other controls. Using static text fields as labels for other controls allows you to provide access-key activation for the control with which it is associated. Make certain that the input focus moves to its associated control and not to the static field.

Other General Controls

The system also provides support for other controls for special types of interfaces and controls designed to organize other controls.

Scroll Bars

Scroll bars are horizontal or vertical scrolling controls you can use to create scrollable areas other than on the window frame or list box, where they are automatically included. Use scroll bars only for supporting scrolling contexts, not for setting values. Instead, you can use a slider or other control, such as a spin box, to set or adjust values. Using a scroll bar to set values may confuse the user as to the purpose or interaction of the control.

While scroll bar controls can support the input focus, avoid defining this type of interface. Instead, define the keyboard interface of your scrollable area so that it can scroll without requiring the user to move the input focus to a scroll bar. This makes your scrolling interface more consistent with the user interaction for window and list box scroll bars.

Sliders

Use a *slider* for setting or adjusting values or position on continuous dimensions, such as volume or brightness. A slider is a control consisting of a bar that defines the extent or range of the adjustment, and an indicator that both shows the current value for the control and provides the means for changing the value, as shown in Figure 2.37.

Figure 2.37   A slider.

The user can move the slide indicator by dragging to a particular location or clicking in the hot zone area of the bar, which moves the slide indicator directly to that location. Arrow keys also move the slide indicator in the respective direction represented by the key.

Sliders support a number of options. You may set a slider as vertical or horizontal and define the length and height of the slide bar component.

Because a slider does not include its own label, use a static text field to create one. You can also add text and graphics to the control to help the user interpret the scale and range of the control.

Progress Indicators

A *progress indicator* is a control you can use to show the percentage of completion of a particular process. The bar "fills" from left to right, as shown in Figure 2.38.

Figure 2.38   A progress indicator.

Display options for progress indicators include height, width, color, solid or segmented bar, and horizontal or vertical orientation. Because a progress indicator displays information, it is noninteractive. However, it may be useful to add static text or other information to help communicate the purpose of the progress indicator.

Tabs

A *tab* is control that looks similar to a notebook divider, as shown in Figure 2.39. You can use this control for navigation between logical "pages" or sections of information.

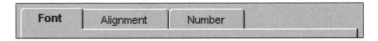

Figure 2.39   A tab control.

Clicking a tab switches to that tab. When the user moves the input focus to a tab, LEFT ARROW or RIGHT ARROW moves between tabs. CTRL+TAB also switches between tabs. Optionally, you can also define access keys for navigating between tabs.

Wells

A *well* is a special field that displays graphical information such as a color, pattern, or image used as a property value, as shown in Figure 2.40. This control is not currently provided by the system; however, its purpose and interaction guidelines are described here to provide a consistent interface.

Figure 2.40   A well control for selection colors.

When the control is interactive, it uses the same border pattern as a check box or text box. If you use the control to choose a value, then the current set value is indicated by a border drawn around the border. Because this control is similar to option buttons, follow the same interaction techniques.

For more information about the option-set appearance, see Chapter 13, "Visual Design."

Group Boxes

A *group box* is a special control you can use to organize a set of controls. A group box is a rectangular frame with an optional label that surrounds a set of controls, as shown in Figure 2.41. Group boxes generally do not directly process any input.

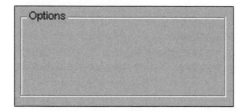

Figure 2.41   A group box.

You can make the label for controls that you place in a group box relative to the group box's label. For example, a group labeled Alignment can have option buttons labeled, Left, Right, and Center.

Column Headings

You can use a *column heading* control to display properties of a selected object in a multicolumn list, as shown in Figure 2.42. The control allows you to define the displayed property and the sort order based on the property for items in the list.

Name	Author	Size	Kind	Modified
Arnold	Arnold	25K	Folder	June 10, 1990
Data Analysis	Nancy	28K	Word	October 18, 1991

Figure 2.42   Column headings.

Property Sheet Controls

A *property sheet control* provides the basic framework for defining a property sheet. It provides the common controls used in a property sheet and accepts dialog box layout definitions to automatically create tabbed property pages.

For more information on property sheets, see Chapter 8, "Secondary Windows."

Topic

Provide help information to users (for example, status bars, tool tips, .HLP files, menu help, F1 key).

Content

User Assistance

User assistance is an important part of a product's design. A well designed Help interface provides the user with assistance upon demand, but the assistance must be simple, efficient, and relevant so that a user can obtain it without becoming lost in the Help interface. A user wants to accomplish a task—a Help interface design should assist in that objective without being intrusive. This chapter provides a description of the system support you can use to create your own user assistance support and guidelines for implementation.

Context-Sensitive Help

Context-sensitive help provides information about a particular object and its context. It answers the question "What is this and why would I use it?" This section covers some of the basic ways to support context-sensitive help in your application.

What's This?

The What's This? command supports a user obtaining contextual information about any object on the screen, including controls in property sheets and dialog boxes. The user can access this command by:

- Choosing the What's This? command from the Help drop-down menu.
- Clicking (for pen, tapping) a What's This? button on a toolbar.
- Clicking a What's This? button on the title bar of a secondary window.
- Choosing the What's This? command on the pop-up menu for the specific object.

Choosing the What's This? command from the Help drop-down menu or clicking a What's This? button sets a temporary mode. This mode is indicated by changing the pointer's image to the contextual Help pointer. SHIFT+F1 is the shortcut key for this mode.

Display the contextual Help pointer only over the window that provides contextual Help; that is, only over the window from which the What's This? command was chosen. In this mode, display a contextual Help pop-up window for the next object that the user explicitly chooses by clicking with the mouse button 1 (tapping with the pen), activating the object using its access key, or pressing the ENTER key when navigating to the object. The contextual Help window gives a brief explanation about the object and how to use it. After the contextual help window is displayed, the pointer and pointer operation return to their normal state.

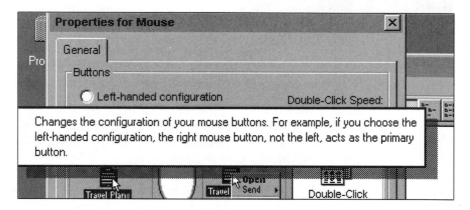

Figure 2.43   A contextual Help pop-up window.

If the user presses a shortcut key that applies to a window that is in contextual Help mode, a contextual Help pop-up window is displayed for the command associated with that shortcut key.

There are some exceptions to this interaction. First, if the user chooses a menu title, either in the menu bar or a cascading menu, maintain the mode and do not display the contextual help window until a menu item is chosen. Second, if the user clicks the item with mouse button 2 and the object supports a pop-up menu, maintain the mode until the user chooses a menu item or cancels the menu. If the object does not support a pop-up menu, the interaction should be the same as clicking it with mouse button 1. Finally, if the chosen object or location does not have support for contextual Help or is otherwise an inappropriate target for contextual Help, then continue to display the contextual Help pointer and maintain the Help mode.

If the user chooses the What's This? command a second time, clicks outside the window, or presses the ESC key, cancel contextual Help mode. Restore the pointer to its normal image and operation in that context.

When the user chooses the What's This? command from a pop-up menu, the interaction is slightly different. Because the object has been identified by clicking mouse button 2, there is no need to enter the contextual Help mode. Instead, immediately display the contextual Help pop-up window for that object.

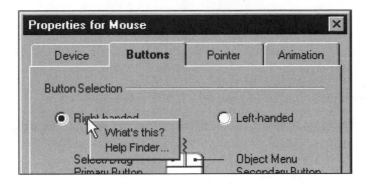

Figure 2.44   A pop-up menu for a control.

The F1 key is the shortcut key for this form of interaction; pressing F1 displays a contextual Help window for the object that has the input focus.

Writing Context-Sensitive Help

When authoring contextual Help information, you are answering the question "What is this?" Start each topic with a verb — for example, "Adjusts the speed of your mouse," "Click this button to close the window," or "Type in a name for your document." When describing a function or object, use words that explain the function or object in common terms; for example, instead of "Undoes the last action," say "Reverses the last action."

In the explanation, you might want to include "why" information. You can also include "how to" information, but this information is better handled by providing access to task-oriented help. Keep your information brief but as complete as possible, so that the Help window is easy and quick to read.

You can provide context-sensitive Help information for the file types supported by your application by registering a What's This? command for the type. This allows the user to choose the "What's This?" command from the file icon's pop-up menu to get information about an icon representing that type. When defining this Help information, include the long type name and a brief description of its function, using the previously described guidelines.

For more information about type names, see Chapter 10, "Integrating with the System."

Tooltips

Other types of contextual user assistance are tooltips. *Tooltips* are small pop-up windows that display the name of a control when the control has no textual label. The most common use of tooltips is for toolbar buttons that have graphic labels.

Display a tooltip after the pointer (or pointing device) remains over the button for a short period of time. Base the time-out on the system timing metric (XXX). It remains displayed until the user presses the button or moves off the control. In the latter case, use the time-out to determine when to remove the tooltip, except if the pointer moves directly to another control supporting a tooltip. In this case, the new tooltip immediately replaces the former one.

For more information about the appearance of tooltips, see Chapter 13, "Visual Design."

Status Bar Help

If a window includes a status bar, you can use the status bar to provide descriptive information about a menu or toolbar button command that the user chooses. You can also use the status bar to provide other forms of descriptive information, such as the state of a process using a progress indicator control. When providing information about a particular menu or control, present the status bar message information when the user presses the mouse button (mouse down transition).

For more information about the status bar control, see Chapter 7, "Menus, Controls, and Toolbars."

Writing Status Line Messages

Use the following guidelines for writing status line messages:

- Begin the message with a verb and use present tense. For example, "Cuts the selection and puts it on the Clipboard."
- Use familiar terms and avoid jargon.
- Be specific when describing a command with a specific function. However, if the scope of the command has multiple functions, try to summarize. For example, "Contains commands for editing and formatting your document."
- Be constructive, not just descriptive. The goal is to inform the user about the purpose of the command.
- Be brief, but avoid truncation. The message needs to be easily read.

The Help Command Button

You can also provide contextual Help for a property sheet, dialog box, or message box by including a Help button in that window.

This is different than the "What's This?" form of Help because it provides an overview, summary assistance, or explanatory information for that window. For example, the Help button on a property sheet provides information about the properties included in the property sheet; for a message box, it provides more information about causes and remedies for the reason the message was displayed.

When the user presses the Help command button, display the Help information in a Help secondary window rather than a contextual help pop-up window.

Task Help

Task Help lists the steps for carrying out a task. It may involve a number of procedures. Task Help topics are organized and displayed in a primary window. The user can size this window like any other primary window.

Note The window style is referred to as a primary window because of its appearance and operation. In technical documentation, this window style may be referred to as a Help secondary window.

A set of command buttons at the top of the window gives the user access to the Content and Index pages of the Help Topics browser, the previously selected topic, and a menu of options, including copying and printing a topic. You can also add buttons by defining them in your Help files.

Figure 2.45   Task Help window.

While you can define the size and location of a task Help window to the specific requirements of your software, consider the following general recommendations:

- Set the window's "always on top" property.
- Size and position the window to minimize what is being covered, but make the window large enough to allow the user to read the topic.
- Set the background color to be XXX.

Writing Task Help Procedures

As with context-sensitive Help, when writing task Help information topics, make them complete but brief. Focus on "how" information rather than "what" or "why." If there are multiple alternatives, pick one method — usually the simplest, most common method for a specific procedure. If you want to include information on alternative methods, provide access to them through other choices or commands.

If you keep the procedure to four or fewer steps, the user will not need to scroll the window. Avoid introductory, conceptual, or reference material in the procedure.

Also, take advantage of the context of a procedure. For example, if a property sheet includes a slider control labeled "Slow" at one end and "Fast" at the other, be contextually concise by stating, "Move the slider to adjust the speed" instead of "To increase the speed, move the slider to the right. To decrease the speed, move the slider to the left." If you refer to a control by its label, capitalize each word in the label, even though the label only has the first word capitalized. .

Shortcut Buttons

Task Help information can also include a "do it" button that offers the user a shortcut or automated way to perform a particular step. For example, use this to automatically open a particular dialog box, property sheet, or other object so that the user does not have to find it.

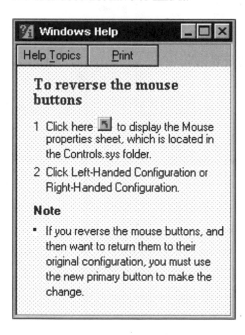

Figure 2.46   **Task Help window with a shortcut button.**

Reference Help

Reference Help is a form of Help information that serves more as on-line documentation. Use the main Help window style, rather than the contextual pop-up windows, topic, or procedure-style windows.

You can provide access to reference Help in a variety of ways. The most common is an explicit menu item in the Help drop-down menu, but you can also provide access by using a toolbar button from the Help Topics browser, or even as a specific file object (icon).

The Help Topics Browser

The Help Topics browser provides user access to Help information. Include a Help Topics menu item on the Help drop-down menu to open this window.

The Help Topic Tabs

Opening the Help Topics window displays a set of tabbed pages. The Contents page displays the list of topics organized by category. A book icon represents a category or group of related topics and a page icon represents an individual topic. You can nest topic levels, but avoid nesting topics too deeply, because this may make access cumbersome.

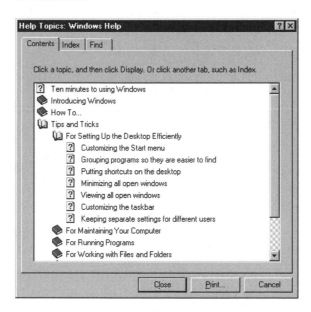

Figure 2.47   The Contents page of the Help Topics browser.

The Help Topics browser window allows a user to expand or collapse the outline. A Print button prints a "book" of topics or a specific topic.

The Index page of the browser organizes the topics by keywords that you define for your topics.

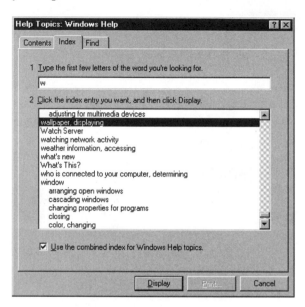

Figure 2.48   Help topics viewed by keyword.

A user can enter a keyword or select one from the list. Choosing the default button displays the topic associated with that keyword. If there are multiple topics that use the same keyword, then another secondary window is displayed that allows the user to choose from that set of topics.

Base the entries listed on the Contents page or the Index page on what you write in your Help files. You can also define additional tabs for the Help Topics browser window.

Writing Content Entries

The purpose of the Contents page is to allow the user to see the organizational relationship between topics. Make the topic titles you include for your software brief but descriptive.

Writing Keywords

Providing an effective keyword list helps users find the information they are looking for. When deciding what keywords to list for your topics, consider the following categories of words: .

- Words that beginning users will think of.
- Words that advanced users will think of.
- Common synonyms of the words you use.
- Words that describe the topic generally.
- Words that describe the topic specifically

Wizards

A *wizard* is a special form of user assistance that automates a task through a dialog with the user. Wizards help users accomplish tasks that may be complex and require experience, but they also provide the interface for streamlining certain tasks.

Wizards may not always appear as an explicit part of the Help interface. You can provide access to them in a variety of ways, including toolbar buttons or even specific objects, such as templates.

For more information about template objects, see Chapter 5, "General Interaction Techniques."

Guidelines for Designing Wizards

Once a wizard is invoked, display it in a secondary window. On the first screen of a wizard include a graphic on the left-hand side of the screen; on the top right portion include a short paragraph welcoming the user to the wizard and explaining what it does.

On subsequent screens you can continue to include a graphic or, if space is critical, use the entire width of the window for displaying instructional text and controls for user input. When using graphics, include pictures that help illustrate the process. For example, you may want to include a conceptual rendering or snapshot of the area of the screen that will be affected, or a preview of the result of the wizard. Where possible, include default values or settings for all controls.

Define your screens so that they are easy to understand. It is important for the user to understand immediately what a wizard screen is about. The user should not have to read it very carefully to be able to understand how to answer. It is better to have several simple screens with fewer choices than to have complex screens with too many options.

Writing Guidelines

Use a conversational rather than instructional writing style for the instructional text you provide on the screens. Use the following guidelines to assist you in writing the textual information.

- Write to the user using words such as "you" and "your".

- Start most questions with phrases such as "Which xxx do you want..." or "Would you like...". Users respond better to a question than to a command. For example, "Which layout do you want?" works better in wizards than "Choose a layout." Think of the type of questions you would ask users to help them do the task.

- Use contractions and short common words. In some cases, it may be acceptable to use slang, but localization should be taken into consideration when doing so.

- Avoid using technical terminology that would be confusing to a novice user.

- Try to use as few words as possible. For example, the question "Which style do you want for this newsletter?" could be written simply as "Which style do you want?"

- Keep the writing clear, concise, and simple, but not condescending.

Wizard Buttons

At the bottom of the window, include the following command buttons, which allow the user to navigate through the wizard.

Command	Action
<Back	Returns to the previous screen. (Disable the button on the first screen.)
>Next	Moves to the next screen in the sequence, maintaining whatever settings the user provides in previous screens.
Finish	Applies user-supplied or default settings from all screens and completes the task.
Cancel	Discards any user-supplied setting, terminates the process, and closes the window.

On the last screen of the wizard indicate to the user that the wizard is prepared to complete the task and instruct the user to press the Finish button to proceed.

Make certain that the design alternatives offered by your wizard provide the user with good results. You may want to limit the options you include in your wizard. Also be sure to make it obvious how the user should proceed when the wizard has completed its process.

CHAPTER 3

Windows Architecture: Fundamentals

Topic

Describe event-driven programming.

Content

Introduction to Windows Programming for MS-DOS Programmers[1]

Summary
This article discusses some differences between programming in the MS-DOS environment and programming in the event-driven Windows environment.

More Information
For the purposes of this discussion, consider the term "traditional programmer" as referring to someone who has not programmed in Windows but who has experience programming in an MS-DOS environment.

As a traditional programmer, you may not only have become comfortable with a particular programming style, but also with certain accepted fundamentals, such as writing an instruction and expecting it to be carried out in a controlled order. Access Basic makes good use of Windows, making it easy to learn to program.

---

[1] The article is also available on the Microsoft Developer Network Development Library under KnowledgeBase and Bug Lists, Microsoft Access Kbase, Related Information. Copyright 1994. Used with permission. All rights reserved.

"One Entry, One Exit" vs. Event-Driven Programming

Consider the following pseudocode of a program designed to get user input, count all the records in a table, and display the result in a box if the user presses 1, or exit if the user presses 2.

```
START PROGRAM
LOOP WHILE TRUE
    GET KEYPRESS INTO X
    IF X IS "1"
        COUNT ALL RECORDS IN THE TABLE INTO Y
        DRAW BOX FROM ROW 10 COLUMN 5 TO ROW 12 COLUMN 7
        DISPLAY Y AT ROW 11 COLUMN 6
    IF X IS "2"
        EXIT LOOP
END LOOP
STOP PROGRAM
```

The purpose of this program is to loop continuously until a key press of a 1 or 2 is detected. At that point, a decision is made to perform some sort of operation, or to ignore the keypress and continue looping. The programmer has full control over what happens.

The Windows programming model is event-driven and graphic object oriented. In other words, programming in Windows involves creating objects and modifying aspects (or properties) of those objects based on different events. Consider the following sample program that presents two buttons to the user. If the user chooses the Count button, the program counts the records in the database and displays the result in a window. The user can press the Exit button to exit from the program.

First, you create the necessary objects. Most of this phase of Access Basic programming is created graphically with the Access Forms designer. The list of controls and properties below defines a form that will be used to illustrate this.

```
Form: MasterForm
---------------------------
   Push Button: CountButton
       Caption: Count
        OnPush: =DisplayCount()
   Push Button: ExitButton
       Caption: Exit
        OnPush: =CloseProgram()
   Text Box: DisplayWindow
```

Note OnPush is a property of Microsoft Access version 1.x command buttons that gives you the ability to invoke an Access Basic procedure or macro. In Microsoft Access 2.0, the property is called OnClick.

You can then create the modules that the objects will invoke. In this case, buttons are the only objects that will have the ability to invoke procedures. The procedures shown below are pseudo-code examples. The first procedure defined is the DisplayCount procedure:

```
PROCEDURE DisplayCount( )
   COUNT ALL THE RECORDS IN THE TABLE INTO Y
   CHANGE THE DISPLAYWINDOW TEXT PROPERTY TO Y
END PROCEDURE
```

Notice that the code did not direct the resulting count to display in a box painted on the screen. Instead, the Text property of DisplayWindow was changed to the resulting count value. The next procedure defined is the CloseProgram procedure.

```
PROCEDURE CloseProgram
   CLOSE MASTERFORM
END PROCEDURE
```

Notice that this procedure does not provide an exit from some kind of loop or other program structure. Instead, it closes the object that contains the buttons and window.

At this point, you have a master form object containing two buttons, a window, and a couple of coded procedures. They are in no special order; they simply exist as part of the form. So where is the loop that checks for button activity? Where is the command to invoke the program?

The answer is that these do not exist as you might expect them to. You "run" the program by opening MasterForm. When you open the form, all the control objects (that is, the buttons and so on) exist on the form waiting for something to happen. In this example, there is no flow of control (no looping to check activity).

While the form is active, Windows constantly checks for events. When an event occurs, the user's input is put in a queue and "waits in line" until it is processed. For example, when you push the "Count" button, Windows detects that the button object you placed on the form has been affected. Windows sends a "Mouse Click" message to Access. Access then translates the message and determines that the DisplayCount() function should be called based on the "On Push" field of the command button.

Advantages

The traditional programmer will find this new approach to programming a bit challenging. There are a few things to learn and "unlearn," but there are many advantages.

Windows Interface

The Windows interface is one that has been regarded throughout the industry as being very user-friendly. Familiar objects such as push buttons, radio buttons, list boxes, and a wide variety of colors and screen fonts are generally more appealing than standard ASCII text characters.

The Windows Standard

Because Access Basic forces you to some extent into the Windows standard, others who are familiar with Windows applications can immediately recognize the "look and feel" of your application. This reduces the learning time because the user does not have to learn entirely new interface controls and prompts.

Advantages Offered by the Windows Environment

You do not have to worry too much about different devices such as monitors, printer drivers, and so on. The Windows operating environment takes care of most device compatibility and user preference issues. In addition, because Windows handles and processes events, you will find it much easier to create and manage many aspects of an application.

See Also

For a treatment of event-driven programming within the Visual Basic environment, see "Introduction to Programming in Visual Basic" on the December 1994 TechNet CD under Conferences, Tech*Ed 1994, Microsoft Visual Basic.

Topic

Identify application design considerations in preemptive versus nonpreemptive environments.

Content

Multitasking[2]

I think multitasking is the single most important new feature that separates 16-bit Windows from Windows NT. Although 16-bit Windows can run multiple applications simultaneously, it runs the applications nonpreemptively. That is, one application must tell Windows it's finished processing before the scheduler can assign another application execution time, which creates problems for both users and application developers.

---

[2] Material excerpted from Chapter Six of *Advanced Windows NT*. *C*opyright Jeffrey Richter 1994. Used with permission. All rights reserved.

For users, it means that control of the system is lost for an arbitrary time period decided by the application (not the user). If an application takes a long time to execute a particular task, such as formatting a floppy disk, the user can't switch away from that task and work with a word processor while the formatting continues in the background. This situation is unfortunate because users want to make the most of their time and not wait for the machine to finish.

Developers for 16-bit Windows recognize this and try to implement their applications so that they execute tasks in spurts. For example, a formatting program might format a single track on a floppy disk and then return control to Windows. Once Windows has control, it can respond to other tasks for the user. When the user is idle, Windows returns control back to the format program so that another track can be formatted.

Well, this method of sharing time between tasks works, but it makes implementing a program significantly more difficult. One way the formatting program can accomplish its tasks is to set a timer for itself using the SetTimer function. The program is then notified with WM_TIMER messages when it's time to execute another part of the process. This type of implementation involves the following problems:

1. Windows offers a limited number of timers for application use. What should the program do if a timer is not available--not allow the user to format a disk until another application using a timer is terminated?

2. The program must keep track of its progress. The formatting program must save, either in global variables or in a dynamically allocated block of memory, information such as the letter of the drive it is formatting, the track that has just been formatted, etc.

3. The program code can't include a function that formats a disk; instead it must include a function that formats a single track of a disk. This means that the functions in the program must be broken up in a way that is not natural for a programmer to implement. You don't usually design an algorithm thinking that the processor needs to be able to jump into the middle of it. You can imagine how difficult implementation would be if your algorithm required a series of nested loops to perform its operations and the processor needed to jump into the innermost loop.

4. WM_TIMER messages occur at regular intervals. So if an application sets a timer to go off every second, WM_TIMER messages are received 60 times every minute. This is true whether a user is running the application on a 25-MHz 386 or a 50-MHz 486. If a user has a faster machine, the program should take advantage of that.

Another favorite method used by 16-bit Windows developers to help their applications behave more courteously towards other applications involves the PeekMessage function. When an application calls PeekMessage, it tells Windows, "I have more work to process, but I'm willing to postpone doing it if another application needs to do something."

Using this method makes the code easier to implement because the implementer can design the algorithms assuming that the computer won't jump into the middle of a process. This method also doesn't require any timers and doesn't have any special system resource requirements. It does have two problems, however: The implementer must sprinkle PeekMessage loops throughout the code, and the application must be written to handle all kinds of asynchronous events. For example, a spreadsheet might be recalculating cell values when another application attempts to initiate a DDE conversation with it. It is incredibly difficult to test your application to verify that it performs correctly in all possible scenarios.

As it turns out, even when developers use these methods to help their applications behave in a friendlier way, their programs still don't multitask smoothly. Sometimes a user might click on another application's window, and a full second or more might go by before Windows changes to the active application. More important though, if an application bug causes the application to never call PeekMessage or to never return control back to Windows, the entire 16-bit Windows system effectively hangs. At this point, the user can't switch to another application, can't save to disk any work that was in progress, and more often than not, is forced to reboot the computer. This is totally unacceptable!

Windows NT solves these problems (and more that I haven't even mentioned) with preemptive multitasking. By adding a preemptive multitasking capability to Windows NT, Microsoft has done much more than allow multiple applications to run simultaneously. The environment is much more robust because a single application can't control all the system resources.

Topic

Describe what a process is.

Content

Multitasking[3]

A *process* is a program that is loaded into memory and prepared for execution. Each process has a private virtual address space. A process consists of the code,

---

[3] Material excerpted from Part 3 of the *Programmer's Reference* in the Win32 Software Development Kit for Windows NT. Copyright 1994. Used with permission. All rights reserved.

data, and other system resources—such as files, pipes, and synchronization objects
—that are accessible to the threads of the process. Each process is started with a
single thread, but additional independently executing threads can be created.

A *thread* can execute any part of the program's code, including a part executed by
another thread. Threads are the basic entity to which the operating system allocates
CPU time. Each thread maintains a set of structures for saving its *context* while
waiting to be scheduled for processing time. The context includes the thread's set of
machine registers, the kernel stack, a thread environment block, and a user stack in
the address space of the thread's process. All threads of a process share the virtual
address space and can access the global variables and system resources of the
process.

A multitasking operating system divides the available CPU time among the threads
that need it. In Windows, the Win32 API is designed for preemptive multitasking;
this means that the system allocates small slices of CPU time among the competing
threads. The currently executing thread is suspended when its time slice elapses,
allowing another thread to run. When the system switches from one thread to
another, it saves the context of the suspended thread and restores the saved context
of the next thread in the queue.

Because each time slice is small (approximately 20 milliseconds), it appears that
multiple threads are executing at the same time. This is actually the case on
multiprocessor systems, where the executable threads are distributed among the
available processors. On a single-processor system, however, using multiple threads
does not result in more instructions being executed. In fact, the system can slow
down if it is forced to keep track of too many threads.

To the user, the advantage of multitasking is the ability to have several applications
open and working at the same time. For example, a user can edit a file with one
application while another application is printing or recalculating a spreadsheet.

To the application developer, the advantage of multitasking is the ability to create
applications that use more than one process and to create processes that use more
than one thread of execution. For example, you can have one thread that handles
interactions with the user (keyboard and mouse input), while other threads with
lower priority perform the other work of the process. The higher priority of the
input thread makes the program responsive to the user, while the other threads
ensure that the processor can be used efficiently during the slices of time between
keystrokes.

When to Use Multitasking

Any thread of any process can use the **CreateThread** and **CreateProcess**
functions to create additional threads or processes. An application might use
multiple processes for functions that require a private address space and private
resources, to protect them from the activities of other threads. Functions that are to

be distributed as separate executable modules, but that can be integrated to form a single application, can benefit from the multiprocess approach.

It is useful for a process to have multiple threads when the application has several tasks to run concurrently. For example, an application that opens more than one window can have a separate thread perform the work of the application in each window. Multiple threads can be a convenient way to structure a program that performs several similar or identical tasks. For example, a named pipe server can create a thread to handle communications with each client process that attaches to the pipe. Other examples of using multiple threads are processes that do the following:

- Handle input for multiple windows.

- Manage input from several communications devices.

- Need to distinguish among tasks of varying priority. For example, a high-priority thread handles time-critical tasks, and a low-priority thread performs other tasks.

It is typically more efficient for an application to implement multitasking by distributing tasks among the threads of a single process, rather than by creating multiple processes, for the following reasons:

- The system can create and execute threads more quickly than it can create processes, primarily because the code for threads has already been mapped into the address space of the process, while the code for a new process must be loaded.

- All threads of a process share the same address space and can access the process's global variables, which can simplify communications between threads.

- All threads of a process can use open handles to resources such as files and pipes.

For both multiple threads and multiple processes, there are costs and dangers to be considered. The system consumes memory for the structures required by both processes and threads. Keeping track of a large number of threads consumes CPU time. With multiple threads accessing the same resources, you must synchronize the threads to avoid conflicts. This is true for system resources (such as communications ports or disk drives), handles to resources shared by multiple processes (such as file or pipe handles), or the resources of a single process (such as global variables accessed by multiple threads). Failure to synchronize multiple threads properly (in the same or in different processes) can lead to program problems such as *deadlock* and *race conditions*. The Win32 API provides a set of synchronization objects and functions you can use to coordinate multiple threads. For more information about synchronization, see "Synchronizing Execution of Multiple Threads" and "Synchronization."

The Win32 API also provides alternative ways to execute multiple tasks that, in some cases, make multithreaded processes unnecessary. The most significant of these are overlapped I/O and the ability to wait for multiple events.

Overlapped I/O enables a single thread to initiate multiple time-consuming I/O requests that can run concurrently. This asynchronous I/O can be performed on files, pipes, serial communications devices, or tape devices. For more information about files, see "Files." For more information about pipes, see "Pipes." For more information about serial communication devices, see "Communications." For more information about tape devices, see "Tape Backup."

Waiting for multiple events enables a single thread to block its execution while waiting for any one of several events to occur. This is much more efficient than using multiple threads, each waiting for a single event, or using a single thread that consumes CPU time by continually checking for an event of interest. For more information about waiting for multiple events, see "Synchronization."

Topic

Describe the relationship between threads and processes.

Content

Processes And Threads[4]

A process is a running instance of an application. Every process consists of blocks of code and data (loaded from EXEs and DLLs) that are located in the process's very own 4-GB address space. A process also owns other resources, such as files, dynamic memory allocations, and threads. The various resources that are created during a process's life are destroyed when the process is terminated.

A thread is the unit of execution in a process. Each thread in a process is associated with a sequence of CPU instructions, a set of CPU registers, and a stack. A process does not execute code—it is simply the address space where the code resides. Code contained in the address space of a process is executed by threads. In fact, threads are often referred to as "threads of execution."

In Windows NT, a process can contain several threads. Each of these individual threads is scheduled CPU time by the Windows NT Kernel. On a single-processor machine, the operating system gives the illusion that all these threads are running concurrently by offering time slices (called quantums) to the threads in a round-robin fashion. (See Figure 3.1 on the following page.)

---

[4] Material excerpted from Chapter One of *Advanced Windows NT*. Copyright 1994 by Jeffrey Richter. Used with permission. All rights reserved.

Windows NT is a giant step forward from 16-bit Windows because it not only offers preemptive multitasking but also runs on machines that contain several CPUs. For example, Sequent is designing a computer system that includes 30 Intel CPUs. Each CPU can be assigned a thread of execution, allowing 30 threads to execute simultaneously. The Windows NT Kernel handles all the management and scheduling of threads on this type of system.

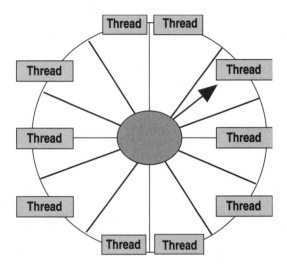

Figure 3.1   Individual threads are scheduled time quantums by the Windows NT Kernel in a round-robin fashion.
When you design your software, you don't need to make any special provisions for multiprocessor systems. However, a process with multiple threads is more likely to malfunction on a multiprocessor system than on a single-processor system. Before shipping a multithreaded application, I strongly suggest that you thoroughly test it on a multiprocessor machine. Any synchronization problems waiting in your application might never show themselves on a single-processor machine.

When a Windows NT process is created, its first thread, called the primary thread, is automatically created by the system. This primary thread can then create additional threads. These additional threads can create even more threads. If you are familiar with OS/2, you know that the primary thread has a special attribute: When the primary thread ends, the whole process terminates even if other threads are still executing. This is not true for Windows NT. In Windows NT, if any thread contained in the process is still running, the process does not die; the process terminates only when all the threads contained in the process have ended.

Using the Win32 API, you can create two types of applications for Windows NT: GUI-based and console-based. A GUI-based application has a graphical front end. GUI applications create windows, have menus, interact with the user using dialog boxes, and use all the standard "Windowsy" stuff. The Program Manager and File Manager are typical examples of GUI-based applications.

Console-based applications more closely resemble MS-DOS text applications. Their output is text based, they don't create windows or process messages, and they don't require a graphical user interface. Al though console-based applications are contained within a window on the screen, the window contains only text characters. The Microsoft C/C++ compiler and linker are typical examples of console-based applications.

Although there are two types of applications, the line between them is very fuzzy. It is possible to create console-based applications that display dialog boxes. For example, the compiler could have a special command-line switch that causes it to display a graphical dialog box, allowing you to select compilation switches instead of typing nonintuitive letter combinations on the command line. You could also create a GUI-based application that outputs character text strings to a console window for debugging. Of the two types, you are certainly encouraged to use a graphical user interface in your applications instead of using the old-fashioned character interface. It has been proven time and time again that GUI-based applications are much more user friendly.

In this chapter, I discuss the mechanics of creating processes and threads. The concepts apply to both GUI-based and console-based applications, but I emphasize GUI-based applications and don't discuss some of the finer details of creating console-based applications. If you want more information on creating console-based applications, please refer to the Win32 SDK documentation.

Content

Preemptive Time Scheduling[5]

16-bit Windows has only one thread of execution. That is, the microprocessor travels in a linear path from functions in one application to functions in another application, frequently dipping into the operating system's code. Whenever the user moves from executing one application, or task, to another, the operating system code performs a task switch. A task switch simply means that the operating system saves the state of the CPU's registers before deactivating the current task and restores the registers for the newly activated task. Notice that I said the operating system is responsible for performing the task switch. Because the system has only one thread of execution, if any code enters an infinite loop the thread can never access the operating system code that performed the task switch, and the system hangs.

---

[5] Material excerpted from Chapter Six of Advanced Windows NT. Copyright 1994 by Jeffrey Richter. Used with permission. All rights reserved.

16-bit Windows uses the concepts of modules and tasks. A module identifies an executable file that is loaded into memory. Every time an instance of the executable file is invoked, 16-bit Windows calls this instance a task. With few exceptions, resources (that is, memory blocks or windows) created (allocated) when the task is executing become owned by the particular task. Some resources, such as icons and cursors, are actually owned by the module, which allows these resources to be shared by all of the module's tasks.

Windows NT still uses the term module to identify an executable file loaded into memory. However, Windows NT takes the concept of a task and breaks it down into two new concepts—processes and threads.

A process refers to an instance of a running program. For example, if a single instance of Clock and two instances of Notepad are running, three processes are running in the system. A thread describes a path of execution within a process. When an executable file is invoked, Windows NT creates both a process and a thread. For example, when the user invokes an application from the Program Manager, Windows NT locates the program's EXE file, creates a process and a thread for the new instance, and tells the CPU to start executing the thread beginning with the C Runtime startup code, which in turn calls your WinMain function. When the application terminates (returns from WinMain), Windows NT destroys the thread.

Every process has at least one thread. Windows NT schedules CPU time among threads of a process, not among processes themselves. After a thread begins executing, it can create additional threads within the process. These threads execute until they are destroyed or until they terminate on their own. The number of threads that can be created is limited only by system resources.

While a thread is executing, Windows NT can steal the CPU away from the thread and give the CPU to another thread. But the CPU cannot be interrupted while it is executing a single instruction (a CPU instruction, not a line of source code). The operating system's ability to interrupt a thread at (almost) any time and assign the CPU to a waiting thread is called preemptive multitasking.

The life span of a process is directly tied to the threads it owns. Threads within a process have lives of their own, too. New threads are created, existing threads are paused and restarted, and other threads are terminated. When all the threads in a process terminate, Windows NT terminates the process, frees any resources owned by the process, and removes the process from memory.

Most objects allocated by a thread are owned by the process that also owns the thread. For example, a block of memory allocated by a thread is owned by the process, not the thread. All the global and static variables in an application are also owned by the process. And all GDI objects (pens, brushes, bitmaps) are owned by the process. Most USER objects (windows, menus, accelerator tables) are owned by the thread that created or loaded them into memory. Only three USER objects— icons, cursors, and window classes—are owned by a process instead of by a thread.

An understanding of ownership is important so that you know what can be shared. If a process has seven threads operating within it and one thread makes a call to allocate a block of memory, the block of memory can then be accessed from any of the seven threads. This access can cause several problems if all the threads attempt to read and write from the same block simultaneously. Synchronizing several threads is discussed further in Chapter 5.

Ownership is also important because Windows NT is much better than 16-bit Windows about cleaning up after a thread or a process after it terminates. If a thread terminates and neglects to destroy a window that it created, the system ensures that the window is destroyed and isn't just sitting around somewhere soaking up precious memory and system resources. For example, if a thread creates or loads a cursor into memory and then the thread is terminated, the cursor is not destroyed. This is because the cursor is owned by the process and not by the thread. When the process terminates, the system ensures that the cursor is destroyed. In 16-bit Windows, a task has the equivalent of one and only one thread. As a result, the concept of ownership is less complicated.

Topic

Define thread priority.

Content

Scheduling Priorities[6]

The scheduling priority of each thread is determined by the following criteria:

- The priority class of its process (high, normal, or idle).
- The priority level of the thread within the priority class of its process (lowest, below normal, normal, above normal, highest).
- The dynamic priority boost, if any, the system applies to the thread's base priority.

By default, the priority class of a process is set to normal. The CreateProcess function allows a parent process to specify the priority class of its child processes. Use **SetPriorityClass** to change the priority class of a process and **GetPriorityClass** to determine the current priority class of a process.

---

[6] Material excerpted from Part 3 of the *Programmer's Reference* in the Win32 Software Development Kit for Windows NT. Copyright 1994. Used with permission. All rights reserved.

There are five priority levels within each priority class. The levels range from lowest (-2) to highest (2). All threads are started with normal (0) priority. The **SetThreadPriority** function enables you to change the priority level of a thread to any of the five levels. Use the **GetThreadPriority** function to determine the current priority level of a thread.

The base priority of each thread is the thread's priority level within the priority class of its process. The scheduler uses this base priority to determine a thread's dynamic priority, which it uses to make scheduling decisions. A thread's dynamic priority is never less than its base priority. The scheduler raises and lowers the dynamic priority of a thread to enhance its responsiveness when significant things happen to the thread. For example, whenever a window receives input (such as timer messages, mouse move messages, keyboard input), the scheduler boosts the priorities of all threads within the process that owns the window. In some cases, the dynamic priority of a waiting thread is raised when a wait is satisfied. For example, a wait associated with disk or keyboard I/O results in a dynamic boost when the input occurs.

After raising a thread's dynamic priority, the scheduler reduces that priority by one level each time the thread completes a time slice, until the thread drops back to its base priority.

In addition to these dynamic priority boosts, the scheduler raises the priority class of the process associated with the foreground window, so it is greater than or equal to the priority class of any background processes. The process's priority class returns to its original setting when it is no longer in the foreground. A user can always make a given window lose the foreground priority boost by clicking on another window or by using the ALT+TAB or CTRL+ESC key combination.

The priority classes are intended to be used as follows.

Priority	Meaning
HIGH_PRIORITY_CLASS	Indicates a process that performs time-critical tasks that must be executed immediately for it to run correctly. The threads of a high-priority class process preempt the threads of normal or idle priority class processes. An example is Windows Task List, which must respond quickly when called by the user, regardless of the load on the operating system. Use extreme care when using the high-priority class, because a high-priority class CPU-bound application can use nearly all available cycles.
IDLE_PRIORITY_CLASS	Indicates a process whose threads run only when the system is idle and are preempted by the threads of any process running in a higher priority class. An example is a screen saver. The idle priority class is inherited by child processes.
NORMAL_PRIORITY_CLASS	Indicates a normal process with no special scheduling needs.
REALTIME_PRIORITY_CLASS	Indicates a process that has the highest possible priority. The threads of a real-time priority class process preempt the threads of all other processes, including operating system processes performing important tasks. For example, a real-time process that executes for more than a very brief interval can cause disk caches not to flush or cause the mouse to be unresponsive.

Use the high-priority class with extreme care. If a thread runs at the highest priority level for extended periods, other threads in the system will be starved for CPU time. If several threads are set at high priority at the same time, the effect of the high priority is neutralized. The high-priority class should be reserved for threads that must respond to time-critical events. If your application has a task that requires the high-priority class while most of its functions are normal priority, use **SetPriorityClass** to raise the priority class temporarily; then reduce it once the time-critical task has been completed. Another strategy is to create a high-priority process that is blocked most of the time, awakening only when the critical task is needed. The important point is that a thread should be high priority and executable only for a brief period, when it has time-critical work to perform.

Having selected a priority class for a multithreaded process, use **SetThreadPriority** to adjust the relative priority of its threads. A typical strategy is to use a higher priority level for the process's input thread, to ensure responsiveness to the user. Other threads, particularly those that are CPU-intensive, can be set to a lower relative priority to ensure that they can be preempted when necessary. However, if you have a higher-priority thread waiting for a lower-priority thread to complete some task, be sure to block the execution of the waiting thread (using a wait function, critical section, or the Sleep) rather than having it iterate in a loop. Otherwise, the process will deadlock, because the lower-priority thread will never get scheduled.

Topic

Explain the difference between asymmetric and symmetric multiprocessing.

Explain how SMP benefits the Microsoft Windows NT operating system.

Content

Symmetric Multiprocessing[7]

Multitasking shares a single processor among multiple threads. When a computer has more than one processor, the multitasking model must be upgraded to a multiprocessing model. While a multitasking operating system appears to execute multiple threads at once, a multiprocessing operating system actually does it, one on each of its processors. Multiprocessing operating systems support either asymmetric or symmetric hardware.

Asymmetric multiprocessing (ASMP) operating systems typically select one processor to execute operating system code, while other processors run user jobs. ASMP operating systems are relatively easy to create by extending existing uniprocessor operating systems. They are especially well-suited to running on asymmetric hardware, such as a processor with an attached coprocessor or two processors that don't share memory. However, it's hard to make ASMP operating systems portable. Hardware from different vendors, and even different versions of hardware from the same vendor, tends to vary in type and degree of asymmetry. Either the hardware vendors must target their products for specific operating systems or the operating system must be substantially rewritten for each hardware platform.

---

[7] Material excerpted from Chapters 1 and 2 of *Inside Windows NT*. Copyright 1993 by Helen Custer. Used with permission. All rights reserved.

Symmetric multiprocessing (SMP) systems, including Windows NT, allow the operating system to run on any free processor or on all processors simultaneously, sharing memory between them. This approach makes better use of multiple processors because the operating system itself can use a significant percentage of a computer's processing time, depending on the application(s) running. Running the operating system on only one processor can tax that processor, leave others idle, and decrease the system's throughput; as the number of processors on the system increases, operating system activities are more likely to bottleneck. SMP systems are also less likely to experience down time than ASMP systems because operating system code can execute on other processors if one fails. Finally, since symmetric hardware is implemented similarly from vendor to vendor, it is possible to create a portable SMP operating system.

Unlike ASMP systems, SMP systems are often designed and written from the ground up, because they must adhere to strict coding guidelines to ensure correct operation. In addition, numerous performance considerations arise in multiprocessing systems that do not occur in single processor systems.

Several Windows NT constructs are crucial to its success as a multiprocessing operating system:

- The ability to run operating system code on any available processor, or on multiple processors at once. With the exception of its kernel component, which handles thread scheduling and interrupts, operating system code can be preempted (forced to give up a processor) when a higher-priority thread needs attention.

- Multiple threads of execution within a single process. Threads allow one process to execute different parts of its program on different processors simultaneously.

- Servers that use multiple threads to process requests from more than one client simultaneously.

- Convenient mechanisms for sharing objects between processes and flexible interprocess communication capabilities, including shared memory and a message-passing facility.

CHAPTER 4

Windows Architecture: Advanced Topics

Topic

Describe virtual memory.

Content

Virtual Memory Manager[1]

The memory architecture for Windows NT is a demand-paged virtual memory system. It is based on a flat, linear address space accessed via 32-bit addresses.

Virtual memory refers to the fact that the operating system can actually allocate more memory than the computer physically has. Each process is allocated a unique virtual address space, which is a set of addresses available for the process's threads to use. This virtual address space is divided into equal blocks, or *pages*. Every process is allocated its own virtual address space, which appears to be 4 gigabytes (GB) in size — 2 GB reserved for program storage and 2 GB reserved for system storage.

Demand paging refers to a method by which data is moved in pages from physical memory to a temporary paging file on disk. As the data is needed by a process, it is paged back into physical memory.

---

[1] Material excerpted from Chapter 1 of the *Resource Guide* in the Windows NT Resource Kit. Copyright 1992 - 1995. Used with permission. All rights reserved.

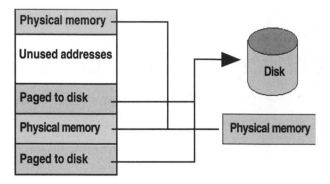

Figure 4.1   Conceptual view of virtual memory.

The Virtual Memory Manager maps virtual addresses in the process's address space to physical pages in the computer's memory. In doing so, it hides the physical organization of memory from the process's threads. This ensures that the thread can access its process's memory as needed, but not the memory of other processes. Therefore, as illustrated by Figure 4.1, a thread's view of its process's virtual memory is much simpler than the real arrangement of pages in physical memory.

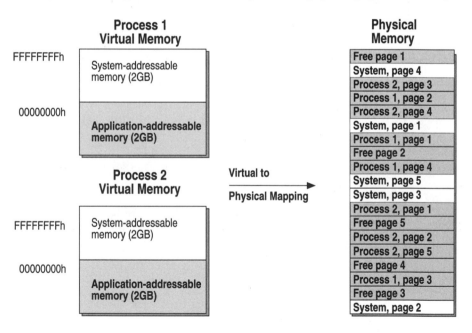

Figure 4.2   Protecting processes' memory.

Because each process has a separate address space, a thread in one process cannot view or modify the memory of another process without authorization.

Topic

Describe memory protection.

Content

Windows 95 Memory Management[2]

In most regards, Windows 95's 32-bit memory management architecture is on the surface very similar to Windows NT. Under the hood, Kernel32 relies heavily on services provided by VWIN32 to implement the Win32 memory management APIs. VMM32.VXD consists of the VMM and a collection of other VxDs. It replaces and extends the Windows 3.1 equivalent, WIN386.EXE. On the 16-bit side of the fence, Krnl386 now also calls directly into the VWIN32 VxD in VMM32.VXD for low-level services such as allocating large memory regions and pagelocking. In Windows 3.1, Krnl386 used DPMI functions from WIN386 for many (but not all) of the same services.

At the level where most programmers work every day, the big news in Win32 and Windows 95 is no more segments! By moving to 32-bit programming, you can finally forget all about near and far pointers. You can also forget about GlobalLock, LocalLock, and anything related to memory models. Everything in a Windows 95 32-bit program is small model. That is, the 32-bit small model. Of course, if you want to perform tricks with the memory manager, the Win32 API and Windows 95 have a whole new set of functions to delight the low-level hacker.

The lowest level of memory manipulation in Windows 95 is the VirtualXxx functions: VirtualAlloc, VirtualFree, VirtualLock, VirtualUnlock, VirtualProtect, and VirtualQuery. VirtualAlloc lets you allocate large chunks of address space with 4KB granularity (the size of an 80386 page). Although there are important differences, the closest equivalent to VirtualAlloc in Windows 3.1 is GlobalAlloc. Both functions are intended for allocating large blocks of memory. Also, the granularity of both functions makes their system overhead relatively high. You probably wouldn't want to use either function in place of malloc or new.

At the time you allocate address space with VirtualAlloc, you can optionally bind that address space to physical RAM by using the MEM_COMMIT flag. Why wouldn't you want an address space allocation to be backed up by memory

---

2 "Stepping Up to 32 Bits: Windows 95's Process, Thread, and Memory Management," by Matt Pietrek is reprinted with permission from *Microsoft Systems Journal* (Vol. 9, No. 8) August 1994, copyright 1994 Miller-Freeman Inc. All rights reserved.

immediately? Sparse memory is one reason. For example, your program might need a great deal of memory for storage (on the order of megabytes). You don't know how much memory you need beforehand. In this situation, you could VirtualAlloc a chunk of address space large enough so that you're confident you won't need more memory. As your program uses up more and more of the address range, you can commit memory as needed by making additional calls to VirtualAlloc. Windows 95's structured exception handling can help automate this. Incidentally, this commit-only-when-needed algorithm is precisely how Windows 95 implements large program stacks while not wasting memory on pages that are never touched.

Just when you finally got the Windows 3.x GMEM_XXX flags straight, VirtualAlloc defines a whole new set of them. The flags are for pages, rather than segments. At any given time, a page in a program's address space is free, reserved, or committed. When VirtualAlloc allocates a range of pages, it changes the MEM_FREE flag to either MEM_RESERVE or MEM_COMMIT depending on what you told VirtualAlloc to do. There are additional flags which hold more specific information about a page. Examples include PAGE_READONLY, PAGE_READWRITE, and PAGE_EXECUTE_READWRITE. The table below shows all the possible flags. The VirtualQuery API retrieves these flags for a range of pages in your process context.

VirtualAlloc Flags

PAGE_NOACCESS	0x01
PAGE_READONLY	0x02
PAGE_READWRITE	0x04
PAGE_WRITECOPY	0x08
PAGE_EXECUTE	0x10
PAGE_EXECUTE_READ	0x20
PAGE_EXECUTE_READWRITE	0x40
PAGE_EXECUTE_WRITECOPY	0x80
PAGE_GUARD	0x100
PAGE_NOCACHE	0x200
MEM_COMMIT	0x1000
MEM_RESERVE	0x2000
MEM_DECOMMIT	0x4000
MEM_RELEASE	0x8000
MEM_FREE	0x10000
MEM_PRIVATE	0x20000
MEM_MAPPED	0x40000
MEM_MAPPED_COPIED	0x80000
MEM_TOP_DOWN	0x100000
MEM_LARGE_PAGES	0x20000000
MEM_DOS_LIM	0x40000000

While VirtualQuery lets you examine the attributes of a block of pages, the VirtualProtect API lets you change page attributes. One "benefit" from this is that you can now easily modify your own code by changing the attributes of a code page to read/write. In 16-bit Windows, code selectors are only as big as the code segment. If you want to modify 16-bit code, you need to create and use an alias data selector that points to the code segment's memory. When Windows 95 initializes the code pages for a 32-bit app in the flat 4-GB segment, it sets the page attributes to read-only. This compensates for the fact that there's no selector-level protection in Windows 95. Windows 95 does all memory protection through paging.

The VirtualLock function is roughly equivalent to the Windows 3.1 GlobalPageLock API. Both functions let you specify a block of memory that's guaranteed never to be paged out (or marked not present). In Win32, you'd want to do this if you have a very heavily used region of memory that could cause a performance hit if it was paged out. Unlike GlobalPageLock, VirtualLock restricts you to a relatively small amount of memory to pagelock. VirtualLock also doesn't have the annoying behavior of moving the block down low (sometimes below 1MB), as does GlobalPageLock.

Higher level Windows 95 memory management comes in the form of heap functions. The Win32 heap functions are as follows: HeapAlloc, HeapFree, HeapReAlloc, HeapSize, HeapCreate, and HeapDestroy. When Windows 95 creates a new 32-bit process, it creates a heap for it within its address space. The 32-bit heap is roughly equivalent to a 16-bit Windows local heap, since every process has one. However, the 32-bit heap certainly isn't limited to 64KB! Windows 95 supports multiple heaps, so you need to pass a handle to the heap function when you want to allocate, free, or otherwise manipulate a heap memory block. A program retrieves the handle to its default process heap with the GetProcessHeap API. This heap handle is nothing more than the starting address of the heap.

Unlike the VirtualXxx functions, allocations from the Win32 heap functions have a much smaller granularity: 4 bytes, rather than 4KB. The overhead for each allocation also appears to be only 4 bytes. This makes the HeapAlloc function a suitable replacement for malloc (or a quick way to implement your own malloc). The 4-byte overhead comes from a DWORD immediately preceding the address returned by HeapAlloc. Ignoring the bottom two bits and the top few bits, this DWORD holds the size of the block including the 4-byte overhead. The bottom two bits are flags (bit 0 off means that the block is in use, bit 0 on means that the block is free). The minimum block size allocated including overhead is 0x10 bytes. If you're familiar with the 16-bit Windows local heap, this way of setting up the heap nodes should ring a bell.

Topic

List and describe the methods available to share data.

Describe shared memory between processes.

Content

Interprocess Communications Options in Win32-based Applications[3]

As computer users become more sophisticated, they demand more power from the applications they use. To meet this demand, developers add more features to their applications, and the applications become larger. At some point, these large applications can become unmanageable, both from a development standpoint and from a user-interface point of view. Therefore, developers now tend to produce highly focused applications that do a good job on a limited number of features and then to enable those applications to communicate and share data with other specialized applications. No longer can any one application meet all user expectations; the age of cooperating and communicating applications has arrived.

The Microsoft Win32 application programming interface (API) provides a rich set of mechanisms for facilitating communications and data sharing between applications. Collectively, the activities enabled by these mechanisms are called *interprocess communications (IPC)*. In addition to facilitating the division of labor among several specialized processes, some forms of IPC can distribute the computational load among cooperating computers on a network.

Typically, cooperating and communicating applications can be categorized as clients or servers. A client is an application or a process that requests a service from some other process. A server is an application or a process that responds to a client request. Many applications act as both a client and a server, depending on the situation. For example, a word processing application might act as a client in requesting a summary table of manufacturing costs from a spreadsheet application acting as a server. The spreadsheet application, in turn, might act as a client in requesting the latest inventory levels from an automated inventory control application.

---

[3] Materials excerpted from Part 6 in the *Win32 Programmer's Reference* of the Microsoft Win32 Software Development Kit for Windows. Copyright 1992 - 1995. Used with permission. All rights reserved. All references to chapter titles in this section refer to the original publication.

Development Considerations

If a developer decides that an application would benefit from IPC, the developer must consider some of the following questions before deciding which of the available IPC methods to use:

- Should the application be able to communicate with other applications running on other computers on a network, or is it sufficient for the application to communicate only with applications on the local computer? In other words, does the application need to be *networkable*? Some IPC methods work either on the local computer or over a network; others work only on the local computer.

- Should the application be able to communicate with applications running on other computers that may be running under different operating systems (that is, MS-DOS , Microsoft Windows Version 3.*x*, UNIX)? In other words, must the application be *interoperable*?

- Should the user of the application have to choose the other application(s) with which the application communicates, or can the application implicitly find its cooperating partners?

- Should the application communicate with many different applications in a general way, such as allowing cut and paste operations with any other application, or should its communications requirements be limited to a restricted set of interactions with specific other applications? Applications that communicate in a general way are called *loosely coupled*; applications that have a more strictly defined interaction are called *tightly coupled*.

- Is performance a critical aspect of the application? All IPC mechanisms include some amount of communications overhead.

- Should the application be a Windows-based application, or will character-mode functionalities be sufficient? Some IPC mechanisms discussed in this chapter do not work in character-mode–only applications. The clipboard, dynamic data exchange (DDE), and object linking and embedding (OLE) all require that the application have at least one window.

The answers to these questions determine whether an application can benefit by using one or more of the IPC mechanisms available in the Win32 API. This chapter discusses the strengths and weaknesses of each of the Win32 IPC mechanisms.

File Mapping

File mapping enables a process to treat the content of a file as if it were a block of memory in the process's address space. Therefore, instead of using file input and output (I/O) operations, the process can use simple pointer operations to examine and modify the contents of the file.

The Win32 API enables two or more processes to access the same *file-mapping object*. Each process receives a pointer to memory in its own address space. With this pointer, the process can read or modify the contents of the file.

There are three ways an application can share a file-mapping object created in one process with another process:

- Inheritance. The first process creates the file-mapping object and then allows the handle of the object to be inherited by a child process.

- Named file mapping. The first process creates the file-mapping object with a well-known name (which can be different from the filename). The second process opens the file-mapping object by specifying the well-known name. Alternatively, the first process can create a file-mapping object with a unique name and communicate that name to the second process through some other IPC mechanism (named pipe, mailslot, and so on).

- Handle duplication. The first process creates the file-mapping object and then passes the handle of the object to the second process. The second process then duplicates the handle to gain access to the shared memory. The original process can communicate the file-mapping handle to the second process through one of the other IPC mechanisms described in this chapter (named pipe, mailslot, and so on). For more information about duplicating handles, see Chapter 44, "Synchronization."

When two or more processes have read-write access to a shared memory block, they must use some sort of synchronization object, such as a semaphore, to prevent data corruption in a multitasking environment.

File mapping is quite efficient and also provides operating-system–supported security attributes that can help prevent unauthorized data corruption. File mapping can be used only between processes on a local computer; it cannot be used over a network. An application can, however, create a file-mapping object to a file on a remotely mounted volume. For example, if a remote server is mounted as the F drive, an application can create a file-mapping object to a file on that volume. However, a process running on a remote server cannot share a file-mapping object with a process running on a local computer.

Key Point File mapping is an efficient way for two or more processes on the same computer to share data, but the developer must provide synchronization between the processes. For more information, see Chapter 47, "File Mapping," and Chapter 44, "Synchronization."

Shared Memory

The Win32 API uses a special case of file mapping to provide shared memory access between processes. If you specify the system swapping file when creating a file-mapping object, the file-mapping object is treated as a shared memory block. Other processes can access the same block of memory by opening the same file-mapping object, as described in Chapter 47, "File Mapping."

Because shared memory is implemented with file mapping, it supports security access attributes and can operate only between processes running on the same computer.

Key Point Shared memory in the Win32 API is implemented by using file mapping. All characteristics of file mapping apply to shared memory. For more information, see Chapter 47, "File Mapping."

Anonymous Pipes

An anonymous (or unnamed) pipe enables related processes to transfer information back and forth as if they were reading from and writing to a file. Typically, anonymous pipes are used for redirecting the standard input and output (I/O) of a child process so that it can exchange data with its parent process.

To use an anonymous pipe, the parent process typically creates the pipe and then allows its read and write handles to be inherited by a child process. The parent process writes data to the pipe; the child process can read the data from the other end of the pipe. Likewise, the child process can write data to the pipe and the parent process can read the data from its end of the pipe. A parent process can also create two or more child processes that inherit the read and write handles to an anonymous pipe. Those child processes can use that pipe to communicate with each other directly, without going through the parent process.

Anonymous pipes cannot be used over a network, nor can they be used between unrelated processes. For information about a pipe mechanism that can be used with unrelated processes and over a network, see "Named Pipes" below.

Key Point Anonymous pipes provide an efficient way to redirect standard I/O to child processes on the same computer. For more information, see Chapter 54, "Pipes."

Named Pipes

Like anonymous pipes, named pipes are used to transfer data back and forth between processes. Unlike anonymous pipes, however, named pipes can operate between unrelated processes and across a network between computers. Typically, a server process creates a named pipe with a well-known name. Client processes that can get the name of the pipe can open the other end of the pipe, subject to access restrictions specified by the pipe's creator. After they are connected, the server and client can exchange data by performing read and write operations on the pipe. Alternatively, the pipe creator can create a pipe and let a child process inherit the handle to the pipe, or it can create a pipe with a unique name and communicate that name to the client through some other IPC mechanism (such as a mailslot maintained by the client).

Key Point Named pipes provide a relatively simple programming interface that makes transferring data across a network no more difficult than transferring data between two processes on the same computer. For more information, see Chapter 54, "Pipes."

Mailslots

Mailslots provide a one-way interprocess communications capability. Any process can create a mailslot and become a mailslot server. Other processes, called mailslot clients, can gain access to the mailslot by its name and send messages to the mailslot server process. A process can be both a mailslot server and a mailslot client, so two-way IPC is possible with multiple mailslots.

Incoming messages are always appended to the mailslot. The mailslot saves the messages until the creating process has a chance to read them.

Mailslots are similar to named pipes, but with a somewhat simplified programming interface and the added ability to broadcast messages to all computers in a specified network domain. A mailslot client can send a message to a mailslot on its local computer, to a mailslot on another computer, or to all mailslots with the same name on all computers in a specified network domain. Messages broadcast to a domain can be no longer than 400 bytes; messages sent to a single mailslot are limited only by the maximum message size specified by the creator of the mailslot (which can be unlimited).

Key Point Mailslots offer an easy way for applications to send and receive short messages. They also provide the ability to broadcast messages across all computers in a network domain. For more information, see Chapter 55, "Mailslots."

Clipboard

The clipboard provides a mechanism for the well-established cut-copy-paste model for simple data sharing between Windows-based applications. It enables an application to read or write data in many different standard and application-defined formats.

The clipboard acts as a central depository for data sharing among applications. When a user performs a cut or copy operation in an application, the application puts the selected data on the clipboard in one or more formats. Any other application can then retrieve the data from the clipboard, choosing from the available formats. The clipboard is a very loosely coupled exchange medium, wherein the two applications need only agree on the data format.

The clipboard mechanism works between applications on the same computer or on different computers on a network. It also works for Windows-based applications only, although 16-bit Windows 3.x applications running with the Microsoft Windows NT operating system can exchange clipboard data with 32-bit applications written for Windows NT.

Key Point All Windows-based applications should support the clipboard for those data formats that they understand. For example, a text editor or word processor should at least be able to produce and accept clipboard data in pure text format. For more information, see Chapter 25, "Clipboard."

Dynamic Data Exchange

Dynamic data exchange (DDE) is a protocol for interprocess communications that enables applications to exchange data in a variety of formats. Applications can use DDE for one-time data exchanges or for ongoing exchanges in which the applications update one another as new data becomes available.

The data formats used by DDE are the same as those used for the Windows clipboard IPC mechanism. DDE can be thought of as an extension of the clipboard mechanism. The clipboard is almost always used for a one-time response to a user command, such as choosing the Paste command from a menu. DDE is also usually initiated by a user command, but it often continues to function without further user interaction.

Three types of data exchange are possible with DDE:

- Cold link: The exchange is a one-time data transfer, like the clipboard.
- Warm link: A server notifies the client when data changes, and the client must then request new data.
- Hot link: A server sends data updates to the client when data changes.

DDE exchanges can occur between applications running on the same computer or on different computers on a network.

Key Point Most major Windows-based applications support DDE. Like the clipboard, DDE support enables an application to exchange data in a variety of standard formats with other Windows-based applications that support DDE. A developer can also define custom DDE data formats for special-purpose IPC between applications with more tightly coupled communications requirements. For more information, see Chapter 26, "Dynamic Data Exchange," and Chapter 77, "Dynamic Data Exchange Management Library."

OLE

OLE applications manage *compound documents*—that is, documents made up of data from a variety of different applications. OLE provides services that make it easy for applications to call on other applications for data editing. For example, an OLE-aware word processor could embed a graph from a spreadsheet. The user could start the spreadsheet automatically from within the word processor by choosing the embedded chart for editing. The OLE libraries would take care of starting the spreadsheet and presenting the graph for editing. When the user quit the spreadsheet, the graph would be updated in the original word processor document. Contrast this with a DDE link involving a spreadsheet graph in a word processor document. With DDE, the user would have to explicitly start the spreadsheet and open the graph document to make changes. With OLE, the spreadsheet appears to be an extension of the word processor.

Like an application using DDE, an OLE-aware application can communicate with a wide variety of other Windows-based applications. Because the OLE protocol includes all necessary context information, the application will be able to hold OLE conversations with all other OLE applications—even those that have yet to be written.

Key Point OLE supports compound documents and enables an application to include embedded or linked data that, when chosen, automatically starts another application for data editing. This enables the application to be extended by any other OLE-aware application.

Dynamic-Link Libraries

It is possible to build a Win32 dynamic-link library (DLL) so that its global data is shared with all processes that call the DLL. Therefore, cooperating processes can call the DLL to examine and modify global data owned by the DLL. For example, process A calls a DLL function with data that the DLL stores in its global data space. Process B calls another DLL function that retrieves that data. Of course, because of the multitasking nature of the Win32 API, the DLL would have to use a semaphore or another synchronization object to control access to the shared memory.

Although shared global data can be used in a DLL, Win32 file mapping is recommended for shared memory. File mapping is more efficient and provides the additional benefit of access protection. (For example, a client can be limited to read-only access to a file-mapping object.)

Key Point Although a developer can use shared global data segments in a DLL to allow two or more applications to share data, it is preferable to use Windows NT file-mapping functions to create shared memory. For more information, see Chapter 50, "Dynamic-Link Libraries."

Remote Procedure Call

The Win32 API provides remote procedure calls (RPC) to enable applications to call functions remotely. With RPC, communication with other processes becomes as easy as calling a function. RPC operates between processes on a single computer or on different computers on a network. One way to think of RPC is as a DLL that works on a network.

The RPC provided by the Win32 API is compliant with the Open Software Foundation (OSF) Distributed Computing Environment (DCE). This means that RPC applications written by using the Win32 API are able to communicate with other RPC applications running with other operating systems that support DCE. RPC automatically supports data conversion to account for different hardware architectures and for byte-ordering between dissimilar environments.

The Win32 development kit includes RPC libraries that support MS-DOS-hosted RPC clients. With this facility, a Windows NT server can provide service to many MS-DOS clients through RPC.

RPC clients and servers are tightly coupled but still maintain high performance. Windows NT makes extensive use of RPC to facilitate a client-server relationship between different parts of the operating system.

Key Point RPC provides IPC with a function interface, with support for automatic data conversion and for communications with other operating systems. Using RPC, a developer can create high-performance, tightly coupled distributed applications. For more information, see the Microsoft Win32 Remote Procedure Call Programmer's Guide and Reference.

The NetBIOS Function

The Win32 API provides the Netbios function to process low-level network control functions. This capability is provided primarily for applications written using the IBM NetBIOS system that must be ported to Windows. It is highly recommended that a developer writing a new application use the other IPC mechanisms described in this chapter rather than the low-level Netbios function. The IPC mechanisms provided in the Win32 API encapsulate and hide an enormous amount of raw NetBIOS functionality that the developer would otherwise have to implement.

Consider, for example, the following list of NetBIOS actions that would be necessary to emulate a Win32 mailslot:

On the server end

- Add the name to the local table.

- Listen for the session connection.

- Read the data upon connection.

- Append the data to the message queue.

- Close the session.

- Listen for another session connection.

- Allow the queued messages to be retrieved.

On the client side

- Open the session.

- Write the data.

- Close the session.

> **Key Point** The Netbios function is provided only for porting an existing application written using the IBM NetBIOS system or for those applications that need specialized access to low-level network functionality. For most applications, it is better to use the higher-level IPC mechanisms available in the Win32 API. For more information, see Chapter 56, "Networks."

Summary

It is likely that an application will support IPC by using several of the mechanisms described in this chapter. For example, all Windows-based applications should provide at least minimal support for the clipboard. In addition, DDE and OLE may offer the application an opportunity to communicate in a loosely coupled way with a wide variety of applications that support these protocols. The great strength of these loosely coupled mechanisms is that a developer can enable an application to share data with other applications without knowing anything about the applications themselves. By supporting the protocols for the clipboard, DDE, and OLE, the developer is assured of a growing number of applications with which the application can share data. As new applications are written that support these protocols, the developer's application will be ready to communicate with them.

As an application becomes more sophisticated, a developer may find it advantageous to break up the application into tightly coupled cooperating processes that use shared memory, pipes, or RPC to communicate. These tightly coupled mechanisms can provide high-performance extensions to the application. But when adding these more specialized IPC methods, the developer should not abandon the more loosely coupled IPC methods that allow the application to share data in a general way with most other Windows-based applications.

Topic

Identify the advantages and disadvantages of using DLLs in Microsoft Win32.

Content

How DLLs Have Changed from 16-Bit Windows to Windows NT[4]

The way the system deals with DLLs has changed from 16-bit Windows to Windows NT in two big ways—how the DLL is made available to a process and

---

how a DLL's local heap facilitates data sharing among processes. DLLs have also changed in other ways, which we'll discuss in this chapter, but let's begin by reviewing how 16-bit Windows works with DLLs and then discuss the changes in DLLs in Windows NT.

How 16-Bit Windows Makes DLLs Available to Applications

In 16-bit Windows, loading a DLL means that, in a sense, the DLL becomes part of the operating system. After the DLL is loaded, any and all applications currently running immediately have access to the DLL and the functions that the DLL contains. An application can determine whether a DLL was loaded by calling the GetModuleHandle function and passing it the name of the DLL:

```
HMODULE GetModuleHandle(LPCSTR lpszModule);
```

If GetModuleHandle returns NULL, the application knows that the DLL isn't loaded into the system yet. If the return value is not NULL, the value is a handle to the loaded DLL. This value is systemwide, meaning that any application can use the handle to manipulate the library.

An application can also load a DLL into memory by calling Load Library:

```
HINSTANCE LoadLibrary(LPCSTR lpszLibFileName);
```

This function causes the system to search the user's hard disk for the library, loads the library into memory, and returns the handle identifying the library. Once loaded, the library acts as though it's part of the operating system—any application can access it. Calling LoadLibrary also increments a usage count associated with the library. If an application calls LoadLibrary to load a DLL that was already loaded into the system, the system simply increments the DLL's usage count and returns the handle that identifies the DLL.

Once an application has the handle of a library, it can get the memory address of a DLL function by calling GetProcAddress and passing it the handle of the library and the name of the function:

```
FARPROC GetProcAddress(HINSTANCE hinst, LPCSTR lpszProcName);
```

When an application no longer needs to access the functions in a DLL, the application calls FreeLibrary:

```
void FreeLibrary(HINSTANCE hinst);
```

This function decrements the usage count for the DLL and, if that usage count reaches 0 (zero), the DLL is removed from the system and is no longer available to any applications.

16-bit Windows has an additional function, GetModuleUsage, that returns the usage count for a loaded DLL: :

```
int GetModuleUsage(HINSTANCE hinst);
```

How Windows NT Makes DLLs Available to Processes

The biggest change in DLLs from 16-bit Windows to Windows NT is how the DLL is made accessible to the different applications. In Windows NT, DLLs don't become part of the operating system; instead, they become part of the process that loads the DLL. When a Windows NT process calls the LoadLibrary function to explicitly load a library into memory, Windows NT creates a file-mapping object for the DLL (as it does when applications are loaded) and maps the DLL into the address space of the process. It is only after the code and data have been mapped into the process's address space that the threads in the process can make calls to functions in the DLL. :

If another process requires the use of the same DLL, Windows NT simply maps another view of the same DLL into the process's address space. Because each process gets its own mapped view of the DLL, it's possible that Windows NT won't map the DLL at the same address in both address spaces.

For example, the DLL function NukeDeficit could get mapped to address 0x12345678 in one process and address 0x77700066 in another process. As a result, a process would not be able to pass the function's address among processes; each process would need to call GetProcAddress individually.

If a thread within a process calls LoadLibrary to load a library that is already mapped into the process's address space, Windows NT doesn't map the library again. Instead, it simply increments a usage count associated with the library and returns the same handle to the library. However, unlike 16-bit Windows, in Windows NT this usage count is maintained on a per-process basis. That is, when a process loads a library for the first time, the usage count for that library becomes 1. If that process calls LoadLibrary to load the same DLL a second time, the usage count for the library with respect to the process becomes 2.

If another process calls LoadLibrary to load a DLL that is being used by another process, the system maps the code and data for the DLL into the calling process's address space and increments the DLL's usage count (with respect to this process) to 1.

When a process no longer needs to access the functions in a DLL, a thread in the process calls FreeLibrary. FreeLibrary decrements the usage count of the DLL and if the usage count reaches 0 (zero), the DLL is unmapped from the process's address space. Both the LoadLibrary and FreeLibrary functions affect the visibility of a DLL only with respect to the process that calls the functions. Neither of these functions can affect the visibility of a DLL with respect to other processes.

The 16-bit Windows GetModuleUsage function is no longer available in the Win32 API. Microsoft dropped this function because GetModuleUsage could no longer report the usage count of the DLL with respect to all processes running in the system. However, I think that Microsoft should have kept the function and made it return the usage count of the DLL with respect to the process. :

Sharing Data Among Processes Using a DLL's Local Heap

In 16-bit Windows, a DLL has its own data segment. This data segment houses all the static and global variables needed by the DLL as well as the DLL's own private local heap. When a DLL function allocates memory using LocalAlloc, the memory that satisfies this request is taken from the DLL's data segment. This segment, like all segments, has a maximum limit of 64 KB.

This design allows applications to easily share data among multiple processes because the DLL's local heap is available to the DLL regardless of which process called the function contained in the DLL. Here is an example of how a DLL can be used for sharing data between two applications:

```
HLOCAL g_hData = NULL;
HLOCAL SetData (LPVOID lpvData, int nSize) {
   g_hData = LocalAlloc(LMEM_MOVEABLE, nSize);
   LPVOID lpv = LocalLock(g_hData);
   memcpy(lpv, lpvData, nSize);
   LocalUnlock(g_hData);
}

void GetData (LPVOID lpvData, int nSize) {
   LPVOID lpv = LocalLock(g_hData);
   memcpy(lpvData, lpv, nSize);
   LocalUnlock(g_hData);
}
```

When SetData is called, it allocates a block of memory out of the DLL's data segment, copies the data pointed to by the lpvData parameter into the block, and saves the handle to the block in a global variable, g_hData. A totally different application can now call GetData. GetData uses the global variable identifying the local memory handle, locks the block, copies the data into the buffer identified by the lpvData parameter, and returns. This is an easy way to share data between two processes in 16-bit Windows.

Unfortunately, this method doesn't work at all in Windows NT for two reasons. First, DLLs in Windows NT don't receive their own local heap. When a process loads a DLL, the system maps the code and data for the DLL into the address space of the process. Any memory allocation calls made by functions in the DLL cause memory to be allocated from the process's address space—no other process has access to this allocated memory.

Second, the global and static variables allocated by a DLL are also not shared among multiple mappings of the DLL. In other words, if two processes use the same DLL, the code for the DLL is loaded into memory once but is mapped into the address space of both processes. However, each process has a separate set of the DLL's global and static variables. The system gives each mapping of a DLL its own set of variables by taking advantage of the copy-on-write mechanism. .

Topic

List and describe how the operating system addresses error handling.

Content

Structured Exception Handling[5]

An *exception* is an event that occurs during the execution of a program, and that requires the execution of software outside the normal flow of control. Hardware exceptions can result from the execution of certain instruction sequences, such as division by zero or an attempt to access an invalid memory address. A software routine can also initiate an exception explicitly.

The Microsoft Win32 application programming interface (API) supports *structured exception handling*, a mechanism for handling hardware- and software-generated exceptions. Structured exception handling gives programmers complete control over the handling of exceptions, provides support for debuggers, and is usable across all programming languages and machines.

---

[5] Materials excerpted from Part 3 of the *Win32 Programmer's Reference* of the Microsoft Win32 Software Development Kit for Windows. Copyright 1992 - 1995. Used with permission. All rights reserved.

The Win32 API also supports *termination handling*, which enables programmers to ensure that whenever a guarded body of code is executed, a specified block of termination code is also executed. The termination code is executed regardless of how the flow of control leaves the guarded body. For example, a termination handler can guarantee that clean-up tasks are performed even if an exception or some other error occurs while the guarded body of code is being executed.

Structured exception and termination handling is an integral part of the Win32 system and it enables a very robust implementation of the system software. It is envisioned that application developers also will use these mechanisms to create consistently robust and reliable applications.

Structured exception handling is made available to application developers primarily through compiler support. For example, the Microsoft compilers provided with the Win32 development kit support the **try** keyword that identifies a guarded body of code, and the **except** and **finally** keywords that identify an exception handler and a termination handler, respectively. Although this topic uses examples from the support available in Microsoft compilers, it is possible for other compiler vendors to provide this support as well.

Exception Handling

Exceptions can be initiated by hardware or software, and can occur in kernel-mode as well as user-mode code. Win32 structured exception handling provides a single mechanism for the handling of kernel-mode and user-mode exceptions, both hardware- and software-generated.

The execution of certain instruction sequences can result in exceptions that are initiated by hardware. For example, an access violation is generated by the hardware when a process attempts to read from or write to a virtual address to which it does not have the appropriate access.

Events that require exception handling may also occur during execution of a software routine (for example, when an invalid parameter value is specified). When this happens, a thread can initiate an exception explicitly by calling the **RaiseException** function. This function enables the calling thread to specify information that describes the exception.

Exception Dispatching

When a hardware or software exception occurs, the processor stops execution at the point at which the exception occurred and transfers control to the system. First, the system saves both the machine state of the current thread and information that describes the exception. The system then attempts to find an exception handler to handle the exception.

The machine state of the thread in which the exception occurred is saved in a CONTEXT structure. This information (called the *context record*) enables the system to continue execution at the point of the exception if the exception is successfully handled. The description of the exception (called the *exception record*) is saved in an EXCEPTION_RECORD structure. Because it stores the machine-dependent information of the context record separately from the machine-independent information of the exception record, the exception-handling mechanism is portable to different platforms. The information in both the context and exception records is available by means of the **GetExceptionInformation** function, and can be made available to any exception handlers that are executed as a result of the exception. The exception record includes the following information:

- An exception code that identifies the type of exception.
- Flags indicating whether the exception is continuable. Any attempt to continue execution after a noncontinuable exception generates another exception.
- A pointer to another exception record. This facilitates creation of a linked list of exceptions if nested exceptions occur.
- The address at which the exception occurred.
- An array of 32-bit arguments that provide additional information about the exception.

When an exception occurs in user-mode code, the system goes through the following search for an exception handler:

1. The system first attempts to notify the process's debugger, if any.
2. If the process is not being debugged, or if the associated debugger does not handle the exception, the system attempts to locate a frame-based exception handler by searching the stack frames of the thread in which the exception occurred. The system searches the current stack frame first, then proceeds backward through preceding stack frames.
3. If no frame-based handler can be found, or no frame-based handler handles the exception, the system makes a second attempt to notify the process's debugger.
4. If the process is not being debugged, or if the associated debugger does not handle the exception, the system provides default handling based on the exception type. For most exceptions, the default action is to call the **ExitProcess** function.

When an exception occurs in kernel-mode code, the system searches the stack frames of the kernel stack in an attempt to locate an exception handler. If a handler cannot be located or no handler handles the exception, the system is shut down as if the **ExitWindows** function had been called.

Debugger Support

The system's handling of user-mode exceptions provides support for sophisticated debuggers. If the process in which an exception occurs is being debugged, the system generates a debug event. If the debugger is using the **WaitForDebugEvent** function, the debug event causes that function to return with a pointer to a DEBUG_EVENT structure. This structure contains the process and thread identifiers that the debugger can use to access the thread's context record. The structure also contains an EXCEPTION_DEBUG_INFO structure that includes a copy of the exception record.

The system's search for an exception handler includes two attempts to notify a process's debugger. The first notification attempt provides the debugger with an opportunity to handle breakpoint or single-step exceptions. The user can then issue debugger commands to manipulate the process's environment before any exception handlers are executed. The second attempt to notify the debugger occurs only if the system is unable to find a frame-based exception handler that handles the exception.

At each notification attempt, the debugger uses the **ContinueDebugEvent** function to return control to the system. Before returning control the debugger can handle the exception and modify the thread state as appropriate, or it can choose not to handle the exception. Using **ContinueDebugEvent** the debugger can indicate that it has handled the exception, in which case the machine state is restored and thread execution is continued at the point at which the exception occurred. The debugger can also indicate that it did not handle the exception, which causes the system to continue its search for an exception handler.

Topic

Design custom applications to address error handling.

Content

Handling Run-Time Errors[6]

Part of application development is to anticipate and plan for the errors users may encounter. While your application is running, external events that you can't prevent or may not anticipate will likely occur. For example, files may be mistakenly

---

[6] Materials excerpted from Part 2 of *Building Applications* in the Office Development Kit 1.0. Copyright 1992 - 1995. Used with permission. All rights reserved.

deleted, disk drives can run out of space, and network drives sometimes disconnect unexpectedly. Such eventualities can cause run-time errors in your code, that is, errors that Microsoft Access can detect only when your application is running. To handle these errors, you need to add error-handling code to your procedures.

Errors and Error Handling

In the world of programming, an error often isn't the same as a mistake. An error may be the result of an event or an operation that doesn't work out as expected, or the result of an attempt to carry out an impossible or invalid maneuver.

Often, you can anticipate the errors that users will encounter when they work with your application. You can shield users from these errors by including *error-handling* code, also known as *error trapping,* in your application. Error-handling code typically *traps* a run-time error by interrupting the default Microsoft Access response to the error and instead executing code that you specify. Your application can correct the error, or give the user an opportunity to correct the error.

Run-time errors occur when the application is actually executing; other types of errors can occur under different circumstances. For example, a syntax error can occur when you enter code in the Module window, and a compile error can occur when you compile code. In Microsoft Access, however, you can trap only run-time errors.

Depending on where it occurs, you can handle a run-time error in one of two ways:

Where error occurs	How to handle the error
Microsoft Access interface or Microsoft Jet database engine	Add code to a form or report's Error event procedure.
Access Basic	Add an **On Error** statement and error-handling code to a procedure

If your application uses Access Basic code, you usually have to use both types of error handling.

For details on using Access Basic to create tables, see Chapter 7, "Objects and Collections," and Chapter 11, "Working with Sets of Records."

Both types of error handling require that you identify each error you want to handle by its error code. You usually declare a constant to represent the numeric error code, and then use the constant to refer to the error. To obtain error codes, first create an Errors Table that contains all error codes and messages used by Microsoft Access by running the following procedure.

```
Sub CreateErrorsTable ()
' Creates a table of error codes and strings used or reserved
' by Microsoft Access.

    Dim Db As Database, ErrTbl As TableDef, Fld As Field
    Dim ErrRs As Recordset, ErrCode As Long

    ' Create errors table with error code and error string fields.
    Set Db = DbEngine.Workspaces(0).Databases(0)
    Set ErrTbl = Db.CreateTableDef("Errors Table")
    Set Fld = ErrTbl.CreateField("Error Code", DB_LONG)
    ErrTbl.Fields.Append Fld
    Set Fld = ErrTbl.CreateField("Error String", DB_TEXT)
    ErrTbl.Fields.Append Fld
    Db.TableDefs.Append ErrTbl

    ' Set the recordset to the Errors Table recordset.
    Set ErrRs = Db.OpenRecordset("Errors Table")

    ' Loop through Microsoft Access error codes, skipping error codes
    ' that generate a "User-defined error" message.
    For ErrCode = 1 To 32767

        DoCmd Hourglass True
        If Error (ErrCode) <> "User-defined error" Then
            'Add each error code and string to the errors table.
            ErrRs.AddNew
            ErrRs("Error Code") = ErrCode
            ErrRs("Error String") = Error(ErrCode)
            ErrRs.Update
        End If

    Next ErrCode

    ' Close the Recordset.
    ErrRs.Close

    DoCmd Hourglass False
    MsgBox "Errors Table created."

End Sub
```

After you create the Errors Table, you can find the error code for an error by
looking up its corresponding error message. To do so, select the Error String
column and choose Find from the Edit menu, and then enter the error string in the
Find dialog box. You can also base a query or report on the table, or sort the Error
String column.

Note The CreateErrorsTable procedure is also included in Help, so you can copy and paste it into a module rather than retype it. To display the procedure, search Help for "error codes" and in the Error Codes topic click "Determining Used Error Codes." To copy the procedure, choose the Copy button.

Guidelines for Complex Error Handling

When you create large applications that use multiple modules, the error-handling code can get quite complex. Keep these guidelines in mind:

- Put an **Error Err** statement in all error-handling code to handle cases in which no code in the error-handling routine deals with the specific current error. This enables your application to try to correct the error in other error-handling routines along the invocation path. It also ensures that Access Basic displays an error message if an error occurs that your code doesn't handle. When you test your code, this helps you uncover the errors you aren't handling adequately.

- If you choose not to use **Error Err**, you can write fail-safe error-handling code that all your error handlers can call as a last resort. For example, such code might attempt to save a user's data before the code terminates.

- If you don't want a previous procedure to trap the error, use the **Stop** statement in the error-handling code to force your application to terminate. Using **Stop** enables you to examine the context of the error while refining your code.

Topic

Explain the role of objects in the I/O system.

Content

Object Manager[7]

Objects are run-time instances of a particular object type that can be manipulated by an operating system process. An object type includes a system-defined data type, a list of operations that can be performed upon it (such as wait, create, or cancel), and a set of object attributes. Object Manager is the part of the Windows NT

---

[7] Materials excerpted from Chapter One of the *Resource Guide* of the Windows NT Resource Kit. Copyright 1992 - 1995. Used with permission. All rights reserved.

Executive that provides uniform rules for retention, naming, and security of objects.

Before a process can manipulate a Windows NT object, it must first acquire a handle to the object. An object handle includes access control information and a pointer to the object itself. All object handles are created through Object Manager.

Note The Executive does not distinguish between a file handle and an object handle. Thus, the same routines that are used to create a file handle can be used to create an object handle.

Like other Windows NT components, Object Manager is extensible so that new object types can be defined as technology grows and changes.

In addition, Object Manager manages the global name space for Windows NT and tracks the creation and use of objects by any process. This name space is used to access all named objects that are contained in the local computer environment. Some of the objects that can have names include the following:

- Directory objects
- Object type objects
- Symbolic link objects
- Semaphore and event objects
- Process and thread objects
- Section and segment objects
- Port objects
- Device objects
- File system objects
- File objects

The object name space is modeled after a hierarchical file system, where directory names in a path are separated by a backslash (\). You can see object names in this form, for example, when you double-click entries in the Event Viewer log, as shown in the following illustration.

Topic

Describe the purpose of the registry.

Content

Registry and Initialization Files[8]

In Microsoft Windows, applications use initialization files to store information that otherwise would be lost when the application closes. These files typically contain such information as user preferences for the configuration of the application. Initialization files, however, have the following inherent limitations:

- Information in initialization files is typically available only to the application that put it there.
- The text format of initialization files allows casual manipulation by potentially naive end users.
- Separate initialization files for many applications can proliferate on a hard disk.
- There is no way to secure initialization files against tampering.
- Initialization files do not support multiple users.
- Initialization files do not support multiple versions of the same application.
- Initialization files are not recoverable.
- Information in initialization files cannot be accessed or administered remotely in any consistent way.

Microsoft Windows version 3.1 included a new feature: a registration database. A registration database contains information that supports shell applications (such as Windows File Manager) and applications that use OLE. Each piece of information in the database is identified by a key, which may have a value (data) associated with it. Windows 3.1 Introduced a set of functions to support querying and setting information in the database. This database was not meant as a place for applications to store private configuration information; initialization files were required for that purpose.

---

[8] Materials excerpted from Part 3 of the *Win32 Programmer's Reference* in the Microsoft Win32 Software Development Kit for Windows. Copyright 1992 - 1995. Used with permission. All rights reserved.

The Win32 application programming interface (API) expands the usefulness of the version 3.1 registration database in two fundamental ways; the database now uses more keys and each key can hold more data. The new database is called the *registry*. The functions that manipulate the registration database in Windows 3.1 work with the Win32 registry, but some of them have been superseded in the Win32 API by extended versions.

The purpose of the registry is to meet the following goals:

- Provide one source for configuration information, making initialization and configuration files (such as CONFIG.SYS and WIN.INI) obsolete.

  Many of these files, however, are maintained for compatibility with previous versions of Windows or Windows apps.

- Enumerate, track, and configure the applications, device drivers, and operating system control parameters.

- Enumerate and track the hardware on a computer.

- Standardize the user interface for configuration information through the use of Windows Control Panel.

- Reduce the likelihood of syntactic errors in configuration information.

- Separate user-, application-, and computer-related information, so that separate data for multiple users can be maintained on a single computer.

- Provide security for configuration data. This security prevents unauthorized changes to critical data but allows users direct control over matters of personal preference.

- Provide a set of network-independent functions for setting and querying configuration information and enable direct examination of configuration data over a network.

- Provide storage that is recoverable after system crashes.

- Provide atomicity of edits.

Applications, device drivers, and the system itself use the registry API to store and retrieve data. The registry stores this data in files which appear in the file system. These files are in a private binary format, and are held open for exclusive access, so apps cannot write to them directly, but must use the API instead.

Structure of the Registry

The registry is stored in binary format in a series of files in the SYSTEM32 directory of Microsoft Windows NT. (Hives that contain user profiles may reside elsewhere.) These files correspond to *hives*; that is, discrete bodies of registry information, rooted at the top of the registry hierarchy. The size of the registry is user-configurable, limited only by system resources. The default registry size limit is one-fourth the size of the system's paged pool size.

Data in the registry is in the form of a hierarchically structured tree. Each entry node in the tree is called a *key*. The registry is something like a file system, in that each key can contain both *subkeys* (analogous to directories) and data entries (analogous to files).

Applications use the registry in much the same way as they use initialization files, as a place where information can be stored and retrieved.

Sometimes, the presence of a key is all the information that an application requires; other times, an application opens a key and uses the data associated with that key. For the Windows 3.1 registration database, this data was in the form of a string. For the Win32 registry, a key can have any number of data entries, and the data can be in any form. Each data entry is called a *value*.

Each key can contain the following items.

Key component	Description
Name	String used to gain access to the key. This name must be unique relative to other subkeys at the same level in the hierarchy (that is, KeyA and KeyB could each have a subkey KeyC, but KeyA could not have two KeyC subkeys). A key name cannot contain backslash (\) or null characters. This key component is required.
Class	Object class name. Intended for use in associating class method code with class instances stored in the registry. Not normally used by apps. This key component is optional.
Security Descriptor	Keys use standard Windows NT security descriptors, and can thus express auditing control and full access control. Normal security inheritance rules apply. This key component is optional.
Last write time	A time stamp indicating the last time the key was modified. Any change to a value is considered a modification of the value's parent key.
Value(s)	Zero or more pieces of information to be stored with the key. This key component is optional. A value consists of the following three parts.

Value component	Description
Name	Identifies the value. The name can be up to 32,767 Unicode characters (65,534 bytes) in size. Backslash characters (\) are legal in value names. A NULL name (that is, "") is also legal to allow compatibility with Windows 3.1.
Type	Defines the type of data stored in this value. In Windows 3.1, this type was always REG_SZ, designating a null-terminated string. In the Win32 API, types are defined for most data formats. Although the system does not use this type information, applications should use the predefined types so that registry tools can find and manipulate the value data. Types with values below 0x7fffffff are reserved for system use.
Data	Specifies user data of arbitrary length and format. May not exceed 1 megabyte in Windows NT 3.1 release.

All name strings in the registry are stored in Unicode format. The registry preserves the case of any strings stored in the registry but ignores the case in all operations. (Data stored in the Data section of values is arbitrary, but strings should be stored as Unicode there as well.) For more information about Unicode, see "String Manipulation" and "Unicode."

The registry enforces a rule of atomicity: for any value entry, a given change either occurs in its entirety, or the change does not occur at all. This means that the name, type, size, and data will always match, and all of the data in the value entry will be consistent. This is true even if the system crashes while a value entry is being updated. Keys are always consistent with the value entries they contain; to repeat, this is true even if the system crashes during an update.

Consistency among multiple values of the same key, or multiple keys, is NOT enforced by the system. Applications that write multiple values and require that they be consistent with one another must build their own transaction mechanism on top of the Registry's atomicity enforcement mechanism.

Whenever an application opens a key, it must supply the handle of another key in the registry that is already open. The system defines four standard handles that are always open. An application can use the following predefined handles as entry points to the registry.

Entry Points	Use
HKEY_CLASSES_ROOT	Registry entries subordinate to this handle define types (or classes) of documents and the properties associated with these classes.
	This is the entry point used in Windows version 3.1; the information it contains has not changed for Windows NT.
	Information stored under this handle is used by Windows shell applications and by OLE applications. Filename extensions are associated with applications that can work with files of that type. The OLE information includes the server command line, appropriate data types, and the action taken by an activated OLE object. This handle is an alias for **HKEY_LOCAL_MACHINE**, Software\Classes.
HKEY_CURRENT_USER	Registry entries subordinate to this handle define the preferences of the current user. These preferences include the settings of environment variables, information about program groups, colors, printers, network connections, and application preferences. The information for this handle is stored under the **HKEY_USERS** key.
HKEY_LOCAL_MACHINE	Registry entries subordinate to this handle define the configuration state of the system, including information about the bus type, system memory, and installed hardware and software.
HKEY_USERS	Registry entries subordinate to this handle define the default user configuration for users on the local computer and the user configuration for the current user. (User profiles appear as subtrees under this handle, the **HKEY_CURRENT_USER** is an alias to the profile of the current user.)

By convention, data in **HKEY_CURRENT_USER** overrides similar data in **HKEY_LOCAL_MACHINE**. That is, per-user preferences should normally override per-machine defaults. However, the system does not enforce this convention; it is the responsibility of application code to do so.

Standardized keys help an application navigate in the registry and make it possible to develop tools that a system administrator can use to manipulate categories of information. Applications that add data to the registry should always work within the framework of predefined keys, so that the administrative tools can find and use the new data. There are many predefined keys in addition to the four entry points already discussed.

To see the contents of the registry, developers can run the Registry Editor (REGEDT32.EXE), a Windows application that ships with Windows NT. This application is not meant to be used as a standard means of modifying the registry. However, using it is an excellent way to get acquainted with the contents of the registry and to monitor changes to the registry's contents.

Note Hives (registry data) saved from a Windows NT 3.5 machine with **RegSaveKey** cannot be restored on a Windows NT 3.1 machine with **RegLoadKey**, because the hive format for Windows NT 3.5 is different than that for Windows NT 3.1. However, Windows NT 3.5 supports both the new and old hive formats, so hives saved from a Windows NT 3.1 machine can be used on a Windows NT 3.5 machine.

Note To save a hive from a Windows NT 3.5 machine for later use on a Windows NT 3.1 machine, use the Win32 registry API functions to read the registry key by key, and save the values in a text file. You can then read the text file on a Window NT 3.1 machine and restore the registry information using the registry API functions.

Mapping and Initialization Files

Many benefits of the registry are available even to applications that do not explicitly write information to it or read information from it. When an application uses a *profile* or private profile function to get or set information in a configuration or initialization file, the function may be mapped to the registry instead of to the specified file. This mapping occurs when the initialization file and section are specified in the registry under the following keys:

HKEY_LOCAL_MACHINE\Software\Microsoft

   Windows NT\CurrentVersion\IniFileMapping

The system is likely to map function calls to the registry if an application modifies system-component initialization files, such as WIN.INI, SYSTEM.INI, CONTROL.INI, and WINFILE.INI. The change in the storage location has no effect on the **GetPrivateProfileInt** function's behavior.

Applications can use the **IniFileMapping** key to simplify their installation procedure. To do this, an application can use an installation routine that calls such functions as **GetPrivateProfileString** and **WritePrivateProfileString**. It can use this routine to write either to the registry or to a private initialization file, depending on whether the host system is running Windows NT. For example, if an application writes to an initialization file named ABC.INI, it can use its standard initialization routine to read from and write to the registry by adding a subkey named **ABC.INI** to the **IniFileMapping** key.

Structure of HKEY_LOCAL_MACHINE

Note The arrangement of registry information may have changed since the publication of this book.

Most applications store information under the **HKEY_LOCAL_MACHINE** key during their installation procedure. This key contains information specific to the local computer, irrespective of the user. Information such as the name and version of the installing software, the capabilities of OLE-enabled applications, and the names and types of device drivers are stored in this key.

The **HKEY_LOCAL_MACHINE** key has five subkeys: Hardware, Security, Sam, Software, and System. Applications can query Hardware, Software, and System. They may write to Software and System.

CHAPTER 5

OLE Fundamentals

Topics

Describe the benefits that component software provides the developer.

Describe the benefits that component software provides the end user.

Identify the features of OLE that can be used to implement a business solution.

Explain how OLE is used to create component software.

List and describe the functionality OLE provides for compatibility and version management.

Explain how OLE components are used to build integrated solutions.

Content

OLE Documents: Technical Backgrounder[1]

OLE is a foundation for component solutions, allowing software components supplied by different vendors to work together. OLE provides an extensible set of

---

[1] This backgrounder is also available on the Microsoft Developer Network Development Library under Backgrounders and White Papers, Operating System Extensions. Copyright 1994. Used with permission. All rights reserved.

component services that allow corporate developers to build business solutions using prefabricated components. One set of services that OLE provides is OLE Documents—a new generation of compound documents that enhance user productivity and allow users to communicate their ideas more effectively.

OLE version 2.0 is a major extension to the OLE version 1.0 technology, which provided some compound document features. OLE 2.0 provides greatly enhanced document services with the Introduction of OLE Documents. OLE 2.0 provides a new level of application interoperability and offers substantial improvements in user-oriented features, providing a more powerful computing environment while retaining full compatibility with OLE 1.0 applications. While OLE 1.0 was solely a document technology, OLE 2.0 is built on the underlying OLE Component Object Model, making OLE 2.0 a foundation for object services that extend well beyond document technologies. As such, OLE provides a single, integrated architecture that addresses the needs of corporate developers building business solutions.

This paper provides an overview of the capabilities of OLE Documents. OLE Document services are described from both the user's and developer's points of view. The first section presents some of the basic OLE concepts and features. The second section presents a brief architectural overview followed by a summary of the technical and user-oriented benefits provided by the OLE Document services. Today over 100 shipping applications support OLE Documents, and as such are compatible components that can be used together to create documents. All major software vendors are incorporating OLE capabilities directly into their applications, and many more OLE-enabled applications will be available over the coming months. This includes applications designed for the Microsoft Windows family of operating systems, and the Apple® Macintosh® System 7 operating system.

Why Use OLE?

OLE is a mechanism that allows applications to interoperate, thereby allowing users to work more productively. End users of OLE container applications can create and manage OLE Documents, an improved form of compound documents. OLE Documents can seamlessly incorporate data, or *objects*, of different formats. Sound clips, spreadsheets, text, and bitmaps are some examples of objects commonly found in OLE Documents. Each object is created and maintained by its object application, but through the use of OLE, the services of the different object applications are integrated. End users feel as if a single application, with all the functionality of each of the object applications, is being used. End users of OLE applications don't need to be concerned with managing and switching between the various object applications; they focus solely on the OLE Document and the task being performed.

What Are Linking and Embedding?

When an object is incorporated into a document, it maintains an association with the object application that created it. *Linking* and *embedding* are two different ways to associate objects in an OLE Document with their object applications. The differences between linking and embedding lie in how and where the actual source data that comprises the object is stored; this in turn affects the object's portability, its method(s) of activation, and the size of the OLE Document.

When an object is linked, the source data, or *link source*, continues to reside physically wherever it was initially created, either at another point within the document or within a different document altogether. Only a reference, or *link*, to the object and appropriate presentation data is kept with the OLE Document. Linked objects cannot "travel" with documents to another machine; they must remain within the local file system or be copied explicitly.

Linking is efficient and keeps the size of the OLE Document small. Users may choose to link when the source object is owned or maintained by someone else because a single instance of the object's data can serve many documents. Changes made to the source object are automatically reflected in any OLE Documents that have a link to the object. From the user's point of view, a linked object appears to be wholly contained within the document.

In addition to simple links, it is possible to create more sophisticated documents by nesting links and combining linked and embedded objects.

Figure 5-1 shows an example of an OLE Document that contains two objects — one linked and one embedded. The table object is linked to a worksheet file stored on disk; the embedded chart object is linked to data in the last two rows of the table. When changes are made to the data in the worksheet file that correspond to the linked table object's last two rows, both the linked table object and the embedded chart object in the OLE Document change as well. When changes are made to data that corresponds to the table object's first three rows, only the linked table object changes.

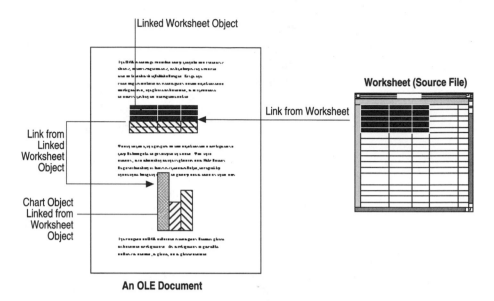

An OLE Document

Figure 5.1   Linked objects in an OLE Document.

With an embedded object, a copy of the original object is physically stored in the OLE Document, as is all of the information needed to manage the object. As a result, the object becomes a physical part of the document. An OLE Document containing embedded objects will be larger than one containing a the same objects as links. However, embedding offers several advantages that may outweigh the disadvantages of the extra storage overhead. For example, OLE Documents with embedded objects may be transferred to another computer and edited there. The new user of the document need not know where the original data resides, because a copy of the objects' source (native) data travels with the OLE Document.

Embedded objects can be edited in place; that is, all maintenance to the object can be done without ever leaving the OLE Document. Since each user has a copy of the object's source data, changes made to an embedded object by one user will not affect other OLE Documents containing an embedding of the same original object. However, if there are links to this object, changes to it will be reflected in each document containing a link.

Figure 5.2 illustrates nested embedding. The OLE Document contains an embedded worksheet object. Inside within the worksheet object is an embedded chart object. Since the chart is contained in the worksheet, the worksheet is said to be the chart's *container* while the OLE Document is said to be the spreadsheet's *container*. A container can be an OLE Document or another object.

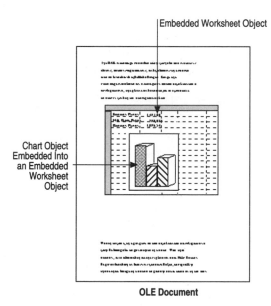

OLE Document

Figure 5.2   Embedded objects in an OLE Document.

OLE Features

The following sections provide an overview of each of the OLE features from the user's perspective.

Visual Editing

With *Visual Editing*, the user can double-click an object in an OLE Document and interact with the object right there, without switching to a different application window. The menus, toolbars, palettes, and other controls necessary to interact with the object temporarily replace the existing menus and controls of the active window. In effect, the object application appears to "take over" the OLE Document window. When the user returns to the OLE Document application, its menus and controls are restored.

Visual Editing (sometimes referred to as in-place activation) can include a variety of operations, depending on the capabilities of the object. Embedded objects can be edited, played, displayed, and recorded in place. Linked objects can be activated in place for operations such as playback and display, but they cannot be edited in place. When a linked object is opened for editing, the object application is activated in a separate window. To return to the OLE Document, the user must either close the object application or switch windows.

Figure 5.3 shows what happens to an application when the user decides to activate an embedded object in place for editing. In the top window, the embedded spreadsheet appears well integrated into the word processing document. However, when the user double-clicks the spreadsheet to start in-place editing, the word processor application undergoes several changes, as demonstrated in the bottom window of Figure 5.3. The title bar changes to reflect the name of the object application; that is, the spreadsheet program. The menu is the result of the word processor and spreadsheet applications merging their individual menus. The spreadsheet changes in appearance; hatch marks surround its border to indicate its activated state. When the user has finished editing and clicks outside the spreadsheet's border, the window once again looks like it belongs to a word processor application.

The advantage of Visual Editing is quickly apparent with OLE Documents consisting of large numbers of objects created by different applications. Instead of switching back and forth between different windows to update objects, users are presented with a single document window that allows them to perform most of their editing and other interaction from a single location. However, a user who prefers editing an embedding object in a separate window can be given the option of activating another window in which to perform the editing.

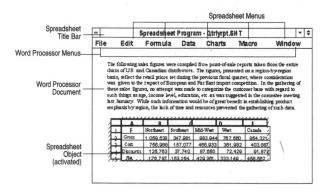

Figure 5.3   Spreadsheet object being activated in place.

Visual Editing represents a fundamental change in the way users interact with personal computers. It offers a more "document-centric" approach by allowing the user to focus primarily on the creation and manipulation of information, rather than on the operation of the environment and its applications. This approach allows users to work within a single context — the OLE Document.

Drag and Drop

The most widely used method for transferring data between applications has been the Clipboard. With the Clipboard method, the user chooses the Copy operation while in the object application, moves to the target application, and chooses Paste to put the object in place. Although effective, a more natural way to exchange data between applications is simply to click an object, drag it to its destination, and drop it in place. OLE supports this drag-and-drop functionality of objects in addition to the traditional Clipboard functionality.

Drag and drop eliminates the traditional barriers between applications. Instead of perceiving window frames as walls surrounding data, users are able to drag information freely to and from a variety of applications. Drag and drop makes OLE Documents easier to create and manage because it provides an interactive model that more closely resembles how people interact with physical objects.

Figure 5.4 demonstrates a typical use of the drag-and-drop feature. The user has selected a range of cells from a spreadsheet that is embedded in a word processor application and is dragging the selection to a destination in another window belonging to another word processor application.

The style of drag and drop illustrated in Figure 5.4, where data is dragged from one application window into another application window, is called *inter-window dragging*.

Two other styles for dragging and dropping objects are:

- *Inter-object dragging*: Objects nested within other objects can be dragged out of their containing objects to another window or to another container object. Conversely, objects can be dragged to other objects and dropped inside them.

- *Dropping over icons*: Objects can be dragged over the desktop to system resource icons such as printers and mailboxes. The appropriate action will be taken with the object, depending on the type of resource the icon represents.

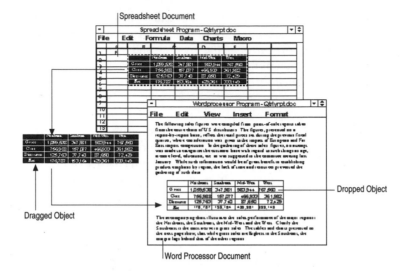

Figure 5.4   Dragging a spreadsheet object from one word processor program and dropping into another word processor program.

Nested Object Support

Objects can be linked to or embedded in another object (or even part of an object) in the same OLE Document. For example, a graph showing sales figures for the month of January may be linked to the part of an embedded spreadsheet which contains January's figures. A change in the spreadsheet figures will automatically affect the linked graph. Nested object linking provides for more efficient use of memory. Users can directly manipulate the nested object. There is no need to launch multiple applications to arrive at the object to be edited.

Figure 5.5 illustrates a word processor OLE Document containing two levels of embedded objects. The pie chart is embedded inside the spreadsheet, which is embedded in the word processor document.

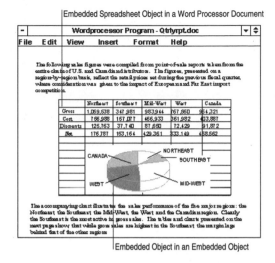

Embedded Spreadsheet Object in a Word Processor Document

Embedded Object in an Embedded Object

Figure 5.5   Nested objects in an OLE Document.

Nested object support gives users additional freedom to manipulate objects in limitless combinations and work with OLE Documents more productively.

Property Inheritance

Objects typically have a set of properties that are relevant to the type of object. For example, a picture might have properties such as background color and line thickness, and a text object might have properties such as font, size, and underlining. Sometimes, when an object is embedded within a container, such as a document, its properties are not consistent with the properties of its container. To make embedded objects take on the look of their containing documents more closely, OLE allows containers to "export" properties to an object. The object then inherits these properties and transforms its appearance to be more consistent with the object's container.

Figure 5.6 illustrates a common use of property inheritance. The user copies a range of cells from a spreadsheet application and embeds them in a word processor OLE Document. The spreadsheet application's italic style and type of font is inconsistent with the word processor's bold style and font. By allowing the embedded object to inherit the characteristics of the containing document's font, the spreadsheet looks as if it were native to the OLE Document.

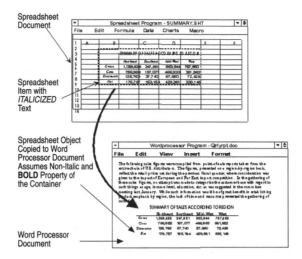

Spreadsheet Document

Spreadsheet Item with *ITALICIZED* Text

Spreadsheet Object Copied to Word Processor Document Assumes Non-Italic and **BOLD** Property of the Container

Word Processor Document

Figure 5.6   Inheriting the properties of the container.

To the user, objects appear "smart" because they know how to transform themselves to match their container. This feature saves users time because they don't have to adjust the object's properties manually before or after embedding it in the target container.

OLE Automation

OLE Automation refers to the ability of an application to define a set of properties and commands and make them accessible to other applications to enable programmability. OLE provides a mechanism through which this access is achieved. OLE Automation increases application interoperability without the need for human intervention.

The public exposure of these properties and commands allows one application to contain code that manipulates another application. It also allows developers to create new applications that can interact with existing applications. OLE Automation is a powerful mechanism that allows OLE-enabled applications to function as components that can be combined into complete applications.

Object Type Conversion and Emulation

The ease with which documents can be transferred between machines, combined with the proliferation of applications that operate on similar types of data, make it desirable for users to be able to convert an object to a different type either temporarily or permanently. OLE provides a mechanism through which applications can perform type conversion and/or emulation.

Type conversion causes a permanent change to an object. A converted object no longer carries any of the traits of its original type; its name and data format reflect the new type. A user may want to convert all objects of one type to another type if the target type's object application provides greater capabilities or the original object application is no longer available.

Type emulation causes an object to take on the characteristics of an object of another type while maintaining its original name and data format. The object is activated using the emulated type's object application and choice of verbs. Users may want to take advantage of type emulation if changes are being made to an OLE Document with multiple machines with different object applications. Type emulation permits all users to interact with the embedded objects using the particular object application on their machine.

Extended Object Layout

OLE provides a sophisticated object placement mechanism that allows large rectangular objects to span more than one page. Figure 5.7 shows a lengthy spreadsheet object which, when embedded into a word processor OLE Document, must be broken into parts. Based on the OLE Document's page size, OLE determines that the object must span three pages. The headings can be presented on each page so that the user need not refer back to the first page.

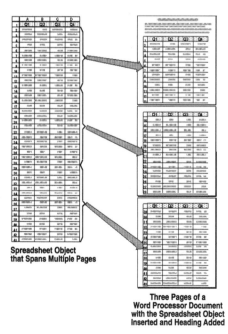

Spreadsheet Object
that Spans Multiple Pages

Three Pages of a
Word Processor Document
with the Spreadsheet Object
Inserted and Heading Added

Figure 5.7   Inserting a large object into a word processor OLE Document.

Searching and Spell Checking

OLE Documents may consist of objects created from two, three, four, or more applications. Since users want the ability to treat a multisource document as a single entity, rather than as a group of disparate objects from different sources, it makes sense to allow some operations to act on entire documents, regardless of where their content was created. Two such operations are searches and spell-checks.

OLE defines a new group of functions that allow string searches and spell-checks to "tunnel" inside embedded objects, and even within objects embedded in other objects. With this new capability, users don't have to invoke multiple applications each time they want to search or spell-check an entire OLE Document. All objects whose applications understand OLE's search and spell-check functions will invoke those functions to perform the operation.

Figure 5.8 demonstrates the search and spell operation for an OLE Document containing nested embedded objects. The search and spell checking begins with the native text belonging to the OLE Document application, a word processor. It then moves hierarchically through the embedded objects, first checking the top level object, the spreadsheet, and then the object contained in the spreadsheet, the pie chart object. When the operation finishes with the spreadsheet and the pie chart, it continues with the text immediately following these objects.

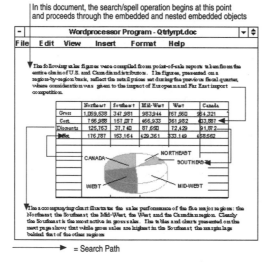

Figure 5.8   Spell checking an OLE Document.

Management

In OLE, objects can contain information about the application that created them, including the name of the application and the version of that application. This allows applications to get more information about the objects they are dealing with, and to handle objects based on the applications or versions of applications that created them.

For example, when an object created by version 1.0 of application X is embedded into a document that is moved to a system having only version 2.0 of that same application and a user tries to edit the object, version 2.0 of the application can determine that the object is from an older version and can take any action it desires. It can, for example, prompt the user to upgrade the object to a new format.

Adaptable Links

OLE provides the mechanism for objects to be linked in a variety of ways and have those links adapt to changing situations. An object may be linked to a complete or partial object, referred to as a *pseudo object*. An example of a pseudo object is a range of spreadsheet cells. The source of a link may reside inside either the same OLE Document as the linked object or in a separate OLE Document. Both the OLE Document containing the linked object and the link source may be stored in a standard disk file or in a file managed by the OLE storage system.

If the linked object is copied to a new location while the link source stays in place, the link remains intact and the linked object points correctly to the source. Similarly, if both the OLE Document containing the linked object and the link source are moved to a new location in the same relative path, the link remains intact.

For example, consider the scenario portrayed in Figure 5.9. The word processor document **SALESRPT.DOC** contains a link to an object in the spreadsheet application file **SALESRPT.XLS**. Both files reside under the **MONTHLY** directory. If the contents of the **MONTHLY** directory are then moved or copied to a new directory named **ANNUAL**, then the link in **SALESRPT.DOC** now points to **SALESRPT.XLS** under **\ANNUAL**. The link is thus updated automatically.

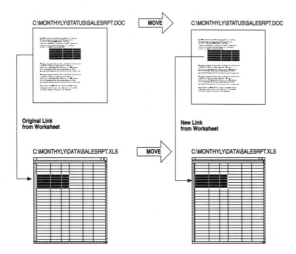

Figure 5.9   Moving a linked object and its link source.

An Overview of the OLE Architecture

Complete compound document services represent just one type of service that OLE supports. Because they are based on a powerful underlying object model, the OLE Component Object Model (COM), all OLE object services are both language independent and platform independent. OLE supports a powerful method of object scripting: the ability of one OLE object to automate at run time the creation or processing of other OLE objects (even those running in different memory spaces). *OLE Automation* allows OLE components to explore the capabilities of other OLE components dynamically at run time and use these components' services to accomplish specific tasks. For instance, an OLE-enabled accounting application could use an OLE-enabled spreadsheet to create charts automatically and embed them in accounting reports. This is just one example— component integrators will be able to assemble fully functional business solutions by combining packaged and custom OLE components through OLE Automation.

In addition, the *OLE Control* architecture is a powerful OLE service that allows ISVs and corporate developers to create specialized custom components that are not complete applications by themselves, but are actually components that can be plugged into existing OLE-enabled applications (both custom applications and shrink-wrapped applications) to extend and customize functionality to meet specific customer needs. The use of such prefabricated OLE components will significantly increase MIS productivity. And because OLE Controls are based on the underlying OLE Component Object Model, they can be incorporated into OLE Documents when desired. OLE Controls won the prestigious "Most Significant New Technology" at the 1994 Spring Comdex in Atlanta.

Major development tools such as the Microsoft Visual Basic programming system, Powersoft PowerBuilder™, Digitalk's PARTS Workbench, and many others will soon fully support OLE Controls. Using these familiar development environments, corporations will be able to integrate prefabricated OLE components into new and exciting business applications. And the development costs and development times for these component-based business applications will be substantially reduced.

Additionally, OLE services are easily extensible as powerful mechanisms to bring component-based solutions to other system-level and business-level services. For instance, OLE can and will be extended as a fully functional object model to address diverse system-level services. In vertical business segments, the OLE software is already being used to extend OLE object services to specific vertical-market applications. For instance, the Windows Open Services Architecture (WOSA) Extensions for Real-time Market Data defines a standard OLE interface for exchanging real-time market data between applications. Using WOSA Extensions for Real-time Market Data, for example, users can insert real-time stock-quote objects into a spreadsheet or other OLE application. This is just a simple example; customers will discover many powerful ways to use WOSA Extensions for Real-time Market Data in their businesses. And OLE will be extended into many other vertical markets including banking and manufacturing (among many others) as the object model of choice for building flexible, component-based solutions.

OLE as an Object-Oriented Design

Object-oriented design is a technique built around ideas that enable developers to write code that can be easily maintained, reused, and extended. These ideas center around the *object class,* or type, a structure consisting of member functions that define the behavior of the object class and object data upon which the member functions operate. To promote reuse, an object class may contain other objects or inherit from other object classes, which means that both the data and the member functions become part of the new object class. In the latter case, the new object class may use just the member functions' names or their full implementation. When only the names are inherited, the new object class provides its own unique implementation of the member functions. A single instance of an object class is called simply an *object*.

The OLE architecture incorporates these design ideas through its own scheme of objects. The OLE libraries define *interfaces*, or sets of member functions, which describe object behavior in an abstract manner without providing an implementation. As defined in C++ terms, interfaces are abstract base classes. The purpose of an abstract base class or interface is to provide member function name inheritance. An object which supports the behavior defined in an interface must provide implementations for all of the member functions specified in the interfaces. These implementations may be shared with other object classes.

The OLE architecture establishes one interface to be the base interface from which all other interfaces are derived. It is through one of the member functions in this interface that communication about all of the other interfaces is achieved. Therefore, implementations for the member functions of this base interface are included in every object. OLE Document services are interfaces designed to handle the creation of OLE Documents. OLE is completely extensible, and additional interfaces, based on the underlying OLE Component Object Model, address important services well beyond OLE Documents. And new interfaces are being defined to address additional services such as database access and other system-level services, making OLE a solid foundation for component solutions.

Interfaces

An interface provides the means by which OLE applications access object services, such as drawing, saving, or Visual Editing. Interfaces are defined by OLE, but can be implemented by OLE, by an object application, and/or by a container application, depending on the service provided by the interface. The services that are standard for all applications are implemented in interfaces provided by OLE. Applications make calls to the member functions in these standard interfaces. Services that are application, document, or object specific (such as pasting from the Clipboard) are supported by interfaces implemented by the application. Implementation involves providing code for each of the member functions defined for the interface.

As indicated in Figure 5.10, both the container application and the object application implement interfaces that allow use of their services or functions. For example, when the user of the container application wants to edit an embedded object, the container makes calls to the appropriate interface (for object editing) implemented by the object application. Similarly, when the object application completes an operation such as changing an object so that it requires more or less space in the container, it calls functions implemented by the container application that change the layout size of the object. The communication between the container and object applications is maintained through the OLE library. The library intercepts calls and provides a variety of services through its own interfaces. Services provided by OLE library interfaces include the packaging and sending of parameters between the different process spaces, providing storage for objects, and translation of object names.

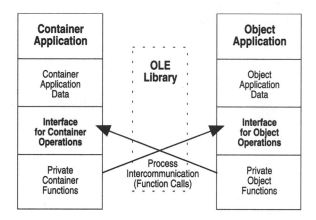

Figure 5.10   Implementation and use of interfaces by OLE applications.

The services provided by interfaces fall into one of four general areas: communication between objects, infrastructure support, basic linking and embedding, and advanced features. An application developer need only implement a few interfaces from those in the first two areas to achieve basic OLE functionality. The specific interfaces required differs somewhat according to whether the application will act as a container, an object, or both. As more features are required, a developer can implement the appropriate additional interface(s) without affecting either the application or those applications that interact with it. Developers should determine which of these features, if any, are important to their users before proceeding with the implementation.

OLE Objects

There are two levels of OLE objects. The more general OLE object, the *component object*, supports the communication interfaces. Component objects are used throughout OLE to provide applications with access to lower-level interfaces implemented by OLE. For example, when a container application calls an interface member function that initiates Visual Editing, a component object is used to pass information to the appropriate object application. The container application is unaware of how this communication is achieved or what this object looks like; the service is provided by the component object and its interface member functions.

The second level of OLE objects is the object that is used in OLE Documents. *OLE Document objects* support both the communication interfaces and at least one of the basic linking or embedding interfaces. OLE associates two types of data with an OLE Document object: *presentation data* and *native data*. The object's presentation data is needed to render the object on a display or other output device, while its native data is needed for an object application to edit the object.

Structured Storage System

OLE includes a hierarchical storage system, which resembles a file system within a file. There are two levels of storage in the OLE storage system: storage objects, which can be viewed as the directory level in a typical file system, and stream objects, which can be viewed as the file level. A storage object may contain streams and/or other storage objects; a stream object contains data. Each OLE object is assigned its own storage object. Access to objects and data within the OLE storage system is through a set of interfaces provided by OLE. OLE provides an implementation of this storage system that it calls *compound files*.

Although OLE applications are not required to use compound files, compound file usage is encouraged because the OLE storage system provides efficient and flexible access to object data. The storage system interfaces allow objects, or portions of objects, to be read from disk to memory without the need to load the entire file. This feature is significant when loading an OLE Document that contains either a large number of objects or a single large object such as a video clip, since it is more efficient to load only the data that is currently needed. That is, applications need not wait for unwanted data to be loaded before the data wanted is made available to the user.

The OLE storage system can be used for a variety of storage needs. Figure 5.11 shows an example of how a simple OLE Document that consists of some text, an embedded worksheet object, and a nested embedded chart object can be stored.

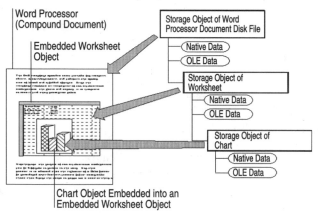

Figure 5.11   How an OLE Document is stored.

When the OLE Document in Figure 5.11 is saved to disk, it is saved as a single file that contains separate "internal" storage areas for each object. The highest level of storage for this file is the storage object for the document, which is the disk file. The document storage object contains stream objects for the document's native data (text in this case) and OLE data, as well as a storage object for the embedded worksheet object. The worksheet object in turn contains streams for its native data and OLE data, plus a storage object for the embedded chart.

For those applications requiring the ability to undo changes made to a document during an edit session, the storage system includes a two-phase commit operation. An application choosing to save in *transacted mode* has both the old and new copies of the document available until the user chooses to save or undo the changes. Applications not needing this feature can choose to save in *direct mode*, in which changes to the document and its objects are incorporated as they are made..

Interprocess Communication

OLE uses a lightweight communication mechanism to transfer data between processes. This communication mechanism is "lightweight" because at present it handles communication between processes on only one machine; in the future, communication will be across machines.

OLE provides transparent communication. An application is unaware of whether a call to a member function remains within its process space or crosses into another process space. Messages and data are grouped so that multiple OLE requests are sent together and traffic between processes is reduced. This mechanism is not a protocol; there is no need for a conversation between the two processes. Data is simply sent to a predefined space on disk where it is read by a process dedicated to that task..

Linking and Naming

The linking and naming services in OLE are implemented through the use of monikers, or aliases. Monikers are names of various types given to objects to maintain a tie between an object and its link source. OLE provides implementations of a set of interfaces and API functions used to manipulate and control monikers.

When the user of an OLE Document needs to access the link source, the application initiates a process known as *binding*. In order to locate the link source, the binding process parses the moniker and interprets each piece according to preestablished rules.

Why Implement OLE?

OLE provides great benefits to both users and developers. OLE is the foundation of a new model of computing, which is more "document-centric" and less "application-centric." Users can focus on the data needed to create their OLE

Documents rather than on the applications responsible for the data. As the user focuses on a particular data object, the tools needed to interact with that object become available directly within the document. Data objects can be transferred within and across documents without the loss of functionality. Documents can share data so that one copy of an object can serve many users. Users can therefore be more productive and manipulate information in a manner that is much more intuitive.

The use of OLE objects and interfaces provides developers with the tools they need to create flexible applications that can be easily maintained and enhanced. OLE applications can specialize in one area, taking advantage of features implemented in other OLE applications to increase their usability.

Since all interfaces are derived from one base interface, applications can learn at run time about the capabilities of other applications that relate to object services. Through this dynamic binding, an application need not have any information about the objects it will use at run time. Support for additional objects and interfaces can be added without affecting either the current application or those applications that interact with it. Because the use of interfaces allows applications to access objects as black boxes, changes to an object's member functions do not affect the code accessing them.

The extensibility that OLE provides will continue to benefit the developer as the computing environment moves more toward object-oriented design. The OLE architecture provides a first step in presenting applications as a collection of independently installable components.

The OLE infrastructure (storage, naming, and communication systems) provides benefits independent of its relationship to OLE Document operations. A storage system that can support transactions and incremental loading and storing promotes efficient usage of memory. The ability to associate a logical name with an object is useful in a variety of situations. The mechanism for interprocess communication, which combines data in a package before sending it, can service all applications regardless of whether they support OLE Documents. Through the sharing of these general-purpose interface implementations, greater commonality between applications is gained.

Applications that support the first version of OLE (OLE 1.0) can be used with applications that support OLE 2.0 and the OLE 2.0 libraries. OLE 2.0 is 100% compatible with OLE 1.0. OLE 1.0 objects look and behave much like OLE 2.0 objects for which Visual Editing is not allowed. Improvements to the infrastructure have no effect on OLE 1.0 applications. These applications can operate on the OLE 2.0 platform without modification and interact with OLE 2.0 applications as if they both supported OLE 1.0.

For developers interested in creating cross-platform applications, OLE 2.0 can be used with Microsoft Windows version 3.1, Microsoft Windows NT, and the Apple Macintosh System 7.

OLE Backgrounders, Technical Summaries, and Technology Comparisons

The following documents (as well as additional documents) can be ordered by contacting the Microsoft Developer Solutions Team at (800) 227-4679.

Strategic Whitepapers	Primary Audience
The Microsoft Object Technology Strategy (098-55163)	MIS, ISVs, System Consultants

Management Backgrounders	Primary Audience
OLE Corporate Backgrounder (098-56457)	Users, MIS, ISVs, System Consultants
The Benefits of Component Software (098-56459)	Users, MIS, ISVs, System Consultants
OLE Documents (098-56352)	Users, MIS, ISVs, System Consultants
OLE Controls (098-55315)	MIS, ISVs, System Consultants
Open Systems: Technology Leadership and Collaboration (098-55058)	MIS, ISVs, System Consultants

Technology Comparisons	Primary Audience
OLE and OpenDoc: Information for Customers (098-56353)	MIS, ISVs, System Consultants
Object Strategies: How They Compare (098-55636)	MIS, ISVs, System Consultants

Technical Documents	Primary Audience
OLE Documents Technical Backgrounder (098-56453)	Developers
Microsoft OLE: Today and Tomorrow (098-56454)	Developers
What is an OLE 2 Application? (098-56455)	Developers
Developing Applications with OLE 2 (098-56456)	Developers
OLE Control Specification Overview (098-56458)	Developers
The Microsoft Foundation Classes (MFC) Whitepaper	Developers
The OLE 2.0 Programmer's Reference (ISBN 1-55615-628-6 and -629-4)	Developers
Inside OLE 2.0 (ISBN 1-55615-618-9)	Developers

Topic

Describe how OLE uses the registration database.

Content

Globally Unique Identifiers: GUIDs, IIDs, and CLSIDs[2]

Every interface is defined by an *interface identifier*, or IID (as in IID_IUnknown), which is a special case of a universally unique identifier, or UUID. The universally unique identifier is also known as the globally unique identifier, or GUID (pronounced goo-id). GUIDs are 128-bit values created with a DEFINE_GUID macro. Every interface and object class uses a GUID for identification. Microsoft will allocate one or more sets of 256 GUIDs for your exclusive use when you request them, or if you have a network card in your machine, you can run a tool named UUIDGEN.EXE that will provide you with a set of 256 GUIDs based on the time of day, the date, and a unique number contained in your network card.

All the code shown in this book uses GUIDs prefixed with *000211*, which are allocated to the author. Do not use these GUIDs for your own products.

OLE defines IIDs for every standard interface along with class identifiers (CLSID) for every standard object class. When we call any function that asks for an IID or a CLSID, we pass a *reference* to an instance of the GUID structure that exists in our process space using the types REFIID or REFCLSID. When passing an IID or a CLSID in C, you must use a pointer--that is, pass &IID_$AO or &CLSID_$AO, where REFIID and REFCLSID are typed as **const** pointers to IID or CLSID. In C++, because a reference is a natural part of the language, you drop the **&**.

Finally, to compare two GUID, IID, or CLSID values for equality, use the **IsEqualGUID**, **IsEqualIID**, and **IsEqualCLSID** functions defined in COMPOBJ.H. There the latter two are simply more readable aliases for **IsEqualGUID**. If you are programming in C++, take a look at COMPOBJ.H, which defines an overloaded "==" operator for the GUID type that, of course, applies equally well to the IID and CLSID types.

---

[2] Materials excerpted from chapters 3 and 4 of *Inside OLE 2* by Kraig Brockschmidt published by Microsoft Press. Copyright 1994. Used with permission. All rights reserved.

Content

Register CLSIDs

Every component object class (but not all types of Windows Objects) must have a unique CLSID associated with it in the Registration Database. The registration entries for a simple object, such as we're implementing here, are few; as you create objects with more features that support linking and embedding, there will be much more information to add. Creating a REG file is the preferred method of registering objects and applications because it can be done at install time instead of programmatically at run time, which is tedious.

The required entries fall under the CLSID key, where OLE stores information about all classes under your spelled-out CLSID, as you can see in the REGEDIT program and as shown in Figure 5.12. OLE also stores information about its standard interfaces and the code that handles parameter marshaling under the Interface key. The following steps describe the necessary registration for DLL-based and EXE-based objects:

1. From **HKEY_CLASSES_ROOT** (the root key of the entire Registration Database), create the entry **CLSID**\{*class ID*}=<*name*>, where {*class ID*} is the value of your CLSID spelled out and <*name*> is a human-readable string for your object. The Koala object has the class ID string {00021102-0000-0000-C000-000000000046} which is not readable. The <*name*> of the Koala object is "Koala Object Chapter 4 ."

2. Create an entry under the CLSID entry in step 1 to point to the object code:

   - For DLL objects, register **InprocServer**=<*path to DLL*>.
   - For EXE objects, register **LocalServer**=<*path to EXE*>.
   - For DLL object handlers, register **InprocHandler**=<*path to DLL*>.

   Note that these entries should always contains full pathnames so that you do not depend on your DLLs or EXEs being on the MS-DOS path. Your application's install program should update the paths when it knows where the installation occurred.*

---

* The sample code with this book does, however, break this rule because the installation program on the companion disks is not capable of modifying all the .REG files in each CHAPxx directory to contain a full pathname. Instead, each DLL and EXE is registered without a full pathname and therefore depends on them being in the path.

3. (Optional) If you want to allow a user to look up your CLSID based on a text string, make an entry under **HKEY_CLASSES_ROOT** of *<ProgID>=<name>*, where *<ProgID>* is a short name without spaces or punctuation, and *<name>* is the human-readable name, identical to that in step 1, of your object. Under this key, create another entry, **CLSID**={*class ID*}, in which {*class ID*} is also the same as in step 1. In this example, *<ProgID>* is Koala and *<name>* is "Koala Object Chapter 4." Note that you can also create a symmetric key under the object's CLSID in the form of *ProgID* = *<ProgID>*.

Entries of the type created in step 3 will be required for Compound Document objects that should appear in the Insert Object dialog box inside a container application. Without those entries from steps 1 and 2, however, the **CoGetClassObject** API function (which **CoCreateInstance** uses, remember) will not be able to locate your object implementation. Note also that the same DLL or EXE can serve multiple CLSIDs, and in such cases you must make a similar entry under each CLSID you support with the **InprocServer** and **LocalServer** keys, although they can all contain the same path to the same server.

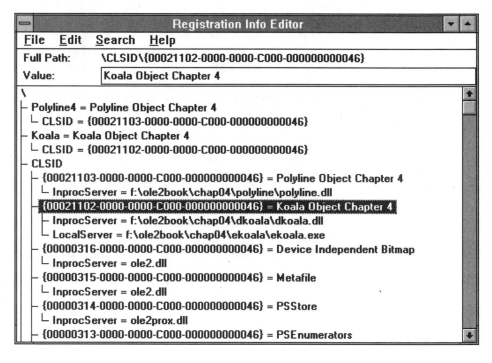

Figure 5.12   The populated CLSID section of the Registration Database, showing the entries for Koala.

Content

Programmatic Identifiers[3]

Every OLE 2.0 object class that is to appear in an Insert Object dialog box (hereafter referred to as an "insertable class") must have a programmatic identifier or *ProgID*. This string uniquely identifies a given class and is intended to be in a form that can be read by humans. Programmatic identifiers are not guaranteed to be universally unique so they can be used only where name collisions are manageable, such as in achieving compatibility with OLE 1.0. Also, the ProgID is the "class name" used for an OLE 2.0 class when it is placed in an object application (OLE 1.0 server).

The ProgID string must:

- Have no more than 39 characters.

- Contain no punctuation (including underscores) except one or more periods.

- Not start with a digit.

- Be different from the class name of any OLE 1.0 application, including the OLE 1.0 version of the same application, if there is one.

Because it is necessary to make a conversion between the ProgId and the CLSID, it is important to note that there are two kinds of ProgIDs. One depends on the version of the object application (the version-dependent ProgID); and one does not (the version-independent ProgID).

The version-dependent ProgID is the string used when OLE 1.0 is trying to contact OLE 2.0 using DDE. Version-dependent ProgID-to-CLSID conversions must be specific, well-defined, and one-to-one.

The version-independent ProgID, on the other hand, can be used when a container application creates a chart or table with a toolbar button. In this situation, the application can use the version-independent ProgID to determine the latest version of the needed object application.

The **CLSIDFromProgID** and **ProgIDFromCLSID** functions can be called to convert back and forth between the two representations. These functions use information stored in the registry to perform the conversion.

The ProgID-to-CLSID conversion is done using the **HKEY_LOCAL_MACHINE\SOFTWARE\Classes\\<*ProgID*>\CLSID** key. The reverse translation is done using the **HKEY_LOCAL_MACHINE\SOFTWARE\Classes\CLSID\\<*clsid*>\ProgID** subkey. This means that the ProgID subkey under **HKEY_LOCAL_MACHINE\SOFTWARE\Classes\CLSID\\<*clsid*>** is version-dependent.

The version-independent ProgID is stored and maintained solely by application code. When given the version-independent ProgID, **CLSIDFromProgID** returns the CLSID of the current version. **CLSIDFromProgID** works on the version-independent ProgID because the subkey, CLSID, is the same as it is for the version-dependent one.

The user must never see the ProgID in the user interface. If you need a short human-readable string for an object, call **IOleObject::GetUserType(USERCLASSTYPE_SHORT, lpszShortName)**.

The ProgID Key and Subkeys

OLE 2.0 classes that belong in the Insert Object dialog box each have a ProgID. The value assigned to this key is the name displayed in the dialog box; it should be the same as the "*MainUserTypeName*" of the class. If this class is insertable in an OLE 2.0 container, the ProgID key must have an immediate subkey named **Insertable**, which must have no value assigned to it.

Note Because OLE 2.0 provides a built-in OLE 1.0/OLE 2.0 compatibility layer, rarely will an OLE 2.0 class that is insertable in an OLE 2.0 container not be insertable in an OLE 1.0 container.

If a particular class is insertable in an OLE 1.0 container, the "ProgID" *root key* will contain a **Protocol\StdFileEditing** subkey with appropriate subkeys **Verb**, **Server**, and so on, as in OLE 1.0. The **Server** that should be registered here is the full path to the executable file of the OLE 2.0 object application. An OLE 1.0 container uses the path and executable file names to launch the OLE 2.0 object application. The initialization of this application, in turn, loads the OLE 2.0 compatibility layer. This layer handles subsequent interactions with the OLE 1.0 container (client), turning them into OLE 2.0-like requests to the OLE 2.0 application. An OLE 2.0 object application doesn't have to take any special action beyond setting up these registry entries to make objects insertable into an OLE 1.0 container.

The ProgID key and subkeys appear in the registry as shown in the following example, where "*<Progid>*" is the key, and **Insertable**, **Protocol**, **StdFileEditing**, **Verb**, and so on are subkeys.

Note   In this registry example and others that follow, **boldface** indicates a literal standard key or subkey, *<italics>* indicates an application-supplied string or value, and *<boldface-italics>* indicates an application-supplied key or subkey. In the first example, "OLE1ClassName," "OLE1UserTypeName," and "CLSID" are all supplied by the application.

```
<ProgID> = <MainUserTypeName>
    Insertable  // class is insertable in OLE 2 containers
    Protocol
        StdFileEditing  // OLE 1 compatibility info; present if, and
only if, objects
            // of this class are insertable in OLE 1 containers.
        Server = <full path to the OLE 2 object application>
        Verb
            0 = <verb 0>// Verb entries for the OLE 2 application must
start with
            1 = <verb 1>// zero as the primary verb and run
consecutively.
    CLSID = <CLSID> // The corresponding CLSID. Needed by GetClassFile.
    Shell   // Windows 3.1 File Manager Info
        Print
        Open
        Command = <appname.exe> %1
```
To summarize, any root key that has either an **Insertable** or a **Protocol\StdFileEditing** subkey is the ProgID (or OLE 1.0 class name) of a class that should appear in the Insert Object dialog box. The value of that root key is the human-readable name displayed in the Insert Object dialog box.

The values of each key in the example below are used for registering the "Ole 2 In-Place Server Outline" sample application. Set these values as required and used by your application.

Long Form String Subkey Entry

The entry to register the string (long form), such as that used in The Insert New dialog box, is as follows. The recommended maximum length for the string is 40 characters.

```
HKEY_CLASSES_ROOT\OLE2ISvrOtl =
    Ole 2 In-Place Server Outline
```

Information for OLE 1.0 Applications Subkey Entries

To maintain compatibility with OLE 1.0, include the following OLE 1.0 information. The "server" key entry should contain a full path to the application. The entries for verbs must start with 0 as the primary verb and be consecutively numbered.

```
HKEY_CLASSES_ROOT\OLE2ISvrOtl\protocol\StdFileEditing\
    server =c:\samp\isvrotl.exe
HKEY_CLASSES_ROOT\OLE2ISvrOtl\protocol\StdFileEditing\
    verb\0 = &Edit
HKEY_CLASSES_ROOT\OLE2ISvrOtl\protocol\StdFileEditing\
    verb\1 = &Open
```

Windows 3.1 Shell Subkey Entries

These entries are for Windows 3.1 shell printing and File Open use. They should contain the path and filename of the object application. The examples below contain simple entries only; more complicated ones could include DDE entries.

```
HKEY_CLASSES_ROOT\OLE2ISvrOtl\Shell\Print\Command =
    c:\svr\isvrotl.exe %1
HKEY_CLASSES_ROOT\OLE2ISvrOtl\Shell\Open\Command =
    c:\svr\isvrotl.exe %1
```

Insertable Subkey Entry

This entry indicates that the object application should appear in the Insert New dialog box's list box when used by OLE 2.0 container applications.

```
HKEY_CLASSES_ROOT\OLE2ISvrOtl\Insertable
```

Entry Point Subkey

This entry points to the application's OLE 2.0 information in the registry. To assign a CLSID for your application, run the UUIDGEN.EXE found in the \TOOLS directory of the OLE 2.0 Toolkit.

```
HKEY_CLASSES_ROOT\OLE2ISvrOtl\CLSID =
    {00000402-0000-0000-C000-000000000046}
```

The CLSID Key and Subkey

Most of the OLE object application information is stored in subkeys under the **CLSID** *root key*. The immediate subkey of the **CLSID** key is a string version CLSID. Subkeys of this version of the CLSID indicate where the code that services this class is found. For more information about converting the CLSID, see **StringFromCLSID**. For other related information see **LocalServer**, **InprocServer**, and **InprocHandler** under The CLSID Key and Subkeys. Most of the **CLSID** information is used by the default OLE handler to return various information about the class when it is in the loaded state. Examples of this include the **Verb**, the **AuxUserType**, and the **MiscStatus** entries. The **Insertable** subkey appears under both this key and the **ProgId** key.

```
CLSID
<CLSID> = <Main User Type Name>
LocalServer = <path to 16- or 32-bit exe>    // local (same machine)
server; see
    // "Server =" under ProgID key.
LocalServer32 = <path to 32-bit exe>    // local (same machine) server;
see
    // "Server =" under ProgID key.
InprocServer = <path to dll>// in process server; relatively rare for
insertable
    // classes.
InprocServer32 = <path to 32-bit dll>    // in process server;
relatively rare for
    // insertable classes.
InprocHandler = <path to dll>    // in process handler. "OLE32.DLL" for
the
    // default OLE 2 handler
InprocHandler32 = <path to 32-bit dll>    // in process handler.
"OLE32.DLL" for
    // the default OLE 2 handler
Verb        // info returned in IOleObject::EnumVerbs.
    verb number = <name, menu flags, verb flags>
    // several examples follow:
        0 = &Edit, 0, 2// primary verb; often Edit; on menu; possibly
dirties object,
                // MF_STRING | MF_UNCHECKED | MF_ENABLED == 0.
        1 = &Play, 0, 3// other verb; appears on menu; leaves object
clean
        -3 = Hide, 0, 1 // pseudo verb for hiding window; not on menu,
opt.
        -2 = Open, 0, 1 // pseudo verb for opening in sep. window; not
on menu, opt.
        -1 = Show, 0, 1 // pseudo verb for showing in preferred state;
not on menu,
                // opt.
AuxUserType // auxiliary user types (main user type above)
    <form of type> = <string>    // See IOleObject::GetUserType(); for
example:
    2 = <ShortName> // key 1 should not be used
    3 = <Application name>    // Contains the human-readable name of the
        // application. Used when the actual name of the app is needed
(for example
```

```
                    // in the Paste Special dialog's result field) Example: Acme
Draw
MiscStatus = <default>   // def status used for all aspects; see
    // IOleObject::GetMiscStatus
    <aspect> = <integer> // exceptions to above;  for example:
    4 = 1           // DVASPECT_ICON = OLEMISC_RECOMPOSEONRESIZE
DataFormats
    DefaultFile = <format>   // default main file/object format of
objects of this
            // class.
    GetSet  // list of formats for default impl. of EnumFormatEtc; very
similar
            // to Request/SetDataFormats in OLE 1 entries
    <n> = <format ,aspect, medium, flag> // in this line,
            // n  is a zero-based integer index;
            // format is clipboard format;
            // aspect is one or more of DVASPECT_*, -1 for "all";
            // medium is one or more of TYMED_*;
            // flag is one or more of DATADIR_*.
            // three examples follow:
        0 = 3, -1, 32, 1     // CF_METAFILE, all aspects, TYMED_MFPICT,
            // DATADIR_GET
        1 = Biff3, 1, 15, 3 // this example shows
            // Microsoft Excel's Biff format version 3,
            // DVASPECT_CONTENT,
            // TYMED_HGLOBAL | TYMED_FILE |
            // TYMED_ISTREAM | TYMED_ISTORAGE,
            // (DATADIR_SET | DATADIR_GET)
        2 = Rich Text Format, 1,1,3
Insertable  // when present, the class appears in the Insert Object
dialog.
                // (not present for internal classes like the moniker
classes)
ProgID = <ProgID>        // the programmatic identifier for this class.
TreatAs = <CLSID>        // see CoGetTreatAs()
AutoTreatAs = <CLSID>    //see CoTreatAsClass
AutoConvertTo = <CLSID>    // see OleGetAutoConvert()
Conversion          // support for Change Type dialog box
    Readable
        Main = <format,format,format,format, ...>
    Readwritable
        Main = <format,format,format,format, ...>
DefaultIcon = <path to exe, index>   // parameters passed to ExtractIcon
Interfaces = <IID, IID, ...> // optional. If this key is present, then
its values are
    // the totality of the interfaces supported by this class: if the
IID is not in this list,
    // then the interface is never supported by an instance of this
class.
VersionIndependentProgID = <VersionIndependentProgID>
```

By default, 32-bit implementations take priority over 16-bit implementations.

Existing 16-bit applications look in the registry for the insertable keyword. This key informs the application that the server supports embeddings. If the insertable keyword exists, 16-bit applications may also attempt to verify that the server exists on the machine. 16-bit applications typically will retrieve the value of the **LocalServer** key from the class, and check to see if it is a valid file on the system. Therefore, to be insertable by 16-bit applications, 32-bit applications should register **LocalServer** in addition to registering **LocalServer32**.

For 32-bit applications, the only required keys are **LocalServer**, **LocalServer32**, **InprocHandler32**, and **Insertable**. **InprocHandler**, **InprocServer**, and **InproServer32** are optional.

For a 32-bit **InprocServer**, the required entries are **InprocHandler32**, **InprocServer**, **InprocServer32**, and **Insertable**. Note that **InprocServer** provides backward compatibility. If missing, the class still works, but isn't insertable in 16-bit applications.

CLSID (Object Class ID) Subkey Entry

The following information creates a CLSID subkey under the **CLSID** key. To obtain a CLSID for your application, run the UUIDGEN.EXE found in the \TOOLS directory of the OLE 2.0 Toolkit.

```
HKEY_CLASSES_ROOT\CLSID\{00000402-0000-0000-C000-
    000000000046} = Ole 2 In-Place Server Outline
```

Note The subkey entries described in this "CLSID Key Entry" section are subkeys to your CLSID subkey. (Not all possible subkeys are described.)

LocalServer Subkey Entry

This subkey designates the application's location. The LocalServer subkey has the same value as the OLE2ISvrOtl\protocol\StdFileEditing\server key and should contain a full path. The entry can contain command-line arguments. Note that OLE appends the "-Embedding" flag to the string, so the application that uses flags must parse the whole string and check for the -Embedding flag.

```
HKEY_CLASSES_ROOT\CLSID\{00000402-0000-0000-C000-
    000000000046}\LocalServer = c:\samp\isvrotl.exe
```
To run an OLE object server in a separate memory space (Windows NT 3.5 only), change the **LocalServer** key in the registry for the CLSID to the following:

```
        cmd /c start /separate <path.exe
```

LocalServer32 Subkey Entry

This subkey designates the location of the 32-bit version of the application. The LocalServer32 subkey has the same value as the OLE2ISvrOtl\protocol\StdFileEditing\server key and should contain a full path name. The entry can contain command-line arguments. Note that OLE appends the "-Embedding" flag to the string, so the application that uses flags will need to parse the whole string and check for the -Embedding flag.

```
HKEY_CLASSES_ROOT\CLSID\{00000402-0000-0000-C000-
    000000000046}\LocalServer = c:\samp\isvrotl.exe
```

When OLE starts a 32-bit local server, the server must register a class object within an elapsed time set by the user. By default, this value must be at least five minutes, in milliseconds, but cannot exceed the number of milliseconds in 30 days. To set this value, add the following entry:

```
HKEY_CLASSES_ROOT\\Software\Microsoft\OLE2\
    ServerStartElapsedTime
```

InprocHandler Subkey Entry

This subkey designates whether the application uses a custom handler. If no custom handler is used, the entry should be set to OLE2.DLL, as shown in the following example.

```
HKEY_-CLASSES_ROOT\CLSID\{00000402-0000-0000-C000-
    000000000046}\InprocHandler = ole2.dll
```

InprocHandler32 Subkey Entry

This subkey designates whether the application uses a custom handler. If no custom handler is used, the entry should be set to OLE32.DLL, as shown in the following example.

```
HKEY_-CLASSES_ROOT\CLSID\{00000402-0000-0000-C000-
    000000000046}\InprocHandler = ole32.dll
```

Verb Subkey Entry

The verbs to be registered for the application must be numbered consecutively. The first value after the verb string describes how the verb is appended by the AppendMenu function call.

The second value indicates whether the verb will dirty the object. It also indicates whether the verb should appear in the menu (as defined by OLEVERBATTRIB_).

```
Verb 0: "Edit", MF_UNCHECKED | MF_ENABLED, no OLEVERATTRIB flags
HKEY_CLASSES_ROOT\CLSID\{00000402-0000-0000-C000-
    000000000046}\Verb\0 = &Edit,0,0
Verb 1: "Open", MF_UNCHECKED | MF_ENABLED, no OLEVERATTRIB flags
HKEY_CLASSES_ROOT\CLSID\{00000402-0000-0000-C000-
    000000000046}\Verb\1 = &Open,0,0
```

AuxUserType Subkey Entry

This key describes the short and actual human-readable names of the application. The short name is used in the menus, including pop-ups, and the recommended maximum length for the string is 15 characters. A short name example follows.

```
HKEY_CLASSES_ROOT\CLSID\{00000402-0000-0000-C000-
    000000000046}\AuxUserType\2 = In-Place Outline
```

The long human-readable name of the application is used in the Results field of the Paste Special dialog box. This string should contain the actual name of the application (such as "Acme Draw 2.0").

```
HKEY_CLASSES_ROOT\CLSID\{00000402-0000-0000-C000-
    000000000046}\AuxUserType\3 = Ole 2 In-Place Server
```

MiscStatus Subkey Entry

The following is an example of a MiscStatus subkey.

```
HKEY_CLASSES_ROOT\CLSID\{00000402-0000-0000-C000-
    000000000046}\MiscStatus = 0
```

DataFormats Subkey Entry

The DataFormats subkey lists the default and main data formats supported by the application. This entry is used by the **IDataObject::GetData**, **IDataObject::SetData** and **IDataObject::EnumFormatEtc** methods.

The values defined in the following example entry are CF_TEXT, DVASPECT_CONTENT, TYMED_HGLOBAL, and DATADIR_GET | DATADIR_SET.

```
HKEY_CLASSES_ROOT\CLSID\{00000402-0000-0000-C000-
    000000000046}\DataFormats\GetSet\0 = 1,1,1,3
```

The values defined in the following entry are: CF_METAFILEPICT DVASPECT_CONTENT, TYMED_MFPICT, DATADIR_GET.

```
HKEY_CLASSES_ROOT\CLSID\{00000402-0000-0000-C000-
    000000000046}\DataFormats\GetSet\1 = 3,1,32,1
```

The values defined in the following entry are: 2 = cfEmbedSource, DVASPECT_CONTENT, TYMED_ISTORAGE, and DATADIR_GET.

```
HKEY_CLASSES_ROOT\CLSID\{00000402-0000-0000-C000-
    000000000046}\DataFormats\GetSet\2 = Embed
    Source,1,8,1
```

The values defined in the following entry are: 3 = cfOutline, DVASPECT_CONTENT, TYMED_HGLOBAL, and DATADIR_GET | DATADIR_SET

```
HKEY_CLASSES_ROOT\CLSID\{00000402-0000-0000-C000-
    000000000046}\DataFormats\GetSet\3 = Outline,1,1,3
```
The following entry declares that the default File Format supported by this application is CF_OUTLINE

```
HKEY_CLASSES_ROOT\CLSID\{00000402-0000-0000-C000-
    000000000046}\DataFormats\DefaultFile = Outline
```

Insertable Subkey Entry

The Insertable entry indicates that this application should appear in the Insert New dialog box's list box when used by OLE container applications. Note that this is a duplicate entry of the one above but is required for future use.

```
HKEY_CLASSES_ROOT\CLSID\{00000402-0000-0000-C000-
    000000000046}\Insertable
```

ProgID Subkey Entry

Every insertable object class has a "programmatic identifier" or ProgID.

```
HKEY_CLASSES_ROOT\CLSID\{00000402-0000-0000-C000-
    000000000046}\ProgID = OLE2ISvrOtl
```

Conversion Subkey Entry

Conversion information is used by the Convert dialog box to determine what formats the application can read and write. A comma-delimited file format is indicated by a number if it is one of the Clipboard formats defined in WINDOWS.H. A string indicates the format is not one defined in WINDOWS.H (private). Note that in this case the readable and writeable format is CF_OUTLINE (private).

Shown below is an entry that registers a file format the application can read (convert from).

```
HKEY_CLASSES_ROOT\CLSID\{00000402-0000-0000-C000-
    000000000046}\Conversion\Readable\Main = Outline,1
```
Shown below is an entry that registers a file format the application can read and write (activate as).

```
HKEY_CLASSES_ROOT\CLSID\{00000402-0000-0000-C000-
    000000000046}\Conversion\Readwritable\Main =
    Outline,1
```

DefaultIcon Subkey Entry

The DefaultIcon subkey provides default icon information for iconic presentations of objects. This entry contains the full path to the executable name of the object application and the index of the icon within the executable. Applications can use this information to obtain an icon handle with **ExtractIcon**.

```
HKEY_CLASSES_ROOT\CLSID\{00000402-0000-0000-C000-
    000000000046}\DefaultIcon = c:\samp\isvrotl.exe,0
```

CHAPTER 6

OLE Documents

Topics

List and identify features and applications for OLE Documents.

Identify the functionality provided by OLE embedding.

Explain how embedded data is saved by an application.

Compare and contrast OLE embedding with OLE linking.

Explain how linked data is saved by an application.

Describe what happens to linked data when an application is moved.

Describe the functionality provided by the types of OLE drag and drop: interwindow dragging, interobject dragging, and dropping onto icons.

Describe the functionality of a container.

Describe the different operations that can be performed on linked objects

Explain how embedded data gets updated

Describe manual and automatic links.

Explain how linked data is updated.

Content

The Interaction Model[1]

As data becomes the major focus of interface design, information content occupies the user's attention rather than the application managing the information. In such a design, data is not limited to its native creation and editing environment (the application); information can be transferred to other types of containers (for example, documents) while maintaining its viewing and editing capability in the new container. The use of the term *document* in this design is not just relevant to word-processing documents. Spreadsheets, charts, drawings, and forms are also documents.

OLE documents are a common example and illustration of the interaction between containers and their components but they are not the only expression of this kind of relationship.

Figure 6.1 is an example of an OLE document. The document includes word-processing text, tabular data from a spreadsheet, a sound recording, and pictures created in other applications.

---

[1] Complete text for the rest of the material in this chapter can be found in Chapter 11 of the *Windows 95 User Interface Design Guide (October 1994 Version)*. All references here to chapter titles and numbers are to that publication. Copyright 1994. Used with permission. All rights reserved.

Classical CD Review

by Thomas D. Becker

The introduction of the Compact Disc has had a far greater impact on the recording industry then anyone could have imagined, especially the manufacturer's of vinyl long play (LP) albums. With the 1991 sales totals in, compact disc is clearly the preferred recording medium for American ears. This month there are several excellent classical CD releases from the Telarc, Deutsche Grammophon, and London lables. My personal choice is Shaw and Atlanta's superb rendering of the Carmina Burana on Telarc. It is a "must-listen" recording. Upcoming reviews will include new Mozart offerings from Alfred Brendel (Philips), the complete flute works of Corelli by Jean-Pierre Rampal (CBS), and the long awaited digital remastering of Horowitz's recitals during the 1940's and 1950's. This year holds much promise. Good Listening. -*TDB*

U.S. Compact Disc vs. LP Sales ($)

	1983	1987	1991
CD's	6,345K	18,652K	32,657K
LP's	31,538K	26,571K	17,429K
Total	37,883K	45,223K	50,086K

Multimedia Mozart: The Dissonant Quartet

The Voyager Company
Microsoft

Performance: ★★★★★
Recording: ★★★★

These two symphonies are separated by no more than twelve years: but during this time Haydn's reputation grew from that of a talented director of music at an obscure provincial court to that of a leading composer whose latest works were in demand all over Eurpoe; and his music changed considerably in character. The Symphony no. 45 seems to be the product of strong personal emotion, and its finale incorporates a coded message on behalf of Haydn's colleagues in the orchestra to his princely employer: Haydn can hardly have imagined it being performed anywehre else, let alone published.

Multimedia Stravinsky: The Rite of Spring

The Voyager Company
Microsoft

Performance: ★★★★★
Recording: ★★★★★

In 1847 Johannes Andreas Schmeller published the complete collection of Latin and German songs released to the public on the secularisation

of the monastery at Benediktbeuern in 1803. Listen to these lyrics on this short sound clip. He called the codex *Carmina Burana*... songs from the beurn (in Latin, *burana*) district. From this single collection, a representative survey of the Latin lyric poetry of the twelfth and thirteenth centuries has been possible, notably in out time with the setting of twenty-five lyrics by the Bavarian composer, Carl Orff.

Multimedia Beethoven: The Ninth Symphony

The Voyager Company
Microsoft

Performance: ★★★★
Recording: ★★★

A source of financial benefit for needy composers in the early part of the nineteenth century was the popular theater, where the demand for special music *sometimes* offered reward. Even the mighty Beethoven, who had a serious respect for money, turned to the stage from time to time to supplement his income. (Let us not forget that he was the kind of man who could title one of his piano pieces *Rage over a Lost Penny*.) But, being Beethoven, it was almost impossible for him not to produce work of quality, no matter how commercial his motive. Though his theater music includes some genuine curiosities

Figure 6.1 An OLE document with OLE linked and OLE embedded objects.

How was this music review actually created? First, a user created a new document and typed in the text. Then a user moved, copied, or linked content from other documents. Data objects that retain their native, full-featured editing and operating capabilities in their new container when moved or copied are called *OLE embedded objects.*

A user can also link information. A *link* is a connection between two objects. Links can be presented in various ways in the interface. For example, a data link propagates a value between two objects, such as between two cells in a worksheet or a series of data in a table and a chart. An *OLE linked object* represents or provides access to another object that resides at another location in the same container or a different, separate container. A shortcut icon is any kind of a link, displayed as an icon, that provides navigational access to another object located elsewhere.

Generally, containers support any level of nested OLE embedded and linked objects. For example, a user can embed a chart in a worksheet which, in turn, can be embedded within a word-processing document. The model for interaction is consistent at each level of nesting.

Displaying Objects

When displaying an OLE embedded or OLE linked object in its presentation or content form (as opposed to displaying the object as an icon), a cached metafile description is generally used (though it is possible for an object to draw itself directly in its container). In this presentation, the object can be visually indistinguishable from native objects.

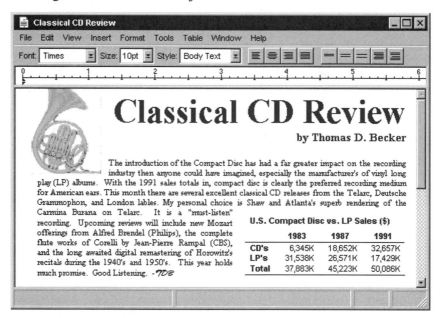

Figure 6.2   Document with linked picture and embedded worksheet objects.

It may be desirable to allow the user to visually identify OLE embedded or OLE linked objects without interacting with them. Therefore, you can provide a Show Objects command that displays a black solid border that is a single pixel wide around the extent of an OLE embedded object—a dotted border around OLE linked objects (shown in Figure 6.3). If the container cannot guarantee that an OLE linked object is up-to-date with its source because of an unsuccessful automatic update or a manual link, the dotted border should be drawn using the inactive title text color of the system to suggest that the OLE linked object is out of date. Show the border around a container's first-level objects only, not objects nested below this level.

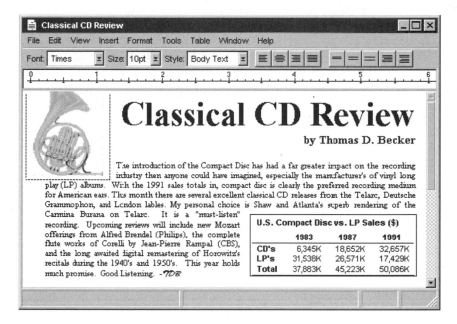

Figure 6.3   Linked and embedded objects after a Show Objects command.

If these border conventions are not adequate to distinguish embedded and linked objects, your container can include additional distinctions; however, make certain that they are clearly distinct from the appearance for the other states, and that you distinguish OLE embedded from OLE linked objects.

Whenever the user creates an OLE linked or OLE embedded object with the Display As Icon check box set, display the icon using its original appearance (unless the user explicitly changes it). A linked icon also includes the shortcut graphic. If an icon is not registered in the system registry for the object, use the system-generated icon.

A default label generally accompanies the icon. If the result is an OLE embedded object, its default label should be one of the following:

- The name of the object, if the object has a name easily read by the user (for example, a filename without its extension).

- The object's registered short type name (for example, Picture, Worksheet, and so on), if the object does not have a name.

- The object's registered full type name (for example, Microsoft Paintbrush 1.0 Picture, Microsoft Excel 5.0 Worksheet), if the object has no name or registered short type name.

- "Document" if an object has no name, short type name, or registered type name.

For more information about registered type names, see Chapter 10, "Integrating with the System."

If a linked object is displayed as an icon, its default label is the source filename as it appears in the file system, preceded by the words "Shortcut to"; for example, "Shortcut to Annual Report." The path of the source is not included, but the user can view it in the property sheet of the object. The filename does not include an extension. If you link only a portion of a document (file) using the Paste Special or Paste Link commands, its default label is derived from its link path (moniker); this is generally sufficient to provide reasonable identification of the object.

Selecting Objects

An OLE embedded or OLE linked object follows the selection behavior and appearance techniques supported by its containing document. For example, Figure 6.4 shows how the linked drawing of a horn is handled as part of a contiguous selection in the document.

For more information about selection techniques, see Chapter 5, "General Interaction Techniques," and for information about selection appearance, see Chapter 13, "Visual Design."

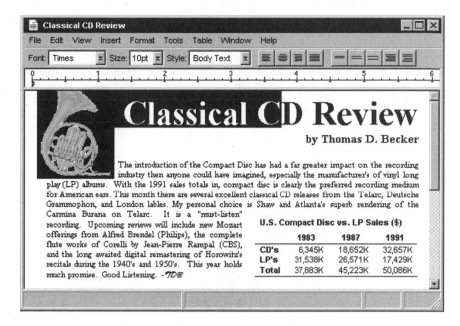

Figure 6.4   A linked object as part of a multiple selection.

When the user individually selects the object, the container displays the object with an appropriate selection appearance for that type. For example for the content view of an object, display it with handles. If the object is displayed as an icon, use the checkerboard selection highlighting used for icons in folders and on the desktop. For linked objects, overlay the content view's lower left corner with the shortcut graphic.

Regardless of what selection appearance applies, the container application always supplies the selection appearance for OLE embedded or OLE linked objects that it contains.

Accessing Commands for Selected Objects

When the user selects an OLE embedded or OLE linked object as part of the selection of native data in a container, the user may select and execute commands supported by the container application that apply to the selection as a whole. When the user individually selects the object, the container offers only operations that apply specifically to the object. The container can retrieve these operations from what has been registered by the object's type in the system registry. The container reflects these operations in the menus it supplies for the object. If the container includes a menu bar, it includes the selected object's commands on a submenu, such as the Edit menu, or as a separate menu on the menu bar. Use the name of the object in the menu item. If you use the short type name as the name of the object, then add the word "Object." For a linked object, use the short type name, preceded by the word "Linked." Figure 6.5 shows these variations.

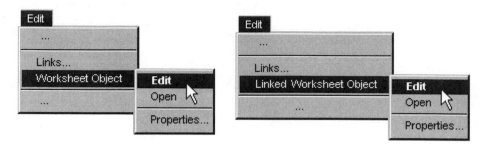

Figure 6.5   Selected object menus.

For more information on registering commands for object types, see Chapter 10, "Integrating with the System."

Define the first letter of the word "Object" (or its localized equivalent) as the access character for keyboard users. When no object is selected, display the command "Object" and disable it.

A container provides a pop-up menu for a selected object (shown in Figure 6.6) which is displayed using the standard interaction techniques for pop-up menus (clicking with mouse button 2). This menu includes the appropriate commands that the container can apply to the object as a whole, such as transfer commands, as well as the object's registered commands. In the pop-up menu, display the object's registered operations as individual menu items rather than in a cascading menu. It is not necessary to include the object's name or the word "Object." In addition, the container application provides a Properties command on the menu that provides access to the property sheet of the selected object.

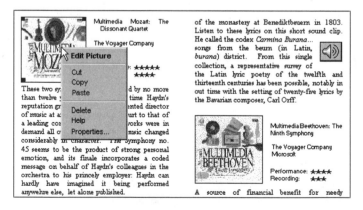

Figure 6.6   Pop-up menu for an embedded picture in a document.

Operations that depend on the state of the object can be enabled and disabled accordingly. For example, a media object that uses Play and Rewind as operations disables Rewind when the object is at the beginning of the media object.

The container can also display the object with appropriate selection appearances, such as handles (for resizing or other operations), that affect the object as a unit with respect to the container.

Note   When the user resizes a selected OLE object, it results in a scaling operation because there is no method through which the container can communicate to the object that another operation, such as cropping, was used.

If the object's type is not registered, the container still supplies any commands that can be appropriately applied to the object as content, such as transfer command, alignment commands, and a Properties command. Also add a Open With command and define it as the default command for the object so that double-clicking executes the command. Open With displays a special dialog box that allows the user to choose from a list of applications to operate on the type or convert the object's type.

Activating Objects

While selecting an object provides access to commands applicable to the object as a whole, it does not provide access for the user to interact with the content of an object. Activating the object allows user interaction with the internal content of the object. There are two basic models for activating objects: outside-in activation and inside-out activation.

Outside-in Activation

Outside-in activation requires an explicit user action. Selecting an object that is already selected simply reselects that object and does not constitute an explicit action. The user can activate the object by using a particular command (usually its default command), such as Edit or Play. Shortcut actions that correspond to these commands, such as double-clicking or pressing a shortcut key, can also activate the object.

Most OLE containers employ this model because it allows the user to easily select objects and reduces the risk of inadvertently activating an object whose underlying code may take a significant amount of time to load and dismiss. Containers display the standard pointer (northwest arrow) over outside-in activated objects when inactive. This indicates that the outside-in object behaves as a single, opaque object.

Inside-out Activation

Using *inside-out activation*, interaction with an object is direct. From the user's perspective, inside-out objects are indistinguishable from native data, because the content of the object is directly interactive and no additional action is necessary.

Use this method for the design of objects that benefit from direct interaction, or because the impact of activating the object is small for performance or use of system resources.

Inside-out activation requires closer cooperation between the container and the object. For example, if the user begins a selection within an inside-out object, the container needs to clear its own selection so that the behavior is consistent with normal selection interaction. An object supporting inside-out activation controls the appearance of the pointer as it moves over its extent and responds immediately to input. Therefore, to select the object as a whole, the user selects the border, or some other handle, provided by its container.

The default behavior for an OLE embedded object is outside-in activation. But information can be registered in the system registry that indicates that an object's type (application class) is capable of inside-out activation (the OLEMISC_INSIDEOUT constant) and prefers inside-out behavior (the OLEMISC_ACTIVATEWHENVISIBLE constant).

Container Control of Activation

A container still determines how to activate its component objects: whether it allows the inside-out objects to handle events directly or whether it intercedes and only activates them upon an explicit action. That is, even though an object may register inside-out activation, it can be treated by a particular container as outside-in. A container uses an activation style that is most appropriate for its specific use and is in keeping with its own native style of activation so that objects can be easily assimilated.

For more information about OLE and the system registry, see the Microsoft Win32 Software Development Kit.

Regardless of the activation capability of the object, a container always activates its content objects of the same type consistently. Otherwise, the unpredictability of the interface is likely to impair its ease of use. The following are four examples of potential container activation strategies:

Activation method	When to use
Outside-in throughout	This is the typical case for containers that often embed large objects and treat them as whole units. Because OLE documents are a popular expression of OLE and many of the available objects are not capable of inside-out activation, to preserve uniformity, most document-type containers use outside-in throughout. This is likely to continue as the common convention until more inside-out objects become available.
Inside-out throughout	The long-term direction is to blend OLE embedded objects with native data to eliminate the distinction. Inside-out throughout containers will become more feasible as increasing numbers of OLE objects support and prefer inside-out activation.
Outside-in plus inside-out preferred objects	Some containers use an outside-in model for large, foreign embeddings but also include some inside-out preferred objects as though they were native objects (by supporting the OLEMISC_ACTIVATEWHENVISIBLE constant). For example, an OLE document might present form control objects as inside-out native data while at the same time activating larger spreadsheet and chart objects as outside-in.
Switch between inside-out throughout and outside-in throughout	Some programming and forms layout design applications have design and run modes. In this type of environment, a container typically holds an object that is capable of inside-out activation (if not preferable) and alternates between outside-in throughout when designing and inside-out throughout when running.

OLE Visual Editing of Embedded Objects

One of the most common uses for activating an object is for editing its content in its current location. Supporting this type of in-place interaction is also called *OLE visual editing*, because the object can be edited within the visual context of its container.

Unless the container and the object both support inside-out activation, the user activates an embedded object for editing by selecting the object and executing its Edit command, either from a drop-down or pop-up menu. You can also support shortcut techniques. For example, if Edit is the object's default operation, you can use double-clicking to activate the object for editing. Similarly, you can support pressing the ENTER key as a shortcut for activating the object.

Note Earlier versions of OLE user interface documentation suggested using the ALT+ENTER key combination to activate an object if the ENTER key was already assigned. However, the ALT+ENTER key combination is now the recommended shortcut key for the Properties command. Alternatively, OLE embedded objects can be activated from the keyboard by supporting the pop-up menu shortcut key, SHIFT+F10. Then the user can select the activation command from the pop-up menu.

When the user activates an OLE embedded object for OLE visual editing, the user interface for its content becomes available and blended into its container's interface. The object can display its frame *adornments*, such as row or column headers, handles, or scroll bars, outside the extent of the object and temporarily cover neighboring material. It can also change the menu interface, which can range from adding menu items existing drop-down menus to replacing entire drop-down menus. Toolbars, status bars, and supplemental palette windows can be added.

The degree of blending varies based on the nature of the OLE embedded object. Some OLE embedded objects may require extensive support and consequently result in dramatic changes to the container's interface. Finer-grain objects that emulate native components of a container may have little or no need to make changes in the container's user interface. The container determines the degree to which an OLE embedded object's interface can be blended with its own, regardless of the capability or preference of the OLE embedded object. A container that provides its own interface for an OLE embedded object can suppress an OLE embedded object's own interface. Figure 6.7 shows how the interface might appear when its embedded worksheet is active.

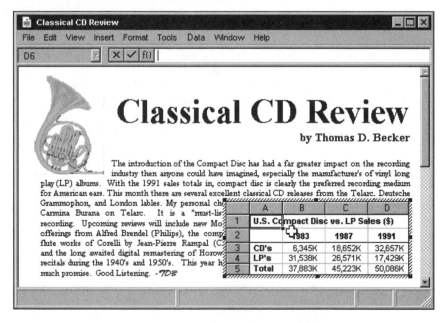

Figure 6.7   A worksheet activated for OLE visual editing.

When the user activates an OLE embedded object, avoid changing the view and position of the rest of the content in the window. While it may seem reasonable to scroll the window, preserving the content's position, the user's focus is not disturbed by the active object shifting down to accommodate a new toolbar and shifting back up when it is deactivated. The exception may be when the activation exposes an area in which the container has nothing to display. However even in this situation, it is possible for the container to render a visible region or filled area that corresponds to background area outside the visible edge of the container.

Activation does not affect the title bar. It always displays the top-level container's name. For example, when the worksheet shown in Figure 6.8 is activated, the title bar continues to display the name of the document in which the worksheet is embedded and not the name of the worksheet. You can provide access to the name of the worksheet by supporting property sheets for your OLE embedded objects.

For more information about property sheets for OLE embedded objects, see "Using Property Sheets" later in this chapter.

A container can contain multiple nested OLE embedded objects. However, only a single level is active at any one time. Figure 6.8 shows a document containing an active embedded worksheet with an embedded graph of its own. Clicking on the graph merely selects it as an object within the worksheet.

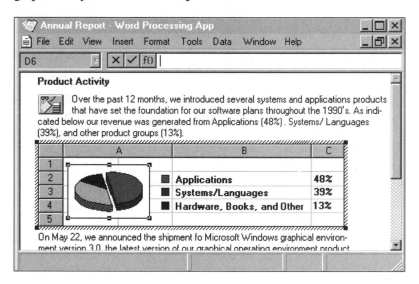

Figure 6.8   A selected graph within an active worksheet.

Activating the embedded graph, for example, by choosing the graph's Edit command, activates the object for visual editing, displaying the graph's menus in the document's menu bar. At any given time, only the interface for the currently active object and the topmost container is presented; intervening parent objects do not remain visibly active.

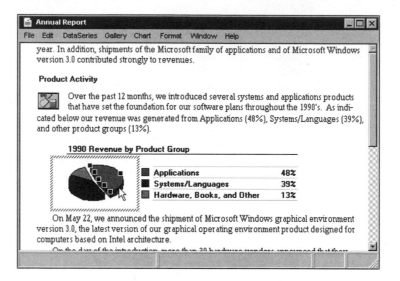

Figure 6.9   An active graph within a worksheet.

Note Ideally, an OLE embedded object supports visual editing on any scale because its container may be arbitrarily scaled. If an object cannot accommodate visual editing in its container's current view scale, or if its container does not support visual editing, the object should open into a separate window for editing. For more information about OLE embedded objects, see "Opening an Embedded Object" later in this chapter.

An interaction, such as selection outside the extent of an active object or activation of another object in the container, deactivates the current object and gives the focus to the new object. This is also true for an object that is nested in the currently active object. The user can also deactivate an active object by pressing the ESC key. If an object uses the ESC key at all times, use SHIFT+ESC to deactivate the object, after which it becomes the selected object of its container.

Edits made to an active object become a part of the container immediately and automatically, just like edits made to native data. Consequently, do not display an "Update changes?" message box when the object is deactivated. Of course, changes to the entire container, embedded or otherwise, can be abandoned if the topmost container includes an explicit command that prompt the user to save or discard changes to the container's file.

OLE embedded objects participate in the undo stack of the window in which they are activated. For more information about embedded objects and the undo stack, see the section "Undo for Active and Open Objects" later in this chapter.

While Edit is the most common command for activating an OLE embedded object for OLE visual editing, other commands can also create such activation. For example, when the user executes a Play command on a video clip, you can display a set of commands that allows the user to control the clip (Rewind, Stop, and Fast Forward). In this case, the Play command provides a form of OLE visual editing.

The Active Hatched Border

If a container allows an OLE embedded object's user interface to affect on its own user interface, then the active object displays a hatched border around itself to show the extent of the OLE visual editing context. That is, if an active object's menus appear in the topmost container's menu bar (the object's request is granted by the container), then display the active hatched border. If the object's menus do not appear in the menu bar (because the object did not require menus or because the container refused its request for menu display) or the object is otherwise accommodated by the container's user interface, it is not necessary to display the hatched border.

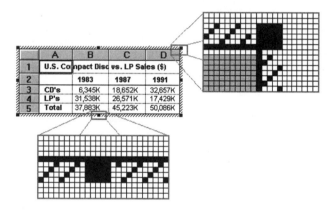

Figure 6.10   Hatched border around in-place activated objects.

The hatched pattern is made up of 45-degree diagonal lines. The active object takes on the appearance which is best suited for its own editing; for example, frame adornments, table gridlines, handles, and other editing aids can appear. The hatched border is part of the object's territory, so the pointer that appears when the mouse is over the border is defined by the active object.

Clicking in the hatched pattern (and not on the handles) is interpreted by the object as clicking just inside the edge of the border of the active object. The hatched area is effectively a hot zone that prevents inadvertent deactivations and makes it easier to select the content of the object.

Opening OLE Embedded Objects

The previous sections have focused on OLE visual editing; that is, editing an OLE embedded object in-place; that is, in its current location. However, as an alternative, the user can also open embedded objects into their own window. This gives the user the opportunity of seeing more of the object, or seeing the object in a different view state. Support this operation by registering an Open command for the object. When the user chooses the Open command of an object, it opens it into a separate window for editing as shown in Figure 6.11.

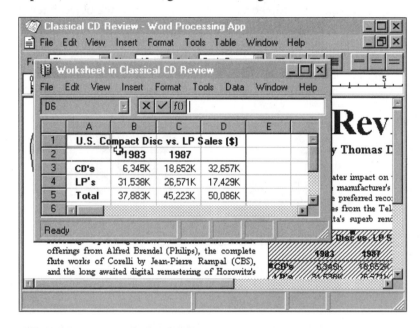

Figure 6.11   An opened worksheet.

After opening an object, its container displays it masked with an "open" hatched (lines at a 45 degree angle) pattern that indicates the object is open in another window as shown in Figure 6.12.

US Compact Disc vs. LP Sales ($)		
1983	**1984**	**1991**
CDs 6,345K	18,652K	32,857K
LPs 31,538K	28,571K	17,428K
Total 37,883K	45,223K	58,088K

Figure 6.12   An opened object.

The format for the open object's window title is "*object name* in *container name*" (for example, "Sales Worksheet in Classical CD Review"). Including the container's name emphasizes that the object in the container and the object in the open window are considered the same object.

OLE presents an open embedded object as an alternate window onto the same object within the container as opposed to a separate application that updates changes to the container document. Therefore, edits are immediately and automatically reflected in the object in the document, and there is no longer the need for displaying an update confirmation message upon exiting the open window.

Nevertheless, you can still include an Update *Source File* command in the window of the open objects to allow the user to explicitly request an update. This is useful if you cannot support frequent "real-time" image updates because of overall system performance. In addition, when the user closes an open object's window, automatically update it in the container's window. You can also include Import File and similar commands in the window of the open object. Importing a file into the window of the open embedded object is conceptually the same as any change to the object.

At the point when the user opens an object, it is the selected object in the container; the selection in the container can be changed afterwards. Like selected OLE embedded objects, the container supplies the appropriate selection appearance together with the open appearance as shown in Figure 6.13. However, if the user chooses to print the container while an OLE embedded object is open or active, use the presentation form of objects; neither the open nor active hatched patterns should appear in the printed document because these patterns are not part of the content.

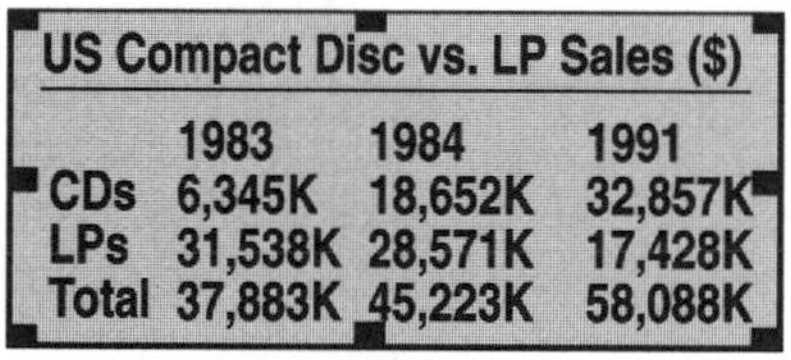

US Compact Disc vs. LP Sales ($)			
	1983	1984	1991
CDs	6,345K	18,652K	32,857K
LPs	31,538K	28,571K	17,428K
Total	37,883K	45,223K	58,088K

Figure 6.13   Selected open object.

While an OLE embedded object is open, it is still a functioning member of its container. It can still be selected or unselected, and respond to appropriate container commands. At any time, the user may open any number of embedded objects. The object is deactivated and its window is closed when the user closes its container window.

When opening an OLE embedded object, if it has file operations, such as Open, remove these in the resulting window or replace them with a command like Import to avoid severing the object's connection with its container. The objective is to present a consistent conceptual model that the object in the opened window is the same as the one in the container.

Editing an OLE Linked Object

An OLE linked object is an object that can be stored in a particular location, moved or copied, and have its own properties. Container actions can be applied in as much as the OLE linked object acts as a unit of content. So an OLE container must supply commands, such as Cut, Copy, and Properties, and interface elements such as handles, menus (menu bar and pop-up), and property sheets, for the linked objects it contains.

For more information about providing access to selected OLE objects, see the section, "Accessing Commands for Selected Objects," earlier in this chapter.

The container also provides access to the commands that activate the OLE linked object, including the commands that allow the content that the OLE linked object represents to be edited. These commands are the same as those that have been registered for the link source's type. Because an OLE linked object represents or provides access to another object that resides elsewhere, editing the content of an OLE linked object always takes the user back to the link source's location. Therefore, the command used to edit an OLE linked object is the same as the command of its linked source object. For example, the menu of a linked object can include both Open and Edit if its link source is an OLE embedded object. The Open command opens the embedded object, just as executing the command on the embedded object does. The Edit command opens the window of the container of the embedded object, and activates the object for visual editing.

Figure 6.14 shows how the linked horn drawing appears in its own window for editing. It is important to note that changes made to the horn are reflected not only in its host container, the "Classical CD Review" document, but in every other document that is linked to that same portion of the "Horns" document. This illustrates the power and the potential danger of using links in documents.

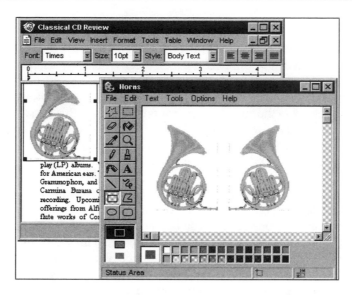

Figure 6.14   Editing a link source.

At first glance, editing an OLE linked object seems to have the same open editing appearance as an OLE embedded object. A separate primary window opens displaying the data. However, the horn does not have the open hatched pattern, nor does the second window's title bar indicate that the object is within "Classical CD Review." The object is actually in a completely independent document. In addition, the container should display a link-loading message to indicate that the source document is loading.

Automatic and Manual Updating

When the user creates an OLE link, by default it is an automatic link; that is, whenever the source data changes, the link's visual representation changes without requiring any additional information from the user. Therefore, you do not display an "Update Automatic Links Now?" message box, but you can display a message box indicating the progress of the update if the update takes significant time to complete.

If the user wishes to exercise control over when links are updated, they can set the linked object's update property to manual. Doing so requires that an explicit command to update the link representation or as a part of a container's "update fields" or "recalc" action.

For more information about updating links automatically or manually, see the section "Maintaining Links" later in this chapter.

Operations and Links

The operations available for an OLE linked object are those supplied by its container and those supplied by its source. When the user chooses a command supplied by its container, the container application handles the operation. When the user chooses a command supplied by its source, the operation is conceptually passed back to the source object for processing. In this sense, activating an OLE linked object actives its source object. In certain cases, the linked object exhibits the result of an operation; in other cases the source object can be brought to the top of the Z-order to handle the operation. For example, executing commands such as Play or Rewind on a link to a sound recording appear to operate on the linked object in-place. However if the user chooses a command to alter the link's representation its source's content (such as Edit or Open), the link's source is exposed and responds to the operation instead of the linked object itself. A link may play in-place, but not be edited in-place. In order for a link source to properly respond to editing operations, fully activate the source object (with all of its containing objects and its container). The common case is when the user double-clicking a linked object whose default operation is Edit. The source (or its container) opens, displaying the link source object ready for editing. If the source is already open, then the window displaying the source becomes active. This follows the standard convention for activating a window already open; that is, the window comes to the top of the Z-order. If necessary, you can adjust the view in the window, scrolling, or changing focus within the window, as necessary, to present the source object for easy user interaction. The linked source window and linked object window operate and close independently of each other.

Note If a link's source is contained within a read-only document, the user cannot save the results of editing the source.

Types and Links

An OLE linked object includes a cached copy of its source's type at the time of the last update. When the type of a link's source object changes, all links derived from that source object contain the old type and operations until either an update occurs or the link source is activated. Because out-of-date links can potentially display obsolete operations to the user, a mismatch can occur. When executing an operation on a link object, the link object compares the cached type with the current type of the link source. If they are the same, the linked object forwards the operation on to the source. If they are different, the linked object informs its container. In response, the container can either:

- Execute the new type's operation, if the operation issued from the old link is syntactically identical to one of operations registered for the source's new type.

- Display a message box, if the issued operation is no longer supported by the link source's new type.

For more information about message boxes, see the section "Message Boxes" later in this chapter.

In both cases, the link adopts the source's new type and subsequently the container displays the new type's operations in the linked object's menu.

Maintaining Links

An OLE linked object has three properties: its type (or class), the name of its source data, and its updating basis, which is either automatic or manual. Include these on a Link page in the linked object's property sheet supplied by the container. A container application can supply a Links command that displays a dialog box for altering the properties of several links simultaneously.

For more information about property sheets for OLE objects, see the section "Using Property Sheets" later in this chapter.

Note The Microsoft Win32 Software Development Kit includes the Links dialog box and other OLE-related dialog boxes that are described in this chapter.

Figure 6.15 shows the Links dialog box. The list box in the dialog box displays the links in the container. Each line in the list contains the link source's name, object type (short type name), and whether it updates automatically or manually. If a link source cannot be found, "Unavailable" appears in the update status column.

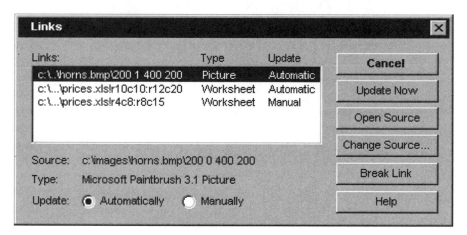

Figure 6.15   The Links dialog box.

If the user chooses the Links command when the current selection includes a linked object (or objects), then display that link (or links) as selected in the Links dialog box and scroll the list to display the first selected link at the top of the list box.

Allow 15 characters for the short type name field, and enough space for Automatic and Manual to appear completely. As the user selects each link in the list, its type, name, and updating basis appear in their entirety at the bottom of the dialog box. Command buttons provide support for the following link operations:

- Break Link effectively disconnects the selected link.
- Update Now forces the selected link to connect to its sources and retrieve the latest information.
- Open Source opens the link source for the selected link.
- Change Source invokes a dialog box similar to the common Open dialog box to allow the user to respecify the link source.

Define the Open Source button to be the default command button when the input focus is within the list of links. Also support double-clicking an item in the list as a shortcut for opening that link source.

The Change Source button allows the user to change the source of a link by selecting a file or typing in a filename. The user can enter a source name that does not designate a presently existing object. When the user chooses OK, display a message box with the following message shown in Figure 6.16.

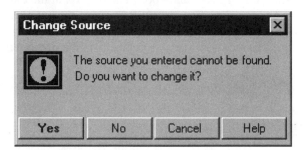

Figure 6.16   Invalid Source message box.

If the user chooses Yes, display the Change Source dialog box to correct the string. If the user chooses No, store the unparsed display name of the link source until the user successfully causes the link to connect to a newly created object that satisfies the dangling reference. The container application can also choose to allow the user to connect only to presently valid links. If the user chooses Cancel, remove the message box and return input focus to the Links dialog box.

If the user changes a link source, and other linked objects in the same container are connected to the same original link source, provide a user option to make the changes for the other references. Figure 6.17 shows how a message box allows users to redirect links, such as when the link source's directory or filename has changed.

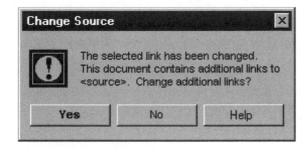

Figure 6.17   Changing additional links with same source.

Using Property Sheets

Like other types of objects, when the user selects an OLE embedded or linked object, provide user access its properties through a Properties command. If the container application already uses some kind of Properties command for its own native data, it can also be used for selected embedded or linked objects. Otherwise, add the command to the Object submenu beneath a separator. In addition, include the Properties command at the bottom of an object's pop-up menu as shown in Figure 6.18.

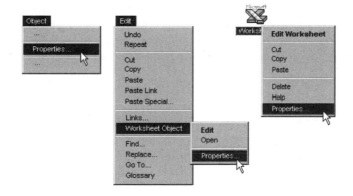

Figure 6.18   The Properties command.

When the user chooses the Properties command, the container displays a property sheet containing all the salient properties and values for the selected object. In general, organize properties by categories or topics. Figure 6.19 shows possible property sheets for an embedded and linked worksheet object.

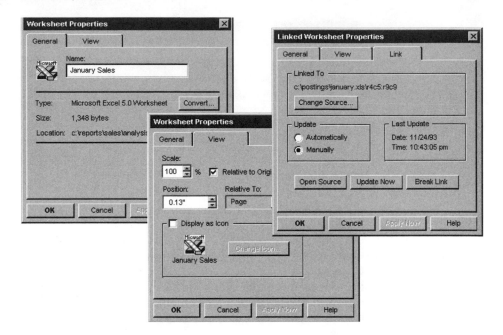

Figure 6.19   OLE embedded and linked object property sheets.

For linked objects, include a Link page in its property sheet containing the essential link parameters. For the typical OLE link, this includes the source name, Change Source command, Update setting (automatic or manual), Last Update timestamp, Open Source, Update Now, and Break Link commands.

C H A P T E R 7

OLE Automation

Topic

Explain what OLE Automation is.

Content

OLE Automation[1]

OLE Automation refers to the ability of an application to define a set of properties and commands and make them accessible to other applications to enable programmability. OLE provides a mechanism through which this access is achieved. OLE Automation increases application interoperability without the need for human intervention.

The public exposure of these properties and commands allows one application to contain code that manipulates another application. It also allows developers to create new applications that can interact with existing applications. OLE Automation is a powerful mechanism that allows OLE-enabled applications to function as components that can be combined into complete applications.

---

1 Excerpted from "OLE Documents: Technical Backgrounder." The complete text of this backgrounder is available on the Microsoft Developer Network Development Library under Backgrounders and White Papers, Operating System Extensions. Copyright 1994. Used with permission. All rights reserved.

Topics

Explain the role of a controller application.

Explain the role of an OLE Automation object/server application.

Content

Choosing a Controlling Application[2]

As stated earlier in this chapter, a popular model for integrated solutions is the Centralized Control model. In this model, the controlling application presents data to the user and provides the context in which the user navigates. In the Single Application model, that single application is the controlling application. The Decentralized Control model uses more than one controlling application.

Because the controlling application plays such a vital role in *all* models of integrated solutions, choosing it wisely is an important part of designing the solution. This choice involves taking several factors into account:

- **Primary data type**   What kinds of data will the integrated solution present or allow access to?

- **Data security**   Are all users of your integrated solution meant only to view information or could some users, after signing on with a password, be allowed to change or enter data? If data is to remain unchanged, how can you protect it?

- **Interapplication communication**   Does the integrated solution combine text, spreadsheet cells or tables, graphics, database data, and other objects from a variety of applications? What are the source applications of your data?

In this section, we examine these factors to consider Microsoft Access, Microsoft Excel, Microsoft Word, and Visual Basic as possible controlling applications for an integrated solution.

Primary Data Type

An integrated solution can present one or more kinds of data to the user. If data is primarily of one type, there may be one application particularly suited to that type.

---

2 Excerpted from *Designing Integrated Solutions with Microsoft Office* in the Office Development Kit 1.0. Copyright 1992 - 1995. Used with permission. All rights reserved.

For example, if relational database data is the only type to be used, Microsoft Access is a good choice for storing, manipulating, and presenting it. Microsoft Access uses its powerful database engine to perform queries of almost any complexity on the data it stores. It also offers all the formatting options needed to create attractive forms and reports used for data input and display. Therefore, when database manipulation and presentation is the goal, Microsoft Access is a good controlling application, especially because its form-creation tools give you precise control over the way data is accessed (the user's context). And since Microsoft Access version 2.0 supports OLE Automation, it can be integrated tightly with Microsoft Excel, which is a good OLE Automation Server.

Other kinds of data suggest other applications. Information consisting largely of tables and charts, such as financial data, is probably best presented in Microsoft Excel. Although Microsoft Access is best used for relational database data, Microsoft Excel can be a highly effective tool for storing or manipulating "flat-file" database data that is not relational. If all your database data can be stored in one or more Microsoft Excel worksheets, and the columns of the data in these worksheets are not related, then Microsoft Excel may be a better choice than Microsoft Access.

Since both Microsoft Access version 2.0 and Microsoft Excel version 5.0 support visual editing, they make excellent controlling applications for a single-context solution. You can link or embed OLE objects into Microsoft Access or Microsoft Excel and allow users to edit these objects visually.

Unlike Microsoft Excel, Microsoft Word, and Microsoft Access, there is no particular type of data that Visual Basic is designed to handle. Because it is an excellent container for both OLE 1 and OLE 2 objects, it can make an excellent controlling application. The forms you create with Visual Basic can have both OLE 1 and OLE 2 objects embedded or linked in them. Visual Basic also supports OLE Automation, thus providing a high level of control over other applications, especially those that expose programmable objects that can be used in OLE Automation.

Interapplication Communication

If information in several data formats needs to be shared, then applications must communicate with each other. The two primary means of sharing information are OLE and OLE Automation.

Since a controlling application is normally required to support the embedding or linking of objects inside its documents, being a good OLE client is a key requirement for a controlling application. And because a controlling application must (by its definition) control the actions of other applications, support for OLE Automation client capability is also an important criteria.

Microsoft Excel, Microsoft Access, Microsoft Project, Microsoft Word, and Visual Basic are all excellent OLE clients. Because Microsoft Excel, Microsoft Access, and Visual Basic support visual editing and allow you to exercise control over the way an object's data is edited, they are usually very good choices for single-context controlling applications.

Because Microsoft Word is an excellent container of OLE objects and has powerful formatting capabilities, it is best used as a controlling application only in circumstances where your integrated solution is used mostly for displaying information rather than allowing users to access or update information.

Being a capable OLE Automation client is more critical than being a capable OLE Automation server (although being both a client and server provides added flexibility). Microsoft Excel and Microsoft Project support not only incoming OLE Automation requests but, using Visual Basic for applications, they can also control other applications. Microsoft Word is an OLE Automation server but not a client. Through Word, you can activate another application and then use its internal macro language, but Word cannot control other applications through OLE Automation. For example, from within Microsoft Excel, a Word document can be opened and text can be formatted using WordBasic, but Word cannot do the reverse— controlling external data, such as data cells in Microsoft Excel.

Microsoft Access can be an OLE Automation client, but not a server. That is, a Microsoft Access application can control other applications using OLE Automation but other applications cannot use OLE Automation to control Microsoft Access.

In summary, because Microsoft Excel, Microsoft Access, and Visual Basic are good OLE clients and support OLE Automation client capabilities, they are suitable as controlling applications. Although Microsoft Project is an OLE client and an OLE Automation client, it is considered to be only a supporting application because of the specialized data it is designed to handle.

Content

Centralized Control

In this model, the controlling application is used as the primary user interface, but additional products may be used to provide data (raw or formatted), carry out commands (such as database queries), or perform other functions. These products, known as supporting applications, can run in the background—hidden from the user—or can be integrated into the user-interface design.

For example, you can use Visual Basic as the primary user interface, and integrate Microsoft Word, Microsoft Excel, and Microsoft Access into the design to provide document processing features, spreadsheet displays, and database connectivity. Normally, users spend most of their time in the controlling application, and in this respect the supporting applications are not treated as peers of the primary application.

Although multiple-application models are not as easy to implement as the Single Application model because of the greater expertise required and the more complex integration requirements, designs based on multiple applications provides a higher degree of power and control.

You can use the Centralized Control model for medium- to large-scale solutions that deal primarily with a single type of information (such as financial data or project data), but include other types of information as well.

To decide which application is best suited for the controlling application in an integrated solution that uses this model, see "Choosing a Controlling Application" in Chapter 7.

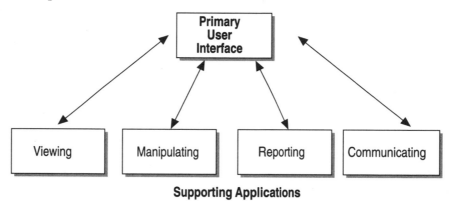

Figure 7.1   Centralized Control model

Content

Automation Servers[3]

An automation server is an application that exposes programmable objects to other applications, which are called "automation controllers." Exposing programmable components enables controllers to "automate" certain procedures by directly

---

3 Excerpted from Part 2 of Visual C++ 2.0 (32-bit) *Programming with the Microsoft Foundation Class Library*. Copyright 1992 - 1995. Used with permission. All rights reserved.

accessing the components and functionality the server makes available.

Exposing components in this way is beneficial when applications provide functionality that is useful for other applications. For example, a word processor might expose its spell-checking functionality so that other programs can use it. Exposure of components thus enables vendors to improve their applications' functionality by using the "ready-made" functionality of other applications.

By exposing application functionality through a common, well-defined interface, OLE automation makes it possible to build applications in a single general programming language like Visual Basic instead of in diverse application-specific macro languages.

Content

Automation Controllers

OLE Automation makes it possible for your application to manipulate components implemented in another application, or to "expose" components so they can be manipulated. An "automation controller" is an application that can manipulate exposed components belonging to another application. The application that exposes the components is called the "OLE Automation server." The controller manipulates the server application's components by accessing those components' properties and methods.

There are two types of OLE Automation controllers:

- Controllers that dynamically (at run time) acquire information about the properties and methods of the component.
- Controllers that possess static information (provided at compile time) that specifies the properties and methods of the component.

Controllers of the first kind acquire information about the component's methods and properties by means of queries to the OLE system's **IDispatch** mechanism. Although it is adequate to use for dynamic clients, **IDispatch** is difficult to use for static controllers, where the components being driven must be known at compile time.

Topic

Describe the contents of a type library.

Content

Automation Clients: Using Type Libraries4

Automation clients must have information about server objects' properties and

---

methods if the clients are to manipulate the servers' objects. Properties have data types; methods often return values and accept parameters. The client requires information about the data types of all of these in order to statically bind to the server object type.

This type information can be made known in several ways. The recommended way is to create a "type library."

For information on Microsoft Object Description Language and MkTypLib, see Chapters 2 and 9 of OLE Programmer's Reference, Volume 2.

Topic

Compare and contrast early and late binding.

Describe the impact of early binding versus late binding on performance.

Content

Exploring Visual Basic for Applications[5]

Editor, browser, debugger to round out toolset for applications programming

Visual Basic, Applications Edition, will work hand-in-hand with the standalone Visual Basic programming system. The first version of Visual Basic for applications will give developers access to objects supplied by applications. Future versions will also allow developers to create forms and use custom controls, just as in the Visual Basic programming system.

Visual Basic for applications is a full-featured version of Basic, designed to be a complete application-hosted development environment, including an editor with support for colorized code (for syntax errors, identifiers, break points, and so on), debugger, and compiler. It will span multiple platforms, including Windows 3.1, Windows NT 3.1, and the Macintosh. Both Visual Basic and object access from Visual Basic will be fully localized in 21 different languages.

Why a new macro language?

It is strategically important for Microsoft to have a consistent macro language across its entire applications product line. With Visual Basic for applications, programmers will only need to learn one core macro language, and extensions to the language that are specific to each application. Programmers will see the same user interface for creating and debugging code in all Visual Basic host applications.

In addition, Visual Basic for applications will help spawn a whole new industry of "solution providers"— independent and corporate developers who can create Visual Basic-based add-ons for many different Microsoft applications.

How will Visual Basic for applications inherit the macro language throne?

Visual Basic for applications won't simply replace current macro languages used in Microsoft products. Microsoft applications will support both Visual Basic and its predecessors. For example, Microsoft Excel 5.0 will provide new enhancements to the Microsoft Excel macro language (XLM) as well as Visual Basic support. And coming versions of Microsoft Excel will allow users to continue to run their old XLM macros.

Both the Access Basic and Visual Basic languages will be completely compatible with Visual Basic for applications, allowing users to easily migrate their code and experience. Future versions of Microsoft Word will provide users with translation tools to help them move their WordBasic code into the Visual Basic environment.

Visual Basic's integration with a host application

Visual Basic will be closely integrated with the native user interface in each host application. Visual Basic's code editor and debug window are displayed in windows that are owned by the host application, and when the code editor is active, the host will switch its menus and toolbar to Visual Basic's. The user interface for the host application will manipulate the modules of Visual Basic code.

A number of options will be available for executing a Visual Basic procedure in a host application, such as pressing a key combination or toolbar button, or selecting a menu item, or choosing a procedure from a dialog box such as the Macro Run dialog box in Microsoft Excel. Visual Basic procedures could also execute automatically during the recalculation of a document or in response to a system event such as the press of a button or receipt of a message.

Object Browser

Using the Object Browser in Visual Basic for applications, the user can quickly search through the object libraries that are exposed by an application, and the methods and properties available for those objects. The user can also look at the routines that are exposed in the modules of another Basic project and can paste the code required to access the objects, including any applicable named parameters.

Advanced debugging

Visual Basic for applications will support stepping (Step Into, Step Over, Set Next Statement) and break points.

The Debug window will have two different modes or panels: the Watch panel allows the user to track variable and expression values; the Immediate panel executes expressions entered by the user. The Debug window also allows users to browse the call stack. The Instant Watch facility allows the user to highlight a variable/expression and then see its value.

Compilation

Visual Basic is a compiled language, but modules are compiled only when they are needed. As a result, compilation can be hidden from someone using a Visual Basic-created application; there is no explicit command that can force compilation of code.

Visual Basic compiles individual modules independently of other modules in a project. This allows a user to work on a new macro in a separate module. Even if errors are introduced inadvertently into a new module, other macros, contained in separate modules, can still be executed.

Visual Basic project model

Visual Basic for applications uses a "project" as a container for the user's code. A project can be compared to an editable dynamic-link library (DLL) that provides access to the procedures defined in it. A project is made up of multiple modules (in the same way that a DLL can be compiled from multiple C files). A project can also access routines defined in other projects.

A project is a single object that can be embedded into a host application's document files. In Visual Basic in Microsoft Excel 5.0, for example, each Microsoft Excel workbook will contain a single project; the project level will be hidden from the user. The workbook is simply a collection of worksheets, charts, modules, and Microsoft Excel 4.0 macros. To the user, each module appears as a page in the workbook; as with all worksheets in Microsoft Excel 5.0, the user can navigate between modules by tabbing.

Identifying objects

Type libraries describe objects in Visual Basic for applications. A type library is created as a component that ships with an application. The type library describes the objects exposed by an application, and the methods and properties supported by those objects. It contains all information necessary to browse, get help on, and access each object.

The type library replaces the Declare statements used in previous Basic syntax. Visual Basic uses type libraries to:

- Gain access to available objects (for example, Cells(1,1).Value)
- Display available objects in Object Browser
- Type-check method parameters and return types

The type library contains the names used to access the abstract functionality made available by an application. For those who use a different language (such as French or Spanish), the type libraries will provide these names (and help information) in the appropriate language.

Accessing objects—OLE Automation

OLE Automation is the pathway for access to all objects. It is an open service provided by OLE that is fundamental to Visual Basic. OLE Automation allows a user to transparently access objects in Visual Basic host applications and other applications, in the same way that they access forms and controls in Visual Basic today. Visual Basic will use OLE Automation on all platforms, including Windows 3.1, Windows NT 3.1, and the Macintosh.

Visual Basic supports both early and late binding to objects. Late binding allows access to objects without needing to know the object type at compile time. This makes it easy to use, since the user doesn't have to understand how to declare types. It is also more flexible because it allows users to manipulate sets of heterogeneous objects (for example, a user could issue a command to print all embedded objects in a document, regardless of their types).

Early binding requires that the object type be declared at compile time. This binding method is type-safe, since checking is done at compile time. It is faster because type checking and conversions are not necessary at run time.

Is Visual Basic for applications in your future?

Microsoft expects Visual Basic for applications to dramatically expand the ranks of programmers and developers of Windows-based applications. For the first time, it will be possible to use any one of an entire family of end-user applications as a development environment. You'll be able to combine many different tools, data types, and objects to create highly customized solutions.

For further information on Visual Basic for applications, see future issues of the Microsoft Developer Network News.

Topic

Describe the performance considerations when building integrated solutions with OLE Automation.

Content

Microsoft OLE Today and Tomorrow: Technology Overview[6]

Introduction

The Microsoft OLE specification offers a variety of ways to integrate application components, including features such as visual editing, drag and drop between applications, OLE Automation, and structured storage for objects.

The capabilities of OLE are powerful and compelling, and OLE has recently received two prestigious industry awards: a Technical Excellence award from *PC Magazine* and the MVP award for software innovation from *PC/Computing*. Moreover, more than 30 applications using OLE are shipping today, with hundreds more scheduled to appear during the next six to twelve months.

There is far more to OLE than desktop application integration. To support its award-winning integration features, OLE defines and implements a mechanism that allows applications to "connect" to each other as software "components"— collections of data and accompanying functions to manipulate the data. This connection mechanism and protocol is called the *Component Object Model*. The many user-oriented and document-centric features of OLE are built on the Component Object Model's simple and fully extensible object architecture. In other words, OLE is a projection into the desktop space of a new and powerful general-purpose technology for building distributed, evolving object systems.

This paper looks briefly at the business reasons for the rapid movement in the computer industry to object-oriented software. It then reviews some of the capabilities of the Component Object Model, with special emphasis on its ability to provide a robust system model for seamless connections between software components running across multiple computers on a network. It concludes with information about the product direction of Microsoft and Digital Equipment Corporation that will result in products that allow OLE-based applications to interact with software objects running on a variety of UNIX-based and other server platforms using the same programming model and communications layer used by OLE between Microsoft-based systems.

---

6 Complete text of this backgrounder is available from the Microsoft Developer Network Development Library under Backgrounders and White Papers, Operating System Extensions. Copyright 1993. Used with permission. All rights reserved.

The Business Benefits of Objects

As its name suggests, the OLE Component Object Model is based on the notion of a *component*. A component is a reusable piece of software that can be "plugged into" other components from other vendors with relatively little effort. For example, a component might be a spelling checker sold by one vendor that can be plugged into several different word processing applications from multiple vendors. Or it might be a specialized transaction monitor that can control the interaction of a number of database servers. In contrast, traditional applications are monolithic, which means that they come prepackaged with a wide range of features, most of which can't be removed or replaced with alternatives.

Component software provides a much more productive way to design, build, sell, use, and reuse software. It has significant implications for software vendors, end users, and corporations:

- **For vendors**, component software provides a single model for interacting with other applications and the distributed operating system. While it can readily be added to existing applications without fundamental rewriting, it also provides the opportunity to modularize applications and to incrementally replace system capabilities where appropriate. The advent of component software will help create a more diverse set of market segments and niches for small, medium, and large vendors.

- **For users**, component software means a much greater range of software choices, coupled with better productivity. As users see the possibilities of component software, demand is likely to increase for specialized components to be purchased at a local software retail outlet and plugged into applications.

- **For corporations**, component software can mean lower costs for corporate computing, helping IS departments work more efficiently, and enabling corporate computer users to be more productive. IS developers may spend less time developing general-purpose software components and more time developing "glue" components or components that solve business-specific needs. Existing applications do not need to be rewritten to take advantage of a component architecture. Instead, corporate developers can create object-based "wrappers" that encapsulate the legacy application and make its operations and data available as an object to other software components in the network.

Objects that conform to the Microsoft Component Object Model are known as *component objects*. As a long-term strategy, the concept of component objects consists of both current and future technologies that are designed to facilitate the development and use of component software. OLE is the first step in the evolution of component objects. Future implementations of OLE will be designed to use the same basic mechanisms of the Component Object Model and be upward-compatible with OLE while providing a range of additional features, including the ability for objects to communicate over the network. The investments that ISVs and IS developers make in implementing OLE technology will be protected in the long term by Microsoft's investments in future versions of OLE and Microsoft Windows.

OLE Today and Tomorrow

OLE and its Component Object Model are the first steps in a major path of innovation for Microsoft systems. OLE is critically important for the following reasons.

- **Binary standard for objects.** OLE defines a completely standardized way for objects to be created and to communicate with one another. Unlike traditional object-oriented programming environments, these mechanisms are independent of the applications that use object services and of the programming language used to create the objects. This binary standard will be used extensively in future versions of the Microsoft Windows operating system and will enable a wide market for component software.

- **Compelling collection of interfaces.** Software architectures become more interesting when useful products are shipping based on the architecture. While other vendors and some consortia have defined high-level object architectures and specifications for language-independent object systems, only ISVs using OLE have delivered to the mass market a compelling set of interoperable applications based on object technology.

- **True system object model.** To be a true system model, an object architecture must allow a distributed, evolving system to support millions of objects without risk of erroneous connections of objects and other problems related to strong typing or definition of objects. OLE's Component Object Model meets those requirements.

- **Distributed capabilities.** Many single-process object models and programming languages exist today, and a few distributed object systems are available. However, none provides an identical programming model for small, in-process objects and potentially large, cross-network objects. Moreover, security is required. Microsoft's OLE has these capabilities factored in.

Binary Standard for Objects

OLE enables interoperability among objects that are written by different programmers from different companies. For example, a spreadsheet object from one vendor can connect to a database object from another vendor and import database records into the cells of its spreadsheet. As long as both objects support a predefined interface for data exchange, the spreadsheet and database don't have to know anything about each other's implementation, other than how to connect through the standard mechanism defined by the Component Object Model and exchange data through the common interface.

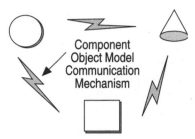

Figure 7.2   The OLE Component Object Model provides a standard way to communicate

Without a binary standard for interobject communication and a standard set of communication interfaces, programmers face the daunting task of writing a large number of procedures, each of which is specialized for communicating with a different type of application, or perhaps recompiling their applications depending on the other components with which they need to interact. Moreover, if the mechanism used for object interaction is not extremely efficient, PC software developers pressured by size and performance requirements simply would not use it. Finally, object communication must be language-independent since programmers cannot and should not be forced to use a particular programming language to interact with the system and other applications.

The OLE Component Object Model meets these challenges. In OLE, applications interact with each other and with the system using collections of function calls or methods, called interfaces. An interface is a strongly typed "contract" between software components that is designed to provide a small but useful set of semantically related operations. All OLE objects support a method called QueryInterface that allows for very efficient negotiation or communication between components to find which interfaces they share. The small portions of functionality defined in the interfaces plus OLE's inherent interface negotiation protocol allow software components to interact with one another in simple or complex ways depending on the needs of the component. They also allow for change and graceful evolution within the object system, since new interfaces can be introduced and discovered safely and efficiently without disturbing existing patterns of interaction between components.

At the lowest level, OLE object interaction is extremely fast and simple. Once the connection between software components is established, method invocations on OLE objects are simply indirect function calls through two memory pointers. As a result, the performance overhead of interacting with an OLE object in the same address space as the calling code is negligible — only a handful of processor instructions slower than a standard function call, and the overhead is even less considering that a typical function call would have to contain some kind of parameter to identify the entity that the caller seeks to act upon. Thus, there is no performance barrier to using OLE objects pervasively, even on low-end PCs.

The simplicity of the OLE model also provides language independence. Any programming language that can create structures of pointers and explicitly or implicitly call functions through pointers — languages such as C, C++, Pascal, Ada, Small Talk®, and the Microsoft Visual Basic programming system — can create and use OLE objects immediately. Other popular languages are being extended to provide direct OLE support since OLE-style programming is planned to be an inherent aspect of future versions of Microsoft Windows. Object-oriented languages can provide their own higher-level mapping between language objects and OLE objects, and can also provide class libraries to make OLE programming easy.

Future versions of the Microsoft Windows operating system are planned to use OLE-style interfaces extensively in areas where new services are defined. Facilities as diverse as visual controls, multimedia services and distributed security are targeted to be defined and programmed through the Component Object Model. The existing Win32 application programming interface will continue to be needed and fully supported; at the same time, object-based capabilities will gradually become pervasive, blurring the distinction between applications and the system and providing for easily replaceable components within the Windows operating system itself.

OLE: A Compelling Collection of Interfaces

Object models are interesting to theoreticians and software designers, but are unimportant to users. As discussed throughout this paper, OLE is based on a powerful, general-purpose object system. Microsoft's Component Object Model provides a language-independent binary standard for object interaction, and strongly typed components that can scale safely to distributed networks comprised of millions of objects. But the primary reason OLE will succeed in the marketplace where many object systems fail is that the immediate benefits of OLE to users are obvious and compelling.

OLE provides visual editing, drag and drop between applications, OLE Automation, and structured storage for objects. Visual editing allows two or more applications to cooperate in the editing of compound documents and display windows such that the user sees only a single document or window, with multiple editors loading themselves dynamically depending on which part of the document is in use. Drag and drop allows users to select an application object such as a document or chart with the mouse and drop in into another application window where it will be copied or moved. OLE Automation provides a standard means for macro and script languages to drive one or more applications by viewing and manipulating a set of internal application-level objects, such as paragraphs, cells, rows, tables, forms, with methods for altering the object's state. Finally, structured storage allows applications to cooperate in the creation of compound files supporting a variety of native data types stored as nested objects within a standard file format.

OLE 2.0 has garnered awards and praise from the industry. According to Michael J. Miller, editor in chief of *PC Magazine,* "Object Linking and Embedding 2.0

offers a far easier, far better method of integration, and it will fundamentally change our expectations for the next generation of software" (*PC Magazine* Dec. 7, 1993, p.78). Columnist Jim Seymour said, "OLE 2.0 is a big, big win for both software developers and PC users. I'd go so far as to say that it's the most important development in PC software of 1993" (*PC Magazine* Dec. 7, 1993 p. 98).

A True System Object Model

Object technology is proliferating and moving outside the realm of object-oriented languages. One area of interest is the development of language-independent class library technology. This kind of technology solves the "C++ in a DLL" problem — the problem of recompiling all code that uses a class whenever changes are made to the class itself — and can be useful for application development. But it is not appropriate for a system object model.

There are several fundamental limitations of class library technology when used to build distributed, evolving object systems.

- **Strong typing.** Distributed object systems have potentially millions of interfaces and software components that need to be uniquely identified. Any system that uses human-readable names for finding and binding to modules, objects, classes, or methods is at risk. The probability of a collision between human-readable names is quite high in a complex system. The result of a name-based identification will inevitably be the accidental connection of two or more software components that were not designed to interact with each other, and a resulting error or crash — even though the components and system had no bugs and worked as designed.

  By contrast, OLE uses globally unique identifiers — 128-bit integers that are virtually guaranteed to be unique in the world across space and time — to identify every interface, type and class. Human-readable names are assigned only for convenience and are locally scoped. This helps ensure that OLE components do not accidentally connect to an object or via an interface or method, even in networks with millions of objects.

- **No implementation inheritance.** Implementation inheritance — the ability of one component to "subclass" or inherit some of its functionality from another component — is a very useful technology for building applications. But more and more experts are concluding that it can create problems in a distributed, evolving object system. The problem is well-documented in academic literature, which calls it "the fragile base-class problem." The problem with implementation inheritance is that the "contract" or relationship between components in an implementation hierarchy is not clearly defined; it is implicit and ambiguous. When the parent or child component changes its behavior unexpectedly, the behavior of related components may become undefined. This is not a problem when the implementation hierarchy is under the control of a defined group of programmers who can make updates to all components simultaneously. But it is precisely this ability to control and change a set of related components simultaneously that differentiates an application, even a complex application, from a true distributed object system. So while implementation inheritance can be a very good thing for building applications, it is risky in a system object model.

OLE does provide a code reuse mechanism called "aggregation." Using this model, a set of objects can work together in a well-defined manner to appear to other software components as a single object. Aggregation provides the benefits of code reuse while maintaining explicit relationships between all objects and avoiding the risks of implementation inheritance.

- **Single programming model.** A problem related to implementation inheritance is the issue of a single programming model for in-process objects and out-of-process/cross-network objects. In the former case, class library technology permits the use of features that don't work outside a single address space, much less across a network. For example, implementation inheritance typically does not work outside a single address space. In other words, the programmer can't subclass a remote object. Similarly, features like public data items in classes that can be freely manipulated by other objects within a single address space don't work across process or network boundaries. OLE's Component Object Model has a single interface-based binding model and has been carefully designed to avoid any differences between the local and remote programming model.

- **Security.** For a distributed object system to be useful in the real world it must provide a means for secure access to objects and the data they encapsulate. While OLE does not currently implement security features, it has been designed to be upwardly compatible with future implementations of OLE that provide a full range of security features. Object servers can be modified to take advantage of secure object invocations, but unmodified OLE clients can participate in fully secure distributed environments.

The issues surrounding system object models are complex for corporate customers and ISVs making planning decisions in this area. OLE meets the challenges, and is a solid foundation for an enterprise-wide computing environment.

Distributed Capabilities for OLE

Today's version of OLE supports a rich set of features for integrating information on a user's desktop computer. But imagine if users could easily integrate objects on different computers as if they were all local. With this capability, a user in San Francisco could, for example, link a range of spreadsheet cells on their desktop to a corporate database in New York. Each time data in the database was updated, the user's spreadsheet would automatically reflect these changes.

To support this level of object integration across different computers, Microsoft is developing a new implementation of OLE that takes full advantage of the inherent capabilities of the Component Object Model. Distributed object communication is the next logical step for OLE. It provides the same kind of standard interobject cooperation as today's OLE, but allows this cooperation to take place *across networks* of computers. For example, an address-book application on a Windows-based computer can connect to a different address-book object on a UNIX-based system and import its address information without the user knowing that the interaction is taking place between different platforms over a network.

Remote services with no added effort

Significantly, the new implementation of OLE requires no changes to existing applications. An existing OLE application can immediately begin linking to other applications on other machines — without any changes the application's source code, and without recompiling the application. In other words, applications automatically receive these remote capabilities without any effort on the part of users or programmers.

Applications don't need to be changed because only the underlying object communication mechanism (which is transparent to applications) is being extended. The new version of OLE makes no changes to the OLE application programming interface (API) and object interfaces, so applications call the same OLE functions in the same way. If the services that support these function calls happen to be located on a different computer, the OLE infrastructure sends the request to the remote service automatically and invisibly.

How distributed OLE works

Distributed capabilities are a natural extension of the OLE Component Object Model. The most significant difference between current and future implementations of OLE is the remote procedure call mechanism used to transfer operations and data between objects. In OLE currently, a "lightweight" remote procedure call mechanism (LRPC) is used for interobject communication within a single computer. LRPC allows objects to pass information across the process boundaries that protect applications from each other within the operating system. In other words, LRPC is an interprocess communication facility that allows processes (such as objects) to talk to one another on the same machine. The new implementation of OLE extends OLE by adding object communication across a network, using Microsoft RPC rather than LRPC.

RPC systems allow applications to call remote procedures as if these procedures were located within the same address space as the calling application. With RPC, an application calls a remote procedure in the same way it would call a local (in-process) procedure, but in reality, that procedure may be located in another process on the same machine, or on a different machine across the network. Since the transfer of data between the calling application and responding procedure is handled transparently, it is possible to build applications that run across multiple processes or computers without changing the programming model used by a non-distributed applications.

Distributed objects will redefine computing

OLE with distributed object support allows a single application to be split into a number of different component objects, each of which can run on a different computer. Since OLE provides network-transparency, these components do not appear to be located on different machines. The entire network appears to be one large computer with enormous processing power and capacity. For example, a database application could be built as a set of components: a query engine, a report engine, a forms builder, and a transaction manager. Each of these components could run on a machine suited to the amount of processing power, I/O bandwidth and disk capacity required for it. As a result, computing can become much more efficient because software can be more closely matched with the exact hardware power required. Computing also becomes much more scaleable, since the virtually unlimited resources of an entire network can be leveraged by a single application or a group of applications.

Common Object Model

Recognizing the need to allow objects on different types of operating systems to interact, Microsoft and Digital have developed an architecture to allow interoperation of OLE and Digital's multi-platform object system, ObjectBroker™. This architecture, called Common Object Model (COM), defines a common DCE RPC-based protocol and a subset of core OLE functions that will be supported by Digital and other interested companies within their products. The Common Object Model is a direct outgrowth of the Component Object Model and provides full upward compatibility with OLE. When OLE and ObjectBroker work together, the Windows, Windows NT and Windows NT Advanced Server operating systems can connect to objects running on a variety of platforms including OSF/1™, HP-UX®, SunOS™, IBM AIX®, Ultrix®, and OpenVMS.

To show how OLE operates across platforms using COM, Microsoft and Digital have demonstrated a sample application that connects an object running on the OSF/1 operating system with objects on a Microsoft Windows NT-based computer. The sample application supports a standard OLE 2.0-compatible "hot link" between Microsoft Excel and a stock quote object running on the OSF/1 server.

Transparently to the user, the OLE elements in ObjectBroker allow the Microsoft Excel spreadsheet to be linked to its source data on the OSF/1 machine. Together, OLE and ObjectBroker hide the new mechanism used to find the OSF/1 server and dynamically transfer stock quote data into the cells of the Microsoft Excel spreadsheet. Users watch the stock data update in real time on their screen, without having to know anything about the different sources of the data.

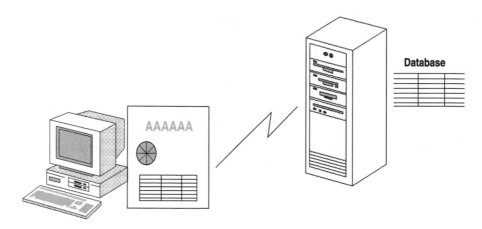

Figure 7.3 Demonstration: OLE allows object links to exist across heterogeneous networks

For users, the benefits are numerous. With the Common Object Model, users can access information on virtually any platform in the enterprise without being concerned about the type of application they are connecting to, or the type of communication mechanism needed to reach that object. Using simple techniques such as OLE's drag and drop, users can manipulate objects throughout the enterprise without knowing or caring where they are located or which application was used to create them.

Microsoft and Digital are committed to following an open process for the Common Object Model that will address broad industry requirements. Design reviews for system integrators, corporate application developers, independent software vendors, and other interested third parties are planned for the first half of 1994. Prior to these reviews, draft publications will be published for review and comment.

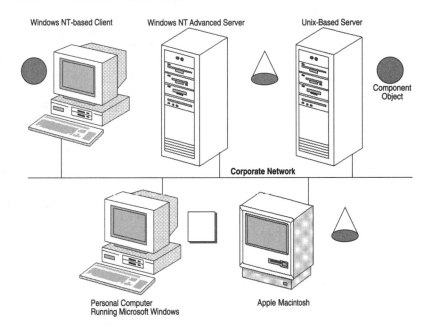

Figure 7.4   OLE and ObjectBroker enable enterprise computing at the object level

An Evolutionary Path for Windows

Today's OLE technology is a major foundation piece in Microsoft's strategy operating system direction. The next major releases of Microsoft Windows NT (code-named "Cairo") and Windows (called Windows 95) will build on OLE and be compatible with it, respectively. Cairo is intended to add a range of capabilities designed to make creating, accessing, manipulating, organizing and sharing information easier for computer users. It will offer an advanced object-oriented environment that focuses users on manipulating information through queries on content and properties, not on manipulating applications or groping around networks. To do this, Cairo will integrate a number of new and existing technologies that change the way people use computers while making computers much more intuitive to use. Similarly, Windows 95 will ship with full OLE support, and future versions of Windows 95 will provide OLE with distributed capabilities as well as other aspects of the Cairo technology.

Although the evolution from OLE to Cairo and Windows 95 offers dramatic changes in the way computers will be used, the path to this functionality will be smooth for existing applications. Much of the advanced technology that will be available in the future will simply be inherited by existing applications, with no changes to the applications themselves. Moreover, the OLE style of object programming will be used extensively in future Microsoft operating systems to implement replaceable and modular system services. Finally, the Microsoft and

Digital Common Object Model helps ensure that OLE's distributed object capabilities will be available on a wide range of UNIX and OpenVMS platforms as well as desktop computers and Windows NT-based servers. Therefore, independent software vendors and corporate IS engineers can begin implementing solutions today using OLE and be assured that this solution can tap into the power of future distributed, heterogeneous object-based computing systems.

CHAPTER 8

OLE Controls

Topic

Compare and contrast Microsoft Visual Basic custom controls and OLE Controls.

Content

OLE Controls: State of the Union[1]

Dale Rogerson

Abstract

OLE Controls are reusable software components designed to work in containers that support OLE. OLE Controls are more powerful and more flexible than the VBX custom controls they will replace. Unlike VBXes, OLE Controls support both 16-bit and 32-bit environments and are not limited to Microsoft Visual Basic. OLE Controls are also easier to develop than VBXes. This article provides an overview of the current state of OLE Controls.

Introduction

VBX custom controls are currently one of the most popular forms of reusable software. Basically, a VBX is a dynamic-link library (DLL) that follows a specification, allowing it to work with Visual Basic and other programming systems. For example, the Microsoft Visual Basic and Visual C++™ development systems understand the interface exported by a VBX, and they can use a VBX by calling its interface.

---

[1] This technical article is also available on the Microsoft Developer Network Development Library under Windows (32-bit) Articles, OLE Articles. Copyright 1994. Used with permission. All rights reserved.

OLE Controls are more powerful than VBXes. They are not a superset of VBXes—they have a completely different architecture. Instead of extending a hardware-specific architecture (VBX) to support multiple platforms (especially 32-bit environments), the OLE Control architecture was developed for both 32-bit and 16-bit platforms. In contrast, VBXes are limited to 16 bits.

Additionally, OLE Controls are not limited to Visual Basic. Rather than developing a Visual Basic-specific VBX replacement, Microsoft chose to bring the benefits of VBXes to a wider audience and to incorporate OLE, a major component of future Microsoft operating systems. OLE Controls are designed to work in any container that supports OLE. This includes not only the next version of Visual Basic, but also OLE-enabled container applications such as Microsoft Office. Additionally, OLE Controls will work in third-party OLE-enabled applications and development tools.

OLE Controls are easier to develop than VBXes. These controls are developed using the Control Development Kit (CDK), which shipped with the recently released Visual C++ version 2.0. The CDK contains new classes from the Microsoft Foundation Class Library (MFC), which simplify OLE Control development, and ControlWizard, which will automatically generate an OLE Control skeleton.

OLE Controls, which will be supported by the next version of Visual Basic, will replace VBXes. If you are a control developer, you may want to consider developing OLE Controls, because they are likely to have the largest market of any type of custom control.

A Little History Lesson

Before we get started, let's review the history of custom controls. In the beginning, we only had DLLs. In fact, Windows consists of a number of DLLs working together.

Custom controls were first defined in Microsoft Windows 3.0. A custom control was a DLL that exported a defined set of functions. These controls were available from third-party developers. Custom controls were neat, but most C developers preferred to write their own. Moreover, the custom control architecture didn't support the Visual Basic development environment because it didn't allow Visual Basic to query the control for information on properties and methods. A new custom control architecture, called the *VBX*, was defined specifically to support Visual Basic.

The VBX has become incredibly popular. Thousands of VBXes, from simple buttons to complicated networking controls, are available for a wide range of uses. VBXes are written in C/C++, so they can automate tasks that are too difficult, time-consuming, or simply impossible in Visual Basic.

The popularity of VBXes increased the demand for reusable components in other programming environments. For example, Visual Basic programmers needed custom controls for the 32-bit platform; Visual Basic for Applications users wanted controls for Microsoft Access, Microsoft Excel, and Word; and C/C++ users wanted controls for MIPS and Alpha® as well as Intel processors. Unfortunately, VBXes are restricted to the 16-bit Visual Basic environment, so it was impossible to extend VBXes to answer these needs.

OLE, on the other hand, provides the perfect environment for building powerful, flexible, and reusable software components. The new OLE Controls will replace VBXes in the next version of Visual Basic as well as answering the need for visual, reusable code libraries in other 16-bit and 32-bit environments.

Desperately Seeking Event Notification

An OLE Control is an **OLE InProc** object (an OLE object that loads into the address space of its container) with some extended functionality. All OLE-compliant containers can already hold OLE Controls. The controls, however, can only get events in containers that support OLE Control events.

This doesn't matter for some controls. Consider the case of a calendar control that lets you click to change the month. If you only need to display the month, you could insert the control and click to the month you want.

The purpose of most controls, however, is to send event notifications to their parent. Most existing OLE containers, such as those generated by AppWizard in Visual C++, don't know how to handle these event notifications. For instance, if you drop an OLE Control push button into a container that doesn't support OLE Controls, you can push the button as much as you want, but the container doesn't know to respond.

In a container that supports OLE Controls, this button control would send events to the container, which would then respond appropriately. For example, you could insert an OLE graph control into a future control-enabled version of Microsoft Word, and the graph control would display the temperature. If the temperature were higher than the record temperature, the control would fire an event to Word. The Word document would have a Visual Basic for Applications function to handle this event. This function would then insert the string "Record temperature reached today" into the document.

OLE Control Containers on the Horizon

The CDK includes Test Container, a sample application that can examine and change the properties of an OLE Control, invoke its methods, and watch it generate events. This is a valuable tool, not only for developing and debugging new controls but also for learning about existing controls.

However, Test Container is limited to being an interactive tool that cannot be programmed. You can manipulate a control only with the mouse. You can't write functions to see how the control works, and you can't actually develop code to direct and respond to the control, so you can't tell whether it is easy or difficult to write a handler for the control you're developing.

Currently, the only released control container that supports OLE Controls (including events) is Microsoft Access 2.0. The large installed base of Microsoft Access provides an immediate potential market for OLE Controls. However, because the current version of Microsoft Access was released before the OLE Control specification was finalized, Microsoft Access is a poor control container.

The next version of Visual Basic will be a full-blown OLE Control container that will support OLE Controls similarly to how Visual Basic currently supports VBXes. You'll be able to simply drop an OLE Control on a form and set its properties. Visual Basic users will become the premier customers for OLE Controls.

Version 3.0 of MFC, which shipped with Visual C++ 2.0, does not directly support OLE containers. In a future version of MFC, however, you will be able to place your control in a dialog box or form, just as you can today with VBXes.

Do I Need OLE Controls Today?

If you are currently using 16-bit Visual Basic, you will want to upgrade to the 32-bit version when it is released. When you buy a new control, make sure you understand whether it is an OLE Control. You do not need to replace your older VBXes with OLE Controls, because future versions of Visual Basic will support both OLE Controls and VBXes. This will allow you to change controls on a case-by-case basis.

To take advantage of 32-bit environments, including Windows NT and the next version of the Microsoft Windows operating system (called Windows 95), you'll want to consider moving to OLE Controls. The added benefit is that the OLE Controls can be used in multiple development environments, greatly enhancing their value over 16-bit VBXes.

For developers who have existing VBX controls, the CDK provides a way to convert these controls to the OLE Control format using the VBX Template Tool. This tool, found in ControlWizard, uses model information in the .VBX file and creates a Visual C++ project file and source code files for creating the OLE Control. These files can be compiled and linked to produce a working skeleton for the OLE Control.

Once this skeleton is built and tested, you can take code from VBX source files and place it in the appropriate areas of the generated OLE source files. The transplanted code will probably require some modification to work in the new source code files.

If you are a C++ developer, you will have to wait a little longer before OLE Control container support is built into MFC. Because MFC does not yet support the construction of OLE containers, you won't be able to use OLE Controls in your C++ applications for a while *unless* you write your own container. In a release to follow Visual C++ 2.0, Visual C++ and MFC will provide integrated support for making your C++ programs into full-blown OLE Control containers.

Whatever course you decide on now, remember that OLE Controls are the future of custom controls.

Further Reading

The articles in the Microsoft Development Library provide an excellent overview of OLE Controls.

Introductory information

- Randell, Scott. "Developing OLE Custom Controls." Presented at the Tech*Ed Conference, (March 1994). (Development Library, Conferences and Seminars, Tech*Ed, March 1994, Visual C++).

  Contains an Introduction and overview of OLE Controls. Also provides implementation details and describes the organization of MFC. The CDK documentation derives some of its content from this article.

- Smith, Erick. "Converting VBX Controls to OLE Custom Controls." *Developer Network News* 3 (July 1994). (Development Library, Books and Periodicals, Microsoft Developer Network News, 1994 Volume 3, July 1994 Number 4, July Features).

  Provides information on converting VBXes to OLE Controls.

- Whittle, Solveig. "OLE Comes to Custom Controls." *Developer Network News* 3 (May 1994). (Development Library, Books and Periodicals, Microsoft Developer Network News, 1994 Volume 3, May 1994 Number 3, May Features).

Provides high-level information and includes some implementation details.

- "Introduction to Microsoft OLE Custom Control Architecture & Tools." Article from the Microsoft Developer Knowledge Base. (In the Development Library, search for "Q113895".)

See the Q&A section at the end for useful information.

- "OLE Custom Controls." Microsoft Backgrounder. Part Number 098-55315 (March 1994). (Development Library, Backgrounders and White Papers, Operating System Extensions.)

High-level strategy document.

In the Development Library, search for "OLE Custom Control" or "OLE Control" (using the quotation marks in your queries) for additional articles on this subject.

Development information

See the Control Development Kit (CDK) in the upcoming Visual C++ 2.0 documentation set for information on developing OLE Controls.

My second article, "OLE Controls: Top Tips", in this two-part series provides guidelines for building OLE Controls, based on my own experiences.

Usage information

The Office Developer's Kit (Development Library, Product Documentation, Office Developer's Kit 1.0) provides useful information. For example, see the "Adding and Manipulating OLE Custom Controls" in the Office Developer's Kit, Microsoft Access 2.0, Advanced Topics, Part 3, Chapter 6 for information on using OLE Controls in a Microsoft Access form.

I expect that the Visual Basic 4.0 Professional Edition, when it becomes available, will also be a good source of information on using OLE Controls. Look for more information on using OLE Controls with Visual Basic in future issues of the Development Library.

Topics

Describe the functionality OLE Controls provide the container in terms of properties, events, and methods.

Explain the benefits of implementing an application that uses OLE Controls.

Content

OLE Comes to Custom Controls

Solveig Whittle

New open architecture allows development of both 16-bit and 32-bit components[2]

Component-based software development is based on the notion of a component, or a reusable piece of software such as a VBX (Visual Basic extension) grid custom control, "plugging" into a development tool "container" or host. The container and component are then used together to create a Windows-based application.

Since the introduction of the Microsoft Visual Basic programming system in 1991, many developers have used Visual Basic custom controls (VBXes), with their point-and-click visual interface, as an easy way to take advantage of component-based software development. The market for VBXes has grown rapidly, and commercially available VBXes now offer a wide range of functionality, from video conferencing to mainframe connectivity.

But VBXes also have some limitations. The VBX architecture was not designed to be an open standard interface, thus the same VBX cannot be used across multiple hardware platforms or multiple operating system platforms, or in multiple development environments. It is also a 16-bit architecture that does not readily port to 32 bits.

The OLE custom control architecture

To help solve these shortcomings, Microsoft recently announced a new 16-bit and 32-bit custom control architecture that joins the benefits of the VBX architecture with OLE.

Because OLE is an open standard, developed with input from companies other than Microsoft, it has the added advantage that a wide range of development tools and applications already support it. But OLE (until now) has not been applied to the world of small, fast components such as VBXes. It seemed inevitable that, especially with the growing importance of cross-platform development, VBXes and OLE would come together.

Microsoft's OLE 2.0, released last year, provides a *standard* means of defining what objects—or components—are and how they can interact with one another. With OLE, a programmer from one company can write components that he or she can be sure will work with other components written by programmers in other companies. In the same way that the standardization of machined parts resulted in tremendous productivity gains during the Industrial Revolution, a standardized

---

[2] Reprinted from *Microsoft Developer Network News*, Volume 3, May 1994, Number 3. Copyright 1994. Used with permission. All rights reserved.

interface for components enables similar benefits for software developers.

The OLE custom control architecture is a set of extensions to the existing OLE interfaces that turn OLE containers and objects into powerful "control containers" and "controls." It adds to the standard OLE compound document interfaces and the concepts of embedded objects, in-place activation, and OLE Automation to meet the specific interaction needs between control and control container. The OLE custom control architecture and these extensions were the focus of a recent design review with third parties as part of the open process for developing this standard.

What are OLE custom controls?

An OLE custom control is an embeddable component, implemented as an in-process server dynamic-link library (DLL), that also supports in-place activation as an inside-out object.

But controls are more than just editable embedded components. They transform end-user events, such as mouse clicks and key strokes, into programmatic notifications to the container, which then can use those transformed events to execute other code. Like a VBX, every OLE custom control has three sets of attributes:

Properties. Named characteristics or values of the control such as color, text, number, font, and so on.

Events. Actions triggered by the control in response to some external actions on the control, such as clicking a mouse button or pressing a key.

Methods. A function implemented in the control that allows external code to manipulate its appearance, behavior, or properties. For example, an edit or other text-oriented control would support methods to allow the control container to retrieve or modify the current text, perhaps performing operations such as copy and paste.

In addition to the OLE interfaces **IOleObject**, **IDataObject**, **IViewObject**, **IPersistStorage**, and **IOleInPlaceActiveObject** (**IOleCache** is optional), the control must also implement the **IPersistStream** and **IDispatch** interfaces to handle the communication of its properties and methods with the container.

A control container also uses the standard OLE interfaces to communicate with the control. These include the **IOleClientSite**, **IOleInPlaceSite**, and **IAdviseSink** interfaces on its site objects, **IOleInPlaceUIWindow** on its document objects, and **IOleInPlaceFrame** on its frame objects. To work properly with controls, the container also implements an **IDispatch** interface for managing a control's events and an **IDispatch** interface for managing ambient properties.

An ambient property is a property of the container itself that generally applies to all controls in the container. Some examples of ambient properties are default colors, font, and whether the container is in "design mode" or "run mode."

The existing compound document interfaces and the use of OLE Automation are almost sufficient to meet all the requirements for controls and control containers. However, these standard mechanisms don't address a few key requirements for controls: mnemonic (ALT key) handling and special accelerator processing for the control; notifications of changes in ambient property values; notification that the container has loaded all of its controls; and a mechanism through which the control obtains the container's event **IDispatch** interface.

The first three requirements are addressed through two new interfaces: **IOleControl** and **IOleControlSite**. The control implements **IOleControl**, while **IOleControlSite** is implemented by the container on the site object, to serve as a notification sink for changes in a control's mnemonics. To take care of the fourth requirement, the control also implements two additional new interfaces called **IConnectionPointContainer** and **IConnectionPoint**. (See Figure 8.2.)

Together these interfaces create the necessary standard mechanisms through which an arbitrary control container can use any arbitrary control to create any type of Windows-based application.

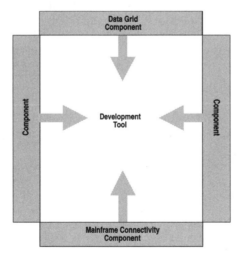

Figure 8.1   Component-based software development is based on "plugging" a component or a reusable piece of software into a development tool "container" or host.

The OLE Control Development Kit to the rescue

Sound complicated? Well, Microsoft is making it easier for independent software vendors (ISVs) and corporate developers of controls to create these controls and also to port their existing VBX controls to the new architecture.

Microsoft will be shipping a new OLE Control Development Kit (CDK) in the summer of 1994. This new CDK is more than a description of the interfaces (like the CDK for VBX controls that is included with Visual Basic today). It is actually an add-on to Microsoft Visual C++, and it provides a set of tools, libraries, and documentation to allow developers to create 16-bit and 32-bit OLE custom controls. A group of third-party development tool vendors has received very early versions of this CDK for their review and to help them incorporate this new technology into their products. Shortly after the new architecture has been fully reviewed and the CDK released, third-party vendors are expected to ship new commercial OLE custom control objects and containers, creating a wave of new tools in the marketplace.

The CDK leverages the existing support in Visual C++ 1.5 for OLE, but adds extensions to the Microsoft Foundation Class Library (MFC) and additions to the Class Wizard as well as a new Control Wizard. An option in the Control Wizard supports the creation of a new OLE custom control template from an existing VBX. The CDK makes it as easy as marking a check box to include support for a variety of control features such as property pages, self-registration, multiple controls in a single OLE custom control file, data binding, and licensing.

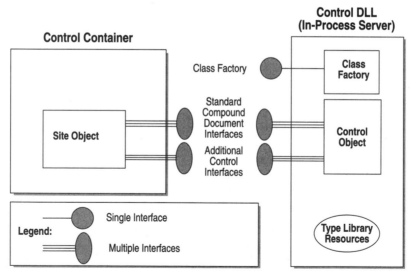

Figure 8.2   OLE control extensions are implemented alongside standard compound document interfaces.

Support for OLE custom controls

To preserve existing customer code bases that use VBX custom controls, Microsoft will continue to support the current 16-bit VBX custom control architecture on future 16-bit versions of Visual Basic and Visual C++.

In the future, however, OLE custom controls will be the extensibility mechanism of choice.

Future versions of Microsoft development tools, including Visual Basic, Visual C++, and the Microsoft Access and Microsoft FoxPro® database management systems, will support OLE custom controls. In addition, a future version of Microsoft Visual Basic for Applications will include support for OLE custom controls, thus bringing OLE custom control capability to the family of Microsoft Office applications.

A key benefit of this open architecture is that third-party development tools and applications will also be able to support OLE custom controls.

The future version of the Microsoft Windows NT operating system, known as Cairo, will also support OLE custom controls, bringing visual component-based development to the desktop.

For more information on OLE custom controls, see the management backgrounder entitled "Microsoft OLE Custom Controls," which can be ordered from Microsoft (part number 098-55315).

Making the corporate gears run smoother

Here are a few ways that OLE custom controls and component-based development can improve corporate computing.

More choices. Because standardized component-based development enables the proliferation of a large number of standard components that work in a variety of containers from different vendors, corporations will have more choices of technology that can be tailored to meet highly specific business needs.

Better quality. Market opportunities for component developers will increase dramatically due to standardization. Broad-based participation in the component software market by small, medium, and large vendors will increase competition. This increased competition should produce more innovative and higher-quality software. This is already happening in the existing VBX marketplace.

Better integration. Because development tools and application containers will support a standard means of component-level communication, products from different vendors will interoperate more fully than today's applications. As a result, users will find it easier to exchange data between applications, and systems analysts will have an easier time building custom business solutions with off-the-shelf tools.

Easier custom solutions. Component-based development will enable the same component to be more easily plugged into a wide range of development tools and applications, allowing a much greater degree of application customization than is possible today. For example, users will be able to plug different OLE custom controls into a database application to provide a range of custom functions such as specialized financial modules, equation editing, scientific analysis, run-time tutorials, charting, data compression, and so on. The same OLE custom controls will also work in other development tools such as languages or programmable applications. Users get the precise functionality they need—in a more cost-effective manner.

Less redundant software on the desktop. Most larger corporations spend millions of dollars on monolithic software. Since component software allows developers and users to get exactly the functionality required in a cost-effective manner, software budgets aren't wasted on capabilities that won't be used. This greater efficiency is one of the most important benefits of VBX custom controls today.

CHAPTER 9

Open Database Connectivity (ODBC) 2.0 Fundamentals

Topics

Describe the role of an application.

Describe the role of the driver.

Describe the services that ODBC provides to the application developer.

Content

Accessing the World of Information: Open Database Connectivity (ODBC)[1]

Abstract

Open database connectivity (ODBC) is Microsoft's strategic interface for accessing data in a heterogeneous environment of relational and non-relational database management systems. Based on the Call Level Interface specification of the SQL Access Group, ODBC provides an open, vendor-neutral way of accessing data stored in a variety of proprietary personal computer, minicomputer, and mainframe databases. ODBC alleviates the need for independent software vendors and corporate developers to learn multiple application programming interfaces. ODBC now provides a universal data access interface. With ODBC, application developers can allow an application to concurrently access, view, and modify data from multiple, diverse databases. ODBC is a core component of Microsoft Windows Open Services Architecture (WOSA). Apple has endorsed ODBC as a key enabling

---

[1] This backgrounder is also available on the Microsoft Developer Network Development Library under Backgrounders and White Papers, Operating System Extensions. Copyright 1992 - 1995. Used with permission. All rights reserved.

technology and has announced the ODBC software developer's kit for Macintosh developers. With growing industry support, ODBC has emerged as the industry standard for data access for both Windows-based and Macintosh-based applications.

Introduction

Providing data access to applications in today's heterogeneous database environment is very complex for software vendors as well as corporate developers. With ODBC, Microsoft has eased the burden of data access by creating a vendor-neutral, open, and powerful means of accessing database management systems (DBMSs).

Note In the context of this paper, DBMS refers to a database product. This may be a relational database, such as ORACLE® or DB2®, or a file-based database, such as dBASE®.

- ODBC is *vendor neutral*, allowing access to DBMSs from multiple vendors.
- ODBC is *open*. Working with ANSI standards, the SQL Access Group (SAG), X/Open, and numerous independent software vendors, Microsoft has gained a very broad consensus on ODBC's implementation, and it has become the dominant standard.
- ODBC is *powerful*—it offers capabilities critical to client/server on-line transaction processing (OLTP) and decision support systems (DSS) applications, including system table transparency, full transaction support, scrollable cursors, asynchronous calling, array fetch and update, a flexible connection model, and stored procedures for "static" SQL performance.

Benefits

ODBC provides many significant benefits to developers, end users, and the industry by providing an open, standard way to access data.

- ODBC allows users to access data in more than one data storage location (for example, more than one server) from within a single application.
- ODBC allows users to access data in more than one type of DBMS (such as DB2, Oracle, MicrosoftSQL Server, DEC™ Rdb, Apple DAL, and dBASE) from within a single application.
- ODBC greatly simplifies application development. It is now easier for developers to provide access to data in multiple, concurrent DBMSs.
- ODBC is a portable application programming interface (API), enabling the same interface and access technology to be a cross-platform tool.

- ODBC insulates applications from changes to underlying network and DBMS versions. Modifications to networking transports, servers, and DBMSs will not affect current ODBC applications.

- ODBC promotes the use of SQL—the standard language for DBMSs—as defined in the ANSI 1989 standard. It is an open, vendor-neutral specification based on the SAG Call Level Interface (CLI).

- ODBC allows corporations to protect their investments in existing DBMSs and protect developers' acquired DBMS skills. ODBC allows corporations to continue to use existing diverse DBMSs, while continuing to "rightsize" applications.

ODBC is the database access component of Windows Open Services Architecture (WOSA), Microsoft's strategic architecture for delivering on "Information At Your Fingertips." This paper describes how ODBC fits into the WOSA framework, the challenges facing developers and users in today's complex computing environment, how ODBC meets these challenges, and why ODBC has become the dominant solution for data access.

The WOSA Solution

In the absence of a formal way to connect front-end applications to various back-end services, application developers are forced to incorporate support for vendor-specific APIs in their applications. Supporting additional services requires that application developers either build new applications or modify existing ones to accommodate diverse APIs—this process is both labor-intensive and expensive.

WOSA provides a single, system-level interface to enterprise computing environments, while hiding the complexities of heterogeneous environments from end users and developers. By taking advantage of the WOSA interface, a Windows-based desktop application does not need to contain special code for any of the types of network in use, the types of computers in the enterprise, or the types of back-end services available in order to gain seamless access to available information. As a result, even if the network, computers, or services should change, the desktop application does not need to be modified. In other words, WOSA enables Windows-based applications to connect to all the services across multiple computing environments.

The Windows operating system presents end users with a single application interface. Once users learn how to use one application, they can quickly learn others. Similarly, WOSA presents developers of distributed applications with a single interface for communicating with back-end services such as DBMSs and messaging. Instead of having to learn a different API for each implementation of a service, developers building applications with WOSA only need to learn a single API for *all* implementations of a particular service. Furthermore, when an existing service is modified or replaced, the front-end application is unaffected as long as the new back-end service communicates through the WOSA interface.

WOSA makes it possible for corporate developers to build stable, long-term enterprise solutions using various combinations of off-the-shelf products and custom packages, while presenting end users with a single, consistent interface. End users are spared having to learn a new application for each new service or each alteration of an existing service. Developers are spared having to constantly modify their applications to communicate with new services. WOSA makes the Windows operating system the single, reliable, strategic platform for end users, application developers, and MIS managers.

What WOSA Does

WOSA provides a single system-level interface for connecting front-end applications with back-end services. Application developers and end users alike do not have to worry about using numerous different services, each with its own protocols and API, because making these connections is the business of the operating system, not of individual applications.

WOSA provides an extensible framework in which Windows-based applications can seamlessly access information and network resources in a distributed computing environment. WOSA accomplishes this magic by making a set of common APIs available to all applications.

ODBC and MAPI (Messaging API) are two of the key components of WOSA, along with the Windows Sockets Library, the Licensing API, and Remote Procedure Calls (RPCs). ODBC addresses database connectivity technology, while MAPI addresses electronic mail and workgroup productivity applications. MAPI, ODBC, and the other WOSA components will become part of the standard Windows and Windows NT operating systems sometime in the future.

The Need for Database Connectivity

Information has become a key asset to corporate competitiveness. To be competitive in the 1990s, corporations need access to accurate and timely information. Companies are striving to achieve a higher level of accuracy and effectiveness in areas such as pricing, quality control, market analysis, capacity planning, inventory management, customer service, and billing. At the same time, users are demanding better tools for accessing this information. Users demand graphical user interfaces, leading edge analytical tools, easy ways of accessing and viewing information—all without having to know the structure or language of the underlying DBMS or the issues unique to their network.

To achieve this goal, corporations must provide better tools for end users to access existing information while providing a migration path for the data and the applications as they evolve or are "rightsized" to the optimum platform. This presents a difficult challenge, given the heterogeneous nature of most corporations' current information technology.

Heterogeneous Database Environments

Historically, database applications have been built to access a single source of data. The range of applications varies from mainframe-based, batch-oriented DBMSs, to terminal-based, interactive applications, to personal computer–based, single-user DBMSs, to the more recent client/server DBMSs. Data typically resides in a variety of file formats, such as VSAM and ISAM, as well as in hierarchical and relational DBMSs.

Corporations typically have applications and data residing on diverse platforms and DBMSs for historical, strategic, and technological reasons. Corporations often have legacy systems that must be maintained because they contain key corporate data. Corporate mergers often bring together diverse information technologies. Systems were often developed using technology that met a specific requirement, such as an engineering application. Departmental users developed their own workgroup and single-user personal computer databases. Over time, data on any of these systems might be summarized for consumption by analysts, copied and distributed geographically, or have many snapshots taken of it.

There is a strong requirement for a common method of accessing, managing, and analyzing data. The heterogeneous nature of database environments is a problem corporations are faced with today. Many firms have discovered that much of the cost associated with application maintenance is related to data access problems. One of the first steps to meeting the needs of information users is database connectivity.

Database Connectivity Components

Database connectivity allows an application to communicate with one or more DBMSs. Database connectivity is a requirement whether the application uses a file-based (ISAM) approach, a client/server model, or traditional mainframe connectivity. The requirement for database connectivity has been hastened by client/server computing. As users increasingly use graphical, personal computer–based tools to analyze, prepare, and present data, they require greater access to the vast volumes of existing corporate data. In the most general sense, client/server computing means that some portion of the application runs on a personal computer. At the very least, this computer is responsible for screen presentation and gathering user input. The server (or host) is responsible for responding to queries; managing concurrency, security, backup and recovery; transaction processing; and so on. This differs from centralized, host-based applications where the entire application runs on the host platform.

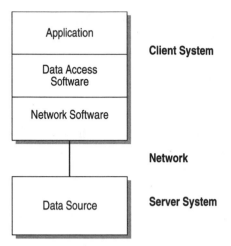

Figure 9.1   ODBC components

Some of the key components involved with database connectivity are explained below.

Application

Allows users to perform a set of functions, such as queries, data entry, and report generation. Examples are Microsoft Excel, Microsoft Works, Aldus PageMaker®, and internally developed applications such as an executive information system or a reporting system.

Client system

The physical system where the client portion of an application runs. In the personal computer world, this may be an IBM PC or compatible or an Apple Macintosh.

Data access software

A service layer on client systems that provides a direct interface for applications. This "middleware" or enabling software plays a key role in client/server data access. This layer accepts data retrieval and update requests directly from the application, and transmits them across the network. This "middleware" also is responsible for returning results and error codes back to the application.

Data source

The data and method of data access. The data may exist in a variety of hierarchical or relational DBMSs, or in a file with a format such as ISAM or VSAM.

Network

The physical connection of the client to the server system.

Network software

The software protocols that allow the client to communicate with the server system.

Server system

The physical system where the DBMS resides (also known as the host system). For example, the server system could be an IBM PC or compatible, a DEC VAX™, or an IBM mainframe.

The Challenge of Database Connectivity

One of the challenges of database connectivity is accessing multiple, heterogeneous data sources from within a single application. A second challenge is flexibility—the application should be able to directly access data from a variety of data sources without modification to the application. For example, an application could access data from dBASE in a stand-alone, small office environment, and from SQL Server or Oracle in a larger, networked environment. Due to these challenges, some Fortune 500 firms have as little as 1 percent of enterprise data in a form that is truly accessible.

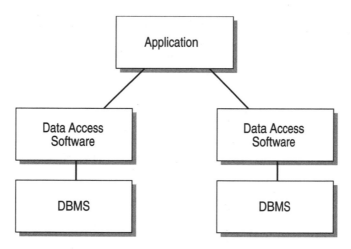

Figure 9.2   The challenge of database connectivity

These challenges are common to developers of off-the-shelf applications, and to corporate developers attempting to provide solutions to end users or to migrate data to new platforms. These challenges grow exponentially for developers and support staff as the number of data sources grows.

The problems of database connectivity are apparent in the differences among the programming interfaces, DBMS protocols, DBMS languages, and network protocols of disparate data sources. Even when data sources are restricted to relational DBMSs that use SQL, significant differences in SQL syntax and semantics must be resolved.

The primary differences in the implementation of each of these components are: .

- **Programming interface.** Each vendor provides his/her own proprietary programming interface. One method of accessing a relational DBMS is through embedded SQL. Another method is through an API.

- **DBMS protocol.** Each vendor uses proprietary data formats and methods of communication between the application and the DBMS. For example, there are many different ways to delineate the end of one row of data and beginning of the next.

- **DBMS language.** SQL has become the language of choice for relational DBMSs, but many differences still exist among actual SQL implementations.

- **Networking protocols.** There are many diverse local area network (LAN) and wide area network (WAN) protocols in networks today. DBMSs and applications must coexist in these diverse environments. For example, SQL Server may use DECnet on a VAX, TCP/IP on UNIX, and Netbeui or SPX/IPX on a PC.

To access various database environments, an application developer would have to learn to use each vendor's programming interface, employ each vendor's SQL, and ensure that the proper programming interface, network, and DBMS software were installed on the client system. This complexity makes broad database connectivity unfeasible for most developers and users today.

Approaches to Database Connectivity

Several vendors have attempted to address the problem of database connectivity in a variety of ways. The primary approaches include using gateways, a common programming interface, and a common protocol.

Gateways

Application developers use one vendor's programming interface, SQL grammar, and DBMS protocol. A gateway causes a target DBMS to appear to the application as a copy of the selected DBMS. The gateway translates and forwards requests to the target DBMS and receives results from it. For example, applications that access SQL Server can also access DB2 data through the Micro Decisionware® DB2 Gateway. This product allows a DB2 DBMS to appear to a Windows-based application as a SQL Server DBMS. Note that an application using this gateway would need a different gateway for each type of DBMS it needs to access, such as DEC Rdb, Informix®, Ingres™, and ORACLE.

The gateway approach is limited by architectural differences among DBMSs, such as differences in catalogs and SQL implementations, and the need for one gateway for each target DBMS. Gateways remain a very valid approach to database connectivity, and are essential in certain environments, but are typically not a broad, long-term solution.

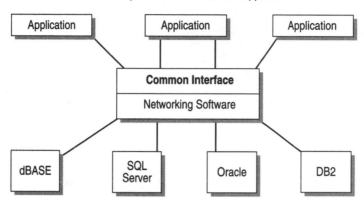

Figure 9.3   Applications accessing heterogeneous data sources concurrently

Common interface

A single programming interface is provided to the developer. It is possible to provide some standardization in a database application development environment or user interface even when the underlying interfaces are different for each DBMS. This is accomplished by creating a standard API, macro language, or set of user tools for accessing data and translating requests for, and results from, each target DBMS. A common interface is usually implemented by writing a driver for each target DBMS.

Common protocol

The DBMS protocol, SQL grammar, and networking protocols are common to all DBMSs, so the application can use the same protocol and SQL grammar to communicate with all DBMSs. Examples are remote data access (RDA) and distributed relational database architecture (DRDA). RDA is an emerging standard from SAG, but not available today. DRDA is IBM's alternative DBMS protocol. Common protocols can ultimately work very effectively in conjunction with a common interface.

There are several current vendor-specific approaches that address database connectivity. These current approaches have several limitations. Many companies expend resources solving the same problem. This results in diverse implementations and duplication of effort. The results are inconsistent interfaces for end users and developers, overlap in effort, and a compromise in functionality and connectivity options. Although some current implementations provide viable solutions, none have the critical mass to emerge as a de facto standard.

Common interfaces, protocols, and gateways may be combined. A common protocol and interface provides a standard API for developers as well as a single protocol for communication with all databases. A common gateway and interface provides a standard API for developers and allows the gateway to provide functionality, such as translation and connectivity to wide area networks, that would otherwise need to be implemented on each client station. Note that a common gateway or protocol still requires a common interface to hide complexities from developers.

The ODBC Solution

ODBC addresses the heterogeneous database connectivity problem using the common interface approach. Application developers use one API to access all data sources. ODBC is based on a CLI specification, which was developed by a consortium of over 40 companies (members of the SQL Access Group and others), and has broad support from application and database vendors. The result is a single API that provides all the functionality that application developers need, and an architecture that database developers require to ensure interoperability. This will result in a rich set of applications that use ODBC, and provide applications with much broader access to data than ever before.

How ODBC Works

ODBC defines an API. Each application uses the same code, as defined by the API specification, to talk to many types of data sources through DBMS-specific drivers. A Driver Manager sits between the applications and the drivers. In Windows, the Driver Manager and the drivers are implemented as dynamic-link libraries (DLLs).

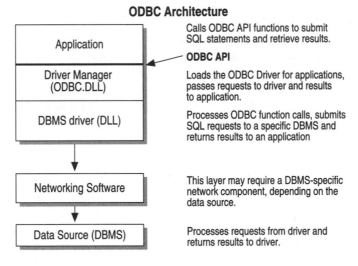

Figure 9.4   ODBC architecture

The application calls ODBC functions to connect to a data source, send and receive data, and disconnect.

The Driver Manager provides information to an application such as a list of available data sources; loads drivers dynamically as they are needed; and provides argument and state transition checking.

The driver, developed separately from the application, sits between the application and the network. The driver processes ODBC function calls, manages all exchanges between an application and a specific DBMS, and may translate the standard SQL syntax into the native SQL of the target data source. All SQL translations are the responsibility of the driver developer.

Applications are not limited to communicating through one driver. A single application can make multiple connections, each through a different driver, or multiple connections to similar sources through a single driver.

To access a new DBMS, a user or an administrator installs a driver for the DBMS. The user does not need a different version of the application to access the new DBMS. This is a tremendous benefit for end users, as well as providing significant savings for IS organizations in support and development costs.

What ODBC Means to the End User

End users do not work directly with the ODBC API, but they benefit in several ways when they use applications written with ODBC. Users may:

- Select a data source from a list of data source names or supply the name of a data source in a consistent way across applications.

- Submit data access requests in industry-standard SQL grammar regardless of the target DBMS.

- Access different DBMSs by using familiar desktop applications. When a requirement arises to access data on a new platform, users will have a common level of functional capabilities while accessing the new data with familiar tools.

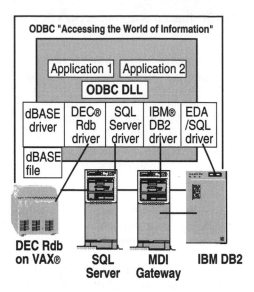

Figure 9.5   ODBC accessing the world of information

What ODBC Means to Application Developers

ODBC was designed to allow application developers to decide between using the least common denominator of functionality across DBMSs or exploiting the individual capabilities of specific DBMSs.

ODBC defines a standard SQL grammar and set of function calls that are based upon the SAG CLI specification, called the *core grammar* and *core functions*, respectively. If an application developer chooses only to use the core functionality, they need not write any additional code to check for specific capabilities of a driver.

With core functionality, an application can:

- Establish a connection with a data source, execute SQL statements, and retrieve results.

- Receive standard error messages.

- Provide a standard logon interface to the end user.

- Use a standard set of data types defined by ODBC.

- Use a standard SQL grammar defined by ODBC.

ODBC also defines an extended SQL grammar and set of extended functions to provide application developers with a standard way to exploit advanced capabilities of a DBMS. In addition to the above features, ODBC includes a set of extensions that provide enhanced performance and increased power through the following features:

- Data types such as date, time, timestamp, and binary.
- Scrollable cursors.
- A standard SQL grammar for scalar functions, outer joins, and procedures.
- Asynchronous execution.
- A standard way for application developers to find out what capabilities a driver and data source provide.

Finally, ODBC supports the use of DBMS-specific SQL grammar, allowing applications to exploit the capabilities of a particular DBMS.

What ODBC Means to Database Developers

One ODBC driver can be developed that provides access to the DBMS. Any ODBC application may then gain access to that DBMS. This provides a wider number and variety of tools that will work with the DBMS, resulting in larger market potential for vendors and a wider variety of tools for corporations to choose from.

Industry Commitment to ODBC

ODBC enjoys a great deal of industry momentum and acceptance as the dominant standard. Database vendors, with the help of third-party developers, have created drivers for their products. Several major application vendors have now shipped products which are ODBC-enabled. ODBC's acceptance to date is due to a variety of reasons:

- It is an implementation of the SAG CLI specification, and is therefore vendor-neutral and open. This open systems approach solves a problem common to everyone in the software industry.
- As a portable API, it can be a common data access language for both the Windows and Macintosh environments, and possibly other operating systems in the future.
- By providing different conformance levels, ODBC allows developers to choose between a least common denominator approach (allowing common access to the broadest set of DBMSs), and being able to fully exploit advanced feature sets in the more robust DBMSs.

The following databases will be supported by one or more database drivers by the end of 1993:

ADABAS SQL Server	IBM DB2/6000™	Quadbase
Btrieve®	IBM SQL/400®	Raima
CA-IDMS	IBM SQL/DS™	R:BASE®
CA-Datacom	Informix	Siemens/Nixdorf SESAM
CA-DB	Ingres	Siemens/Nixdorf UDSD
DAL	Integra SQL	SQL Server
dBASE	Interbase	SupraServer
DEC Rdb	Microsoft Access	Systems 2000
DEC RMS	Microsoft Excel	Tandem NonStop™ SQL
Focus®	Microsoft FoxPro	Teradata®
Formatted Text	Model 204	Text files
Gupta SQLBase®	NetWareSQL	UNIFY
HP® ALLBASE/SQL	Nomad Gateway	WATCOM SQL for Windows
HP Image®/SQL	ORACLE	White Cross 9000
IBI EDA/SQL™	Paradox™	XDB
IBM DB2	PICK	
IBM DB2/2™	Progress	

The following application vendors have released ODBC-enabled products or have publicly endorsed ODBC technology as of July 1993:

Andyne	JYACC
Approach Software	Knowledgeware
Blue Sky Software	LABTECH
Blyth	Lotus Development
Brio	mdbs
Bull HN	Micro Design International
Canaan Analytics	Microsoft Corporation
Cincom Systems, Inc.	Natural Language
Computer Corporation of America	Neuron Data
Clear Access	PageAhead Software Corp.
Cognos	Parcplace Systems
Computer Associates	Pilot Technologies
Coromandel	Pioneer Software Systems Corp.
CSA	Powersoft
DataEase International	Progress Software
Dharma Systems	Revelation
EASEL	SPC
Fairfield Software	SPSS
FileNet	Sterling Software
Genus Software	SoftwareTechnologies
Great Plains Software	The Dodge Group
Guild Software	Trinzic
Gupta Technologies, Inc.	Visionware
Hewlett-Packard Company	Winclient
Icons International	Xdb

Future Plans for ODBC

The next release of the ODBC Software Development Kit, version 2.0, will be available in the first quarter of 1994, and will provide considerable enhancements based on input from software vendors and corporate developers. The new version will support the 32-port technology of Windows NT, scrollable cursors independent of driver capability, additional sample applications, and sophisticated debugging tools.

Apple has endorsed ODBC technology and will continue to enable developers to exploit the power of ODBC. Apple has announced their ODBC Software Developers Kit and will announce additional ODBC-compatible drivers later this year. ODBC is a completely portable API, and may be ported to other major operating system environments in the future:

The Current Status of ODBC

ODBC is available for software vendors and corporate developers. The ODBC SDK includes development tools, documentation, a dBASE test driver for developing and testing ODBC applications, and an application for testing ODBC drivers. ODBC will be included in future versions of the Windows operating system. Microsoft has shipped numerous Windows-based applications with ODBC technology, and these products will continue to provide data connectivity through ODBC in future releases.

ODBC SDK

The Microsoft ODBC SDK contains everything necessary for developing Windows-based ODBC applications and drivers. The ODBC SDK version 1.0 includes the following:

- ODBC Programmer's Reference
- ODBC SDK Guide
- Sample source code
- Driver Manager DLL
- ODBC administrator (for configuring data sources)
- ODBC test program (for testing drivers)
- Visual Basic demonstration application
- dBASE test driver
- On-line Help

Apple has announced its ODBC Software Developers Kit, which enables Macintosh developers to build applications and drivers using ODBC. The kit consists of an installer disk, ODBC test application, a test DBMS driver, and other components to assist in the development of ODBC-compatible applications for the Macintosh. Please contact Apple for availability and pricing information.

Driver Catalog

The Microsoft *ODBC Driver Catalog* provides a quick reference for driver availability. This catalog contains key information on vendors that provide ODBC drivers, pricing, availability, and contacts.

Information Resources for ODBC

CompuServe provides the Windows Extension forum, which has an ODBC section. Please refer to this forum for updates on ODBC's status. The library in this section contains relevant files that may be downloaded. To access the forum from CompuServe, type GO WINEXT, and then select the ODBC section.

Technet, Microsoft's technical information network, is a community of support professionals, system integrators and solution builders, many of whom have experience implementing ODBC technology.

The Microsoft Developer Network publishes technical information for all developers who write applications for Microsoft operating systems or who use Microsoft development tools. ODBC-experienced developers contribute information to the network, which helps speed the acceptance and implementation of ODBC technology.

Summary

Providing data access to applications in today's heterogeneous database environment is very complex for software vendors as well as corporate developers. ODBC solves this data access problem for software vendors and corporations by providing a standard, open, and vendor-neutral API. ODBC allows corporations and software vendors to protect their investments in existing DBMSs, and protect developers' acquired DBMS skills. ODBC benefits users as more end-user applications connect to additional data sources, making the vast volumes of corporate data more readily available. ODBC is a portable API, which allows it to be a cross-platform tool. It is based upon the SQL Access Group (SAG) Call Level Interface (CLI) and provides a standard SQL language based upon ANSI standards. With ODBC, Microsoft provides many benefits to developers, end users, and the industry by creating a vendor-neutral, open, and powerful means of accessing data.

Topic

Describe the role of the Driver Manager.

Content

Role of the Driver Manager[2]

ODBC function calls are passed through the Driver Manager to the driver. An application typically links with the Driver Manager import library (ODBC.LIB) to gain access to the Driver Manager. When an application calls an ODBC function, the Driver Manager performs one of the following actions:

- For **SQLDataSources** and **SQLDrivers**, the Driver Manager processes the call. It does not pass the call to the driver.

- For **SQLGetFunctions**, the Driver Manager passes the call to the driver associated with the connection. If the driver does not support **SQLGetFunctions**, the Driver Manager processes the call.

- For **SQLAllocEnv**, **SQLAllocConnect**, **SQLSetConnectOption**, **SQLFreeConnect**, and **SQLFreeEnv**, the Driver Manager processes the call. The Driver Manager calls **SQLAllocEnv**, **SQLAllocConnect**, and **SQLSetConnectOption** in the driver when the application calls a function to connect to the data source (**SQLConnect**, **SQLDriverConnect**, or **SQLBrowseConnect**). The Driver Manager calls **SQLFreeConnect** and **SQLFreeEnv** in the driver when the application calls **SQLFreeConnect**.

- For **SQLConnect**, **SQLDriverConnect**, **SQLBrowseConnect**, and **SQLError**, the Driver Manager performs initial processing, then sends the call to the driver associated with the connection.

- For any other ODBC function, the Driver Manager passes the call to the driver associated with the connection.

If requested, the Driver Manager records each called function in a trace file after checking the function call for errors. The name of each function that does not contain errors detectable by the Driver Manager is recorded, along with the values of the input arguments and the names of the output arguments (as listed in the function definitions).

The Driver Manager also checks function arguments and state transitions, and for other error conditions before passing the call to the driver associated with the connection. This reduces the amount of error handling that a driver needs to

---

[2] Materials excerpted from Part 3 of the *ODBC 2.0 Programmer's Reference* in the Open Database Connectivity Software Development Kit 2.0. Copyright 1992 - 1995. Used with permission. All rights reserved.

perform. However, the Driver Manager does not check all arguments, state transitions, or error conditions for a given function. For complete information about what the Driver Manager checks, see the following sections, the Diagnostics section of each function in Chapter 22, "ODBC Function Reference," and the state transition tables in Appendix B, "ODBC State Transition Tables."

Topic

Describe the role of the data source.

Content

Role of Data Sources[3]

A data source consists of the data a user wants to access, its associated DBMS, the platform on which the DBMS resides, and the network (if any) used to access that platform. Each data source requires that a driver provide certain information in order to connect to it. At the core level, this is defined to be the name of the data source, a user ID, and a password. ODBC extensions allow drivers to specify additional information, such as a network address or additional passwords. The data source is responsible for:

- Processing SQL requests received from a driver.
- Returning results to a driver.
- Performing all other functions normally associated with a DBMS (concurrency control, transactions, and so on).

Topic

List the information necessary to connect to a data source.

Content

Accessing ODBC Data[4]

Using the methods and properties described earlier in this chapter, you can access

---

[3] Materials excerpted from "ODBC: Architecture, Performance, and Tuning," a backgrounder located on the Microsoft Developer Network Development Library. Copyright 1994. Used with permission. All rights reserved.
[4] Materials excerpted from Part 2 of *Advanced Topics* in the Office Developer's Kit 1.0. Copyright 1992 - 1995. Used with permission. All rights reserved.

data in ODBC databases such as SQL Server. The procedures for accessing the data in ODBC databases are similar to the procedures used to access data in the other external data sources. Special considerations and examples for using ODBC data are provided in the following sections.

Configuration

Before you can access external ODBC data sources using Microsoft Access, you may need to configure the following items on your workstation:

- Data source names
- Drivers and other associated software
- Timeout values

Data Source Names

As described earlier in this chapter, each ODBC data source is identified by an entry in the ODBC.INI file. Each data source name entry in the ODBC.INI file specifies connection information for the external data source, including network location, drivers, and attributes.

To add a data source name to your ODBC.INI file, you can use the ODBC option in the Windows Control Panel, the ODBC Administrator application (if you're using Windows 3.0), or the **RegisterDatabase** method of the **DBEngine** object.

To add a data source name using the ODBC option

1. In the Program Manager group containing the Control Panel, choose the Control Panel icon.
2. In the Control Panel window, choose the ODBC option.
3. Choose the Add button.
4. Follow the on-screen instructions. If you need help in completing any of the dialog boxes, choose the Help button.

To add a data source name using the RegisterDatabase method

- Use the following syntax:

   DBEngine.RegisterDatabase *dbname*, *driver*, *silent*, *attributes*

The **RegisterDatabase** arguments are as follows.

Argument	Description
dbname	A string expression indicating the data source name to add, for example, "SQLTEST". Often, the *dbname* is the name of the server.
driver	A string expression indicating the ODBC driver to use, for example, "SQL Server". The *driver* argument is the name of the driver, *not* the name of the DLL file, for example, *not* "SQLSRVR.DLL". To use **RegisterDatabase** to add a data source name using a particular driver, you must have already installed ODBC and the indicated driver.
silent	A Boolean value that is **True** if you don't want to display the ODBC driver dialog boxes that prompt for driver-specific information or **False** if you want to display the ODBC driver dialog boxes. If *silent* is **True**, then *attributes* must contain all the necessary driver-specific information.
attributes	A string expression indicating the list of keywords to be added to the ODBC.INI file. Each keyword in the list is delimited by a carriage return. If the database is already registered in the ODBC.INI file, the entry is updated. If **RegisterDatabase** fails, no changes are made to the ODBC.INI file, and an error occurs.

Here is an example of how to use the **RegisterDatabase** method to add a data source name for a SQL Server on the server \\PTLUDLOW:

```
Dim Attribs As String

'Build keywords string.
Attribs - "Description-SQL Server on server PtLudlow" & Chr$(13)
Attribs - Attribs & "OemToAnsi-No" & Chr$(13)
Attribs - Attribs & "Server-PtLudlow" & Chr$(13)
Attribs - Attribs & "Database-NWIND"
'Update ODBC.INI.
DBEngine.RegisterDatabase "PtLudlow", "SQL Server", True, Attribs
```

Note When adding a data source name for a Sybase SQL Server or a Microsoft SQL Server listening on an alternate pipe, in addition to the Server keyword shown in the preceding example, you must also include the Network and Address keywords in the keyword string. For example:

```
Atrribs - Attribs & Network=DBNMP3 & Chr$(13)
Atrribs - Attribs & Address-\PTLUDLOW\PIPE\ALT\QUERY & Chr$(13)
```

You can confirm that the entry was added by using either the ODBC option in the Windows Control Panel or the Microsoft ODBC Administrator application (if you're using Windows 3.0).

Drivers and Other Associated Software

Microsoft Access uses ODBC drivers when accessing tables in ODBC databases. Before you can connect to an ODBC database, the appropriate drivers and DLLs must be installed.

You install the appropriate ODBC driver for a database by running the ODBC Setup program. You can also install drivers for SQL Server using the Setup program on the ODBC disk included with Microsoft Access.

Important The ODBC driver must be Level 1 compliant.

After you install ODBC, you can change ODBC driver information at any time using either the ODBC option in the Windows Control Panel or the ODBC Administrator application (if you're using Windows 3.0).

For additional information, search Help for "ODBC drivers." For additional information about driver requirements for SQL Server, see the online Help file DRVSSRVR.HLP in the \WINDOWS\SYSTEM directory.

Timeout Values

Microsoft Access provides two timeout properties that you can set to control timeout values for connecting to external ODBC databases and for running queries that access external ODBC databases:

- LoginTimeout

  The LoginTimeout property indicates the number of seconds that Microsoft Access waits for an external ODBC server to respond to a connection request. This feature is especially useful when the default login timeout of 20 seconds is too short. Setting a higher timeout value is essential when using local area networks that rely on modems or long-distance bridges or in situations where network or server load prevent the server from responding in the allotted time. Setting the timeout to 0 causes no timeout to occur.

  To set a login timeout value, use the **DBEngine** object's LoginTimeout property. For example:

  ```
  DBEngine.LoginTimeout = 60
  ```

If you need to use different login timeout values for different databases, you can change the LoginTimeout property between calls to the **OpenDatabase** method.

- QueryTimeout or ODBCTimeout

Either the QueryTimeout or the ODBCTimeout property indicates the number of seconds that Microsoft Access waits for an external ODBC server to complete a query. After a query times out, the external server is told to stop processing the query, and your application receives an error. At this point you can re-run the query or inform the user that the query can't be completed.

If your ODBC server supports this functionality, you can use one of these properties to find out when queries have been blocked by heavy use or by locking problems on the external server. The default query timeout is 60 seconds. Setting a value of 0 causes no timeout to occur.

To set a query timeout value, you use the QueryTimeout property of the **Database** object or the ODBCTimeout property of the **QueryDef** object. For example:

```
CurrentDatabase.QueryTimeout = 120
:
```

Connection Information

When specifying connection information for ODBC data, use the following specifications.

For	Use
Data source name	A data source name from the ODBC.INI file
Source database type	ODBC
Database name	Zero-length string
Source table name	The object identifier for the table

Note If the connection string to an external ODBC data source is missing any information, when you first attempt to connect you're prompted for the missing information.

For syntax information, see "Specifying Connection Information" earlier in this chapter..

Topic

Describe where configuration information for each data source is stored for Microsoft Windows version 3.*x* and Microsoft Windows NT.

Content

Structure of the ODBC.INI File[5]

The ODBC.INI file is a Windows initialization file used in Windows 3.1 and Windows on Win32 (WOW). It is created by the installer DLL when data sources are first configured and contains the following sections:

- The [ODBC Data Sources] section lists the name of each available data source and the description of its associated driver.
- For each data source listed in the [ODBC Data Sources] section, there is a section that lists additional information about that data source.
- An optional section that specifies the default data source.
- An optional section that specifies ODBC options.

On Windows NT, this information is stored in the registry. The key structure in which it is stored is:

HKEY_CURRENT_USER
    Software
        ODBC
            ODBC.INI

A subkey of the ODBC.INI subkey is created for each section of the ODBC.INI file. A value is added to this subkey for each keyword-value pair in the section. The value's name is the same as the keyword, the value's data is the same as the value associated with the keyword, and the value's type is REG_SZ.

Note This section uses terminology for Windows initialization files. For the registry, you should substitute *ODBC.INI subkey* for *ODBC.INI file*, *subkey* for *section*, *value* for *keyword-value pair*, *value name* for *keyword*, and *value data* for *value*.

---

[5] Materials excerpted from Part 2 of the *ODBC 2.0 Programmer's Reference* in the Open Database Connectivity Software Development Kit 2.0. Copyright 1992 - 1995. Used with permission. All rights reserved.

For information on the general structure of Windows initialization files, see the Windows SDK documentation. For information on the Windows NT registry, see the Windows NT SDK documentation.

[ODBC Data Sources] Section

The [ODBC Data Sources] section lists the data sources specified by the user. Each entry in the section lists a data source and the description of the driver it uses. The driver description is usually the name of the associated DBMS. The format of the section is:

[ODBC Data Sources]
data-source-name1=driver-desc1
data-source-name2=driver-desc2

          .
          .
          .

For example, suppose a user has three data sources: Personnel and Inventory, which use formatted text files, and Payroll, which uses an SQL Server DBMS. The [ODBC Data Sources] section might contain the following entries:

```
[ODBC Data Sources]
Personnel=Text
Inventory=Text
Payroll=SQL Server
```

Topic

Describe the four scrollable cursor types in ODBC: static, keyset-driven, dynamic, and mixed.

Content

Using Block and Scrollable Cursors[6]

As originally designed, cursors in SQL only scroll forward through a result set, returning one row at a time. However, interactive applications often require forward and backward scrolling, absolute or relative positioning within the result set, and the ability to retrieve and update blocks of data, or *rowsets*.

---

[6] Materials excerpted from Part 2 of the *ODBC 2.0 Programmer's Reference* in the Open Database Connectivity Software Development Kit 2.0. Copyright 1992 - 1995. Used with permission. All rights reserved.

To retrieve and update rowset data, ODBC provides a *block* cursor attribute. To allow an application to scroll forwards or backwards through the result set, or move to an absolute or relative position in the result set, ODBC provides a *scrollable* cursor attribute. Cursors may have one or both attributes.

Block Cursors

An application calls **SQLSetStmtOption** with the SQL_ROWSET_SIZE option to specify the rowset size. The application can call **SQLSetStmtOption** to change the rowset size at any time. Each time the application calls **SQLExtendedFetch**, the driver returns the next *rowset size* rows of data. After the data is returned, the cursor points to the first row in the rowset. By default, the rowset size is one.

Scrollable Cursors

Applications have different needs in their ability to sense changes in the tables underlying a result set. For example, when balancing financial data, an accountant needs data that appears static; it is impossible to balance books when the data is continually changing. When selling concert tickets, a clerk needs up-to-the minute, or dynamic, data on which tickets are still available. Various cursor models are designed to meet these needs, each of which requires different sensitivities to changes in the tables underlying the result set.

Static Cursors

At one extreme are *static* cursors, to which the data in the underlying tables appears to be static. The membership, order, and values in the result set used by a static cursor are generally fixed when the cursor is opened. Rows updated, deleted, or inserted by other users (including other cursors in the same application) are not detected by the cursor until it is closed and then reopened; the SQL_STATIC_SENSITIVITY information type returns whether the cursor can detect rows it has updated, deleted, or inserted.

Static cursors are commonly implemented by taking a snapshot of the data or locking the result set. Note that in the former case, the cursor diverges from the underlying tables as other users make changes; in the latter case, other users are prohibited from changing the data.

Dynamic Cursors

At the other extreme are *dynamic* cursors, to which the data appears to be dynamic. The membership, order, and values in the result set used by a dynamic cursor are ever-changing. Rows updated, deleted, or inserted by all users (the cursor, other cursors in the same application, and other applications) are detected by the cursor when data is next fetched. Although ideal for many situations, dynamic cursors are difficult to implement.

Keyset-Driven Cursors

Between static and dynamic cursors are *keyset-driven* cursors, which have some of the attributes of each. Like static cursors, the membership and ordering of the result set of a keyset-driven cursor is generally fixed when the cursor is opened. Like dynamic cursors, most changes to the values in the underlying result set are visible to the cursor when data is next fetched.

When a keyset-driven cursor is opened, the driver saves the keys for the entire result set, thus fixing the membership and order of the result set. As the cursor scrolls through the result set, the driver uses the keys in this *keyset* to retrieve the current data values for each row in the rowset. Because data values are retrieved only when the cursor scrolls to a given row, updates to that row by other users (including other cursors in the same application) after the cursor was opened are visible to the cursor.

If the cursor scrolls to a row of data that has been deleted by other users (including other cursors in the same application), the row appears as a *hole* in the result set, since the key is still in the keyset but the row is no longer in the result set. Updating the key values in a row is considered to be deleting the existing row and inserting a new row; therefore, rows of data for which the key values have been changed also appear as holes. When the driver encounters a hole in the result set, it returns a status code of SQL_ROW_DELETED for the row.

Rows of data inserted into the result set by other users (including other cursors in the same application) after the cursor was opened are not visible to the cursor, since the keys for those rows are not in the keyset.

The SQL_STATIC_SENSITIVITY information type returns whether the cursor can detect rows it has deleted or inserted. Because updating key values in a keyset-driven cursor is considered to be deleting the existing row and inserting a new row, keyset-driven cursors can always detect rows they have updated.

Mixed (Keyset/Dynamic) Cursors

If a result set is large, it may be impractical for the driver to save the keys for the entire result set. Instead, the application can use a *mixed* cursor. In a mixed cursor, the keyset is smaller than the result set, but larger than the rowset.

Within the boundaries of the keyset, a mixed cursor is keyset-driven, that is, the driver uses keys to retrieve the current data values for each row in the rowset.

When a mixed cursor scrolls beyond the boundaries of the keyset, it becomes dynamic, that is, the driver simply retrieves the next *rowset size* rows of data. The driver then constructs a new keyset, which contains the new rowset.

For example, assume a result set has 1000 rows and uses a mixed cursor with a keyset size of 100 and a rowset size of 10. When the cursor is opened, the driver (depending on the implementation) saves keys for the first 100 rows and retrieves data for the first 10 rows. If another user deletes row 11 and the cursor then scrolls to row 11, the cursor will detect a hole in the result set; the key for row 11 is in the keyset but the data is no longer in the result set. This is the same behavior as a keyset-driven cursor. However, if another user deletes row 101 and the cursor then scrolls to row 101, the cursor will not detect a hole; the key for the row 101 is not in the keyset. Instead, the cursor will retrieve the data for the row that was originally row 102. This is the same behavior as a dynamic cursor.

Specifying the Cursor Type

To specify the cursor type, an application calls **SQLSetStmtOption** with the SQL_CURSOR_TYPE option. The application can specify a cursor that only scrolls forward, a static cursor, a dynamic cursor, a keyset-driven cursor, or a mixed cursor. If the application specifies a mixed cursor, it also specifies the size of the keyset used by the cursor.

Note To use the ODBC cursor library, an application calls **SQLSetConnectOption** with the SQL_ODBC_CURSORS option before it connects to the data source. The cursor library supports block scrollable cursors. It also supports positioned update and delete statements. For more information, see Appendix G, "ODBC Cursor Library."

Unless the cursor is a forward-only cursor, an application calls **SQLExtendedFetch** to scroll the cursor backwards, forwards, or to an absolute or relative position in the result set. The application calls **SQLSetPos** to refresh the row currently pointed to by the cursor.

Specifying Cursor Concurrency

Concurrency is the ability of more than one user to use the same data at the same time. A transaction is *serializable* if it is performed in a manner in which it appears as if no other transactions operate on the same data at the same time. For example, assume one transaction doubles data values and another adds 1 to data values. If the transactions are serializable and both attempt to operate on the values 0 and 10 at the same time, the final values will be 1 and 21 or 2 and 22, depending on which transaction is performed first. If the transactions are not serializable, the final values will be 1 and 21, 2 and 22, 1 and 22, or 2 and 21; the sets of values 1 and 22, and 2 and 21, are the result of the transactions acting on each value in a different order.

Serializability is considered necessary to maintain database integrity. For cursors, it is most easily implemented at the expense of concurrency by locking the result set. A compromise between serializability and concurrency is *optimistic concurrency control*. In a cursor using optimistic concurrency control, the driver does not lock rows when it retrieves them. When the application requests an update or delete operation, the driver or data source checks if the row has changed. If the row has not changed, the driver or data source prevents other transactions from changing the row until the operation is complete. If the row has changed, the transaction containing the update or delete operation fails.

To specify the concurrency used by a cursor, an application calls **SQLSetStmtOption** with the SQL_CONCURRENCY option. The application can specify that the cursor is read-only, locks the result set, uses optimistic concurrency control and compares row versions to determine if a row has changed, or uses optimistic concurrency control and compares data values to determine if a row has changed. The application calls **SQLSetPos** to lock the row currently pointed to by the cursor, regardless of the specified cursor concurrency.

Topic

Define bookmarks.

Content

Using Bookmarks[7]

A bookmark is a 32-bit value that an application uses to return to a row. The application does not request that the driver places a bookmark on a row; instead, the application requests a bookmark that it can use to return to a row. For example, if a bookmark is a row number, an application requests the row number of a row and stores it. Later, the application passes this row number back to the driver and requests that the driver return to the row.

---

[7] Materials excerpted from Part 2 of the *ODBC 2.0 Programmer's Reference* in the Open Database Connectivity Software Development Kit 2.0. Copyright 1992 - 1995. Used with permission. All rights reserved.

Before opening the cursor, an application must call **SQLSetStmtOption** with the SQL_USE_BOOKMARKS option to inform the driver it will use bookmarks. After opening the cursor, the application retrieves bookmarks either from column 0 of the result set or by calling **SQLGetStmtOption** with the SQL_GET_BOOKMARK option. To retrieve a bookmark from the result set, the application either binds column 0 and calls **SQLExtendedFetch** or calls **SQLGetData**; in either case, the *fCType* argument must be set to SQL_C_BOOKMARK. To return to the row specified by a bookmark, the application calls **SQLExtendedFetch** with a fetch type of SQL_FETCH_BOOKMARK.

If a bookmark requires more than 32 bits, such as when it is a key value, the driver maps the bookmarks requested by the application to 32-bit binary values. The 32-bit binary values are then returned to the application. Because this mapping may require considerable memory, applications should only bind column 0 of the result set if they will actually use bookmarks for most rows. Otherwise, they should call **SQLGetStmtOption** with the SQL_BOOKMARK statement option or call **SQLGetData** for column 0.

Before an application opens a cursor with which it will use bookmarks, it:

- Calls **SQLSetStmtOption** with the SQL_USE_BOOKMARKS option and a value of SQL_UB_ON.

To retrieve a bookmark for the current row, an application:

- Retrieves the value from column 0 of the rowset. The application can either call **SQLBindCol** to bind column 0 before it calls **SQLExtendedFetch** or call **SQLGetData** to retrieve the data after it calls **SQLExtendedFetch**. In either case, the *fCType* argument must be SQL_C_BOOKMARK.

Note To determine whether it can call **SQLGetData** for a block (more than one row) of data and whether it can call **SQLGetData** for a column before the last bound column, an application calls **SQLGetInfo** with the SQL_GETDATA_EXTENSIONS information type.

−Or−

Calls **SQLSetPos** with the SQL_POSITION option to position the cursor on the row and calls **SQLGetStmtOption** with the SQL_BOOKMARK option to retrieve the bookmark.

To return to the row specified by a bookmark (or a row a certain number of rows from the bookmark), an application:

- Calls **SQLExtendedFetch** with the *irow* argument set to the bookmark and the *fFetchType* argument set to SQL_FETCH_BOOKMARK. The driver returns the rowset starting with the row identified by the bookmark.

Topic

Describe the cursor library in ODBC.

Content

ODBC Cursor Library[8]

The ODBC cursor library (ODBCCURS.DLL on Windows 3.1 and ODBCCR32.DLL on Windows NT) supports block scrollable cursors for any driver that complies with the Level 1 API conformance level; it can be redistributed by developers with their applications or drivers. The cursor library also supports positioned update and delete statements for result sets generated by **SELECT** statements. Although it only supports static and forward-only cursors, the cursor library satisfies the needs of many applications. Furthermore, it provides good performance, especially for small- to medium-sized result sets.

The cursor library is a dynamic-link library (DLL) that resides between the Driver Manager and the driver. When an application calls a function, the Driver Manager calls the function in the cursor library, which either executes the function or calls it in the specified driver. For a given connection, an application specifies whether the cursor library is always used, used if the driver does not support scrollable cursors, or never used.

To implement block cursors in **SQLExtendedFetch**, the cursor library repeatedly calls **SQLFetch** in the driver. To implement scrolling, it caches the data it has retrieved in memory and in disk files. When an application requests a new rowset, the cursor library retrieves it as necessary from the driver or the cache.

To implement positioned update and delete statements, the cursor library constructs an **UPDATE** or **DELETE** statement with a **WHERE** clause that specifies the cached value of each bound column in the row. When it executes a positioned update statement, the cursor library updates its cache from the values in the rowset buffers.

---

[8] Materials excerpted from Part 6 of the *ODBC 2.0 Programmer's Reference* in the Open Database Connectivity Software Development Kit 2.0. Copyright 1992 - 1995. Used with permission. All rights reserved.

CHAPTER   10

Open Database Connectivity (ODBC) 2.0 Advanced Topics

Topics

List and describe the ODBC API and SQL conformance levels.
Describe the differences between Core, Level 1, and Level 2 ODBC interfaces at the API level.

Content

ODBC Conformance Levels[1]

ODBC defines conformance levels for drivers in two areas: the ODBC API and the ODBC SQL grammar (which includes the ODBC SQL data types). Conformance levels help both application and driver developers by establishing standard sets of functionality. Applications can easily determine whether a driver provides the functionality they need. Drivers can be developed to support a broad selection of applications without being concerned about the specific requirements of each application.

To claim that it conforms to a given API or SQL conformance level, a driver must support all the functionality in that conformance level, regardless of whether that functionality is supported by the DBMS associated with the driver. However, conformance levels do not restrict drivers to the functionality in the levels to which they conform. Driver developers are encouraged to support as much functionality as they can; applications can determine the functionality supported by a driver by calling **SQLGetInfo**, **SQLGetFunctions**, and **SQLGetTypeInfo**.

---

[1] Materials excerpted from Part 1 of the *ODBC 2.0 Programmer's Reference* in the Open Database Connectivity Software Development Kit 2.0. Copyright 1992 - 1995. Used with permission. All rights reserved.

API Conformance Levels

The ODBC API defines a set of core functions that correspond to the functions in the X/Open and SQL Access Group Call Level Interface specification. ODBC also defines two extended sets of functionality, Level 1 and Level 2. The following list summarizes the functionality included in each conformance level.

Important Many ODBC applications require that drivers support all of the functions in the Level 1 API conformance level. To ensure that their driver works with most ODBC applications, driver developers should implement all Level 1 functions.

Core API

- Allocate and free environment, connection, and statement handles.
- Connect to data sources. Use multiple statements on a connection.
- Prepare and execute SQL statements. Execute SQL statements immediately.
- Assign storage for parameters in an SQL statement and result columns.
- Retrieve data from a result set. Retrieve information about a result set.
- Commit or roll back transactions.
- Retrieve error information.

Level 1 API

- Core API functionality.
- Connect to data sources with driver-specific dialog boxes.
- Set and inquire values of statement and connection options.
- Send part or all of a parameter value (useful for long data).
- Retrieve part or all of a result column value (useful for long data).
- Retrieve catalog information (columns, special columns, statistics, and tables).
- Retrieve information about driver and data source capabilities, such as supported data types, scalar functions, and ODBC functions.

Level 2 API

- Core and Level 1 API functionality.
- Browse connection information and list available data sources.
- Send arrays of parameter values. Retrieve arrays of result column values.
- Retrieve the number of parameters and describe individual parameters.
- Use a scrollable cursor.

- Retrieve the native form of an SQL statement.
- Retrieve catalog information (privileges, keys, and procedures).
- Call a translation DLL.

For a list of functions and their conformance levels, see Chapter 21, "Function Summary."

Note Each function description in this manual indicates whether the function is a core function or a level 1 or level 2 extension function.

SQL Conformance Levels

ODBC defines a core grammar that roughly corresponds to the X/Open and SQL Access Group SQL CAE specification (1992). ODBC also defines a minimum grammar, to meet a basic level of ODBC conformance, and an extended grammar, to provide for common DBMS extensions to SQL. The following list summarizes the grammar included in each conformance level.

Minimum SQL Grammar

- Data Definition Language (DDL): **CREATE TABLE** and **DROP TABLE**.
- Data Manipulation Language (DML): simple **SELECT**, **INSERT**, **UPDATE SEARCHED**, and **DELETE SEARCHED**.
- Expressions: simple (such as **A > B + C**).
- Data types: CHAR, VARCHAR, or LONG VARCHAR.

Core SQL Grammar

- Minimum SQL grammar and data types.
- DDL: **ALTER TABLE, CREATE INDEX, DROP INDEX, CREATE VIEW, DROP VIEW, GRANT,** and **REVOKE**.
- DML: full **SELECT**.
- Expressions: subquery, set functions such as **SUM** and **MIN**.
- Data types: DECIMAL, NUMERIC, SMALLINT, INTEGER, REAL, FLOAT, DOUBLE PRECISION.

Extended SQL Grammar

- Minimum and Core SQL grammar and data types.
- DML: outer joins, positioned **UPDATE**, positioned **DELETE, SELECT FOR UPDATE**, and unions.

> **Note** In ODBC 1.0, positioned update, positioned delete, and **SELECT FOR UPDATE** statements and the **UNION** clause were part of the core SQL grammar; in ODBC 2.0, they are part of the extended grammar. Applications that use the SQL conformance level to determine whether these statements are supported also need to check the version number of the driver to correctly interpret the information. In particular, applications that use these features with ODBC 1.0 drivers need to explicitly check for these capabilities in ODBC 2.0 drivers.

- Expressions: scalar functions such as **SUBSTRING** and **ABS**, date, time, and timestamp literals.
- Data types: BIT, TINYINT, BIGINT, BINARY, VARBINARY, LONG VARBINARY, DATE, TIME, TIMESTAMP
- Batch SQL statements.
- Procedure calls.

For more information about SQL statements and conformance levels, see Appendix C, "SQL Grammar." The grammar listed in Appendix C is not intended to restrict the set of statements that an application can submit for execution. Drivers should support data source–specific extensions to the SQL language, although interoperable applications should not rely on those extensions.

For more information about data types, see Appendix D, "Data Types."

Topic

Describe the advantages and disadvantages of using native SQL versus ODBC SQL.

Content

Native SQL versus ODBC SQL[2]

Native SQL, or Transact-SQL, is typically passed directly through to SQL Server using DB-Library. By directly passing native T-SQL commands using the DB-Library API, a programmer gains a higher degree of SQL-Server specific functionality. ODBC SQL, in contrast, consists of a generic SQL language that is

---

[2] Copyright 1995 Microsoft Corporation. Used with permission. All rights reserved.

not specific to SQL Server. Using SQL pass-through with ODBC does not require the programmer to know the intricacies of Transact-SQL. Instead, generic ODBC SQL commands are translated by the ODBC driver into an understandable Transact-SQL language which is then passed on to the SQL Server for processing. In ODBC SQL the user is shielded from learning a specific flavor of SQL language and can apply the generic language to many other products that use ODBC SQL.

Topics

List and describe the different types of multiple-tier drivers.

Describe the impact of single-tier versus multiple-tier drivers on performance.

Describe performance issues related to prepared execution versus those related to direct execution.

Describe performance issues related to opening and closing connections.

Content

ODBC: Architecture, Performance, and Tuning[3]

Colleen Lambert

Abstract

Open database connectivity (ODBC) is Microsoft's strategic interface for accessing data in a heterogeneous environment of relational and nonrelational database management systems (DBMSs). Even though ODBC has enjoyed growing industry support, various reports of poor performance have surfaced among MIS professionals, analysts, and engineers. Most of these reports are based on a lack of understanding of the ODBC architecture, improper use of ODBC within applications, and poorly optimized ODBC drivers.

---

[3] This backgrounder is also available on the Microsoft Developer Network Development Library under Backgrounders and White Papers, Operating System Extensions. Copyright 1994. Used with permission. All rights reserved.

This article first outlines some of the causes of poor performance, and presents the architecture of ODBC as an overview. A cross-section of applications is discussed with respect to how each utilizes ODBC. Inspection of these applications provides an insight into situations in which performance may suffer.

Finally, the article suggests various techniques for optimizing performance of applications using ODBC and ODBC drivers.

Introduction

Many MIS decision-makers, analysts, field engineers, and independent software vendors (ISVs) believe that open database connectivity (ODBC) performance is poor. The overall effect of this perception has been that ODBC is being positioned as a low-performance solution for decision support to be used only when connectivity to multiple databases is an absolute requirement. This article will review the architecture of ODBC and applications using ODBC. To adequately explore these topics, it is necessary to discuss the Microsoft Jet database engine used by Microsoft Access and Visual Basic version 3.0. The latter part of the article discusses various application and driver optimizations to promote better performance.

Functionality Versus Performance

Oddly, the perception of poor ODBC performance was, in part, perpetuated by a lack of understanding of the Jet architecture. Jet, used in Microsoft Access and Visual Basic 3.0, is an advanced database management system (DBMS) technology that provides a means of accessing desktop databases as well as remote client-server databases. As an advanced DBMS, Jet requires a very rich and functional cursor model. Although ODBC does not utilize Jet, Jet makes heavy use of ODBC for accessing remote databases. Figure 10.1 illustrates the relationship of Jet to ODBC and applications such as Microsoft Access and Visual Basic.{}

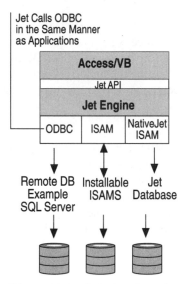

Figure 10.1   Relationship of Jet to ODBC.

Many of the performance issues attributed solely to ODBC were likely caused by:

- Inappropriate selection of development tools for the desired level of functionality (ODBC versus Microsoft Access or Visual Basic).
- Under-utilization of the database technology used by the development tools.
- The state of many of the ODBC drivers. Some were not optimized and thus clouded the whole performance issue.

Further adding to the confusion has been the theorizing of many analysts. They surmise that because ODBC adds more layers, it is therefore slower than using a proprietary interface. While some drivers do add additional layers by mapping to the proprietary interface, other drivers, such as Microsoft SQL Server, bypass the proprietary interface and emit the database protocol directly. However, even with extra layers, the overhead in a client-server application on the network and at the server far exceeds any overhead at the client in terms of overall performance and is therefore insignificant.

Some developers have also suggested that ODBC performance is poor. They cite the lack of static SQL (structured query language) support in ODBC as a cause of poor performance. Without this feature they conclude that the same level of performance cannot be achieved. This argument is not any different from comparing a proprietary, embedded API to a typical call-level interface. Vendors that support both, such as Sybase and Oracle, have moved to using stored procedures to achieve the same performance benefits. Since ODBC supports stored procedures, ODBC can make the same claim.

When to Expect Decreased Performance

The assertion that ODBC's performance is always equal to if not better than all other solutions is false. There are a few instances where ODBC may be slower. For example, depending on the driver's implementation for loading and connecting, ODBC may take longer to connect to the data source than using a proprietary API. This is related to the amount of work done under the covers during connection in order to support ODBC capabilities.

Specifically, there is the time for the Driver Manager to load the driver DLL (dynamic-link library); this time will vary depending on how the driver writer specified that segments should be loaded. Also, some drivers such as the Microsoft SQL Server driver, by default, request information (such as user-defined data type information and system information) from the server at connect time. Usually the driver will expose an option to disable retrieval of such information for applications where those items are not important, which gives equivalent performance to native API connections.

Drivers to non-SQL databases such as dBASE will, in fact, be slower than going through dBASE directly in certain cases. Some people expect ODBC to have the same performance with this data going through SQL as with using the native interface. This is simply not true in all cases. On the other hand, using SQL as the interface provides operations that are not available in non-SQL databases.

PC databases are built on ISAMs, which have a different data model than SQL. Some things are much easier and faster with ISAMs, such as scrolling, single table operations, and indexed operations. But others are difficult if not impossible, such as joins, aggregations, expressions, and general Boolean queries. Neither model is better; it depends on the features required by the application. For example, when an application looks for all the people in the EMPLOYEE table ordered by an index on NAME, the ISAM interface will have better performance than a SQL engine every time. But if an application needs to calculate the average age of EMPLOYEEs in all the DEPARTMENTs with more than 20 employees, SQL is much easier to program. In this example, you could accomplish the operation with an aggregate and a GROUP BY and a HAVING clause, and would have performance equivalent to the code required in the native interface, such as dBASE.

The Purpose of This Article

The goal of this article is to demystify the ODBC architecture and to suggest techniques to tune applications and drivers for optimal performance.

ODBC Architecture

Part of the perception of poor performance is related to a lack of understanding of the architecture of ODBC. Without an understanding of the architecture, performance issues become matters of speculation. By understanding the architecture, applications and drivers may be tuned in very specific ways to enhance performance.

Architectural Overview

The ODBC architecture has four components: .

- Application: performs processing and calls ODBC functions to submit SQL statements and retrieve results.

- Driver Manager: loads drivers on behalf of an application.

- Driver: processes ODBC function calls, submits SQL requests to a specific data source, and returns results to the application. If necessary, the driver modifies an application's request so that the request conforms to syntax supported by the associated DBMS.

- Data source: consists of the data the user wants to access and its associated operating system, DBMS, and network platform (if any) used to access the DBMS.

The Driver Manager and driver appear to an application as one unit that processes ODBC function calls. Figure 10.2 illustrates the relationship among the four components.

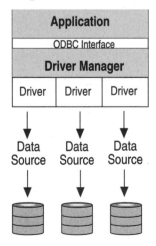

Figure 10.2   ODBC architecture.

Role of Applications

To interact with a data source, an application:

- Connects to the data source. It specifies the data source name and any additional information needed to complete the connection.
- Processes one or more SQL statements:
    - The application places the SQL text string in a buffer. If the statement includes parameter markers, it sets the parameter values.
    - If the statement returns a result set, the application assigns a cursor name for the statement or allows the driver to do so.
    - The application submits the statement for prepared or immediate execution.
    - If the statement creates a result set, the application can inquire about the attributes of the result set, such as the number of columns and the name and type of a specific column. It assigns storage for each column in the result set and fetches the results.
    - If the statement causes an error, the application retrieves error information from the driver and takes appropriate action.
- Ends each transaction by committing it or rolling it back.
- Terminates the connection when it has finished interacting with the data source.

The following diagram (Figure 10.3) lists the ODBC function calls that an application makes to connect to a data source, process SQL statements, and disconnect from the data source. Depending on its needs, an application may call other ODBC functions.

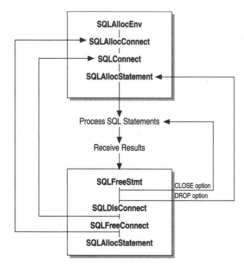

Figure 10.3   ODBC application function calls.

Additionally, an application can provide a variety of features external to the ODBC interface, including mail, spreadsheet capabilities, online transaction processing, and report generation. The application may or may not interact with users.

Role of the Driver Manager

The Driver Manager exists as a dynamic-link library (DLL). The primary purpose of the Driver Manager is to load ODBC drivers. In addition, the Driver Manager:

- Processes several ODBC initialization and information calls.
- Passes ODBC function calls from application to driver.
- Performs error and state checking.
- Logs function calls made by applications (optional).

Process ODBC initialization calls

The Driver Manager processes all or a large part of many ODBC functions before passing the call to the driver (if ever). This is the case with many of the information and connection functions.

Information functions

SQLDataSources and **SQLDrivers** are processed exclusively by the Driver Manager. These calls are never passed to the driver. For **SQLGetFunctions**, the Driver Manager processes the call if the driver does not support **SQLGetFunctions**.

Connection functions

For **SQLAllocEnv, SQLAllocConnect, SQLSetConnectOption, SQLFreeConnect**, and **SQLFreeEnv**, the Driver Manager processes the call. The Driver Manager calls **SQLAllocEnv, SQLAllocConnect**, and **SQLSetConnectOption** in the driver when the application calls a function to connect to the data source (**SQLConnect, SQLDriverConnect**, or **SQLBrowseConnect**). The Driver Manager calls **SQLFreeConnect** and **SQLFreeEnv** in the driver when the application calls **SQLFreeConnect**.

For **SQLConnect, SQLDriverConnect, SQLBrowseConnect**, and **SQLError**, the Driver Manager performs the initial processing, then sends the call to the driver associated with the connection.

Pass function calls from application to driver

For any other ODBC function, the Driver Manager passes the call to the driver associated with the connection.

Perform error and state checking

The Driver Manager also checks function arguments and state transitions, and checks for other error conditions before passing the call to the driver associated with the connection. This reduces the amount of error handling that a driver needs to perform. However, the Driver Manager does not check all arguments, state transitions, or error conditions for a given function. For complete information about what the Driver Manager checks, see the "Diagnostics" section of each function in the ODBC *Function Reference* and the state transition tables in Appendix B of the ODBC Software Development Kit (SDK).

Log function calls made by applications

If requested, the Driver Manager records each called function in a trace file after checking the function call for errors. The name of each function that does not contain errors detectable by the Driver Manager is recorded, along with the values of the input arguments and the names of the output arguments (as listed in the function definitions).

Role of Drivers

A driver is a DLL that implements ODBC function calls and interacts with a data source.

The Driver Manager loads a driver when the application calls the **SQLBrowseConnect**, **SQLConnect**, or **SQLDriverConnect** function.

A driver performs the following tasks in response to ODBC function calls from an application:

- Establishes a connection to a data source.
- Submits requests to the data source.
- Translates data to or from other formats, if requested by the application.
- Returns results to the application.
- Formats errors into standard error codes and returns them to the application.
- Declares and manipulates cursors if necessary. (This operation is invisible to the application unless there is a request for access to a cursor name.)
- Initiates transactions if the data source requires explicit transaction initiation. (This operation is invisible to the application.)

Role of Data Sources

A data source consists of the data a user wants to access, its associated DBMS, the platform on which the DBMS resides, and the network (if any) used to access that platform. Each data source requires that a driver provide certain information in order to connect to it. At the core level, this is defined to be the name of the data source, a user ID, and a password. ODBC extensions allow drivers to specify additional information, such as a network address or additional passwords. The data source is responsible for:

- Processing SQL requests received from a driver.

- Returning results to a driver.

- Performing all other functions normally associated with a DBMS (concurrency control, transactions, and so on).

Driver Architecture

There are two basic types of drivers in ODBC: single tier and multiple tier. With single-tier drivers, the driver processes both ODBC calls and SQL statements. In this case, the driver performs part of the data source functionality. With multiple-tier drivers, the driver processes ODBC calls and passes SQL statements to the data source. One system can contain both types of configurations. Let's take a more detailed look at the architecture of these drivers.

Single-Tier Drivers

Single-tier drivers are intended for non-SQL–based databases. The database file is processed directly by the driver. The driver processes SQL statements and retrieves information from the database. SQL statements, once parsed and translated, are passed to the database as basic file operations. A driver that manipulates an Xbase file is an example of a single-tier implementation.

A single-tier driver may limit the set of SQL statements that may be submitted. The minimum set of SQL statements that must be supported by a single-tier driver is defined in the ODBC SDK *Programmer's Reference* in Appendix C, "SQL Grammar."

Single-tier drivers are generally slower than using the native DBMS tools such as Microsoft FoxPro® because they parse and translate the SQL statements into basic file operations. The degree to which they are slower depends on how optimized this process is. Difference in speed between two different single-tier drivers is usually attributed to the method of optimization.

Figure 10.4 illustrates a typical situation in which the data source resides on the same computer as the other components of ODBC. Note that the driver contains logic to access the data source.

· Application
· Driver Manager
· Driver (Includes Data Access Software)

   ↕ File I/O
· Data Source, i.e. dBASE®

Figure 10.4   Single-tier driver and data source on same computer.

With the use of single-tier drivers, the data source need not be restricted to the same computer. These drivers can also be used in classic file/server configurations, as Figure 10.5 illustrates.

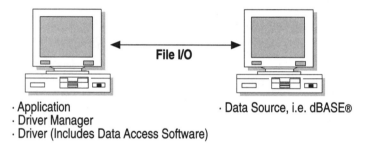

· Application   · Data Source, i.e. dBASE®
· Driver Manager
· Driver (Includes Data Access Software)

Figure 10.5   Single-tier driver using a client-server.

Multiple-Tier Drivers

In a multiple-tier configuration, the driver sends requests to a server that processes these requests. The requests may be SQL or a DBMS-specific format. Although the entire installation may reside on a single system, it is more often divided across platforms. Typically, the application, driver, and Driver Manager reside on one system, called the client. The database and the software that controls access to the database reside on another system, called the server. There are two types of multiple-tier drivers: two-tier and three-tier (or gateway).

Two-tier drivers

Among two-tier drivers, there are two variations. The variations are conveniently defined in terms of SQL functionality, being either SQL-based or non-SQL–based.

Drivers for SQL-based DBMSs, such as Oracle or Sybase, lend themselves to a fairly straightforward implementation. The ODBC driver on the client side passes SQL statements directly to the server-based DBMS using the database's data stream. The DBMS handles all processing of the SQL statements. Figure 10.6 illustrates the relationship of the ODBC driver to the SQL-based DBMS.

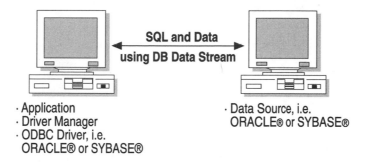

· Application
· Driver Manager
· ODBC Driver, i.e.
  ORACLE® or SYBASE®

· Data Source, i.e.
  ORACLE® or SYBASE®

Figure 10.6   ODBC driver for SQL-based DBMS.

Non-SQL–based DBMSs require extra code on the server side to parse and translate the SQL to the native database format. There are currently two significant implementations of this. In the first (Figure 10.7), SQL is completely parsed and translated to basic file I/O operations. These file operations act on proprietary data on the client side.

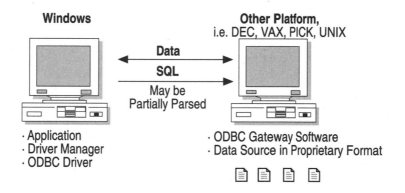

· Application
· Driver Manager
· ODBC Driver

· ODBC Gateway Software
· Data Source in Proprietary Format

Figure 10.7   Non-SQL DBMS ODBC implementation using client-side SQL engine.

In the second implementation, SQL statements are parsed and translated into the native database format on the server side. There may be some partial parsing on the client side as well. Figure 10.8 illustrates this implementation.

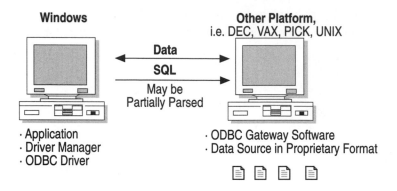

Figure 10.8 **Non-SQL DBMS ODBC implementation using server-side SQL engine.**

Three-tier (gateway) drivers

Another type of multiple-tier configuration is a gateway architecture. The driver passes SQL requests to a gateway process, which in turn sends the requests to the data source residing on a host. Gateway drivers may support both SQL-based and non-SQL–based gateways.

Often the gateway is simply a network communications-level gateway such as in Figure 10.9. In this case, SQL is passed all the way to the host. This is the architecture of the Information Builders Inc. EDA/SERVER product.

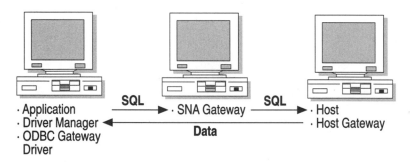

Figure 10.9 **Network communications-level gateway**

In other implementations, the gateway parses and translates SQL into DBMS-specific SQL or DBMS-specific format. Gateway code on the host is also typically required. Figure 10.10 illustrates this architecture. MicroDecisionware provides an ODBC driver based on this architecture.

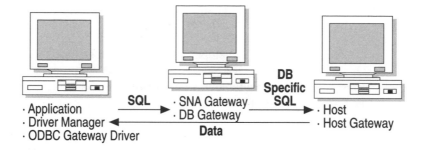

Figure 10.10   Three-tier driver using database gateway.

Yet another architecture is the distributed relational database architecture (DRDA). Wall Data™ has written an ODBC driver that accommodates DRDA. Figure 10.11 depicts the implementation.

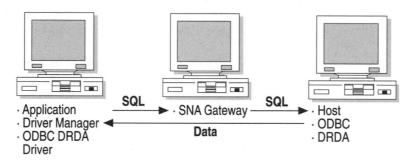

Figure 10.11   ODBC DRDA implementation.

Applications Architecture

Many Microsoft and third-party applications and libraries exploit ODBC functionality. Understanding how they utilize ODBC is useful when exploring ODBC performance issues related to use of these applications.

Microsoft Query and Microsoft Word

These applications call ODBC directly via the ODBC API. Word also uses ODBC for mail merges utilizing data sources. This is transparent to the user.

Microsoft Query is a tool that queries ODBC data sources. It is intended as an end-user application and is written in such a manner that it calls ODBC directly.

Performance of Microsoft Query is affected only by the level of optimization of the driver.

The Microsoft Word Developer's Kit provides ODBC extensions for WordBasic. This permits direct ODBC access to any DBMS that supports ODBC via ODBC drivers. The kit is available from Microsoft Press, and includes a disk that contains the ODBC extensions for WordBasic. When using WordBasic and ODBC, performance will depend on the user's coding techniques (with respect to ODBC) and the level of optimization within the ODBC driver.

Jet

Like ODBC, Jet provides transparent access to any database in your environment, regardless of the data's location and format. Jet is built around a keyset-driven cursor model. This means data is retrieved and updated based on key values. A key value is a value that uniquely identifies each record in a table.

The keyset model introduces complexities in how Jet operates against ODBC data sources. Traditional relational database environments use a dataset-driven model; that is, the data in a result set is thought of as one set of records. A DBMS may provide cursor capability on the set of records within the DBMS itself, enabling the client to scroll around in the data and update specific records, but typically this is not the case. So Jet itself must implement this functionality.

Visual Basic and Microsoft Access both use the Jet engine. Remember Figure 10.1? It overstated Visual Basic's use of the Jet engine. The following figure (Figure 10.12) clarifies the relationship.

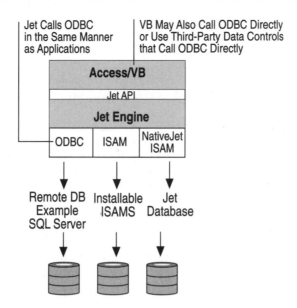

Figure 10.12   Microsoft Access/Visual Basic relationship to Jet.

So what is it that makes Jet different from ODBC? It is helpful to answer this in terms of functionality. One difference is ease of use. The use of Jet is generally transparent to users of Visual Basic and Microsoft Access. Another difference is found in the cursor model. Although the ODBC API provides the same level of functionality that Jet cursors do, not all ODBC drivers support that functionality. The ODBC cursor library in ODBC 2.0 provides a subset of the existing ODBC functionality. The ODBC cursor library supports only the snapshot cursor model with limited update capability. With Jet, both snapshot and keyset cursors are provided, and the update capabilities are more extensive.

Jet cursors

When Jet executes a query, the result set returned is either a dynaset or a snapshot. A dynaset is a live, updatable view of the data in the underlying tables. Changes to the data in the underlying tables are reflected in the dynaset as the user scrolls, and changes to the dynaset data are immediately reflected in the underlying tables. A snapshot is a nonupdatable, unchanging view of the data in the underlying tables. The result sets for dynasets and snapshots are populated in different manners.

Result set population

A snapshot is populated by executing a query that pulls back all the selected columns of the rows meeting the query's criteria. A dynaset, on the other hand, is populated by a query that selects only the key columns of each qualifying row; and the actual data is retrieved via a separate query using the key values to select the row data. In both cases, these result sets are stored in memory (overflowing to disk if very large), allowing you to scroll around arbitrarily

Microsoft Access and Visual Basic populate the result set slightly differently. Microsoft Access is optimized to return answers to you as quickly as possible; as soon as the first screen of result data is available, Microsoft Access paints it. The remainder is fetched as follows:

- User scrolling: Many user actions (for example, page down, go to last record, and search) require Microsoft Access to partially or completely populate the query's result set. A snapshot fetches all data up to the position scrolled to; a dynaset fetches keys up to that point and then fetches a small amount of data surrounding that position.

- Idle time: While you are inactive, Microsoft Access populates the query's result set in the background. This allows faster operations when you become active again. A snapshot fetches and stores all selected columns; a dynaset fetches and stores only keys, and no other data. You can control how quickly this idle-time population occurs, using the MSysConf server-based options table.

When the population query reaches the end of the result set, a snapshot does no further data fetching; a dynaset does no more key fetching but will continue to fetch clusters of rows based on those keys, as you scroll around (see below). In addition, if a connection is needed solely for this key-fetching query, it is closed, unless either:

- There are pending results.
- There are pending transactions.

Visual Basic populates the result set in the same manner with the exception that it does not use background cycles to further populate the result set. User scrolling is the only manner in which population proceeds.

Data fetching

When rows of data are needed (for example, to paint a datasheet), a snapshot has the data available locally. A dynaset, on the other hand, has only keys and must use a separate query to ask the server for the data corresponding to those keys. Microsoft Access asks the server for clusters of rows specified by their keys, rather than one at a time, to reduce the querying traffic.

The dynaset behind a Microsoft Access datasheet/form does in fact cache a small window of data (roughly 100 rows). This slightly reduces the "liveness" of the data but greatly speeds moving around within a small area. The data can be refreshed quickly with a single keystroke and is periodically refreshed by Microsoft Access during idle time. This contrasts with a snapshot, which caches the entire result data set and cannot be refreshed except by complete reexecution of the query.

In addition to background key fetching, a dynaset also fills its 100-row data window during idle time. This allows you to page up or down "instantly" once or twice, provided you give Microsoft Access at least a little idle time.

The Jet data access objects (DAO) expose this caching mechanism (the 100 rows of data) in Microsoft Access 2.0 through two new recordset properties (CacheStart and CacheSize) and a new recordset method (FillCache). These apply only to dynasets (not snapshots or pass-through queries), and only when the dynaset contains at least some ODBC data. CacheStart and CacheSize indicate the beginning and length (in rows) of the local cache, while FillCache fills the cache with remote data, fetched in chunks rather than a single row at a time.

Performance implications

Snapshots and dynasets differ in several performance characteristics due to their different methods of retrieving and caching data. Several points are worth noting:

- Snapshots may be faster to open and scroll through than dynasets. If your result set is small, contains no Memo or BLOB data, and you don't need to update data or see changes made by other users, use a snapshot. In Microsoft Access, set the form's Allow Updating property to "No Tables" to force the form to run on a snapshot. In Visual Basic, use a Snapshot object.

- For larger result sets, a dynaset is faster and more efficient. For example, moving to the end of a snapshot requires the entire result set to be downloaded to the client. But a dynaset downloads only the key columns and then fetches the last screen of data corresponding to those keys.

- Dynaset open time and scrolling speed are affected most negatively by the number of columns you select and the number of the query's tables that are output. Select only the columns you need; outputting all columns using Table.* is more convenient but slower. Sometimes joins are used simply as restrictions and don't need to be output at all.

- When a dynaset fetches the data for a given set of keys, Memo/BLOB columns are not fetched unless they are visible on the screen. If scrolling causes them to become visible, they are then fetched. You can improve performance by designing your form so that, by default, Memo columns are not visible. Either place the Memo off the right-bottom edge of the screen or add a button that renders the Memo visible when clicked. In any case, Memos are cached within the dynaset caching window, once fetched.

- OLE objects are never fetched in bunches, nor are they stored in the dynaset caching window, because they tend to be quite large. When a row is displayed, the OLE objects are fetched if they are visible. However, the current row's OLE objects are cached, so simple screen repainting does not require refetching.

Improvements to client-server data access in Jet version 2

As noted previously, version 2 implements several improvements to enhance access to client-server data. Among these are:

- Remote transaction management. You can now use transactions in data access objects (DAO) that properly propagate to the server. For example, these cases now work whereas they previously did not:

```
BeginTrans
Set ds = d.CreateDynaset("select * from authors")
ds.Delete
ds.Close
CommitTrans/Rollback

BeginTrans
d.Execute ("UPDATE Accounts1 SET Balance = Balance + 10")
d.Execute ("UPDATE Accounts2 SET Balance = Balance - 10")
CommitTrans/Rollback
```

  This allows development of true client-server transactional applications, and highly modular code.

- Integrated SQL pass-through, row-returning, and non-row-returning. Pass-through queries are populated on demand, as rows are requested, for faster open and less network traffic.

- A row-returning pass-through query is just like a snapshot; you can use it as the basis for queries, forms, reports, list and combo boxes, and in DAO.

- Pass-through queries can optionally log server warning and informational messages into a Jet table.

- Pass-through queries that return multiple result sets can be used. Their results are stored in multiple Jet tables.

- Connect-string builder: relieves the user of having to enter arcane ODBC connect strings.

- Attached views can be made updatable by creating a "fake unique index" on them. Using a data definition language (DDL) query, create a unique index on the attachment. This index can also be dropped using DDL. Note: the server's view updatability restrictions are not violated; attaching tables and creating Jet queries allow greater view updatability.

- Custom update: updates in datasheets/forms no longer update all columns. Only the columns actually edited will be included in the UPDATE statement sent to the server. This lessens network traffic (especially when Memos and OLE Objects have not been changed), and prevents gratuitous server-based trigger firing.

- Custom insert: inserts in datasheets/forms no longer insert all columns. Only the non-NULL columns will be included in the INSERT statement sent to the server. This reduces network traffic and prevents overwriting of server-based default values. The server-based default values will appear in the datasheet as soon as the new row is saved.

- Row reselect: if a server-based trigger changes the primary key of a table when a record is inserted, Jet will automatically reselect the new row, based on the other values entered in the row. This prevents it from appearing as "#Deleted" in a datasheet, thus allowing better handling of server-side counter columns or triggers that simulate such counter columns.

- ODBC drivers with a CURSOR_COMMIT_BEHAVIOR or CURSOR_ROLLBACK_BEHAVIOR value of zero were read-only in Jet. This restriction has been lifted; you may update tables—provided, of course, that they have unique indexes. Multiple connections, however, may be needed.

- If an ODBC driver supports only a single connection, ever, and doesn't allow multiple statements on that connection, then Jet ignores unique indexes when attaching tables in order to force snapshot-only mode, which requires only a single connection.

- The ODBC type SQL_TIME is now mapped to Text rather than to DateTime. Also, restrictions involving constant date-values and time-values work properly.

- More aggressive connection timeout: connections will now be timed out even if they are being used by a datasheet, form, DAO, and so on. Only two things prevent a connection from being timed out:

  - A pending transaction
  - Unfetched results on a query

  Connections that have been timed out will automatically be reconnected when needed. This allows developers to write applications that leave datasheets and forms on the screen, without worrying about extensive consumption of server connections.

- More MSysConf settings: two new settings in the server-based MSysConf configuration table control how fast Microsoft Access does background population of query results:

  - FetchDelay: indicates how often to fetch another chunk of query results
  - FetchRows: indicates how many rows to fetch

  These two settings have defaults, in case MSysConf doesn't exist: 100 rows are fetched every 10 seconds of idle time. These settings allow a system administrator to trade server locking against network traffic, and not allow ordinary users to override these settings.

- Servers that do not allow multiple statements on a connection (such as SQL Server) require two connections to browse a dynaset. A new delayed-connection algorithm allows small dynasets (fewer than 100 rows) to be browsed on a single connection, even against such servers.

- Remote data caching is available through DAO, using the CacheStart and CacheSize properties and the FillCache method. This also allows for more efficient "chunk-fetching" of dynaset results in DAO.

- A new optimization called "Remote Index Join" dramatically speeds heterogeneous queries and reduces network traffic. When a large server table is joined to a small local table on an indexed column, the large server table is not completely fetched and joined locally as in version 1.1. Rather, only the rows needed are fetched, based on the keys in the small local table. Any additional restrictions on the remote table are also sent to the server.

- It's no longer necessary to declare query parameters against ODBC data. Jet now infers the parameter type from its surrounding expression context and sends such restrictions to the server for processing.

- Constant subexpressions are internally changed into query parameters. This means that a user-defined function, expression, or domain function not involving any remote columns will be evaluated once and sent to the server as a query parameter. This allows queries such as:

```
SELECT RemoteTable.*
FROM RemoteTable
WHERE RemoteColumn1 = UserDefinedFunc([QueryParameter1]) AND
      RemoteColumn2 = IIF([QueryParameter2] = "foo", 1, 2)
```

   to be sent completely to the server for processing. This is useful when the server table contains code but you wish to prompt the user for a string; the user-defined function would translate the user's string into the proper code value.

- Other operations are now sent to the server, including:

  - Queries containing subqueries.

  - Unions.

  - Conversion functions (CInt, CLng, CSng, CDbl, CCur, CStr, CVDate).

- A few more Basic intrinsic functions than version 1.1:

  - Multicolumn outer joins (version 1.1 supported only single-column outer joins).

  - A single outer join along with any number of inner joins. Version 1.1 sent only multiple inner joins or a single outer join, but did not send both in the same query to the server.

  - The LIKE operator is always sent to the server, if supported. Version 1.1 sent only simple LIKE expressions.

  - Wildcard characters in LIKE expressions are always translated from "*" and "?" to "%" and "_", even if they are entered as query parameter values by the user. Version 1.1 only translated wildcards in literal strings. This allows queries such as:

```
SELECT RemoteTable.*
FROM RemoteTable
WHERE RemoteColumn LIKE [QueryParameter]
```

to be sent completely to the server, even if the user types "*" and "?" wildcards.

Visual Basic and Jet

The professional edition of Visual Basic 3.0 includes ODBC support and a variety of data-aware controls. Visual Basic developers using the data-aware controls are intrinsically bound to the Jet engine to access ODBC. The high-level controls that ship in Visual Basic 3.0 have no way of connecting directly to the ODBC API, but must pass through the Jet engine (see Option 1 of Figure 10.13). This provides the benefits of enabling distributed/heterogeneous joins, dynaset technology, and so on. It also introduces overhead to Visual Basic applications when remote access via ODBC is required.

Since Visual Basic is such a flexible tool, there are several options available when attempting to access remote databases:

- Use the Visual Basic 3.0 custom controls, the Jet engine, and ODBC. If performance is a problem, look at the material contained in the EXTERNAL.TXT and PERFORM.TXT files shipped with Visual Basic 3.0. In addition to providing basic information about opening and accessing external databases, EXTERNAL.TXT also provides performance-related information. The PERFORM.TXT file contains performance tuning tips for Visual Basic and Microsoft Access.

- Use "attach table" rather than directly opening remote data sources.

- Use third-party custom controls (VBXs) and the associated third-party data-aware controls (for example, Coromandel or Q+E®). This approach typically has less overhead than the Jet engine.

- Call the ODBC API directly from Visual Basic. Since DLLs can be called from Visual Basic, any of the ODBC APIs may be called by first declaring the API as an external function and then referencing the function as any other Visual Basic function call. The ODBC SDK includes sample Visual Basic programs that provide the subroutines and declarations, and a sample application that uses the ODBC API directly.

- Call the proprietary API similar to Option 3 in Figure 10.13. The SQL Server group provides Visual Basic/SQL libraries that allow Visual Basic developers to write front-end applications to SQL Server.

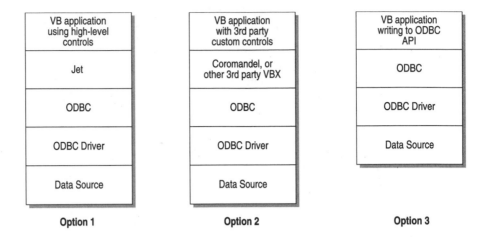

Figure 10.13   Data management options in Visual Basic 3.0.

Microsoft Access and Jet

Visual Basic and Microsoft Access use Jet differently. One notable difference is that Microsoft Access uses Jet exclusively, whereas Visual Basic provides options such as use of Jet through data controls, use of third-party data controls, and direct access to ODBC. Another significant difference is the ability of Microsoft Access to process queries asynchronously. This is in contrast to Visual Basic, where all queries are synchronous.

Asynchronous query execution

Jet executes ODBC queries asynchronously if this is supported by the ODBC driver, the network software, and the server. This allows you to cancel a long-running query in Microsoft Access or to switch to another task in the Windows operating system while the query runs on the server. Jet asks the server if the query is finished every m milliseconds, where m is configurable (the default is 500 milliseconds).

When you cancel a query (or simply close a query before all results have been fetched), Jet calls the ODBC **SQLCancel** function, which discards any pending results and returns control to the user. However, some servers (or their network communication software) do not implement an efficient query-canceling mechanism, so you might still have to wait some time before regaining control.

Asynchronous processing might cause unpredictable results with some network libraries and some servers. These network libraries are often more robust when operating synchronously, owing chiefly to the added complexities of handling multiple asynchronous connections. Client applications are often written to operate fully synchronously, even if interactive; this is simpler to implement and test. You can force Jet to operate synchronously by setting DisableAsync to 1 in the

MSACC20.INI file. Also notify your network/server vendor; an upgrade or patch might be available for these problems.

Jet will automatically cancel a long-running query after a configurable amount of time (the default is 60 seconds). If this happens, it does not necessarily mean that the server did not respond during that time or that you have become disconnected. It simply means the query did not return results in the time allotted. If you know a certain query will take a very long time to execute, increase the query's "ODBC Timeout" property. Each query can have its own timeout setting.

When designing a Microsoft Access application that will interact with remote databases, you need to consider potential performance obstacles

Designing with remote databases in mind

Elements of Microsoft Access applications that performed acceptably against local data may be too slow against a server, cause too much network traffic, or use excessive server resources. Examples include:

- Forms with many list boxes, combo boxes, and subforms, and controls containing totals: each control requires a separate query. Against local data, performance may be adequate due to data caching and in-memory query processing. Against remote data, each query must be sent to the server and a response returned, resulting in an unacceptably long delay when opening the form.

- Very large combo boxes: presenting a combo box of hundreds or even thousands of choices based on a local table may yield reasonable response time, especially if you define an appropriate index on the local table. Against a remote table, such a combo box will be sluggish and will drain server and network resources as it fetches the data to fill the list.

- Jet optimizes record searching (the Find command on the Edit menu in the user interface) to work well against local recordsets of almost any size, and remote recordsets of reasonable size. When working with large remote recordsets (thousands of records), use a filter or query, and be careful to use restrictions that your server can process.

Q+E Database Library 2

One key to a good performing ODBC application requires that the application exploit the capabilities of the database driver. In addition, the application should be aware of the capabilities and specifics of each data source. The Q+E Database Library 2 (QELIB) architecture was designed to address these issues. Figure 10.14 illustrates how QELIB provides data handling and driver leveling features to applications.

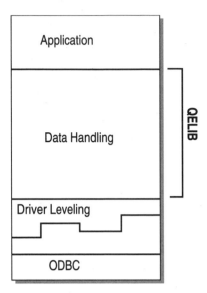

Figure 10.14   QELIB architecture.

QELIB data handling

QELIB's data handling capabilities provide the developer with the functions to manage the data access requirements. These include:

- Functions that simplify the creation, modification, and execution of SQL statements.

- Q+E Query Builder: a DLL that provides a user interface to build SQL statements. The resulting SQL statement is generated, checked for any conditions that may cause problems, and executed.

- Query by example (QBE): allows the developer to provide the user with the ability to choose data that is similar to what they want from a field and build a query.

- Find functions: allow the developer to locate a record from a result set by searching for the value supplied to the Find function, much like the search function in a word processor. Once you have executed an SQL SELECT statement, current-record functions let you position to individual records and update or delete the current record, or insert new records.

- Predefined query: SQL queries can be written and read to files.

- Stored procedures: several functions are provided that assist application developers in using stored procedures that assure proper operation and integration with the application.

- Scrolling in SQL data sources.

- Data conversion: conversion functions permit the developer to convert values from any of the eight standard data types to any other data type.
- Data formatting.
- Utility functions, including data dictionary, SQL parsing, and ODBC handle conversion functions.
- Transaction processing and record locking.

QELIB ODBC driver leveling

Two important issues in ODBC are data-source-specific attributes and ODBC driver compliance. To solve different ODBC driver variances, QELIB queries the capabilities of each driver and provides for missing functionality wherever possible. By using QELIB, applications are isolated from the problems that arise because of limited ODBC driver compliance, as shown in Figure 10.15.

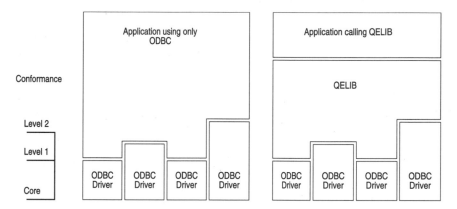

Figure 10.15   QELIB driver leveling.

Suggestions for Enhancing Performance

Driver Manager

There is nothing in the Driver Manager that can be "tuned" by the application or driver writer. However, Microsoft has optimized the Driver Manager in two significant ways.

The Driver Manager for ODBC 2.0 does not unload driver DLLs until either the connection handle is dropped or a connection is made to a different driver on a given connection's handle. This eliminates overhead where frequent connects/disconnects are performed through a given driver. This is in contrast to the

Driver Manager for ODBC 1.0, which automatically unloaded driver DLLs on **SQLDisconnect**.

In the Driver Manager 2.0, the **SQLGetFunctions** function now uses an array in which to store a map of all driver-supported ODBC functions. This is in contrast to ODBC 1.0, where a call was required for each ODBC function. This was done by the use of a new symbolic constant, SQL_API_ALL_FUNCTIONS. When this argument is passed to **SQLGetFunctions**, *pfExists* (the third parameter of the function) is treated as a pointer to an array of 100 elements.

Taken from the ODBC 2.0 *Programmer's Reference*, the following two examples show how an application uses **SQLGetFunctions**. The first example illustrates how the function was used in ODBC 1.0. The second illustrates the use of the array of support driver functions new to ODBC 2.0.

In the first example, **SQLGetFunctions** is used to determine whether a driver supports **SQLTables**, **SQLColumns**, and **SQLStatistics**. If the driver does not support these functions, the application disconnects from the driver. **SQLGetFunctions** is called once for each function. This is the method that was used for ODBC 1.0.

```
UWORD TablesExists, ColumnsExists, StatisticsExists;

SQLGetFunctions(hdbc, SQL_API_SQLTABLES, &TablesExists);
SQLGetFunctions(hdbc, SQL_API_SQLCOLUMNS, &ColumnsExists);
SQLGetFunctions(hdbc, SQL_API_SQLSTATISTICS, &StatisticsExists);

if (TablesExists && ColumnsExists && StatisticsExists) {

    /* Continue with application. */

}

SQLDisconnect(hdbc);
```

The next example calls **SQLGetFunctions** a single time and passes it an array in which **SQLGetFunctions** returns information about all ODBC functions.

```
UWORD fExists[100];

SQLGetFunctions(hdbc, SQL_API_ALL_FUNCTIONS, fExists);

if (fExists[SQL_API_SQLTABLES] &&
    fExists[SQL_API_SQLCOLUMNS] &&
    fExists[SQL_API_SQLSTATISTICS]) {

    /* Continue with application. */

}

SQLDisconnect(hdbc);
```

Overall, the Driver Manager is written for performance by keeping overhead to a minimum. An analysis and benchmarking of the **SQLFetch** function sheds some light on the overhead associated with the Driver Manager:

- 23 lines of C code
- 95 assembler instructions
- 332 clock ticks per execution
- Single execution time of 6.64 microseconds on a 486/50

Given that the blink of a human eye takes .01 seconds, **SQLFetch** can be called 10,000 times in the time it takes to blink.

Applications

Many things can be done in applications to enhance performance. In general, an application should use all of a given driver's capabilities. This is done by querying the API and SQL conformance levels of the driver. To check the SQL conformance level, use the **SQLGetInfo** function with the SQL_ODBC_SQL_CONFORMANCE flag. To test the API conformance level, use the **SQLGetFunctions** function as described above. The following techniques will help reduce overhead, thereby resulting in enhanced performance:

- Don't call data source catalog routines (**SQLTables**, **SQLColumns**, **SQLPrimaryKeys**, and so on) unless it is absolutely necessary. If you do need to call them, do so once and cache the results locally. If you subsequently need them, retrieve the results from the local cache.

- Address scalability in your program design. Be prepared to handle huge result sets. For example, don't dump all the **SQLTables** results into a single list box. It is not uncommon to have thousands of rows returned by **SQLTables**. Let the user choose if VIEW or SYNONYM table types should be displayed.

- Backward scrolling by use of **SQLFetch** is very time consuming. The application must close the cursor by calling **SQLFreeStmt** with the SQL_CLOSE option, reexecute the SELECT statement, and fetch rows with **SQLFetch** until the target row is retrieved. The better approach is to use **SQLExtendedFetch** for scrolling if the driver supports it. This function is used to retrieve result sets utilizing a scrollable cursor.

- Positioned updates and deletes will be faster on some databases (for example, DB2), but be aware that SELECT FOR UPDATE may cause records to be locked. You might update multiple rows if the primary key is not in the SELECT list, thereby increasing time and reducing performance.

- Use **SQLPrepare** and **SQLExecute** for any statement that will be executed more than once. The use of prepared statements is much faster than unprepared statements. Once a statement has been prepared, it is associated with the statement handle (hstmt) until that handle is freed. Reexecuting it is just a matter of calling **SQLExecute** with that statement handle.

- When using **SQLPrepare** and **SQLExecute**, avoid retrieving meta-data (via **SQLDescribeCol, SQLColAttributes, SQLNumResultCols**) for a query until after **SQLExecute**. Some DBMSs do not support the prepare and execute model. In this case, meta-data is not available following the prepare. Some drivers support return of meta-data following prepare by executing a dummy version of the query to force return of meta-data. This permits higher functionality, but it lowers performance.

- Use **SQLBindCol** rather than **SQLGetData**. **SQLGetData** returns the result data for a single unbound column. **SQLBindCol** assigns the storage and data type for a column in a result set. The difference is found in the number of calls to each, and the associated overhead. Although this overhead is somewhat small, it can add up. In the following code samples (taken from the ODBC 2.0 SDK *Programmer's Reference*), it is easy to see that **SQLGetData** is called *n* times (where *n* is the number of rows in the result set) for each column, whereas **SQLBindCol** is called only once for each column.

```
#define NAME_LEN 30
#define BDAY_LEN 11

UCHAR     szName[NAME_LEN], szBirthday[BDAY_LEN];
SWORD     sAge;
SDWORD    cbName, cbAge, cbBirthday;

retcode = SQLExecDirect(hstmt,
            "SELECT NAME, AGE, BIRTHDAY FROM EMPLOYEE ORDER BY 3, 2, 1",
            SQL_NTS);

if (retcode == SQL_SUCCESS) {
  while (TRUE) {
    retcode = SQLFetch(hstmt);
    if (retcode == SQL_ERROR || retcode == SQL_SUCCESS_WITH_INFO) {
      show_error();
  }
  if (retcode == SQL_SUCCESS || retcode == SQL_SUCCESS_WITH_INFO){

      /* Get data for columns 1, 2, and 3. */
      /* Print the row of data.            */

      SQLGetData(hstmt, 1, SQL_C_CHAR, szName, NAME_LEN, &cbName);
      SQLGetData(hstmt, 2, SQL_C_SSHORT, &sAge, 0, &cbAge);
      SQLGetData(hstmt, 3, SQL_C_CHAR, szBirthday, BDAY_LEN,
                  &cbBirthday);
```

```
      fprintf(out, "%-*s %-2d %*s", NAME_LEN-1, szName, sAge,
            BDAY_LEN-1, szBirthday);
  } else {
    break;
  }
 }
}
```

This sample demonstrates the use of **SQLBindCol**. Notice that it is called once for each column prior to the data fetching loop.

```
retcode = SQLExecDirect(hstmt,
            "SELECT NAME, AGE, BIRTHDAY FROM EMPLOYEE ORDER BY 3, 2, 1",
            SQL_NTS);

if (retcode == SQL_SUCCESS) {

  /* Bind columns 1, 2, and 3. */

  SQLBindCol(hstmt, 1, SQL_C_CHAR, szName, NAME_LEN, &cbName);
  SQLBindCol(hstmt, 2, SQL_C_SSHORT, &sAge, 0, &cbAge);
  SQLBindCol(hstmt, 3, SQL_C_CHAR, szBirthday, BDAY_LEN, &cbBirthday);

  /* Fetch and print each row of data. On */
  /* an error, display a message and exit. */

  while (TRUE) {
    retcode = SQLFetch(hstmt);
    if (retcode == SQL_ERROR || retcode == SQL_SUCCESS_WITH_INFO) {
      show_error();
    }
    if (retcode == SQL_SUCCESS || retcode == SQL_SUCCESS_WITH_INFO){
      fprintf(out, "%-*s %-2d %*s", NAME_LEN-1, szName,
            sAge, BDAY_LEN-1, szBirthday);
  } else {
      break;
    }
  }
}
```

- Avoid calling **SQLTypeInfo** more than once. Cache it locally. In some databases it is an expensive stored procedure call.

- Don't design your application so that it requires more than one active connection. Many data sources limit you to one.

- Use block fetches (**SQLExtendedFetch**) wherever possible to reduce trips across the network for multiple-tier drivers.

- Connecting is often expensive. Avoid making and breaking connections repeatedly if it isn't necessary. Each time an application calls **SQLConnect**, **SQLDriverConnect**, or **SQLBrowseConnect**, the Driver Manager calls **SQLAllocEnv**, **SQLAllocConnect**, and **SQLSetConnectOption** in the driver. This can introduce significant overhead if these functions are called frequently.

- If you are not using vendor escape clauses, the *fOption* of **SQLSetStmtOption** should be set to SQL_NOSCAN and the *vParam* set to SQL_NOSCAN_ON. This instructs the driver not to scan for escape clauses. The driver sends the statement directly to the data source.

Drivers

It is easy to write ODBC drivers. Conversely, it is time consuming to write highly optimized drivers. However, there are cases where a non-optimized driver is more than adequate for a particular need. When writing drivers, a general principle is that the driver should make use of all the underlying capabilities of the data source.

Single-tier drivers

Performance tuning a single-tier driver involves three basic techniques. First, make the file I/O as fast and efficient as possible. Second, have a good sort engine. Third, have a good query optimizer.

PageAhead Software Corporation, developers of the Simba ODBC driver tools, provides some insight into the importance of query optimizers in the following excerpt taken from the PageAhead white paper "Introduction to ODBC Driver Development"

"SQL statements describe the operation to be performed, not how to perform the operation. Effective optimization of a query is crucial. Optimized queries that take seconds or minutes to perform can take hours if left unoptimized. Optimization is more of an art than a science. Cost-based optimization is used in many client-server SQL implementations and is the method discussed here. Essentially, the query planner/optimizer will analyze the query tree created by the parser and will attempt to determine an optimal method of execution. A number of methods are used to do this, including:

- General "rules of thumb" or heuristics are applied first. For example, the optimizer can:

  - Apply row selection filters to tables prior to joining them in order to minimize the number of rows in the join product table.

  - Work with as few columns as possible while doing intermediate operations.

  - Combine any Cartesian product operations and select operation into a single join operation.

- A number of candidate access plans are produced to solve the SQL request. Cost estimates are produced for each. Cost is estimated using information about how the database information is actually stored on disk. Variables examined include the number of database rows, availability of primary and secondary indexes, and variability of data within columns. The access plan that results in the least cost (time) is the one selected for execution.

A good query planner/optimizer can yield an order of magnitude performance improvements relative to non-optimized access plans. The product of this phase is a detailed list of execution steps, described at the record and index level, that can be executed by a record-oriented process."

Multiple-tier drivers

Several points can be made about enhancing performance of multiple-tier drivers. When writing multiple-tier drivers, you need to decide who should be doing the work, the client or the server. What makes sense in your particular situation or market? Consider the following as you write your driver:

- Be frugal in the refresh of static catalog information using **SQLGetTypeInfo**. Perhaps only on initialization (not with each connect/disconnect), or implement **SQLGetTypeInfo** directly in the driver.

- Tune catalog queries carefully to optimize access to the DBMS.

- Preprocess SQL strings as little as possible. Do the minimum preprocessing, including looking for vendor escape sequences and standardizing of quotation characters.

- Use the highest performance access to DBMS; for example, Microsoft SQL Server driver goes to TDS instead of DB-Library; Oracle makes use of higher performance options in OCI in their ODBC driver.

- Support block fetch (**SQLExtendedFetch**) to permit applications to minimize network traffic and function calls.

- Fetch the data in the datatype of the server. Make the server do the work if this makes sense.

- Support canonical functions to enable the maximum amount of processing to be off-loaded to the data source. Many data sources directly support commonly used functions. When an application sends an ODBC canonical function to the driver, the driver is responsible for translating the canonical syntax into the data-source-specific syntax before sending the query on to the server. Without canonical functions, the data is pulled back from the server in order to operate on it. For example, consider the **Date** function in Access Basic. Almost every data source supports a **Date** function that returns the current date, but they all use different syntax. So, consider the following Microsoft Access query:

```
SELECT *
FROM table
WHERE column = Date()
```

If ODBC could not use the canonical syntax for **Date,** and *table* referred to a SQL Server table, all records would be pulled back from the server. The **Date** function would then run locally to find the matching records. Using the canonical function, a query is sent to the SQL Server driver, which translates the canonical into SQL Server syntax. SQL Server processes the request and returns the proper records. No local processing is involved.

Summary

ODBC provides a means of accessing data in a heterogeneous environment of relational and nonrelational database management systems. It can do so in an efficient, high-performance manner. However, attaining this performance requires an understanding of the tools that are being used to access the data. Are the tools actually using ODBC? If they are using ODBC, are they doing so in an efficient way? Does the architecture of the tool enhance performance or become and obstacle to it? Should you even be using ODBC? These are just a few of the questions that you need to address when you implement your ODBC projects. As with any client-server application, the application needs to be tuned with the knowledge of the underlying tools, the database, and the user requirements.

Topic

Discuss the approach to writing an interoperable database application that uses ODBC.

Content

Writing Interoperable Applications with ODBC[4]

Richard Schwartz

---

[4] This backgrounder is also available on the Microsoft Developer Network Development Library under Backgrounders and White Papers, Operating System Extensions. Copyright 1993. Used with permission. All rights reserved.

Overview

This technical article provides information to application developers on writing interoperable ODBC-enabled applications. The first section begins by exploring the challenges inherent to heterogeneous data access. It looks at ways of approaching these challenges and discusses the open database connectivity (ODBC) solution. It then discusses the ODBC programming paradigm, which application developers need to work within when coding to ODBC. The second section provides a high-level "recipe" for writing interoperable applications. It enumerates the steps involved in the development process, from planning through coding and testing, and includes information about issues a development team needs to address at each step. The third section contains detailed scenarios that illustrate proper usage of the ODBC paradigm and programming interface. The final section ties together the main ideas of this technical article.

The reader is presumed to have application development experience, but no knowledge of the ODBC API or experience writing applications for heterogeneous data access is necessary. Readers who are familiar with ODBC and the issues involved in writing applications that access multiple DBMSs may want to skip to the more technical sections, starting with "A Recipe for Writing Interoperable Applications."

Introduction to Interoperability

Microsoft developed the open database connectivity (ODBC) interface as a means of providing applications with a single application programming interface (API) through which to access data stored in a wide variety of database management systems (DBMSs). Prior to ODBC, applications written to access data stored in a DBMS had to use the proprietary interface specific to that database. If application developers wanted to provide their users with *heterogeneous data access* (access to data in more than one data source), they needed to code to the interface of each data source. Applications written in this manner are difficult to code, difficult to maintain, and difficult to extend. ODBC was created to overcome these difficulties.

The ODBC architecture has four components:

- **Application.** Calls ODBC functions to submit SQL statements and retrieve results.
- **Driver Manager.** Loads drivers on behalf of an application.
- **Driver.** Processes ODBC function calls, submits SQL requests to a specific data source, and returns results to the application.

- **Data Source.** Consists of the data the user wants to access and its associated operating system, DBMS, and network platform (if any) used to access the DBMS.

This architecture is designed to permit maximum *interoperability*: It allows application developers to create an application without targeting a specific DBMS. End users can then use the application with the DBMS that contains their data by adding modules called *database drivers*, which are dynamic-link libraries (DLLs) available from the database vendor or third-party driver developers.

This technical article provides information to application developers on writing interoperable ODBC-enabled applications. Note that the concept of interoperability is a relative one. To one developer it might mean being able to access data in each of two known data sources using the same application. To a second developer, it might mean writing applications that work with DB/2 today, but might at some future date need to work with ORACLE. To another developer it might mean providing access to any data stored in a desktop-database format. And to a fourth developer, interoperability might mean giving access to any data for which there exists an ODBC driver. ODBC can meet the interoperability needs of all of these developers.

If ODBC Is the Solution, What Is the Question?

Heterogeneous data access is very appealing to developers and end users alike. Independent software vendors (ISVs) would like to be able to provide users of their shrink-wrapped applications with the ability to use data that is stored in one of the many commercially available databases. Corporate developers want easy ways to access data that is stored in different DBMSs. These same developers want the ability to write code to one DBMS and reuse it on a second (or a third, or. . .). Database vendors see data access to their DBMS from popular applications as a way of increasing use of (and demand for) their product. And for end users, interoperability means there is a simple way to access their data and process it from a familiar, easy-to-use interface.

The Hurdles to Interoperability

The benefits of (and need for) heterogeneous data access are well-defined. However, the hurdles to accessing data in multiple DBMSs from a shrink-wrapped application, or writing code with one DBMS in mind and having it work on another DBMS without modification, are many. The crux of the problem is that each DBMS provides its own interface, its own manner of handling and storing data, its own version of SQL, its own set of functionality, and so forth. Any attempt to create interoperable applications has to address these differences head-on.

Let's look more closely at the hurdles to interoperability.

Programming interfaces

Each DBMS typically has its own call-level programming interface through which it communicates with client applications. For example, SQL Server provides an interface called DB-Library™, while ORACLE® Server provides the Oracle Call Interface (OCI). Any client application that wishes to access more than one DBMS must therefore be able to translate requests and data transfers into each interface it needs to access. After the application has been completed, if developers wish to provide access to a new DBMS, they need to learn a new programming interface, write and test new code for accessing the new DBMS, and recompile and redistribute the application.

Functionality

Although database users have come to expect a certain set of functionality for defining, updating, and working with their data (and there is much overlap from one product to another), there is no agreement on what is the proper set of functionality. Even databases that follow the relational database model, use SQL as a query language, and run on client-server architecture have no consensus on functionality. On the contrary, database vendors take pride in the ways their product *differs* from the others on the market, and users purchase the products partially due to the extended functionality that the product offers. But what is good for a single database is a nightmare for interoperability. Interoperable applications must contend with the fact that they cannot know what functionality to expect from any given DBMS. This problem is further compounded by the fact that users want an application to access data in both relational and non-relational databases (be they hierarchical, object-oriented, ISAM, or just plain text), providing the same interface and functionality for each. This raises the question of whether or not there can be a "standard" set of functionality, and if not, what can be done about it.

SQL syntax and semantics

While most DBMSs support SQL, and while the SQL they support is typically based on an ANSI or ISO standard, each DBMS has its own idiosyncratic implementation of the language. Although these differences are often small, they are huge impediments to interoperability, as SQL statements must be tailor-made for each DBMS.

System catalogs

Relational database management systems (RDBMSs) use system catalogs to hold information about the data being stored, such as the column names, data types, and permissions. Applications need catalog information to create databases, to make changes to data, and to provide a clean user interface. Although ANSI has defined standard system views that contain this system data, these are not yet implemented by most database vendors. Until they are implemented, each RDBMS will continue to have an incompatible manner of providing information from its system catalog. Consider, for example, that the names of data types differ across DBMSs: SQL Server refers to alphanumeric data as CHAR, ORACLE uses CHARACTER, and Paradox™ calls it ALPHANUMERIC. Because of these differences, an application needs to make specific, individual reference to the system catalog of each DBMS it supports. Once again, there is the issue of writing DBMS-specific code, and the problem of portability.

Solving the Interoperability Problem

As stated above, ODBC was created to permit maximum interoperability between applications and databases. Its primary design goal is to facilitate the process of applications communicating with multiple, different DBMSs. This may ease the initial development burden on the developer, allow developers to write code that is easily extensible and portable, and broaden the application support for databases.

ODBC achieves its goals through its driver-based architecture and by defining a set of standards that mitigate the differences among databases, thereby eliminating DBMS-specific code.

- ODBC provides a single API for communicating with any DBMS for which there is a driver, eliminating the need for DBMS-specific calls. Included in the API is a standard way to connect with and log on to a DBMS, and a standard set of error codes that can be handled in a generic fashion.

- ODBC defines a minimum level of functionality that is expected to be supported by all drivers and represents the capabilities of most DBMSs. At the same time, ODBC utilizes as many features of a DBMS as possible, and provides a standard way of querying a driver to see whether some particular functionality is supported. For a discussion of this solution, see "Addressing the Issue of Differing Database Functionality" below.

- ODBC recommends an industry-standard SQL grammar (syntax and semantics) based on the X/Open and SQL Access Group (SAG) SQL CAE specification (1992). Additionally, ODBC provides a way to handle specific extensions to standard SQL. All SQL statements are written the same way; it is no longer the application developer's responsibility to fine-tune SQL statements to meet the needs of the DBMS.

- ODBC provides catalog functions, such as **SQLTables**, **SQLColumns**, and **SQLStatistics**, to enable an application to obtain information about the system catalogs in a standard, interoperable fashion. ODBC also defines a standard means for describing a DBMS's data types, so that applications can take advantage of its data type characteristics. .

Addressing the issue of differing database functionality

In addressing the issue of differing functionality, there were a number of approaches for ODBC to choose from. One solution would have been to limit the functionality available through ODBC to only that which all DBMSs have in common. This solution is often referred to as the lowest-common-denominator approach. Under this approach, an application would be assured of a given set of functionality. Although this may seem appealing at first, it turns out that there is very little functionality that all databases have in common. Many application developers would have found this lowest common denominator to be insufficient for meeting their users' needs, and it would be unacceptable to users of advanced databases.

A second approach would have been to define a guaranteed functionality that was somewhat larger than the lowest common denominator. Any functionality that a DBMS could not provide would be handled by ODBC. ODBC would essentially need a database engine of its own to provide this functionality. (This is the model used by Microsoft Access.) Although the functionality provided by the engine would go further to meeting the needs of end users, there are still applications that would find this solution too constricting, since not all of a DBMS's functionality would be utilized.

Still another approach would have been to not worry about providing common functionality at all. Instead, the ODBC API would provide a way to get to all features of all databases, but it would make no guarantees about any of it. This would maximize functionality available to applications, but at the cost to developers of having to write much conditional code to deal with functionality that might not be available.

In the end, ODBC has chosen a hybrid approach to handling database functionality. As stated above, ODBC provides a minimum level of functionality that is expected to be supported by all drivers, while utilizing as many features of a DBMS as possible. Application developers have to decide to either use the minimum level of functionality, or write the conditional code to test for extended functionality. Applications that make the latter choice are responsible for handling any missing DBMS functionality in the way they best see fit. The process of compensating for differing functionality is the heart of the "ODBC programming paradigm."

ODBC Programming Paradigm

ODBC has chosen to use as much functionality of the DBMS as possible. Because no DBMS provides all functionality, ODBC has provided a standard way for an application to check what functionality is available from any data source it is connected with. Available functionality is communicated by way of conformance levels and capabilities.

Even though DBMSs can differ greatly from one to the next, many of them have sets of functionality in common. Therefore, ODBC has defined *conformance levels*, both for the API and for SQL statements. There are three ODBC API conformance levels defined in the *Programmer's Reference*: Core, Level 1, and Level 2. Driver writers are encouraged to support Level 1 API (at a minimum), as most interactive applications require much of the functionality defined in that conformance level. But an application should not make any assumptions about the conformance level of a driver. Developers should use the **SQLGetInfo** function to explicitly check for API conformance.

Note Information about what functions are contained within each conformance level can be found in the ODBC *Programmer's Reference* in the documentation for **SQLGetFunctions**.

ODBC also defines three SQL conformance levels: Minimum, Core, and Extended. Applications should use **SQLGetInfo** to check for SQL conformance.

Note Information about SQL conformance level can be found in Appendix C of the ODBC *Programmer's Reference*.

Although drivers are required to report their conformance levels, they are not limited to the functionality defined by those levels. On the contrary, driver writers are encouraged to support as much of the API and SQL grammar as they are able. In order to learn what functionality is provided by a given driver, an application can check for specific *capabilities* using **SQLGetInfo**.

ODBC also provides a standard means of executing extended functionality. For example, although most DBMSs provide scalar functions such as SUBSTRING and ABS, there is no consensus on the syntax of those functions. ODBC defines a canonical syntax that the application can use to access this extended functionality of the data source. Similarly, while most databases support time and date data types, there are many different ways to represent those data types. ODBC defines a standard way of representing times and dates.

By design, all ODBC applications have a similar structure. An application begins by connecting to a data source. Next, it queries the data source for information about conformance levels and individual capabilities that the application will take advantage of if available. Then it typically sends one or more SQL statements to the DBMS for processing. Next, the application retrieves the results sent by the DBMS, checking for errors along the way. Finally, the application terminates the connection when it has finished interacting with the data source.

The primary feature of the ODBC programming paradigm is the shift from writing DBMS-dependent code to writing capability-dependent code. Any application that is not written for a particular driver, even one that only uses functionality listed as Core API or Minimum SQL, needs to actively query the DBMS for supported features, and respond appropriately to those queries.

A Recipe for Writing Interoperable Applications

This section examines the process of writing an interoperable application from the planning phase through development and testing. It gives a step-by-step account of the issues that need to be addressed, providing some specific solutions along the way. The primary focus of the section is on the planning phase. This is partly due to the scope of this paper, but mostly due to the belief that interoperable applications are the result of good planning.

Note that although the issues to address are given in a linear order, the reality of planning, developing, and testing the application tells us that these steps are not always taken in a specific order. Often more than one step will be addressed at a time. Do not take the "recipe" metaphor too literally, to the detriment of your development process.

Step 1: Understand ODBC and Its Applications

The first step in developing an ODBC-enabled application is understanding the ODBC programming paradigm, including the problems that ODBC was designed to solve. The discussion in the above sections describes this paradigm. Another source for this information is the ODBC *Programmer's Reference*.

Part of understanding ODBC is knowing when its use is appropriate and when it is best to look for other solutions. ODBC is not a panacea for all database programming problems. As discussed above, ODBC was designed primarily as a tool for heterogeneous data access. Although ODBC exposes much of the functionality of any given DBMS, and serves as an alternative to coding directly to a particular DBMS's API, it is more advantageous to use the proprietary DBMS interface for some applications, particularly those applications that perform administrative tasks on the database and those that are written for only one DBMS.

An example of an administrative application that is best written in the native API is SQL Administrator for SQL Server. This application allows a user to create SQL Server devices; create databases; move the log segment to a separate device; create and maintain log-in IDs, user names, and remote log-ins; obtain statistics information; view the error log; and provide other administrative functions in addition to being an ad-hoc querying tool. Almost all of this functionality can be achieved using the ODBC API, but if one knows enough about the SQL Server architecture to write SQL Administrator (a SQL Server-specific administrative utility), it is definitely easier to use the DB-Library API.

Step 2: Determine Which Databases You Need to Connect to and the Conformance Levels of Those Drivers

The second step in writing interoperable applications is to determine which databases you need to be able to connect to. Many applications use ODBC to access only one or two specific DBMSs. If you have a limited, known set of databases you need to connect to, you may be able to take advantage of features specific to those databases. This may cut down on the amount of capability-checking the application needs to perform, thereby lessening the application's complexity. On the other hand, if you are writing an off-the-shelf application, or you are uncertain which databases you need to communicate with, then you will need to program for maximum interoperability, making no assumptions about the databases you are connected to.

Once the data sources have been determined, it can be helpful to know the conformance levels of the drivers that access those data sources. For applications that are written for a limited number of data sources, knowing conformance levels can give you some idea of what functionality to expect, which might decrease the amount of work you need to do (particularly relating to Steps 3 and 4 below). For applications that need to be interoperable with many or unknown data sources, it is useful to know the general conformance levels of currently available drivers when planning the application.

Accessing a known and limited set of data sources

If the set of data sources to be accessed is known, as is often the case when writing custom applications, the developer needs to consider the constraints imposed by existing hardware and software and by cost considerations. For example, are drivers available for the data sources? Do these drivers require additional software, such as network components or gateways? Will the drivers work with the existing network and server hardware? Although ODBC allows applications to ignore these questions, developers writing software to work in a specific environment must ensure that all components are available and fit cost constraints before they begin writing code.

For example, the only commercially available ODBC driver for ORACLE at the time of this writing comes from Microsoft. To communicate with ORACLE, this driver uses SQL*Net, a network component from Oracle Corporation. Although SQL*Net is available in both TSR and DLL form, the Microsoft ORACLE driver can only use SQL*Net DLLs. Furthermore, although there is a SQL*Net TSR for DECnet™, there is not a SQL*Net DLL for DECnet. Therefore, before users can use an ODBC application to access ORACLE data, a company currently using DECnet and ORACLE must either change their network or wait for an ORACLE driver that can communicate across DECnet.

Overall driver conformance

Microsoft has encouraged driver writers to support Level 1 API conformance, and to date, most drivers do. In response, there are applications being written that require Level 1 conformance in order to connect with the driver (Microsoft Access being a notable example). As for SQL conformance, most server databases provide Core conformance, while most desktop databases (Microsoft Access, Paradox, text, and so on) provide only Minimum SQL conformance. This is because the desktop databases do not possess an engine to parse SQL statements, so the SQL support must be implemented in the driver.

Determining the conformance level of drivers

There are a number of ways to determine the conformance levels of ODBC drivers. First, you can check the documentation that comes with the drivers. Alternatively, you can access the drivers through ODBC Test (a utility provided in the ODBC SDK) and confirm conformance there. A shortcut could be to check the driver's conformance in the ODBC Driver Catalog, if it is listed.

Differences between desktop and server databases

Part of understanding the conformance issue is understanding the fundamental differences between data stored in a relational database on a server or mainframe and data stored in ISAM format in a desktop database. Developers who are familiar with relational databases need to understand that some of the basic concepts from the relational model, such as transactions and system catalogs, are not present in desktop databases. Also, as pointed out above, desktop databases do not use SQL as their native query language. On the other hand, developers familiar with desktop databases need to realize that some of the functionality they depend on, such as the rich capabilities for navigating (moving) through a result set, is not present in the relational model. Although ODBC makes it possible for interoperability between the two models, and developers should be able to present an interface to the user that masks the differences, there is an impact to the application developer. ODBC enables interoperability, and decreases complexity, but it does not eliminate all of the issues.

Step 3: Determine the Functionality Requirements of the Application

Together with Step 4 below, this is the major focus of the planning phase. Functionality here refers to the capabilities of the driver you are connected to. It might be the same as the functionality your application offers the end user, but not necessarily.

Note In some cases, the application will compensate for functionality not provided in the driver. See Step 4, below.

As discussed above, the fact that each DBMS provides a unique set of functionality is one of the major hurdles to creating interoperable applications. The functionality required by your application will determine which drivers it is compatible with (or, as seen below, the amount of work you need to do to make your application compatible).

When determining the functionality required by your application, you might want to consider each of the following:

- Is there a minimum level of API or SQL conformance needed by the application to work at all?

- What are the specific SQL statements the DBMS needs to support?

- Does the application need access to features such as outer joins, unions, and procedures?

- Will users need to create and drop tables?

- What are the data types that the application needs to have supported? Does it need support for very long data types (such as memo/text, blob/image, and so on)?

- Does the application require that the data be modified in any way, or only that it be browsed?

- What level of transaction support does the application require?

- What degree of security does the application require?

- What type of concurrency control mechanisms are available to the application? Can it explicitly lock a table or a set of tables? Can it lock a certain row?

- Does the application require block and/or scrollable cursors? If so, can it make do with static cursors or does it need dynamic cursors?

- Does the application need to have multiple connections to the same driver? Multiple active statements per handle?

- Does the application need to use asynchronous processing?

- What versions of the DBMS does the application need to access? Are there drivers that support those versions?

It is virtually impossible to know all the ways in which DBMSs can vary from one to the next. The best way to get an idea is to look over the options for **SQLGetInfo**, the primary function provided for querying DBMS capabilities. Familiarity with **SQLGetInfo** greatly increases the likelihood of creating interoperable applications.

Step 4: Determine How to Handle Functionality That Is Not Supported

Many applications will require functionality that is not supported by the DBMS. There are essentially five options available to the application at that time:

- Provide the unsupported functionality in the application.

- Make the feature available to the user on a conditional basis.

- Provide an alternative to the unsupported functionality.

- Determine that the application cannot communicate with the data source, and terminate the connection.

- Drop the feature from the application.

Handling these situations involves weighing the tradeoffs. Will your users miss the functionality if you don't provide it? Are you eliminating important data sources by not communicating with them? Will your application be less interoperable if you provide the functionality yourself? Is there a clean way to implement an alternative without frustrating or confusing the end user? These are tough choices, but they are inevitable when writing complex, interoperable applications.

The *Programmer's Reference* from the ODBC SDK 1.0 provides a good illustration of this kind of situation: Assume your application displays data in a table. It uses **SQLColumnPrivileges** to determine which columns a user can update and dims those columns the user cannot update. Assume further that not all drivers support **SQLColumnPrivileges**. What are your options?

- Locally implement **SQLColumnPrivileges**. This allows you to provide full functionality for all data sources, with the application behaving the same for all. However, in order to implement **SQLColumnPrivileges**, you need to know how to retrieve column privileges from the data source you are connected to. The only way to do this is to write data-source–specific code, and hence your application will be less interoperable. Also, the development time for this solution is longer.

- Dim the columns that the user cannot update for data sources that support **SQLColumnPrivileges**, as planned. For those that don't support **SQLColumnPrivileges**, warn the user that he or she might not have update privileges on all columns. If the user attempts to update a column for which he or she does not have privileges, display an error message. This solution provides the desired functionality, is maximally interoperable, and allows for use of all data sources. However, users may feel it is an inelegant solution, since the only way they can find out the columns for which they have privileges is through trial and error, and the interface is inconsistent across data sources.

- Try UPDATE statements from the application against all columns of the table (being careful not to change any data!). Dim any column for which the update fails. This solution provides the desired functionality without causing interoperability problems. However, running the queries each time a table is opened can be very time-consuming, so the application may have unacceptable performance.

- Use only those drivers that support **SQLColumnPrivileges**. The application has consistent behavior and full functionality for all supported data sources. But the application is not maximally interoperable; it has eliminated some set of drivers.

- Drop the column-dimming feature from the application. Instead, simply warn users that they may not have update privileges on all columns, as in the second alternative above. This provides consistent behavior for all data sources and maximum interoperability, but at the price of reduced functionality.

Step 5: Determine Appropriate Places for Data-Source–Specific Code

There are times when it is appropriate to write data-source–specific code in applications. Although this will probably not be an option for shrink-wrapped interoperable applications, there are cases in which it might be useful for applications written to known data sources. In particular, a developer may choose to write directly to the data source's interface to gain access to features of the DBMS that are not exposed through ODBC.

ODBC drivers generally support any SQL that the DBMS supports, including SQL that is not covered by ODBC SQL. If an application sends SQL to the driver that is not supported by ODBC, the driver will pass the statement through to the DBMS. In this manner, an application can use data-source–specific code.

For example, SQL Server supports a USE *database* statement, with which a user can change the current SQL Server database. An application developer writing an application specific to SQL Server can change the database by calling **SQLExecDirect** and sending it this statement. The SQL Server driver will pass the statement through to SQL Server, which will execute the statement.

Here is another example of when an application may choose to write data-source–specific code. Suppose the application is a table builder that allows users to create tables and insert values into them. One of the things such an application has to keep in mind is domain integrity. Defaults are a common way of enforcing domain integrity constraints. Assume that the underlying drivers do not support the Integrity Enhancement Facility (IEF). Now the developer must use data-source–specific SQL for defining defaults.

In ORACLE, the SQL looks like this:

```
create table employees (name char(20), deptno number(5) default 100)
```

In SQL Server, the SQL looks like this:

```
create table employees (name char(20), deptno int)
create default deptno_default as 100
sp_bindefault deptno_default, 'employees.deptno'
```

The driver will pass these data-source–specific SQL statements through to the DBMS.

Step 6: Code the Application

Once the design decisions have been made, it is time to code the application. The primary obstacle to writing interoperable applications is using data-source–specific code. As seen above, there are some cases in which writing code particular to a data source is appropriate. However, much data-source–specific code is not written intentionally, and it generally comes in the form of making assumptions about the functionality of DBMSs.

Using SQLGetInfo

The key to avoiding driver-specific code is **SQLGetInfo**. There are more than 70 values for the **SQLGetInfo** *fInfoType* parameter, each representing a DBMS feature that might or might not be present. All applications need to check the capability of the driver before using a feature. To omit to do so is to open the application up to interoperability problems. There are dozens of examples in which developers have neglected to check for capabilities, mostly because it did not occur to them that some functionality would not be supported. Here are some tips on avoiding data-source–specific code.

Multiple active statement handles per connection

Many developers assume that all drivers support multiple statement handles per connection. However, the SQL Server driver from Microsoft does not. This feature needs to be checked with an *fInfoType* value of SQL_ACTIVE_STATEMENTS.

Transaction capability

As noted above, some data sources, particularly desktop databases, do not support transactions. Others provide transaction support but have differing behavior in response to data definition language (DDL) statements within a transaction. Use an *fInfoType* value of SQL_TXN_CAPABLE to check transaction support and behavior.

Cursor behavior on COMMIT and ROLLBACK

No assumptions can be made about the behavior of a cursor following a COMMIT or ROLLBACK operation. In some cases cursors will be closed and deleted, in other cases they will be closed but not deleted, and in other cases they will be preserved. To find out about cursor behavior, use **SQLGetInfo** with *fInfoType* values of SQL_CURSOR_COMMIT_BEHAVIOR and

SQL_CURSOR_ROLLBACK_BEHAVIOR.

Support for NOT NULL in CREATE TABLE statement

Some data sources, such as dBASE and FoxPro, do not support the NOT NULL column constraint of the CREATE TABLE statement. Use an *fInfoType* value of SQL_NON_NULLABLE_COLUMNS to check for availability.

Support for scalar functions

Virtually all data sources will support scalar functions, but no assumptions can be made about which ones are supported and what syntax is used. Call **SQLGetInfo** with *fInfoType* values of SQL_NUMERIC_FUNCTIONS, SQL_STRING_FUNCTIONS, SQL_TIMEDATE_FUNCTIONS, and so on, to determine what scalar functions are supported, and use the ODBC canonical syntax for scalar functions.

Data type support

Do not make any assumptions about what types are supported by the DBMS and what their names are. Use **SQLGetTypeInfo** to find this information. Be sure to check their precision and other characteristics to find out about data-source–specific behavior.

Identifier naming conventions

Application developers should not assume that all data sources support the same identifier naming convention. In addition to a single identifier (usually a table or column name), identifiers can be extended by the owner's name and the use of qualifiers. ODBC supports one-, two-, and three-part naming conventions. To determine if, and in what statements, a data source supports owner names, an application calls **SQLGetInfo** with an *fInfoType* of SQL_OWNER_USAGE. To determine if, and in what statements, a data source supports qualifiers, an application calls **SQLGetInfo** with an *fInfoType* of SQL_QUALIFIER_USAGE. In addition, different data sources use different characters as the separator between a qualifier name and the element that follows it. To find out what character is being used, call **SQLGetInfo** with an *fInfoType* of SQL_QUALIFIER_NAME_SEPARATOR.

Once again, there is no way to know all the ways in which one DBMS differs from another. The best way to become familiar with the capability issues that your application might need to address is to look over the possible values for the *fInfoType* parameter of **SQLGetInfo**.

Using ODBC SQL

A second major step in writing generic code is to be certain to use the ODBC SQL syntax and data types. ODBC provides these standards to mitigate the incompatibilities among DBMSs. Consider the syntax for performing outer joins. (**Note**: ANSI has defined a standard syntax for outer joins, but this standard has not been implemented by most database vendors.) Here are two versions of the same request for an outer join. The first is written for ORACLE Server, the second for SQL Server:

```
SELECT EMPLOYEE.NAME, DEPT.NAME
FROM EMPLOYEE, DEPT
WHERE (EMPLOYEE.PROJID = 544) AND (EMPLOYEE.DEPTID = DEPT.DEPTID (+))

SELECT EMPLOYEE.NAME, DEPT.NAME
FROM EMPLOYEE, DEPT
WHERE EMPLOYEE.PROJID = 544 AND EMPLOYEE.DEPTID *= DEPT.DEPTID
```

Rather than writing conditional code to fine-tune this SQL SELECT statement for the appropriate DBMS, the programmer should send the SELECT statement using the SQL syntax defined in Appendix C of the ODBC *Programmer's Reference*. Using this syntax, the SQL statement sent to the DBMS will look like one of the following (the escape syntax is given first, the shorthand syntax second):

```
select employee.name, dept.deptname from
--(*vendor(Microsoft),product(ODBC)oj employee left outer join
dept on employee.deptid=dept.deptid*)--
where employee.projid =544

select employee.name, dept.deptname from
{oj employee left outer join dept on employee.deptid=dept.deptid}
where employee.projid =544
```

It is then the driver's responsibility to translate the ODBC SQL grammar to the SQL native to the data source. (Note that before using outer joins, the application must first call **SQLGetInfo** with an *fInfoType* value of SQL_OUTER_JOINS to determine whether the data source even supports the feature.)

Performance issues

Somewhat off the topic of writing interoperable applications, but directly relevant to the topic of coding ODBC applications, are some misunderstandings developers have had about the proper use of certain ODBC constructs. The consequences of these misuses have been significant performance problems for these applications. To avoid future problems, here are descriptions of the proper use of two of the misunderstood constructs, prepared execution and opening and closing connections.

Prepared vs. direct execution

ODBC provides two ways to submit an SQL statement to the DBMS for processing: direct execution (using **SQLExecDirect**) and prepared execution (using **SQLPrepare** and **SQLExecute**). Prepared execution is useful if a statement will be executed many times, or if an application needs information about a result set prior to the execution of the statement. Under prepared execution, upon receiving the **SQLPrepare** function the data source will compile the statement, produce an access plan, and return the access plan to the driver. The data source will then use this plan when it receives a **SQLExecute** statement. For statements that are executed multiple times, prepared execution creates a performance advantage because the access plan need only be created once. But for statements that are executed just once, prepared execution creates added overhead, and hence there is a performance hit. Direct execution is the proper choice for statements that are executed a single time. Using the correct execution strategy is one way of optimizing application performance.

Opening and closing connections

Opening and closing connections can be very time-consuming. Under ODBC 1.0, upon opening a connection, the driver manager loads the driver DLL and calls the driver's **SQLAllocEnv** and **SQLAllocConnect** functions, plus the driver's connect function corresponding to the connection option chosen by the application. Upon closing a connection, the driver manager unloads the DLL and calls all the disconnect functions: **SQLDisconnect**, **SQLFreeConnect**, and **SQLFreeEnv**.

Note   Under ODBC 2.0, the driver manager will not unload the DLL or call **SQLFreeConnect** or **SQLFreeEnv** upon receiving a **SQLDisconnect** call; instead it waits until the application calls **SQLFreeConnect** or requests a connection to a different data source.

For this reason, from a performance perspective, it is preferable to leave connections open, rather than closing and re-opening them each time a statement is executed. However, there is a cost to maintaining open, idle connections. Each connection consumes a significant amount of resources on the server, which can cause problems on PC-based DBMSs that have limited resources. Therefore, applications must use connections judiciously, weighing the potential costs of any connection strategy.

Step 7: Test the Application

In most ways, testing an ODBC application is no different than testing any other application. However, the only way to discover how interoperable an application truly is to test it against multiple drivers. For applications that are written for a known set of drivers, it is critical to test against all of them. For applications that are generically interoperable, it is advised that application developers test with as many drivers as they can. At a minimum, developers should test with at least one driver with limited capabilities (many single-tier drivers fall into this category) and one driver having extensive capabilities (many multiple-tier drivers fall into this category).

The ODBC Test utility that comes with the ODBC SDK version 1.0 can be an aid to the testing process. It can be particularly helpful when tracking down interoperability problems with specific drivers: ODBC Test can help the application developer determine whether the problem is with the application or with the driver. For the ODBC SDK version 2.0, there will be an expanded version of the Test tool, plus a second utility called ODBC Spy that will capture the communication between application and driver. ODBC Spy will be a valuable debugging tool, providing information on what ODBC functions were called in what sequence, including parameter and return information.

Application Development Scenarios

Although much of the discussion of interoperability pertains to all applications, the specific issues that a developer needs to address are very much dependent upon the nature of the application. ODBC-enabled applications are many and varied. However, for the purposes of this article, it is possible to categorize these applications according to the number of data sources they need to be able to connect with, and the amount of functionality they require of the data source.

Below are four scenarios that examine the interoperability issue in more detail. Each scenario typifies a subset of applications and discusses approaches to planning and testing.

- Scenario 1 addresses the needs of applications that communicate with a known, limited set of drivers.

- Scenario 2 depicts a mail-merge application, one that needs to use many drivers but does not make heavy demands of those drivers.

- Scenario 3 describes an application that only connects with a small subset of drivers, but that makes use of more functionality than either of the first two scenarios.

- Scenario 4 shows some of the logic of a generic query application that has been designed to expose maximum DBMS functionality and to work with all available drivers.

Note These scenarios are presented solely to illustrate the process of determining how ODBC can best be employed to meet different types of data access challenges. They are by no means intended to represent complete product specifications.

Scenario 1: Merging Data from Two Known Data Sources

Description

A mid-sized manufacturing firm needs a small, custom application that accesses sales data stored in both Microsoft SQL Server and dBASE IV. The company's primary DBMS is SQL Server. It contains tables with information concerning inventory, personnel, customers, sales, and so forth. The dBASE database is used in the field by sales representatives to record information about individual sales. The application in question will run queries against SQL Server based on the data in dBASE and generate summary reports. Assume that there are no plans for using other DBMSs, so the application can ignore many interoperability issues.

Planning the application

The developer could accomplish his or her goal by writing directly to the SQL Server API and retrieving data directly from the dBASE files. However, assume this developer is not very familiar with the SQL Server API or the structure of dBASE files, and prefers to learn a single interface (ODBC) for accessing both data sources. Because the focus of the project is heterogeneous data access, the application seems well-suited for ODBC.

The databases this application needs to connect with are a fixed set: The company uses only SQL Server and dBASE IV®. Because the SQL Server driver is multiple-tier and the dBASE driver is single-tier, the developer might have some concerns about the capabilities of the dBASE driver. However, the functionality requirements of the application are not very demanding. The drivers in question should pose no particular problems due to functionality deficiencies.

The dBASE database contains data regarding sales that the salespeople have made, both basic invoice information and notes particular to a given sale. In order to produce reports from this data, information is needed from SQL Server. For example, the dBASE database contains only product code numbers, but the report will need full product descriptions, which are located in the PRODUCTS database on SQL Server.

What are the specific functionality requirements of the application? From the perspective of ODBC, the application needs to do the following:

- Connect with both data sources.
- Perform simple queries against the data sources, using the data it retrieves from dBASE to generate the queries against SQL Server. As the data is retrieved, the application creates the desired reports.
- Disconnect from the data sources.

Because the drivers have adequate functionality, the developer need not be concerned about having to code around deficiencies. In fact, because the data sources are known and not subject to change, the application can take full advantage of any DBMS-specific features that it wants. For example, the application can prompt the user for the name of the local database using a standard File/Open dialog box with the file extension set for dBASE (.dbf), as opposed to asking the user to identify a data source using the standard ODBC SQL Data Sources dialog box.

Coding and testing the application

From the perspective of ODBC, the coding of the application is very straightforward. After the user selects a dBASE file from the File/Open dialog box, the application uses **SQLAllocEnv** to allocate an environment handle, **SQLAllocConnect** to get connection handles for both data sources, and **SQLDriverConnect** to connect with the drivers.

The application builds a SELECT statement to run against the selected dBASE file. Because the application knows the structure of the databases in advance (things such as the names of the columns and their data types), it need not query for this information. It allocates a statement handle with **SQLAllocStmt**, sends the SELECT statement to the DBMS via **SQLExecDirect**, and binds the columns using **SQLBindCol**. The results are retrieved one row at a time using **SQLFetch**. The data from each row of the result set is used to generate the SELECT statement for the SQL Server database. To retrieve data from SQL Server, the application needs to allocate another statement handle, generate the query, and bind and fetch results. One report is printed for each row of data fetched.

After all data have been retrieved, the application frees the statement handles by calling **SQLFreeStmt**, disconnects from the data sources by calling **SQLDisconnect**, and cleans up after itself by calling **SQLFreeConnect** and **SQLFreeEnv** to free the connection and environment handles.

Because the application is not designed to be interoperable, it need not pursue any ODBC-specific test strategies, other than making certain it works properly with the SQL Server and dBASE drivers.

Scenario 2: Generic Mail Merge Utility

Description

ProseWare Corporation, a small, independent software vendor, wants to use ODBC to increase the data access capabilities of the mail-merge feature of their low-end, Windows-based word-processing program. In the current release, the program can perform mail merge only with data in text format. They hope that ODBC will allow for mail merge with information stored in any desktop database format.

Planning the application

After examining the ODBC *Programmer's Reference*, the developers at ProseWare believe that ODBC will meet their needs. They will design their application to connect with all desktop databases for which there exists a driver (such as Microsoft Access, text, Microsoft Excel, and dBASE). As mail merge does not use any complex or advanced SQL statements and does not make great demands of the ODBC API, this will not be a difficult goal to meet.

Here is how the application's mail-merge feature works from the end user's perspective: After indicating that he or she wants to create a mail-merge document, the user is prompted for the data source using a standard File/Open dialog box. (ProseWare recognizes that their users are familiar with this dialog box, and will find it easier to use than an ODBC data source connection prompt). The file extensions (filters) are listed in a drop-down combo box in the dialog box. The user selects the data source type by choosing the appropriate file filter, and then selecting the file to connect with. For data sources that contain more than one table per file (such as Microsoft Access), the user receives a second dialog box through which he or she indicates the correct table.

The user now begins entering text into her/his document. To insert a data field, he or she selects "Insert Data Field" from the menu. This brings up another dialog box with the list of fields to choose from. The user selects a field, and it is placed in the document. In addition to inserting data fields, users can also indicate simple selection criteria by choosing "Selection Criteria" from the menu. This invokes another dialog box for entering the criteria. When they are finished composing their document, inserting fields, and entering selection criteria, users can select "Print Merge" from the menu, and the document is printed once for each record that meets the criteria.

In terms of ODBC functionality required by the DBMS, the application needs to connect to the data source and retrieve information about the columns it contains so it can populate the selection list. If it is unable to get column information from the DBMS, the application displays an error message indicating to the user that it is unable to communicate with the file. After the user has finished inserting fields and entering selection criteria, the application needs to send a SQL SELECT statement to the DBMS and retrieve the results. Once the results are retrieved, the application can terminate the connection.

Coding and testing the application

The ODBC logic for this feature is more complex than that for Scenario 1, but it is still fairly straightforward. As described above, the application uses a File/Open dialog box to allow the user to select a data source. After the user has selected a data source, the application uses **SQLAllocEnv**, **SQLAllocConnect**, and **SQLDriverConnect** to connect with the driver. **SQLDriverConnect** is called with the option of SQL_DRIVER_PROMPT in case the user needs to indicate further information to access the data source.

The file selected by the user may represent a single table, as is the case for Xbase, or it may represent an entire database, as is the case for Microsoft Access. To find out how the data source treats files, the application needs to call **SQLGetInfo** with an *fInfoType* of SQL_FILE_USAGE. In cases where the data source uses files as databases, the application needs to call **SQLTables** to generate a list of tables for the user to select from. Once the table is known (either because the file itself is a table or because the user has selected one from the list), the application calls

SQLColumns to populate the drop-down combo box that displays the names of the columns the user will place in her/his document.

SQLAllocStmt is called to allocate a statement handle. The application uses a SQL expression builder to transform the user's selection criteria into a SQL SELECT statement written with ODBC syntax. It keeps track of the columns that have been chosen and places them in the SELECT statement. The selection criteria are placed in the WHERE clause. Once the SQL SELECT statement is built, it is sent to the DBMS via a **SQLExecDirect** call.

After the SQL statement has been executed, the application needs to fetch the results and display the retrieved data in the document. To simplify the processing of the results, all data returned from the DBMS is cast to strings. The application uses **SQLBindCol** to bind the columns and **SQLFetch** to retrieve the rows. It can free the statement handle when all data have been returned.

When the user quits the mail-merge feature, the application calls **SQLDisconnect** to terminate the connection, **SQLFreeConnect** to free the connection handle, and **SQLFreeEnv** to free the environment handle.

When debugging the application, the ProseWare developers should test their application against all available desktop-database drivers from all vendors, since their goal is to be interoperable with all of them.

Scenario 3: Report Writer for SQL Server and ORACLE

Description

An independent consultant wants to write a single report writer to sell to two different clients, one of whom has SQL Server and the other, ORACLE Server. The report writer will perform cross-tabulation and feature a "wizard" for helping users generate reports in a step-by-step manner.

Planning the application

This seems to the consultant to be a perfect use of ODBC technology: Rather than write the same application twice to two different APIs, he or she can write the application once to reach both data sources. Although the application uses more DBMS functionality than the first two scenarios, neither the SQL Server nor the ORACLE driver has any trouble providing the necessary level of functionality.

The application enables the user to generate reports from a single table. The user can either use a previously saved report or create a new one. To create a new report, the user begins by selecting a data source and providing any extra information needed to make a connection (for example, password). Next the user is asked which table he or she wants to generate the report from. If the data source uses a three-part table-naming convention, the user is also prompted to select from a list of available table qualifiers. In the case of SQL Server, which uses the database name as the table qualifier, the user is given a list of the available databases. In the case of ORACLE, the user simply selects a table. Once the table has been selected, the user is prompted to provide each of the following in turn:

- The fields that go across the top of the report and the order to display them in (these will be selected from a list)
- The fields by which to group the report, also selected from a list
- The fields to aggregate and which aggregation operations to use (SUM, COUNT, AVG, and so on)
- The selection criteria to impose on the table
- Any scalar functions to be used in building expressions (selected from a list box; only those that are supported by the DBMS are included)
- General formatting information (header and footer, font and point size, document orientation, and so on)

After the user provides the application with all the information, the application builds and executes the SQL SELECT statement and generates the report.

In order to provide the user interface described here, the application needs to gather information about the data in the data source. Some of the things it needs to know are:

- Whether or not qualifiers are used
- Information about field types in order to construct the selection criteria properly
- Which scalar functions are available

Coding and testing the application

Both drivers are Level 1 API conformant, and hence provide support for **SQLColumns** and **SQLTables**, two functions the application needs in order to provide the described functionality. The wizard begins by prompting the user for connection information. Connections are made using **SQLDriverConnect** with a value of SQL_DRIVER_PROMPT for the *fDriverCompletion* parameter. This provides users with the standard SQL Data Sources dialog box.

After connection the user needs to select a table from the data source. The application displays a dialog box that contains two lists. The first list is the available qualifiers; the second is the available tables corresponding to the selected qualifier. If qualifiers are not supported, the first list will be dimmed. To set up the dialog box, the application first calls **SQLGetInfo** with an *fInfoType* of SQL_QUALIFIER_TERM to find out the native term for a qualifier. If the function returns a valid string, as is the case with SQL Server, it will use that string to label the list of qualifiers. It then calls **SQLGetInfo** with an *fInfoType* of SQL_QUALIFIER_NAME_SEPARATOR to find out what character is used between the qualifier and the table name when referring to the table. The separator character is used later when qualifying the table in the FROM clause of the

SELECT statement. For SQL Server, the character is "." (a period). Now the application calls **SQLTables** to generate the list of qualifiers. The "current" qualifier is set by default to the first item in the list. Finally, using the current qualifier if it exists or the empty string if it does not, the application calls **SQLTables** again to populate the list of available tables. Note that the application needs to call **SQLTables** whenever the user selects a new qualifier from the qualifier list in order to repopulate the table list.

As the wizard moves on, it needs to display the columns available in the selected table. These can be populated by calling **SQLColumns**. In addition to providing the names of the columns, **SQLColumns** also provides information on the ODBC SQL data type of the column. Data type information is used elsewhere by the application, such as when prompting the user for fields to aggregate: Only numeric fields are offered as choices.

The application will want to make available a set of scalar functions that are supported by the DBMS. To check if a particular scalar function is supported, the application calls **SQLGetInfo** using the *fInfoType* values for scalar functions (SQL_NUMERIC_FUNCTIONS, SQL_STRING_FUNCTIONS, SQL_TIMEDATE_FUNCTIONS, and so on). These functions will then be placed in a list from which the user can make a selection. When the user selects a scalar function, he or she is prompted for whatever function arguments are required by the ODBC SQL syntax.

For example, suppose the user wishes to select only those rows in which the postal code is "97405", and he or she knows that some of the data contains the full nine-digit postal code. The user can use the SUBSTRING function to extract the first five digits from the POSTAL_CODE field. After selecting SUBSTRING from the list, the application prompts the user for the function arguments—the string, the starting position, and the length of the substring.

Once all the information for the report has been obtained from the user, the application builds a SELECT statement using the ODBC SQL syntax. The SELECT statement includes WHERE and GROUP BY clauses, plus the aggregated fields. Scalar functions are placed in escape clauses, where they can be easily found and parsed by the driver.

Note   Escape clause syntax is used because DBMSs vary in their use of scalar functions. See "The Hurdles to Interoperability" above for further discussion.

For the postal code example, the SUBSTRING portion of the SELECT statement will look like this:

```
{fn SUBSTRING(POSTAL_CODE, 1, 5)}
```
The SELECT statement is sent to the DBMS the same way it was for the Mail Merge application described in Scenario 2. The data is fetched from the DBMS, and the report generated on the screen. If the user is satisfied with the report, he or

she can print it out; otherwise, he or she can regenerate it. Before exiting, the user will have the opportunity to save the report. Upon exiting, or starting a new report, the application closes the connection.

When testing the application, the developer needs to be certain that it works for both data sources for which it was written.

Scenario 4: Generic Query Application

Description

Winmark Enterprises is developing a generic query application that provides users with a means of constructing complex queries against multiple DBMSs. It includes the ability to scroll through result sets; to create new tables; and to add, update, and delete data in the data source.

Planning the application

Winmark's query application pushes ODBC to its limits. It attempts to take advantage of all DBMS-specific functionality, and provide some missing functionality itself. Here are some of the features it provides, and the issues it needs to address in providing them:

- The ability to build complex SQL queries. The application therefore must understand the DBMS's data types, identifier quote characters, and literal prefixes/suffixes, in addition to knowing exactly what SQL statements are supported by the DBMS.

- Creation of tables and indexes. The application needs to know more about data types (such as their native names), whether or not the DBMS supports NOT NULL in the CREATE TABLE statement, and usage of owner names and qualifiers when referring to database objects.

- Access to stored procedures, if available. The application needs to find out if stored procedures are supported, and if so, which ones are available to the user.

- Update, delete, and insert data in the database. The application employs multiple statements (or connections if necessary), one for reading and one for writing. It takes advantage of column privilege information, if it is available. In addition, the application has to address the data integrity issues that are raised in a multi-user environment.

- Scrollable cursors. If they are not available, the application provides this functionality itself.

Note The ODBC SDK 2.0 comes with a cursor library that provides cursor functionality for all drivers. Applications such as this one need to determine whether the cursor library meets their needs. If not, the application will still have to provide the functionality itself.

- Transaction support. If the data source supports transactions, the application supports the transaction semantics of the DBMS. It can query the driver for the supported transaction isolation levels and the default transaction isolation level by calling **SQLGetInfo**.

- Allow aliasing of field names and use of correlation names, if the DBMS does.

Coding and testing the application

Exploring the full logic of an application of this magnitude is beyond the scope of this paper. Instead, here are some of the development issues the programmers would need to address in writing this application.

Creating tables

To provide support for table creation, the application needs to know the data types that the DBMS supports, which can be obtained through **SQLGetTypeInfo**. This same function provides the application with other information it needs, including the parameters for the data types and the DBMS-specific data type names. (**Note**: There has been some confusion about the result set returned by **SQLGetTypeInfo**. The data type names to be used in the CREATE TABLE statement are in the TYPE_NAME column. The LOCAL_TYPE_NAME column is provided for labelling purposes only.) In order to enforce limits such as the maximum number of columns in a table, characters in a column name, and characters in a table name, the application needs to call **SQLGetInfo**. Other information the application may want to gather about the characteristics of the data source includes how qualifiers can be used (**SQLGetInfo** with an *fInfoType* of SQL_QUALIFIER_USAGE), how owner names can be used (**SQLGetInfo** with an *fInfoType* of SQL_OWNER_USAGE), and whether the data source supports non-nullable columns (**SQLGetInfo** with an *fInfoType* of SQL_NON_NULLABLE_COLUMNS).

Updating data

To allow for updates, the application needs access to multiple active statement handles per connection, one for reading and one for writing. It needs to query the DBMS for this capability (by calling **SQLGetInfo** with an *fInfoType* of SQL_ACTIVE_STATEMENTS). If multiple active statements are not supported, the application can open a second connection under the covers, using the connection information it received to make the first connection. Before allowing updates, the application can check if the data source is read-only (**SQLGetInfo** with an *fInfoType* of SQL_DATA_SOURCE_READ_ONLY).

Deleting data

Here is the logic for supporting a DELETE, taking advantage of transactions if they are available, and working around their absence if they are not. When the user attempts to delete a row of the database, the application attempts to build a

WHERE clause for the DELETE statement that uniquely identifies the row. To do so, the application first calls **SQLSpecialColumns**. If **SQLSpecialColumns** indicates that the row can be uniquely identified, the application can build a WHERE clause using the data from the SQL_BEST_ROWID columns(s) and submit a DELETE statement.

If the record cannot be uniquely identified, the application will try to set the connection option to Manual Commit by calling **SQLSetConnectOption** with an *fOption* of SQL_AUTOCOMMIT and a *vParam* of FALSE. If this is successful, the application issues a searched DELETE statement using a WHERE clause that contains all the columns in the row. It then uses **SQLRowCount** to determine how many rows were deleted. If more than one row was deleted, the row was not uniquely identified, and the user needs to be made aware of how many items will be deleted. The application displays a dialog box informing the user that *n* rows will be deleted, and prompts for continuation. If the user chooses to continue, the application issues the COMMIT manually. Otherwise, the transaction is rolled back.

If the application is unable to set the connection option to Manual Commit, the application can perform a SELECT COUNT(*) using the same WHERE clause as the DELETE statement. If the number of rows selected is not equal to 1, the row was not uniquely identified, and the application displays the same alert box as above. If the row is unique, or the user says it is okay to delete more than one, then the application issues the DELETE statement.

Data consistency

Because this application will be running in a multi-user environment, it needs to address the data consistency issues that arise when two users access the same data simultaneously. For example, suppose User 1 and User 2 have both retrieved data from the CUSTOMERS table. It is quite possible that when User 2 attempts to UPDATE one of the records on her/his screen, User 1 has already changed or deleted that record, since there is a lag time between the time when User 2 issued the SELECT and when he or she issued the UPDATE. Some approaches to handling these kinds of problems include:

- Locking the entire table(s) that the user is browsing.
- Locking only the record on which the user's cursor is positioned.
- Checking to see whether the record has been modified and rolling back the UPDATE if it has.

Each method has its own advantages and disadvantages. Note that setting the transaction isolation level to SQL_TXN_SERIALIZABLE guarantees that such anomalies do not occur. However, most data sources implement serializable transactions by a locking protocol, so choosing this option can cause a significant reduction in concurrency. The actual approach chosen by an application depends on the cursor model it uses, the transaction and locking capabilities of the data source, and other factors.

Scalar functions and stored procedures

The application supports any scalar functions available from the data source. As described in Scenario 3, it calls **SQLGetInfo** to find out which are available, if any. The application also provides access to stored procedures if they are supported by the DBMS. It can check to see whether the DBMS supports stored procedures by calling **SQLGetInfo** with an *fInfoType* of SQL_PROCEDURES. If they are not supported, the procedures feature can be disabled (by dimming a menu item). If procedures are supported, the application uses **SQLProcedures** to get the list of those that are available. Some procedures that are returned in this list may not be available to the user; this case can be tested by calling **SQLGetInfo** with an *fInfoType* of SQL_ACCESSIBLE_PROCEDURES. Before using a procedure, the application calls **SQLProcedureColumns** to gather important column and parameter information.

Testing

Because this is a generic application that is designed to connect with any driver, the developers need to test the application with as many drivers as they can procure.

Summary

In discussing ODBC as a tool for heterogeneous data access, this paper has provided the following information:

- A definition of interoperability.
- The approach ODBC has taken to enabling interoperability.
- Guidelines for the application developer to follow when creating interoperable applications, be they custom solutions for in-house use in a corporate environment or commercially available, shrink-wrapped products.
- A discussion of the "ODBC programming paradigm," pointing out issues that developers need to consider when writing their applications, functionality that may differ from one data source to the next, and common pitfalls to be avoided.
- Testing strategies for checking interoperability.
- Development scenarios that demonstrate the use of the ODBC programming paradigm.

The key to writing interoperable applications is to make no assumptions about the functionality or behavior of the DBMS. ODBC encourages driver writers to provide Level 1 API conformance, but not all drivers meet that conformance level. Application developers must query the driver for the capabilities it supports, and respond accordingly based on the information they get back. Although ODBC does not eliminate all conditional code from the application, by shifting the focus from DBMS-dependent code to capability-dependent code, ODBC provides a cost-effective solution for application developers who need to reach multiple DBMSs with a minimum of programming effort.

CHAPTER 11

Messaging API (MAPI): Fundamentals

Topics

Describe the role of the Windows Messaging System and each of its components.

Describe the services that MAPI provides to the application developer.

List the functions of the server messaging system.

Describe folders, messages, recipient lists, and attachments and how they work together.

Describe the role of the address book.

Content

Microsoft Messaging Application Program Interface (MAPI)[1]

Abstract

This article provides an overview of the electronic messaging standard for the Microsoft Windows Open Services Architecture (WOSA).

---

[1] A complete version of this backgrounder is also available on the Microsoft Developer Network Development Library, under Backgrounders and White Papers, Operating System Extensions. Copyright 1993. Used with permission. All rights reserved.

Overview

The information revolution of the 1980s and 1990s has created a serious challenge for organizations. Workers use a greater variety of information in their daily activities than ever before—voice mail, fax, documents, and visual presentations, to name only a few. In addition, workers use this information in a variety of often incompatible software programs, each with different features and commands.

How can information from all these systems be integrated and made easily accessible to users across the entire organization? Many organizations are looking to their electronic messaging system to take on the role of a central communications backbone, used not just for electronic-mail (e-mail) messages, but to integrate all types of information.

With the emergence of powerful enterprise-wide workgroup applications for scheduling, forms routing, order processing, project management, and more, the need for such a communications backbone has never been greater.

Microsoft is committed to making a reality of this vision of electronic messaging as the "central nervous system" for organizational communication. However, achieving this goal requires that messaging applications be plentiful, easy to use, and compatible with each other and with a multitude of messaging systems.

Unfortunately, today's messaging systems and applications have vastly different user interfaces, many are hard to use, and the systems and development tools are largely incompatible with one another. Not surprisingly, developing and deploying a new enterprise-wide program such as a scheduling workgroup application in this mixed-bag scenario can be a nightmare.

Microsoft offers a solution to this dilemma with the Windows operating system and a new messaging industry standard. In consultation with independent software vendors and industry consultants, Microsoft created the messaging application program interface (MAPI) standard to help ensure complete system independence for messaging applications.

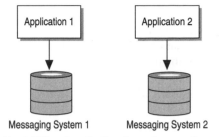

Alternative 1: Different applications for each messaging system

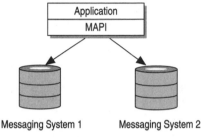

Alternative 2: One application for multiple messaging systems

Figure 11.1   Alternative Application Designs for Addressing Messaging Systems: MAPI allows developers to save time and leverage their efforts by writing a single messaging application that will work without modification on multiple messaging systems. And because users of different systems can share the same client application, an organization can dramatically reduce training and support costs.

MAPI solves a critical development problem. To date, if developers wanted to create a widely usable scheduling workgroup application, they had to write a version for each messaging system on the market. Or else write their own messaging system to go with the application. Neither option is attractive and both demand a tremendous amount of resources. The result is to discourage the development of a variety of messaging applications, especially by smaller vendors.

MAPI offers an alternative by providing a layer of functionality between applications and the underlying messaging systems, allowing each to be developed independent of the other.

The impact on enterprise-wide messaging systems is tremendous. With the MAPI subsystem, adding messaging features to any Windows-based applications is easy for developers, making basic workgroup activities, such as electronically sharing charts and reports, easy for the end users. MAPI also encourages the development of advanced workgroup applications that give workers a better way to exchange information in a corporate setting—from schedules and timesheets to automated forms processing. MAPI does this by acting as a broker between the PC client application and the underlying messaging services. As a result, developers can spend less time trying to fit round pegs into square holes and more time creating applications that let people work in more productive, natural ways.

MAPI also gives organizations the freedom to choose messaging systems and applications according to what best meets the organization's needs, rather than choosing from the few that happen to be compatible. And with the Windows operating system, all of the messaging systems and applications—whether host-based or LAN-based, e-mail, fax, workgroup, and more—are united on the user's desktop with familiar graphical tools.

The Origins of MAPI (WOSA)

MAPI is part of the Microsoft Windows open services architecture (WOSA), a comprehensive design created to hide programming complexities from both users and application developers while providing seamless access across a variety of systems.

WOSA defines a common set of application program interfaces (APIs) that allow developers to write applications and back-end services with the confidence that these products can be easily connected in a distributed computing environment.

WOSA is a critical part of the Microsoft vision of computing in the future, a vision based on the concept of *information at your fingertips*. The goal of this vision is to make information easier to find and use, with the desktop PC serving as the entrance into corporate information, wherever the information resides.

WOSA standards are being developed for database, directory, security, and messaging functions to provide superior PC integration across a variety of platforms. More information on WOSA is available in the WOSA specification on the Microsoft Developer Network CD (Specs and Strategy, Specifications).

As the messaging component of WOSA, MAPI is the result of an effort among Microsoft and more than a hundred independent software vendors (ISVs), messaging system providers, corporate developers, and consultants from around the world. The goal was to develop a messaging API that truly met the needs of developers and vendors while providing the greatest flexibility and power for future messaging applications, allowing workgroup computing to succeed.

MAPI is an open API; it can support virtually any client messaging-enabled application—including advanced workgroup solutions—on any messaging system.

In this white paper, we'll explain the innovative dual (client and messaging-service) API approach of MAPI, its ability to leverage the power of the Windows operating system, and the benefits of this architecture for developers, users, and organizations using electronic messaging.

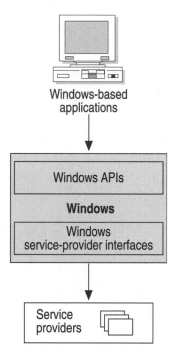

Figure 11.2   **WOSA Architecture: Windows APIs provide the link for Windows-based applications. Windows service provider interfaces provide the link for service providers. Together they enable Windows-based applications to access a wide range of services across multiple environments.**

Requirements for an Open Messaging API

During the development of MAPI, a variety of vendors with a wide range of industry knowledge provided Microsoft with a clear picture of the "must-have" capabilities for any open messaging industry standard.

Open Client and Server Interfaces

It is not enough to be open on the front end, or client-application side, if you can only connect to a single, or at best a few, predefined messaging services. The messaging system API must also be open to a variety of independent message services, whether host-based or LAN-based. In addition, the capabilities of the system should be consistent, regardless of the underlying messaging system. Client applications must be able to communicate across varied messaging systems, giving the customer the greatest freedom to mix and match different client applications with different messaging systems and to choose the "best of breed" products in each category.

Integration with the Operating System

The goal is clear: messaging will be a natural part of all applications, simply another way of exchanging information just as printing from a computer is today. However, the only way this can occur is for the messaging APIs to be closely integrated with the features of the underlying operating system. The operating system itself should include messaging functions and interfaces tailored to its distinctive strengths. There are several benefits to this approach. Consistent messaging functions are always available on every desktop because they are a part of the operating system itself, rather than being an optional add-in that some users may not have. Developers can write to the operating system and exploit advanced features already programmed into every desktop. And finally, messaging functions will look and feel like applications that users and developers are already familiar with.

Cross-Platform Availability

Taking advantage of the distinctive strengths of a specific operating system is crucial for advanced enterprise-wide messaging. So, too, is the ability to communicate cross-platform with other operating systems. Consequently, any operating system-based messaging API should also support a cross-platform industry standard that provides basic messaging functions such as sending and receiving mail on multiple platforms.

Rich, Easy-to-Use Features

Finally, an industry-standard messaging API must be sophisticated enough to handle the needs of a wide range of applications while being easy enough to encourage widespread use to solve a variety of messaging challenges.

MAPI is designed specifically to address each of these critical requirements for an industry-standard messaging API while meeting the needs of the different development communities—from corporate developers to messaging-system developers.

MAPI is open on both the client and server sides. In addition, MAPI is highly integrated with the operating system and will, in fact, ship as a part of the Windows operating system in future releases. Plus, MAPI will support the XAPIA industry-standard cross-platform messaging API effort.

More Than APIs: The Messaging Subsystem

As operating systems become more sophisticated in the 1990s, messaging subsystems will be as important as industry-standard APIs for electronic messaging.

APIs

In any messaging application, there are common functions such as sending, receiving, saving, and reading mail. Each function is controlled within the application by a command or function call. These commands are the Application Programming Interfaces, or APIs. They tell the underlying messaging system what to do; that is, they trigger an action.

Messaging Subsystems

A *messaging subsystem*, which is part of the computer's operating system, responds to the API calls and performs the requested actions. It is called a subsystem because it is a set of code that is a subset of the entire operating system.

In the past, all messaging functions have been handled by the particular messaging service that is running on the LAN or host system. A messaging subsystem does not replace a messaging system such as MS® Mail, Novell MHS, X.400, or IBM PROFS®, but rather acts as a central clearinghouse to unify the various messaging services and shield the user from their differences. Typical functions handled by the subsystem include:

- Providing common user interfaces for message sending, receiving, saving, and so on.

- Managing different message stores.

- Managing different address books.

- Managing the different transports required to send messages to different messaging systems.

- Storing messages in an out box when the intended message system is not connected, and automatically forwarding the message at a later time.

- Notifying applications when events such as mail delivery or mail sending occur.

The Advantages of Messaging Subsystems

The advantage of having a messaging subsystem is that messaging applications do not have to rely on the particular code of each vendor's messaging product. Instead, developers can create applications that will work reliably and consistently for all customers who are using the operating system, regardless of the underlying messaging services or network system.

Developers can rely on the common user interfaces and message functions available on every user's computer (via the messaging subsystem of the operating system). Consequently, the developer of a desktop publishing program who wants to add "Send Mail" as a menu option is assured that this command will always look and work the same for every user, regardless of which messaging or network system is running in the background.

The Best of Both Worlds

MAPI is much more than a set of industry-standard API calls. It is also a messaging subsystem present in the Windows operating system. This innovative architecture allows true independence for both front-end messaging applications and back-end messaging systems.

The MAPI messaging subsystem works just like the print subsystem in the Windows operating system. All Windows applications share common dialog boxes to prompt the user for printing their documents and selecting printers. Different print drivers, which work with the Windows operating system rather than directly with each application, allow applications to work with a variety of printers. The Print Manager and Spooler let a word-processing application print to a network laser printer, for example, while a spreadsheet is printing to a local dot-matrix printer. MAPI's messaging subsystem works in the same way, allowing different messaging applications to communicate to a variety of messaging services.

Because electronic messaging on the desktop PC is relatively new, very few PC operating systems provide a built-in messaging subsystem. MAPI and its messaging subsystem is one of the first messaging systems created as an integral part of a microcomputer's operating system.

MAPI Architecture

In the past, developers had to write messaging and workgroup applications to proprietary platforms. This created obvious limitations, allowing a vendor to support only those users with a particular messaging system. The single alternative was for developers to write their own comprehensive messaging services (including complete facilities for storing, transporting, and addressing messages) in order to be independent. This demands tremendous resources and frequently creates unnecessary duplication of the messaging system.

The MAPI architecture is designed to make it easy to write powerful messaging-enabled applications that are truly independent of the messaging system. To achieve this, MAPI provides two "faces": the application program interfaces (client APIs), which form the client-to-MAPI link, and the service-provider interfaces, which complete the MAPI-to-messaging system link. MAPI provides a set of common function calls that, together with its messaging subsystem, act as brokers between the front-end (client) applications and the back-end (network-messaging) system.

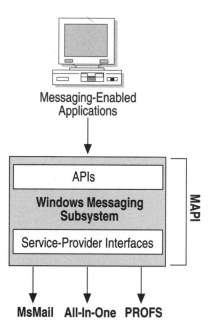

**Figure 11.3   MAPI Open Architecture: MAPI's innovative architecture provides
separate APIs for both the client applications (front end) and for the messaging
systems (back end), allowing true independence between the two and freeing
developers and vendors from compatibility concerns.**

This dual interface helps ensure true openness on both the client and server sides.
Using MAPI calls, any messaging application can use any messaging service (see
"Separating Messaging Services" later in this paper). The application developers
are freed from the messaging-system concerns, and messaging-system vendors are
freed from application-specific concerns.

The MAPI architecture not only makes development easier, but in many cases
makes it possible on a large scale for systems that do not have APIs, such as many
host-based systems. Once a MAPI driver is written for a host system (by either
Microsoft, a third party, or the system vendor itself), developers simply write
applications to the MAPI calls, which in effect become the host APIs.

Finally, the MAPI architecture offers an easy way to tie all of these development
efforts together for the everyday messaging user; namely, the consistent graphical
user interface of the Windows operating system.

The following sections explain the three levels of MAPI architecture: the client
(front-end) APIs, the messaging subsystem of the Windows operating system, and
the service provider (back-end) interfaces.

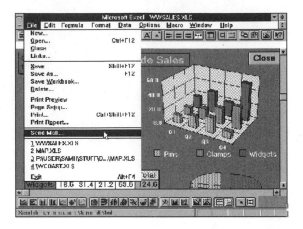

Figure 11.4   MAPI UI Dialog in Microsoft Excel Spreadsheet: Simple MAPI and its common dialog boxes make it easy to add messaging functions to applications for Windows, such as spreadsheets or word processors.

Client APIs

The MAPI front-end, or client, APIs are available in two parts: Simple MAPI, for those applications that require only the most common messaging functions, and Extended MAPI, for creating advanced messaging-based applications.

Simple MAPI

Simple MAPI contains the 12 most common API calls and is designed to make it easy for developers to build powerful custom messaging applications. The types of application that can be created with Simple MAPI include a forms routing program that automatically sends a purchase request form to various workers for their completion and approval. Another example is a calendar and scheduling program that lets users view the schedules of other workers and make requests for meetings. Simple MAPI can also be used to add message capabilities to applications that normally do not provide message services, such as spreadsheets and word processors. Simple MAPI includes an optional common user interface (dialog boxes) so that developers can easily add a consistent look to their applications with very little work.

Whether creating a custom messaging application or adding message capabilities to an existing application, developers do not have to worry about the underlying messaging system or the network platform.

The 12 Simple MAPI calls, listed below, enable an application to send, address, and receive messages. Messages can include data attachments and Windows object linking and embedding (OLE) objects.

Common Messaging Calls (CMC)

The Common Messaging Call Application Program Interface (CMC API) provides a set of ten high-level functions for mail-enabled applications to send and receive electronic messages. It is very easy to add mail capability to an application with CMC, since an important consideration in the design of the API is to minimize the number of function calls needed to send or receive a message. For example a mail-enabled application can send a message with a single function call and receive a specific message with two calls.

The CMC API is designed to be independent of the actual messaging service used. It is also independent of the operating system and underlying hardware used by the messaging service and will allow a common interface over virtually any electronic messaging service. The CMC API is a good choice for applications to use when:

- Multiple computing platforms need to be supported
- Multiple messaging services need to be supported
- Detailed knowledge of the underlying message service is not needed or known

The CMC API was developed in conjunction with the X.400 API Association (XAPIA) standards organization and electronic mail vendors and users. As a cross-platform API, applications on Windows, DOS, OS/2, Macintosh and UNIX platforms can benefit from this simple, easy-to-implement messaging API.

CMC or Simple MAPI?

Since Simple MAPI and CMC provide similar basic messaging functionality for applications, which is the right API to use? As described above, CMC offers many benefits, such as messaging service independence and cross-platform support, so many applications developers would find that API to be the best choice. Simple MAPI is available to support existing applications which have been written to that API. The chart below lists all of the CMC functions, their Simple MAPI equivalents and the purpose of each function.

CMC call	MAPI call	Result
CMC_Logon	MAPILogon	Establishes a session with the messaging service.
CMC_Logoff	MAPILogoff	Terminates a session with the messaging service.
CMC_Free	MAPIFree	Frees the memory allocated by the messaging service.
CMC_Send	MAPISendMail	Sends a standard mail message. Messages can be sent without any user interaction or can be prompted via a common user interface (dialog box).
CMC_SendDocuments	MAPISendDocuments	Sends a standard mail message. This call always prompts with a dialog box for the recipient's name and other sending options. It is primarily intended for use with a scripting language such as a spreadsheet macro.
CMC_List	MAPIFindNext	Lists information about messages meeting specific criteria.
CMC_Read	MAPIReadMail	Reads a specified mail message.
CMC_ActOn	MAPISaveMail, MAPIDeleteMail	Saves or deletes a specified mail message.
CMC_LookUp	MAPIAddress, MAPIDetails, MAPIResolveName	This group of functions handles addressing chores, such as creating addresses, looking up addresses and resolving friendly names with e-mail names.
CMC_QueryConfiguration		Determines information about the installed CMC service.

Extended MAPI

Extended MAPI goes beyond Simple MAPI to provide even greater interaction with the messaging services. Extended MAPI is the additional API set, intended for complex messaging-based applications such as advanced workgroup programs that use the messaging subsystem extensively. Such applications are likely to handle large and complex messages in large numbers, and require sophisticated addressing features. Extended MAPI supports advanced message features such as *custom forms* and *smart forms*. With custom forms, an organization can replace a standard send and receive mail form with its own timesheet or calendar form, with its own predefined fields of information. Smart forms take this one step further, letting you link the information that is entered into those fields with other applications. So, for example, the timesheet entries could all be pulled off the message system automatically and sent to a host-based payroll program.

The message-store and address-book capabilities provided by Extended MAPI are discussed as follows.

Message Store

Extended MAPI provides powerful message store capabilities with its use of folders to organize messages. Folders contain messages, and messages can contain attachments. Folders, messages, and attachments all have properties such as the time sent, type (binary, integer), and so on.

Folders are organized in a hierarchical tree, allowing applications to store messages in any subtree. In addition, wastebasket or out-box folders can be created. Table operations are provided to enable a user to scroll through the folder structure and to view the messages in each folder by subject or other property. Multiple folders can also be searched for specific information. Criteria can be entered to locate messages with particular properties such as subject, sender or recipient, or message text.

Received messages can be modified and stored back in their folders. For example, a user could rotate a fax message that arrived upside down and store it right side up for later viewing. In the Windows operating system, a person who has received a Microsoft Excel spreadsheet as an OLE object in a message can launch Microsoft Excel from within the message, edit the file, and then store the changed file as part of the message.

Address Book

Address books, as defined by MAPI, are a collection of one or more lists of message recipients. Each list is called a *container*. Recipients can be either a single user or a distribution list—that is, a group of recipients that are commonly addressed together. Depending on the features of the service providers available on the network system, address books can be organized to have just a single container, a list of containers, or a hierarchy of containers.

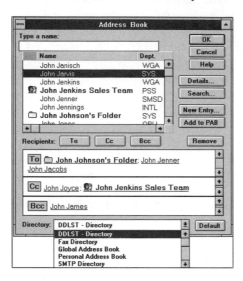

Figure 11.5   Address Book: Even when different messaging systems are being used together, each with their own directories, MAPI can present a single master address book that combines all of the directories, hiding the complexities of the system from the user.

MAPI supports custom address-book providers. For example, a corporate phone book could be created listing all of a company's employees. When a name is selected as a message recipient, additional information could appear such as the person's office location, title and department, supervisor's name, and more.

Even if multiple service providers are installed, MAPI allows access to the different service directories and provides a common interface to give the appearance of a single address book to the client application. This hides the complexities of the multiple back ends from the user. MAPI also provides a specialized container in the address book called the *personal address book*. Users can store copies of frequently used addresses in this container and can also maintain entries for e-mail recipients who are not in the main address book of the underlying messaging system.

With MAPI's support for robust messaging functions, message-service developers can be confident that their existing and future message-store, address-book, and transport services will be fully supported by any MAPI application.

For more information on the types of messaging applications that can be created by Simple and Extended MAPI, refer to the section "MAPI and Messaging Applications" later in this document.

The MAPI Messaging Subsystem

The Common Messaging Calls (CMC), Simple MAPI and Extended MAPI provide the required API calls for messaging applications. These calls work with a second level of MAPI features that are actually built into the Windows operating system: the messaging subsystem. The MAPI messaging subsystem and a MAPI dynamic-link library (DLL) are responsible for dividing the tasks of handling multiple transport-service providers. Drivers for each transport exist in the form of a Windows DLL to provide the interface between the MAPI messaging subsystem message spooler and the underlying back-end messaging system(s) or services (see the "Service Provider Interfaces (SPIs)" section later in this paper for more information on drivers). The message spooler is similar to a print spooler except that it assists with the routing of messages instead of print jobs. The spooler, MAPI.DLL, and the transport drivers work together to handle the sending and receiving of messages.

When many different transport drivers are installed on a Windows-based desktop, messages from client applications can be sent to a variety of transport services. When a message is sent from a client application, the MAPI.DLL responds to the CMC, Simple or Extended MAPI calls first, routing the message to the appropriate message store and address book service providers. When a message is marked for sending, it is handled by the message spooler where it is delivered to the appropriate transport driver.

The message spooler looks at the message's address to determine which transport to use to send the message. Depending on the recipients, the message spooler may call upon more than one transport provider. The spooler performs other message-management functions as well, such as directing inbound messages to a message store and catching messages that are undeliverable because no transport provider can handle them. The spooler also provides an important *store and forward* function, maintaining a message in a store if the needed messaging service is currently unavailable. When connection to the service is reestablished, the spooler automatically forwards the message to its destination.

Except for dialog boxes at the initial transport login, the spooler and transport providers operate in the background, transferring messages among various messaging services. The spooler does its work and makes its calls to the transport providers when the foreground applications are idle, so users don't have to wait while they are working with the messaging application.

Windows application developers enjoy the benefits of the spooler and other messaging subsystem features without having to write additional code beyond the MAPI calls. MAPI automatically assigns the appropriate tasks to the appropriate service providers.

In addition to the common functions for sending and receiving messages, MAPI and its subsystem can support file attachments and Windows OLE objects.

Message Security

MAPI provides tremendous flexibility for message security while supporting multiple message services. MAPI gives complete freedom to each service provider to implement an appropriate level of security for access to the underlying messaging system(s). The service provider (driver) can either prompt for a user's credentials every time a message is sent, or can remember a user's login and forgo the prompting.

In the Windows operating system, MAPI gives each service provider the option of sharing its security responsibilities with the messaging subsystem. The security features MAPI can provide will vary according to what is offered by the operating system. The Windows NT operating system, for example, provides more sophisticated security capabilities than Windows.

Typically, however, the Windows messaging subsystem can, if the provider so requests, store users' credential sets for the service provider. The service provider can also choose how much information is to be retained by the subsystem for each user. It might be as little as the user's network address with no name or password, all the way up to a complete credential set. The subsystem also supports *unified logons*; that is, with a single initial logon to the messaging system, the user can gain access to multiple workgroup applications. Users don't have to enter their name and password for each application they wish to use.

The MAPI messaging subsystem encrypts any security information it stores for a service provider.

Service Provider Interfaces (SPIs)

The third level of MAPI features is the innovative use of a back-end architecture to provide true messaging-system independence for applications. MAPI does this by carrying the concept of printer drivers into the messaging arena. Just as a word-processing program can print to many different printers as long as the necessary drivers are installed, so can any MAPI-compliant messaging application communicate with any messaging service.

The back-end or service-provider interfaces to MAPI are called service provider *drivers*. These drivers can be written by either the service vendor or third-party developers.

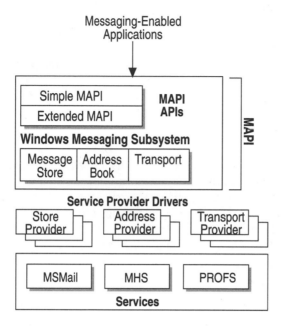

Figure 11.6   MAPI Open Architecture: Information from a variety of services—fax, bulletin boards, host e-mail, LAN e-mail, and more—can be easily used with any MAPI client application. From the Windows desktop, users simply choose the service provider drivers for the desired back-end services. A single in box can present messages from all of the different services.

Because of these drivers, client applications can work with multiple messaging systems such as MS MAIL, Novell MHS, and IBM PROFS at the same time, without having to be customized for each system. On a Windows-based desktop, the user simply selects the desired drivers from the control panel as easily as if installing different printers. Once a driver is installed, the user is never again concerned with the underlying messaging system.

MAPI supports more than just LAN-based electronic-mail systems. Communication in an organization typically includes fax, host services such as DEC All-In-1™, voice mail, public services such as EasyLink®, CompuServe, MCI MAIL®, and others. Drivers can be written for each of these systems and installed by users according to their needs, providing true transport independence. In addition, all of these back ends can share a single, Windows-based user interface. For example, the same client mail application can receive messages from a fax, bulletin board system, host-based e-mail system, and a LAN-based e-mail system. Mail from all of these systems, each with a different transport, can arrive in one universal in box. A single client application handling all of these systems not only reduces development costs, but also reduces costs for application purchases, user training, and system administration.

MAPI's back-end driver approach creates a truly open future. As new technologies provide unforeseen communication tools, vendors can write a driver for the messaging system and it immediately becomes compatible with any existing or future MAPI client applications. Users simply load the new driver to access the new system.

Separating Messaging Services

Most messaging systems include three types of back-end services—message store, address book or directory, and message transport. MAPI supports each type of service independently, allowing a vendor to offer, for example, a specialized addressing service. Or a customer could create its own corporate phone-book directory of employees. In addition, by writing a MAPI driver, a customer could use one of an organization's existing databases to act as a message store. In all these cases, the customer simply loads and selects the appropriate driver for the specialized message service and begins using it with any MAPI-compatible client application.

The MAPI Programming Model

MAPI uses object-oriented programming methods for its messaging functions. Messages, folders, and attachments are all accessed through MAPI object structures. When one of these objects is opened, the calling program gets a pointer to the MAPI object; it uses the pointer to further manipulate the object. Each type of object allows different calls, or operations, to be made to it. Many MAPI objects support *polymorphism*, which means that the same set of calls can be made to different objects. This can reduce the time it takes to write an application by reducing the amount of code required. For example, an application can use the same code to browse a list of messages and to browse a list of attachments.

The MAPI object model is consistent with both present and future object-oriented models for Windows, recognizing each service-provider dynamic-link library (DLL) as a separate object.

Multiplatform Support

MAPI is the messaging standard for the Windows operating system. As an integral part of the Windows operating system, MAPI will pave the way for powerful network-independent messaging capabilities for workgroup applications. Tight integration with the operating system is vital to achieve advanced messaging functions with the benefits of the graphical Windows operating system.

In an enterprise-wide messaging system, the ability to support the basic messaging features common to other operating systems is also important. As a member of the X.400 Application Program Interface Association (XAPIA), Microsoft is working with other messaging vendors and end users to define a cross-platform API set for basic messaging functions such as sending and receiving mail. Microsoft will deliver Simple MAPI on some other platforms such as MS-DOS and Macintosh to aid developers until the universal XAPIA calls are available for these basic cross-platform messaging functions.

Solutions to Customer Messaging Problems

MAPI's architecture provides organizations with tremendous flexibility to respond to the challenges of enterprise-wide messaging systems. Because the client messaging applications are truly independent of the underlying network services, MAPI helps solve three critical messaging problems facing organizations today. The problems: supporting multiple messaging services with a common client, integrating services at the desktop, and choosing specialized service providers.

Migrating from Multiple Messaging Services

Typically, an organization running multiple e-mail systems linked by gateways must use tremendous development and support resources in order to maintain compatibility among the systems. Users are often stuck with the proprietary mail application that came with each messaging system. With users in the same organization working on different applications to accomplish the same tasks, training and support demands can be greatly increased. Alternatively, a single messaging system, with a universal client application, can provide significant benefits. MAPI makes it easier for an organization to migrate to a single messaging system by allowing a gradual, phased migration.

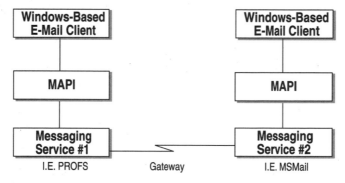

Figure 11.7   Migration/Mulitple Back Ends: MAPI lets an organization use the same client mail application with a variety of messaging systems, providing a consistent user interface during a migration to a single messaging system.

Because MAPI eliminates the dependence between the client application and the server messaging system, there is true transport independence. As a result, an organization can continue to use its different messaging systems while migrating all users to the same client e-mail application. The organization is free to choose the client application that best meets its needs.

An organization can then consolidate its multiple messaging systems to a new single system at its own pace, without disrupting the users and their common client application.

The move to a single client application provides an additional benefit for organizations running different e-mail systems. A common client application gives an organization a consistent API on every desktop. This makes it easier to develop custom messaging applications that will run the same for every user, despite the different back-end messaging systems.

Integrating Services at the Desktop

MAPI makes it possible to integrate multiple, diverse messaging services at the desktop. This means that an e-mail, fax, voice mail, and bulletin-board service could all be reached through a single client application acting as a master communications window. Rather than have a separate in box for each messaging system, users can enjoy the simplicity of a single universal in box to consolidate all of the various message types.

The user simply installs the drivers for the appropriate services, just like printer drivers for different printers.

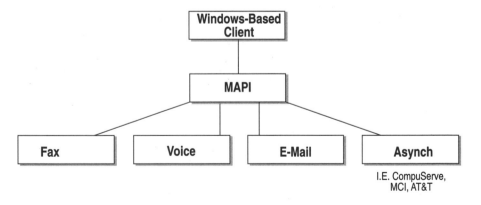

Figure 11.8   Integration of Services at Desktop: By simply installing MAPI drivers for each desired service, users can access a variety of communication services—from e-mail to fax—through a single client interface.

Choosing Specialized Service Providers

Today, when choosing a messaging system for their networks or host systems, organizations are faced with an all-or-nothing choice. Either take all of the system's services—the directory/address service, the message-store and database functions, and the transport agent—or take nothing at all. And rarely is one system equally strong in all three areas.

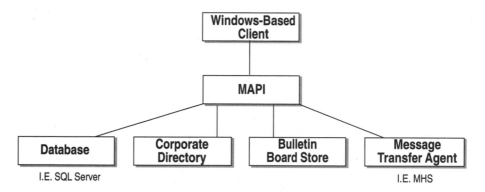

Figure 11.9   Provide for Service Provider Specialization: Because MAPI supports each part of a messaging system separately—the address book, transport, and message store—an organization can choose from the best specialized back-end services while maintaining a consistent client front-end for users.

MAPI, because it defines each aspect of the messaging system independently, supports specialized service providers. Independent developers can focus on just one type of service. A directory developer doesn't have to worry about writing a transport, for example. The customer benefits with a choice of powerful, specialized services.

Any organization can mix services from its own corporate resources and from outside vendors to customize a messaging system for its own needs. For example, an existing database could be used for the message-store facility in conjunction with an off-the-shelf directory service. Using MAPI drivers, any service or combination of services from different sources can work together without modification and without affecting any existing MAPI-compatible client applications.

MAPI and Messaging Applications

Messaging-Aware Applications

MAPI allows basic messaging capabilities to be easily integrated into virtually any desktop application. Using the Common Messaging Calls or Simple MAPI, developers can add message capabilities to their applications' own user interfaces.

A word-processing program could be enhanced to include a Send Message option next to the print selection. Such an option would send the document as a mail message to a recipient.

MAPI also supports application macro languages, such as those in Microsoft Excel and Word. This method of incorporating message capabilities into existing applications is extremely flexible. For example, a spreadsheet macro could be written that automatically sends a monthly budget spreadsheet to a designated recipient when the file is updated with new sales figures.

Applications are called *messaging-aware* when they do not depend upon messaging for their functions. That is, the basic messaging capabilities provide an additional value to the regular features of that application.

Sales Report Automation Macro

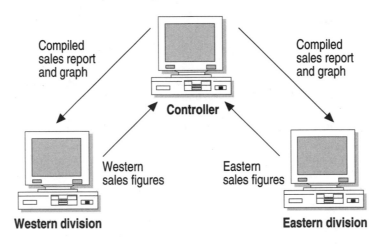

Figure 11.10   Using Microsoft Mail and Microsoft Excel: The Eastern and Western sales divisions create sales reports that are automatically sent to the controller machine at the corporate office. The controller machine automatically consolidates the two reports and sends the combined report back to the sales divisions.

Simple MAPI and CMC are designed for messaging-aware applications.

Messaging-Enabled Applications

Unlike messaging-aware applications, *messaging-enabled* applications require some type of messaging capability in order to function. One example is a scheduling application in which users can view the schedules of their coworkers and send meeting requests to the coworkers' calendars. Another example is a forms-routing application that sends an expense report to a series of recipients and records their approval or disapproval.

Simple MAPI and CMC are designed for messaging-enabled applications.

Messaging-Based Workgroup Applications

The most advanced type of messaging application is the workgroup application, which requires full access to all of the back-end messaging services, including the message-store, address-book or directory, and transport functions. These applications include e-mail clients, workflow automation programs, and bulletin board services. For example, a workflow application might allow a user to inspect a message stored in a certain project folder to see if the appropriate workers have signed off on their tasks. This application could also include a sophisticated search-and-store feature that retrieves relevant files from a bulletin board system and stores them in the folders of certain recipients.

A workgroup application could also be created for an advanced expense-report system in which the application selects the appropriate managers to send the report to based on the type of expense. In addition, this application could search the schedules of the appropriate managers, identify who is available to approve the expense report, and automatically route the report to that manager.

For these advanced workgroup applications, we recommend that developers also use Extended MAPI.

MAPI Developer Resources

Developers can be assured of having the tools and resources they need to develop any MAPI-compatible application.

Software Development Kits (SDKs)

Simple MAPI is available today in the Windows SDK. Simple MAPI is also included in MS Mail for PC Networks and is available for MS Mail for AppleTalk Networks.

The Simple MAPI SDK and the Common Messaging Call (CMC) SDK are available on CompuServe. Type Go MSWRKGRP at any CompuServe prompt and move to section 17.

Because the full MAPI functionality will be built into future releases of the Windows operating system, all of MAPI will eventually be available in the Windows SDK itself.

MAPI functions are designed to be called from C programs as well as through scripting packages such as Microsoft Visual Basic programming system and various application macro languages such as Microsoft Excel and Word.

Summary

In order to take advantage of their messaging systems as powerful communication backbones, organizations need a messaging standard that is open on both the client and messaging-system ends. Because MAPI provides both a client API and a service-provider API, it is possible to insulate application developers from the details of the underlying messaging system. MAPI's use of service provider interfaces and its support for industry-standard, cross-platform messaging APIs ensures interoperability with other messaging systems on other leading operating systems. By providing a standard that is easy for both service providers and application developers to adopt, MAPI encourages the creation of a new generation of exciting workgroup applications."

Topics

Describe the role of the address book.

Describe the role of the message store.

Describe the role of the message spooler.

Describe the role of the transport provider.

Content

Understanding and Using Extended MAPI[2]

Ted Stamps

Ted Stamps is a Program Manager for Microsoft Corporation. He is a technical architect for Microsoft's Messaging Application Programming Interface (MAPI).

---

[2] A complete version of this presentation is also available on the Microsoft Developer Network Development Library, under Conferences and Seminars, Tech*Ed March 1994, Workgroup Applications. Copyright 1994. Used with permission. All rights reserved.

Session Objective

This session covers Microsoft MAPI 1.0. MAPI 1.0 is Microsoft's messaging architecture for connecting applications to a diverse array of messaging services. Many people are familiar with Simple MAPI, which Microsoft has been shipping since 1992. Simple MAPI is just one component of the MAPI architecture, so this paper will discuss how Simple MAPI fits in with Extended MAPI and MAPI 1.0, and how to build applications to take advantage of the new features in the MAPI messaging architecture. Most of the information about Extended MAPI is technically oriented for the intermediate C or C++ developer

What's Covered

- Uses for MAPI
- MAPI architecture
- Using extended MAPI to access:
  - Message stores
  - Address books
  - Transports
- Demo
- Developer information

Uses for MAPI

What types of problems was MAPI designed to solve? What's a good use for MAPI? Since MAPI offers more of an architecture approach than just APIs, this paper will look into how that approach benefits the user and developer.

MAPI Architecture

By understanding the MAPI architecture, we'll be able to see more clearly how different messaging applications and components can fit together. The MAPI architecture will also be a good place to help us understand the differences between Simple MAPI, Extended MAPI, and MAPI 1.0

Using Extended MAPI to Access...

Using Extended MAPI, you have much greater control over messaging services like message stores, address books, and message transports. So we'll be looking into the interfaces that Extended MAPI provides us to interact with these services when building our applications.

Demo

We'll be demonstrating MAPI and several MAPI components. On the client side, we're going to connect Microsoft's forthcoming MAPI-compliant messaging client to several services, using MAPI service providers. We'll also show a messaging client from a company called Isocor connecting to those same services, demonstrating MAPI's open mix-and-match architecture.

Developer Information

We'll cover the various tools that you would use to add messaging features to your applications or to write MAPI applications and service providers.

Messaging Problems in the Past

Up to this point, if developers wanted to create a widely-used workgroup application such as scheduling package, they had to write a different version for each messaging system that their customers were likely to use. This meant getting familiar with APIs like Simple MAPI, VIM, MHS, and others. Developers ended up spending a large amount of time adding repetitive support for different messaging systems, rather than focusing on end-user features or capabilities of their application. Another alternative was to write a messaging system to go along with the application, which forced developers to focus on solving back-end messaging, rather than application problems.

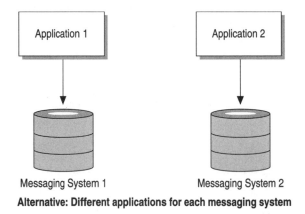

Alternative: Different applications for each messaging system

Figure 11.11   Different applications for each messaging system.

Neither option is attractive and both demand a tremendous amount of resources. This situation discouraged the widescale development of messaging applications, especially by smaller vendors.

Unfortunately, the customer email landscape did not make life easy for messaging developers. Most corporations have many different messaging systems installed, because email has often been installed on an ad-hoc, departmental basis. A typical example might be a workgroup like the marketing department that decides to install email and chooses Microsoft Mail. The Finance department also wants to install email and installs cc:Mail. Many people in the Engineering group are still connected to the mainframe and use host-based mail.

This situation creates many problems. Not only are support and training issues difficult because of the variety of features and user interfaces, but rolling out a single application throughout the company is nearly impossible. There are few selections from among commercial applications, and corporations find it difficult and costly to develop their own in-house applications.

Only now are corporations beginning to transition to a unified LAN-based email system, but they will have an investment in various existing systems for a long time.

The last problem caused by the lack of system-based messaging APIs is that few workgroup applications were developed. Because existing messaging APIs were limited in functionality and supported only one mail system, most messaging systems were used only for simple messaging or file attachments, rather than for workgroup computing.

Solution: MAPI

MAPI offers an alternative to today's messaging API approach by providing a layer of functionality between applications and underlying messaging systems, allowing each to be developed independently of the other.

The impact on enterprise-wide messaging systems is tremendous. MAPI is a messaging architecture approach, rather than a limited messaging API. Because adding messaging features to any Windows-based application is easy for developers, basic workgroup activities, such as electronically sharing charts and reports, become easier for end users. MAPI also encourages the development of advanced workgroup applications that give workers a better way to exchange information in a corporate setting—from schedules and timesheets to automated forms processing. MAPI does this by acting as a broker between the PC client application and the underlying messaging services. As a result, developers can spend less time trying to fit round pegs into square holes and more time creating applications that let people work in more productive, natural ways.

MAPI Goals

MAPI has three main goals as an operating system-based messaging architecture. The first is to separate client applications from the underlying messaging services. By doing this, MAPI reduces application development cost by allowing developers to focus their time on adding user features and refining interfaces rather than adapting their product for additional messaging systems or building their own messaging support. Client applications will be able to communicate across varied messaging systems, giving the customer the greatest freedom to mix and match different client applications with different messaging systems and to choose the "best of breed" products in each category.

The second goal is to make basic mail-enabling a standard feature of all applications. Mail-enabling is a useful feature because users can send files and other information without having to exit an application like Microsoft Excel and begin a message in their mail application. By having a consistent, easily implemented messaging interface in the operating system, developers will add messaging functionality to a wide range of desktop productivity products.

Finally, MAPI is designed to enable not just simple messaging access, but the rich features required by messaging-reliant, workgroup applications. These applications need to interact with the messaging system very closely to file and retrieve messages and documents, send and route messages, and maintain user and address lists. MAPI provides the rich services required by the most demanding messaging applications.

Migrating from Multiple Messaging Services

Typically, an organization running multiple email systems linked by gateways must use tremendous development and support resources in order to maintain compatibility among the systems. Users are often stuck with the proprietary mail application that came with each messaging system. With users in the same organization working on different applications to accomplish the same tasks, training and support demands can be greatly increased.

Alternatively, a single messaging system, with a universal client application, can provide significant benefits. MAPI makes it easier for an organization to migrate to a single messaging system by allowing a gradual, phased migration.

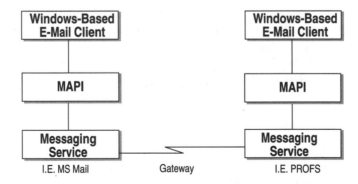

Figure 11.12   Migration/Multiple Backends MAPI lets an organization use the same client mail application with a variety of messaging systems, providing a consistent user interface during a migration to a single messaging system.

Because MAPI eliminates the dependence between the client application and the server messaging system, there is true transport independence. As a result, an organization can continue to use its different messaging systems while migrating all users to the same client email application. The organization is free to choose the client application that best meets its needs.

An organization can then consolidate its multiple messaging systems to a new single system at its own pace, without disrupting the users and their common client application.

The move to a single client application provides an additional benefit for organizations running different email systems. A common client application gives an organization a consistent API on every desktop. This makes it easier to develop custom messaging applications that will run the same for every user, despite the different back-end messaging systems.

Integrating Services at the Desktop

MAPI makes it possible to integrate multiple, diverse messaging services at the desktop. This means that an email, fax, voice mail, and bulletin-board service could all be reached through a single client application acting as a master communications window. Rather than have a separate Inbox for each messaging system, users can enjoy the simplicity of a single universal Inbox to consolidate all the various message types.

The user simply installs the drivers for the appropriate services, just like printer drivers for different printers.

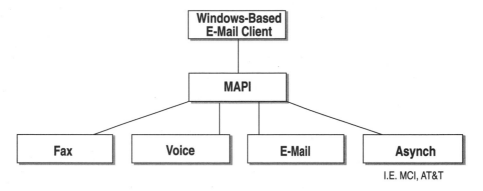

Figure 11.13   Integration of Services at Desktop: By simply installing MAPI drivers for each desired service, users can access a variety of communication services—from email to fax—through a single client interface.

MAPI Components

The MAPI architecture is designed to make it easy to write powerful messaging-enabled applications that are truly independent of the messaging system. To achieve this, MAPI provides two "faces": the application program interfaces (client APIs), which form the client-to-MAPI link, and the service-provider interfaces, which complete the MAPI-to-messaging system link. MAPI provides a set of function calls that, together with its messaging subsystem, act as brokers between the front-end (client) applications and the back-end (network-messaging) system.

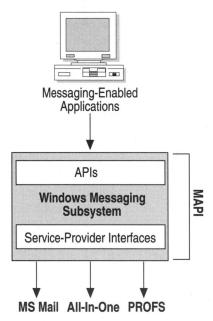

Figure 11.14   MAPI Open Architecture: MAPI's innovative architecture provides separate APIs for both the client applications (front end) and for the messaging systems (back end), allowing true independence between the two and freeing developers and vendors from compatibility concerns.

This dual interface helps ensure true openness on both the client and server sides. Using MAPI calls, any messaging application can use any messaging service. The application developers are freed from the messaging-system concerns, and messaging-system vendors are freed from application-specific concerns.

The MAPI architecture not only makes application development easier, but in many cases makes it possible for systems that don't have APIs, such as many host-based systems. Once a MAPI driver is written for a host system (by either Microsoft, a third party, or the system vendor itself), developers simply write applications to the MAPI calls, which in effect become the host APIs.

The application components for MAPI include: Simple MAPI which means that all existing Simple MAPI applications will continue to operate; Common Messaging Calls to support applications written for the standard XAPIA cross-platform API, and Extended MAPI, which is the new client API for workgroup and mail-reliant applications.

For messaging services, MAPI provides separate interfaces for address books, message stores (or "databases") and message transports. These messaging service providers are Windows Dynamic Linked Libraries (DLLs) that run on the Windows desktop.

Taken together, the entire architecture is called MAPI 1.0. The messaging API that is shipping today, Simple MAPI is in fact just one component integrated into MAPI 1.0. Similarly, CMC, which is also shipping, and Extended MAPI, are other integrated components. All of the interfaces taken together form MAPI 1.0, a complete messaging architecture for connecting messaging applications with services.

API Features
Store Centric
Many people will be surprised to find that MAPI has extremely strong database and data handling capabilities. This isn't so unusual when you stop to think that every messaging system has storage and organizational capabilities for messages. MAPI's message stores go beyond handing email messages. They are built to handle everything from email messages to documents and other data files to OLE objects, video and sound clips, and so on. Also, most workgroup applications make rich use of shared databases. With this in mind, having strong data handling capabilities in a messaging architecture is critical.

Multiple Providers
MAPI is also about transparently accessing diverse messaging systems. Even though MAPI has a lot of new, powerful capabilities, it's not difficult to write MAPI applications. By writing to either Simple MAPI, CMC, or Extended MAPI, MAPI client applications will work interoperably with any MAPI provider. Similarly, users will find that using one interface to access a variety of different messaging systems reduces the effort to learn new systems.

Common User Interface
MAPI provides some common user interface code, which will be examined later in this paper. Just like the common dialog boxes in Windows (for opening and saving files, printing, and so on) MAPI's common user interface adds some consistency between different applications as they access mail services. Common user interface dialog boxes also make it easier for developers to add messaging capabilities to

their applications, because for many functions they can use predefined dialog boxes.

Different APIs for Different Needs

The most important point to remember about MAPI is that, although there are several different options when it comes to client application programming interfaces, it shouldn't be difficult to decide which one is the best to use.

Simple MAPI and CMC are very similar in their construction and in their intended use. They are for mail-enabling applications, that have occasional use of the mail system. Mail-enabling might include adding a File.Send command to an application to easily send a document or report over the mail system. Although mail-enabled applications use the mail system, they aren't often oriented towards workgroup computing.

Extended MAPI is for an entirely different audience. It is a more complex, object-oriented API that is intended for applications that need to make frequent, heavy use of the mail system. These applications are usually called mail-reliant applications because they require access to a messaging system in order to perform their function and often need to closely interact or control the messaging function. These applications could include messaging clients, workgroup applications, rules processors, or Electronic Data Interchange (EDI) clients, among others.

Common Messaging Calls

The Common Messaging Calls are new (they were announced in June, 1993) and may be unfamiliar to some people. Although this paper is mostly about Extended MAPI and MAPI 1.0, some brief information about CMC is useful.

Microsoft worked with other vendors and corporate email users in the X.400 Application Programming Interface Association (XAPIA) to define a cross-platform API for mail-enabling applications. Similar in construction and target use to Simple MAPI, this API can be used by applications on a variety of platforms such as Windows, the Macintosh, UNIX, and others.

The API is relatively easy to implement; there are 10 function calls for things like addressing messages, sending messages, and receiving messages. Developers can also implement forms-based solutions using the CMC. When used on Windows with the MAPI architecture, CMC applications can take advantage of MAPI's common user interface dialogs boxes.

Here is a quick chart comparing the functions in Simple MAPI and CMC:

CMC call	MAPI call	Result
CMC_Logon	MAPILogon	Establishes a session with the messaging service.
CMC_Logoff	MAPILogoff	Terminates a session with the messaging service.
CMC_Free	MAPIFree	Frees the memory allocated by the messaging service.
CMC_Send	MAPISendMail	Sends a standard mail message. Messages can be sent without any user interaction or can be prompted via a common user interface (dialog box).
CMC_SendDocuments	MAPISendDocuments	Sends a standard mail message. This call always prompts with a dialog box for the recipient's name and other sending options. It is primarily intended for use with a scripting language such as a spreadsheet macro.
CMC_List	MAPIFindNext	Lists information about messages meeting specific criteria.
CMC_Read	MAPIReadMail	Reads a specified mail message.
CMC_ActOn	MAPISaveMail, MAPIDeleteMail	Saves or deletes a specified mail message.
CMC_LookUp	MAPIAddress, MAPIDetails, MAPIResolveName	This group of functions handles addressing chores, such as creating addresses, looking up addresses and resolving friendly names with email names.
CMC_QueryConfiguration		Determines information about the installed CMC service.

Extended MAPI

Extended MAPI is a new interface for messaging client applications and is the focus of this paper. This paper looks at the Object Interfaces that Extended MAPI provides, the Common Base interfaces to tables and properties, and the interfaces for message stores and address books.

Object Oriented

MAPI uses object-oriented programming methods for its messaging functions. Messages, folders, and attachments are all accessed through MAPI object structures. When one of these objects is opened, the calling program gets a pointer to the MAPI object; it uses the pointer to further manipulate the object. Each type of object allows different calls, or operations, to be made to it. Many MAPI objects support polymorphism, which means that the same set of calls can be made to different objects. This can reduce the time it takes to write an application by reducing the amount of code required. For example, an application can use the same code to browse a list of messages and to browse a list of attachments.

The MAPI object model is consistent with both present and future object-oriented models for Windows, recognizing each service-provider dynamic-link library (DLL) as a separate object.

Object Dependency Tree

The diagram below shows how messaging objects are accessed through MAPI object methods. The top-level interface is MAPISession, where the logon/logoff process takes place to initialize or end a messaging session. Once an application has logged on and started a MAPI session, that application makes requests to MAPI services and receives pointers to those service objects. Common classes of service objects include message stores and address books. We'll look at some of the available methods for each type of service object in the following pages.

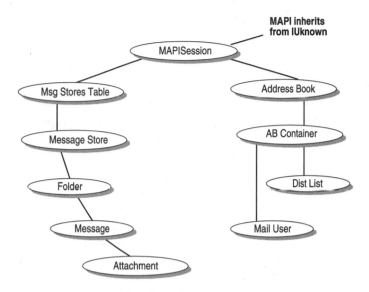

Figure 11.15   Object dependency tree

Public Interfaces

There are two types of public interfaces that are very important to MAPI applications: properties and tables.

Rich Property Model

Messages, attachments and other objects in MAPI are principally composed of data called *properties*. Examples of properties include the subject line of a message, the name of a user, or the body of an attachment. Each property contains a value of interest to the recipient who receives a message or the transport that handles a message during delivery. Objects having accessible properties typically have a pair of "Get/Set" functions that allow you to get (read) or set (write) the property of interest. Properties can consist of many different types of data, including currency figures, date/time, text, integers, real numbers, binary information and objects.

It's important that MAPI has a strong property model because using properties, it can exchange messages with other types of messaging services. For example, when creating a message destined for an X.400 messaging system, the application that creates the message will add X.400-specific properties to the message so that the message can be received and understood by other non-MAPI X.400 applications. Also, properties can be used to hold important information about message attachments, such as the file name, date, time, size, and icon.

Properties can also be used to form the basis of useful workgroup applications. By adding custom properties to a message or other object, the receiver will be able to file, search, and retrieve that message or object by more meaningful information than simply the message subject, sender, and so on.

Table Interface

The MAPI table interface (IMAPITable) allows applications to examine an object composed of rows of information, where each row contains a number of columns, much like a spreadsheet contains rows and columns of data. The interface allows display of tables within a dialog box or window user interface.

The table interface is quite useful for dealing with large amounts of data, typically found in an address book with thousands or millions of entries, or a message store, having a similar amount of information. One of the benefits of MAPI's object implementation, is that once code is written for a table viewer that handles addresses, for example, that same code can be used to view other tables of data.

The table interface has methods for quickly sorting tables, for navigating within the table, and for seeking particular locations or rows.

Message Store

As discussed, MAPI is very store-oriented. The message store, or rather the collection of message stores, is the center of the MAPI universe. We say "collection of stores" because most users will likely have at least two message stores to access, and perhaps more. All users will have the local message store, which comes with MAPI and is a MAPI component, as well as one or more network-based or remote message stores.

Between the stores, it is very easy to copy and move messages and folders, just as users today copy and move files and directories. Users can have access to messages when they are disconnected from the network by copying them into a folder in the local message store.

The folder storage is hierarchical, which means that you can have folders, then sub-folders, and more subfolders and on. Messages can be stored at any level. Developers have access to all of the folders and messages, which is more control than provided by Simple MAPI or CMC. Those APIs only give access to the Inbox.

MAPI provides developers with search folders, which can be used to locate messages. Just as today's Microsoft Mail offers the Message Finder, MAPI has a rich search capability that allows users based on any property (such as time/date, user, subject or custom property) that is carried by a MAPI message.

MAPI provides a rich notification engine, which is an improvement over the polling process used by many of today's mail products. These products check for a specific event (like new message arrival) at a specified time interval. With MAPI, messaging clients and providers can register their interest with MAPI regarding many system events, like new message arrival, message deletion, or creating a new address entry, and so on. When this event happens, the MAPI subsystem notifies the messaging applications and providers, which then take the appropriate action. By moving the notification responsibilities to MAPI, MAPI can consolidate notification responsibilities and improve system response and performance.

Message Submission

It may be helpful to walk through the process of creating and submitting a message to see how all of the MAPI services interact.

The messages are initially created in a message store. The store is also used for creating messages, not just for storing and organizing them.

The recipients of a message are chosen by the user or by a messaging application from the various address books installed on the system. The message is then submitted.

The spooler, which is an active process in MAPI, examines the message and reads the table of recipients contained within the message. Based on the message systems on which the message will be transmitted, the spooler exposes the message to the appropriate transports. For example, if the message was addressed to a fax user (as in "FAX:1-206-555-1212") then the spooler would expose the message to the fax transport, and only to the fax transport. Other transport providers would not be aware that a message was being processed.

Through this example of an outgoing message, we can see how a messaging application would interact in a simple way with the message store, the address books, and the message transports.

IFolder

A folder object (or just folder) is an organized collection of messages and possibly other folders. Folders are used to group and arrange the messages in a message store so users can more easily locate and access the messages. Each message store has at least one folder, called the root folder. Additional folders can be created for the message store and placed in the root folder or in other folders that exist.

You create and manage folders and messages in folders using the functions of the IFolder interface. These functions are available whenever you create or open a folder object. Here are some of the most common functions.

Function	Description
GetContentsTable	Returns a pointer to a table of summary information
GetHierarchyTable	Returns a table object with information about the child folders of the current folder
Create/Delete/Copy Folder	Performs management on folder objects
Create/Delete/Copy Messages	Performs management on messages in folders
Get/Set SearchCriteria()	Reads or sets the search criteria for a particular search results folder

IMessage

A message object provides access to the contents of a message within a message store. A message consists of properties, attachments, and recipients. A message object supports the IMAPIProp interface for access to properties in the message as well as additional operations specific to messages.

All messages support the IMessage interface. Here are some of the common functions:

Function	Description
GetAttachmentTable()	Returns the attachment table in a message.
Create/DeleteAttach()	Creates a new attachment or deletes an attachment in a message.
Get/ModifyRecipientTable()	Returns the recipient table, or adds, deletes, or modifies the table.
SubmitMessage()	Saves all changes to a message and its attachments. Marks the message as ready for sending.
AbortSubmit()	Attempts to cancel the send process

IAttach

Attachments objects are a way of delivering additional data, beyond that of the message itself, through the messaging system to a recipient. While there are a variety of attachment types, most application writers use the following types:

- An attached file, by reference or with the full contents embedded in the attachment

- An attached OLE object, by reference or with embedded contents
- An attached MAPI message (possibly containing more attachments)
- Arbitrary binary data (such as sound or images)

Properties in the attachment object indicate the position where the attachment appears in the message, the attachment type, and other information describing the attachment.

Address Books

The address book object is the highest level of access to lists of recipients that are selected when addressing a message. It represents a collection of possible recipients usually (except in the case of the Personal Address Book) grouped together by the type of message service on which the addresses are found.

Just as with folders, the address books are structured as a hierarchy. Each address book can contain distribution lists, which can contain additional distribution lists and individual addressees. Address books are often viewed as a table, perhaps using the same table viewer code constructed to view a table of messages and folders in a message store.

Users will see individual address books installed on the system, and will be able to open various address books to build a message recipient table. The view of multiple address books helps to logically organize users instead of viewing one immense list. Messaging applications however, are more efficient at making sense of vast amounts of information and thus view the entire set of address entries available as a single, unified table. This allows a single message to be simultaneously addressed and sent to multiple users on multiple messaging systems.

MAPI provides users and developers with a rich container for addresses called the Personal Address Book. The PAB is a collection of address book entries from other address books. So, even if a LAN-based address service is not connected or not available, users will have access to frequently used addresses and address information in their Personal Address Book.

Address Book Common UI

The address-related functions provide most of the common user interface dialogs in MAPI. The common messaging dialogs are optional for an Extended MAPI application (they are required in Simple MAPI or CMC) but fulfill the useful purpose of providing consistency between different messaging applications and speeding up application development.

Address()

The Address method is used to address a new message, or to perform maintenance on the Personal Address Book. It generates the following dialog box which contains both individual users and distribution lists.

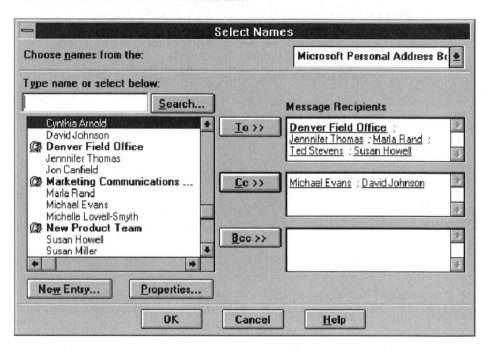

Figure 11.16   Select Names dialog

ResolveName()

The Resolve Name method is used to resolve a "friendly" name, or display name, into the email name required by the underlying messaging system. For example, a user might address a message by typing "Marla Rand" but the Resolve Name method would then match that name against a specific email address in an address book.

The Resolve Name function is also used to choose between ambiguous entries. For example, if there were more than one Marla Rand in the address book, the ResolveName method would generate a dialog box from which the user would pick the appropriate addressee.

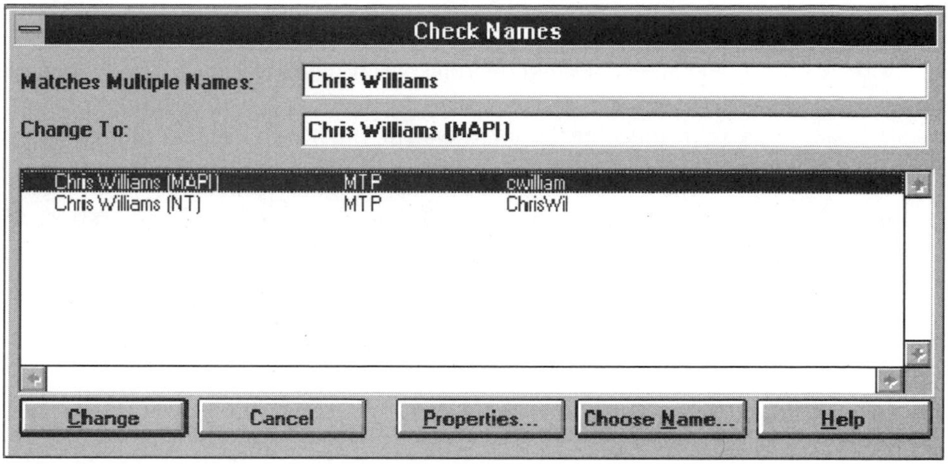

Figure 11.17   Check Names dialog box

Details()

The Details method displays a dialog box which provides the underlying information for a specific address entry. For example, in the Personal Address Book, the Details method would show a dialog box which would include the user's display name, their email name, and the email type. On other address book types, more detailed information may be available, such as the office address, a phone number, or a picture of the employee.

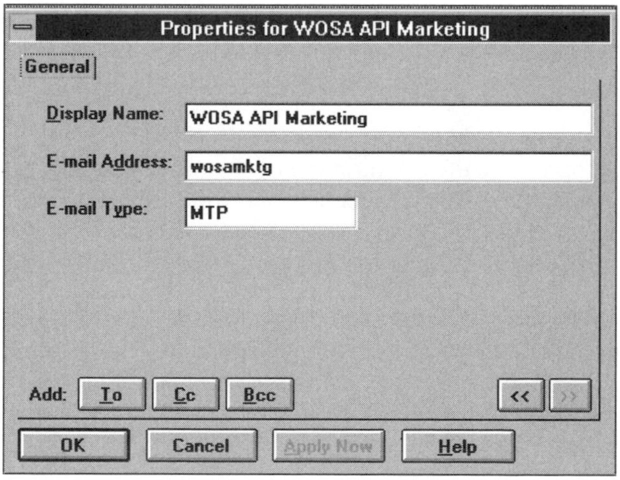

Figure 11.18   Properties for WOSA API Marketing dialog box

The MAPI Spooler

The spooler and the transport provider work together to handle the responsibilities of sending and receiving messages. You can have multiple installed transports installed on the same system, but MAPI supplies the one spooler required.

Drivers for each transport exist in the form of a Windows DLL to provide the interface between the MAPI messaging subsystem spooler and the underlying back-end messaging systems or services. The message spooler is similar to a print spooler except that it assists with the routing of messages instead of print jobs. The spooler, MAPI, and the transport drivers work together to handle the sending and receiving of messages.

When many different transport drivers are installed on a Windows-based desktop, messages from client applications can be sent to a variety of transport services. When a message is sent from a client application, MAPI responds to the CMC, Simple, or Extended MAPI calls first, routing the message to the appropriate message store and address book service providers. When a message is marked for sending, it is handled by the message spooler where it is delivered to the appropriate transport driver.

The message spooler looks at the message's address to determine which transport to use to send the message. Depending on the recipients, the message spooler may call on more than one transport provider. The spooler performs other message-management functions as well, such as directing inbound messages to a message store and catching messages that are undeliverable because no transport provider can handle them. The spooler also provides an important store and forward function, maintaining a message in a store if the needed messaging service is currently unavailable. When connection to the service is reestablished, the spooler automatically forwards the message to its destination.

Except for dialog boxes at the initial transport logon, the spooler and transport providers operate in the background, transferring messages among various messaging services. The spooler does its work and makes calls to the transport providers when the foreground applications are idle, so users don't have to wait while they are working with the messaging application.

Windows application developers enjoy the benefits of the spooler and other messaging subsystem features without having to write additional code beyond the MAPI calls. MAPI automatically assigns the appropriate tasks to the appropriate service providers.

MAPI Transports

Message transports maintain the actual connection to the underlying messaging system. They are also responsible for implementing any communications services that are required for that system. For example, a message transport that would provide services to a dialup service would provide the code necessary to interact with a modem, make a connection and send data in and out of the serial port. In the same way, a provider to a host-based system like IBM PROFS might implement SNA connectivity. Because transports provide the necessary communications, messaging applications are not required to implement their own communications support and are independent of the communications services implemented.

Message Security

MAPI provides tremendous flexibility for message security while supporting multiple message services. MAPI gives complete freedom to each service provider to implement an appropriate level of security for access to the underlying messaging systems. The service provider can either prompt for a user's credentials every time a message is sent, or can remember a user's logon and forgo the prompting.

In the Windows operating system, MAPI gives each service provider the option of sharing its security responsibilities with the messaging subsystem. The security features MAPI can provide will vary according to what is offered by the operating system. The Windows NT operating system, for example, provides more sophisticated security capabilities than Windows.

Typically, however, the Windows messaging subsystem can, if the provider so requests, store users' credential sets for the service provider. The service provider can also choose how much information is to be retained by the subsystem for each user. It might be as little as the user's network address with no name or password, all the way up to a complete credential set. The subsystem also supports unified logons; that is, with a single initial logon to the messaging system, the user can gain access to multiple workgroup applications. Then, users don't have to enter their name and password for each application they wish to use.

The MAPI messaging subsystem encrypts any security information it stores for a service provider.

Address Information

The transports register with MAPI the address types that they can handle. MAPI then maintains this information in a table structure for use by other applications.

For example, a specific provider such as a fax transport might be able to handle only one type of address. However, providers for public mail systems such as CompuServe, MCI, and so on would notify MAPI that they are able to handle messages with fax addresses, Internet addresses, addresses for other service users, and so on.

Recipient/Message Options

The transport providers register with MAPI both the per-recipient and the per-message options for the address types supported. The information is used by the system to support common user interface dialogs. Most email address types offer the same per-message options as per-recipient options, but some, such as X.400, cannot.

Slow-Link Services

MAPI supports slow-link providers as well as those that make near-instantaneous access to the messaging system through a LAN connection, for example. Slow-link services are those such as dialup or wireless which have relatively limited data capacity.

Applications should be aware of slow-link services and offer good support, through MAPI, for these types of providers. One example of good slow-link support is to prompt the user before beginning a download of new messages. The application could provide status information (message subject, sender name, date/time, and so on) about waiting messages and then allow the user to choose interactively which messages should be retrieved.

Transmitting/Receiving Messages

The transport providers have several responsibilities when it comes to sending and receiving messages. The transport providers:

- Perform any verification of credentials required by the remote messaging system
- Access outbound messages using the **IMessage** object passed by the spooler
- Translate the message format as required by the underlying messaging system
- Generate a delivery report (DR) or non-delivery report (NDR) as required
- Inform the spooler when an incoming message needs to be handled
- Pass incoming data to the spooler using the **IMessage** object
- Fill in all required MAPI properties on incoming messages
- Provide status information and the appropriate interface for the spooler and client application

Encapsulation Services

MAPI 1.0 offers a rich message content model to the Windows client. In many cases, this model exceeds the ability of underlying messaging systems to represent it. In order to promote interoperability, a relatively "standard" method of passing message data (both text and binary information) is provided: the MAPI Transport Neutral Encapsulation Format (TNEF). This format wraps up unsupported MAPI properties in a binary attachment file that accompanies the message through the transport and can be decoded on the receiving side to reconstitute the MAPI properties.

This encapsulation scheme has the following qualities:

- Full support of all MAPI 1.0 properties without affecting the native message properties.
- Compatibility with Windows for Workgroups 3.1 encapsulation
- A Help DLL, which simplifies the process of creating TNEF attachment files
- A TNEF file format, available to developers of mail applications on non-Windows platforms for examining or creating MAPI properties.

Windows Message Manager

The Windows Message Manager is a component of the Windows Messaging System as it will be delivered with Chicago. The Message Manager will be a fully-MAPI-compliant mail client, meaning that it will be able to freely interoperate with other MAPI applications and service providers.

The Windows Message Manager is designed to be good enough for day-to-day use, although it will not implement every feature a user could ever want. It will allow users to create, reply to, and forward messages, much as users do today in Windows for Workgroups. However, developers will have the opportunity to either extend the system messaging client through documented interfaces, or replace the Windows Messaging Manager with a MAPI messaging client of their own design.

Microsoft believes that the presence of a mail client in Chicago will rapidly expand the development of mail-enabled and workgroup applications. At the same time, MAPI's open APIs provide developers with access to rich messaging services and allow them to replace the Windows Message Manager with their own products as necessary to respond to customer needs.

Windows Message Manager UI

This looks much like the Windows for Workgroups messaging client. There are several cosmetic differences, but the main benefit is that as a MAPI application, it can access various messaging services through MAPI providers. This example shows the Windows Message Manager accessing two different message stores: the MAPI Local Message Store and a Microsoft Mail 3.0-based MMF file, which is the local message database used by Microsoft Mail. In the right pane, users can see the messages that are contained within a specific folder.

Message Stores and Folders   Messages

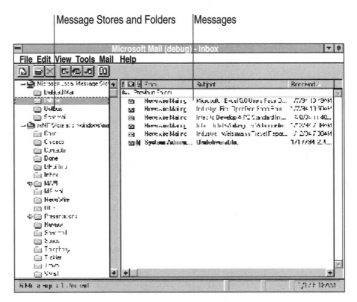

Figure 11.19   **Message store and folders**

Developer Information

Developers can be assured of having the tools and resources they need to develop any MAPI-compatible application.

All of the MAPI interfaces will be available in both 16-bit and 32-bit versions to support the Windows family of platforms. Applications written to 16-bit interfaces will run unchanged on any Windows platform, while 32-bit applications will run on Windows NT and Chicago.

In addition to the choice of platform, MAPI also provides developers with a choice of development tools. MAPI functions are designed to be called from C or C++ programs as well as through scripting packages such as the Microsoft Visual Basic programming system and various application macro languages such as Microsoft Excel and Microsoft Word for Windows.

We're currently working with about 500 developers who will be providing service providers to access messaging systems, or messaging clients and workgroup applications written to Extended MAPI. By the time MAPI 1.0 is available, we're convinced that there will be a broad range of provider and application support available from third parties.

MAPI 1.0 will ship as a system component with the next version of Windows, code-named Chicago. Every Windows user will have open access to messaging as a central component of their computing experience.

MAPI will also be available to users on other Microsoft platforms, although it will not be delivered in the system. On the Windows 3.1 and Windows NT platforms, developers will have a royalty-free license to redistribute the MAPI components. So a developer of a messaging application, for example, would be able to provide Windows 3.1 users with the required MAPI components on their product's Setup disks. .

Software Development Kits (SDKs)

Simple MAPI is available today in the Windows SDK. Simple MAPI is also included in Windows for Workgroups and Microsoft Mail for PC Networks.

The Simple MAPI SDK and the Common Messaging Call (CMC) Software Development Kits are available on Microsoft's Developer Network (MSDN) Level II. The Microsoft Developer Network is the official source of development toolkits (SDKs and DDKs), operating systems, and development-related technical, strategic, and resource information from Microsoft. The Developer Network is an annual membership program, ensuring that members are kept up-to-date with the latest toolkits and information. Developers that join receive regular deliveries of information via the Development Library and the Developer Network News, and toolkits and operating systems via the Development Platform. To join the Developer Network in the U.S. and Canada, call (800) 759-5474, 7 days a week, 24 hours a day.

Because the MAPI 1.0 functionality will be built into future releases of the Windows operating system, MAPI will eventually be available in the Windows SDK.

What Should You Do Today?

The appropriate course of action is really quite simple and depends on what type of application you're developing.

The vast majority of applications today should become mail-enabled to benefit from the integrated messaging within Windows. Generally, these applications would use either Simple MAPI or the Common Messaging Calls APIs in order to provide messaging features. These APIs are simple and easy to implement. Developers should particularly look towards CMC, as it is a standards-based API with wide support in the industry and the benefit of a cross-platform approach.

Other developers are targeting messaging-reliant applications which require a greater level of interaction with or control over the messaging system. Examples of these applications might include messaging clients or workgroup applications. These applications will require using Extended MAPI and will also benefit from finding the rich messaging interfaces available on every Windows desktop.

Other developers may be focusing on developing a MAPI service provider, so that they can provide access to database, address book, or transport services from the Windows desktop. These developers also need the MAPI SDK and will be able to deliver their unique services to a broad market of Windows users.

Finally, corporate developers may choose any of the paths discussed above. In many cases their needs are met by mail-enabling APIs like Simple MAPI or CMC. However, many of the developers are becoming quite sophisticated and are looking to create their own workgroup applications or messaging providers with MAPI. The benefit to this group is that as they create a workgroup application, they can be sure of it running on any messaging service installed within their organization.

Summary

In order to take advantage of their messaging systems as powerful communication backbones, organizations need a messaging standard that is open on both the client and messaging-system ends. Because MAPI provides both a client API and a service-provider API, it is possible to insulate application developers from the details of the underlying messaging system. MAPI's use of service provider interfaces and its support for industry-standard, cross-platform messaging APIs ensures interoperability with other messaging systems independent of platform. By providing a standard that is easy for both service providers and application developers to adopt, MAPI encourages and makes possible the creation of a new generation of exciting workgroup applications.

Topic

Content

Describe the role of the profile provider.

Profile Provider[3]

All of the activity associated with logging a user on to a specific profile is carried out by the profile provider that is loaded with the system. There is a minimum set of

---

[3] Excerpted from MAPI (Messaging Application Programming Interface), *Provider Developer Guide,* MAPI Software Development Kit, Appendix D: Messaging Services and Profiles. Copyright 1994. Used with permission. All rights reserved.

features that a profile provider must have in order to allow the system to run properly. MAPIincludes a profile provider that has features beyond this minimal set that takes advantage of the operating system to provide features such as user security.

If the user is trying to open a new profile (not piggyback on an existing one), MAPI will send the profile name and password entered during **MAPILogon** directly to the profile provider. The profile provider will open the requested profile if necessary credentials are provided. If no profile name is entered the profile provider can optionally open a default profile if requested or provide UI for selecting the profile to open.

The minimum feature set for a MAPI profile provider is shown below:

1. Used to logon—Needs to expose Logon UI - no other UI required.
2. Implement all profile methods as defined in MAPI.
3. Not required to allow profile manipulation.
4. Section/Property creation/modification allowed.
5. Provides storage of secure information based on its security needs.

Additional features in the WMS profile provider:
1. Profile Passwords.
2. Stores a default profile for the user.
3. Profile manipulation access to configuration clients.
4. Allows setting a default profile to be opened when no profile name is entered.
5. Logon UI provides a picklist of profiles.
6. Use system registry to allow multi-user access where per-user registry exists. This implies that on systems with user security, if the user has not logged on to system, the profile provider we ship will force the user to log on so that we have the reg information.
7. Use system password cache where available.
8. If the user calls **MAPILogon** (**OpenProfile** in the profile provider) and no profile exists, a default profile set to the name of the current user and with no password will be created. MAPI will be responsible for adding default services based on the entries in [Default Services] in SERVICE.INI.

CHAPTER 12

Messaging API (MAPI): Advanced Topics

Topic

Describe the difference between Simple MAPI and CMC.

Content

Simple MAPI[1]

Simple MAPI contains the 12 most common API calls and is designed to make it easy for developers to build powerful, custom messaging applications. The type of application that can be created with Simple MAPI includes a forms routing program that automatically sends a purchase request form to various workers for their completion and approval. Another example is a calendar and scheduling program that lets users view the schedules of other workers and make requests for meetings. Simple MAPI can also be used to add message capabilities to applications that normally do not provide message services, such as spreadsheets and word processors. Simple MAPI includes an optional common user interface (dialog boxes) so that developers can easily add a consistent look to their applications with very little work.

Whether creating a custom messaging application or adding message capabilities to an existing application, developers do not have to worry about the underlying messaging system or the network platform.

---

[1] Excerpted from "Microsoft Messaging Application Program Interface (MAPI)." A complete version of this white paper is located on the Microsoft Developer Network Development Library, under Backgrounders and White Papers, Operating System Extensions. Copyright 1993. Used with permission. All rights reserved.

The 12 Simple MAPI calls enable an application to send, address, and receive messages. Messages can include data attachments and Windows object linking and embedding (OLE) objects.

Common Messaging Calls (CMC)

The Common Messaging Call Application Program Interface (CMC API) provides a set of ten high-level functions for mail-enabled applications to send and receive electronic messages. It is very easy to add mail capability to an application with CMC, since an important consideration in the design of the API is to minimize the number of function calls needed to send or receive a message. For example a mail-enabled application can send a message with a single function call and receive a specific message with two calls.

The CMC API is designed to be independent of the actual messaging service used. It is also independent of the operating system and underlying hardware used by the messaging service and will allow a common interface over virtually any electronic messaging service. The CMC API is a good choice for applications to use when:

- multiple computing platforms need to be supported.
- multiple messaging services need to be supported.
- detailed knowledge of the underlying message service is not needed or known.

The CMC API was developed in conjunction with the X.400 API Association (XAPIA) standards organization and electronic mail vendors and users. As a cross-platform API, applications on Windows, DOS, OS/2, Macintosh and UNIX platforms can benefit from this simple, easy-to-implement messaging API.

CMC or Simple MAPI?

Since Simple MAPI and CMC provide similar basic messaging functionality for applications, which is the right API to use? As described above, CMC offers many benefits, such as messaging service independence and cross-platform support, so many applications developers would find that API to be the best choice. Simple MAPI is available to support existing applications which have been written to that API. The chart below lists all of the CMC functions, their Simple MAPI equivalents and the purpose of each function.

CMC call	MAPI call	Result
CMC_Logon	MAPILogon	Establishes a session with the messaging service.
CMC_Logoff	MAPILogoff	Terminates a session with the messaging service.
CMC_Free	MAPIFree	Frees the memory allocated by the messaging service.
CMC_Send	MAPISendMail	Sends a standard mail message. Messages can be sent without any user interaction or can be prompted via a common user interface (dialog box).
CMC_SendDocuments	MAPISendDocuments	Sends a standard mail message. This call always prompts with a dialog box for the recipient's name and other sending options. It is primarily intended for use with a scripting language such as a spreadsheet macro.
CMC_List	MAPIFindNext	Lists information about messages meeting specific criteria.
CMC_Read	MAPIReadMail	Reads a specified mail message.
CMC_ActOn	MAPISaveMail, MAPIDeleteMail	Saves or deletes a specified mail message.
CMC_LookUp	MAPIAddress, MAPIDetails, MAPIResolveName	This group of functions handles addressing chores, such as creating addresses, looking up addresses and resolving friendly names with e-mail names.
CMC_QueryConfiguration		Determines information about the installed CMC service.

Topics

Describe extended MAPI.

Define unified logons.

Describe store-and-forward functionality.

Content

Extended MAPI[2]

Extended MAPI goes beyond Simple MAPI to provide even greater interaction with the messaging services. Extended MAPI is the additional API set, intended for complex messaging-based applications such as advanced workgroup programs that use the messaging subsystem extensively. Such applications are likely to handle large and complex messages in large numbers, and require sophisticated addressing features. Extended MAPI supports advanced message features such as *custom forms* and *smart forms*. With custom forms, an organization can replace a standard send and receive mail form with its own timesheet or calendar form, with its own predefined fields of information. Smart forms take this one step further, letting you link the information that is entered into those fields with other applications. So, for example, the timesheet entries could all be pulled off the message system automatically and sent to a host-based payroll program.

The message-store and address-book capabilities provided by Extended MAPI are discussed as follows.

Message Store

Extended MAPI provides powerful message store capabilities with its use of folders to organize messages. Folders contain messages, and messages can contain attachments. Folders, messages, and attachments all have properties such as the time sent, type (binary, integer), and so on.

Folders are organized in a hierarchical tree, allowing applications to store messages in any subtree. In addition, wastebasket or out-box folders can be created. Table

---

[2] Excerpted from "Microsoft Messaging Application Program Interface (MAPI)." A complete version of this white paper is located on the Microsoft Developer Network Development Library, under Backgrounders and White Papers, Operating System Extensions. Copyright 1993. Used with permission. All rights reserved.

operations are provided to enable a user to scroll through the folder structure and to view the messages in each folder by subject or other property. Multiple folders can also be searched for specific information. Criteria can be entered to locate messages with particular properties such as subject, sender or recipient, or message text.

Received messages can be modified and stored back in their folders. For example, a user could rotate a fax message that arrived upside down and store it right side up for later viewing. In the Windows operating system, a person who has received a Microsoft Excel spreadsheet as an OLE object in a message can launch Microsoft Excel from within the message, edit the file, and then store the changed file as part of the message.

Address Book

Address books, as defined by MAPI, are a collection of one or more lists of message recipients. Each list is called a *container*. Recipients can be either a single user or a distribution list—that is, a group of recipients that are commonly addressed together. Depending on the features of the service providers available on the network system, address books can be organized to have just a single container, a list of containers, or a hierarchy of containers.

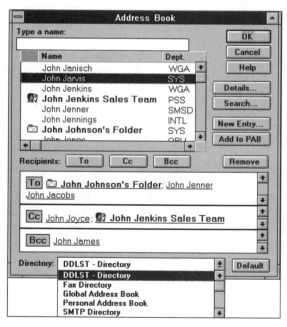

Figure 12.1   Even when different messaging systems are being used together, each with their own directories, MAPI can present a single master address book that combines all of the directories, hiding the complexities of the system from the user.

MAPI supports custom address-book providers. For example, a corporate phone book could be created listing all of a company's employees. When a name is selected as a message recipient, additional information could appear such as the person's office location, title and department, supervisor's name, and more.

Even if multiple service providers are installed, MAPI allows access to the different service directories and provides a common interface to give the appearance of a single address book to the client application. This hides the complexities of the multiple back ends from the user. MAPI also provides a specialized container in the address book called the *personal address book*. Users can store copies of frequently used addresses in this container and can also maintain entries for e-mail recipients who are not in the main address book of the underlying messaging system.

With MAPI's support for robust messaging functions, message-service developers can be confident that their existing and future message-store, address-book, and transport services will be fully supported by any MAPI application.

For more information on the types of messaging applications that can be created by Simple and Extended MAPI, refer to the section "MAPI and Messaging Applications" later in this document.

The MAPI Messaging Subsystem

The Common Messaging Calls (CMC), Simple MAPI and Extended MAPI provide the required API calls for messaging applications. These calls work with a second level of MAPI features that are actually built into the Windows operating system: the messaging subsystem. The MAPI messaging subsystem and a MAPI dynamic-link library (DLL) are responsible for dividing the tasks of handling multiple transport-service providers. Drivers for each transport exist in the form of a Windows DLL to provide the interface between the MAPI messaging subsystem message spooler and the underlying back-end messaging system(s) or services (see the "Service Provider Interfaces (SPIs)" section later in this paper for more information on drivers). The message spooler is similar to a print spooler except that it assists with the routing of messages instead of print jobs. The spooler, MAPI.DLL, and the transport drivers work together to handle the sending and receiving of messages.

When many different transport drivers are installed on a Windows-based desktop, messages from client applications can be sent to a variety of transport services. When a message is sent from a client application, the MAPI.DLL responds to the Simple or Extended MAPI calls first, routing the message to the appropriate message store and address book service providers. When a message is marked for sending, it is handled by the message spooler where it is delivered to the appropriate transport driver.

The message spooler looks at the message's address to determine which transport to use to send the message. Depending on the recipients, the message spooler may call upon more than one transport provider. The spooler performs other message-management functions as well, such as directing inbound messages to a message store and catching messages that are undeliverable because no transport provider can handle them. The spooler also provides an important *store and forward* function, maintaining a message in a store if the needed messaging service is currently unavailable. When connection to the service is reestablished, the spooler automatically forwards the message to its destination.

Except for dialog boxes at the initial transport login, the spooler and transport providers operate in the background, transferring messages among various messaging services. The spooler does its work and makes its calls to the transport providers when the foreground applications are idle, so users don't have to wait while they are working with the messaging application.

Windows application developers enjoy the benefits of the spooler and other messaging subsystem features without having to write additional code beyond the MAPI calls. MAPI automatically assigns the appropriate tasks to the appropriate service providers.

In addition to the common functions for sending and receiving messages, MAPI and its subsystem can support file attachments and Windows OLE objects.

Message Security

MAPI provides tremendous flexibility for message security while supporting multiple message services. MAPI gives complete freedom to each service provider to implement an appropriate level of security for access to the underlying messaging systems. The service provider can either prompt for a user's credentials every time a message is sent, or can remember a user's logon and forgo the prompting.

In the Windows operating system, MAPI gives each service provider the option of sharing its security responsibilities with the messaging subsystem. The security features MAPI can provide will vary according to what is offered by the operating system. The Windows NT™ operating system, for example, provides more sophisticated security capabilities than Windows.

Typically, however, the Windows messaging subsystem can, if the provider so requests, store users' credential sets for the service provider. The service provider can also choose how much information is to be retained by the subsystem for each user. It might be as little as the user's network address with no name or password, all the way up to a complete credential set. The subsystem also supports unified logons; that is, with a single initial logon to the messaging system, the user can gain access to multiple workgroup applications. Then, users don't have to enter their name and password for each application they wish to use.

The MAPI messaging subsystem encrypts any security information it stores for a service provider.

Topic

Describe what it means for an application to be an advanced workgroup application and which API or APIs are applicable.

Content

The Microsoft Workgroup Computing Strategy[3]

A discussion of Microsoft's strategy and tools for helping people work together more effectively

Overview

If the 1980s were the decade of the personal computer, the 1990s are becoming the decade of the interpersonal computer. Advances in local area networks (LANs), client-server computing, graphical operating systems, electronic messaging, and more have changed the PC from an individual's tool to one that helps people work together to accomplish group tasks more effectively.

Of course, people working together isn't a new phenomenon. People have long collaborated on projects and participated in group processes. What is relatively new is the use of everyday desktop PCs to help people work closely together in their jobs, whatever those jobs may be—from several project members each contributing to a group status report, to thousands of sales and manufacturing people sharing sales and inventory information around the world.

The stakes are high. In this era of limited budgets, increased competition, and pressure to do more with less, giving people easy-to-use tools to improve communication, automate work processes, and allow the sharing of expertise and information resources can add up to a significant advantage.

---

[3] A complete version of this white paper is also available on the Microsoft Developer Network Development Library, under Backgrounders and White Papers, Operating Systems. Copyright 1992 - 1995. Used with permission. All rights reserved.

Unlike others in the industry, we don't see workgroup computing as a separate category of computing. Instead of creating specialized applications just so people can work together, Microsoft is committed to making workgroup features available in all applications. In this way, workgroup computing becomes a natural part of the way people use computers, just as printing from an application is. In this white paper, we'll discuss Microsoft's markedly different approach to the fast-growing and often ill-defined area of workgroup computing.

It's an open, flexible approach that stands apart from the proprietary-product approach of other vendors. It's a strategy that gives you the freedom to leverage your existing computer system investments—in hardware, software, data, and user knowledge—as you build workgroup solutions that meet your specific needs.

But before we discuss the elements and benefits of Microsoft's workgroup computing strategy, we should first define what we mean by workgroup computing.

What Is Workgroup Computing?

It seems as if everyone in the personal computer industry today has a different definition of workgroup computing. Some argue it is a new, cutting-edge category of applications called groupware. Others say that workgroup computing is something that requires entirely new systems or radically different user environments. Still others claim that workgroup computing requires customers to adopt new databases and data structures in order to develop solutions. The theme consistently promoted by many in the industry is that workgroup computing is revolutionary new technology.

Workgroup computing, however, is really about extending and evolving the tools people already have in order to support the ways they already work. Consequently, any complete definition of workgroup computing should be based first on an understanding of people and how they work together.

Activities should define workgroup solutions

Most people depend, directly or indirectly, on help from others to get their jobs done. There are myriad structured and ad hoc ways in which people work together, forming teams around any number of activities. Indeed, virtually any process that involves a group of people collaborating on work is by definition a workgroup activity.

These individual workgroup activities should define their own corresponding software solutions. Defining workgroup computing this way, with an activity-based approach, means that "What business problems do we want to solve?" is the most important question an organization can ask itself.

Consequently, Microsoft defines workgroup computing as open, flexible software solutions that build on existing, industry standard technology to help people work together more effectively. What might these solutions do? Here are a few of the many possibilities:

- Department expense tracking. Managers approve, consolidate, and track expense reports from department members.

- Enterprise-wide budgeting. People from several different departments contribute to the process of creating a master budget for an entire organization.

- Collaborative report creation. A team of people collaborate to create a report requiring input from different groups within an organization.

- Enterprise information systems. Coworkers access, share, and manipulate critical business information to help them make better, more timely decisions.

- Project planning, scheduling, and tracking. Project members allocate tasks, manage schedules, and monitor status of projects involving multiple team members and resources.

- Corporate information management systems. Marketing and sales personnel call an information management system and request or submit updated sales reports, documents, files, and other information.

- Loan or claim processing. Loan or insurance claim applications are electronically routed for review and approval in line-of-business workflow applications.\sgml Just these few examples demonstrate that workgroup computing solutions are tremendously diverse. Consequently, a single, proprietary, one-size-fits-all product cannot meet the many needs facing an organization today and might, in fact, limit an organization's flexibility in the future. The right approach to workgroup computing involves many different software products and vendors working together within an open architecture to deliver the best solutions for real-world business problems.

Workgroup Computing Is Strategic Information Technology

Workgroup computing is not an information technology area to be taken lightly. There are several important reasons why choosing the right workgroup strategy is one of the most important technology decisions an organization must make.

First, workgroup computing decisions will have a direct impact on an organization's long-term competitiveness. In what ways? The right workgroup computing strategy can make group and multiuser processes more efficient, enabling everyone in an organization to concentrate on productive work instead of struggling through a bureaucratic and inefficient manual processes. Adopting the right workgroup computing strategy can reduce the time-to-action required for a company to act in its markets, whether that action involves more responsive customer service or bringing products to market faster. The right strategy can also preserve an organization's flexibility in the future—the flexibility to react quickly to changes in the competitive marketplace by implementing new workgroup solutions and the flexibility to adopt new information technology as it becomes available from any computer industry vendor.

Second, workgroup computing affects all of an organization's computing investments, whether workgroup solutions are built directly on top of existing computer systems or must simply access existing data assets. In this way, an organization's workgroup computing strategy, much like its electronic messaging and database strategies, is a decision about the technology infrastructure of the organization.

Finally, choosing a workgroup computing strategy means, fundamentally, choosing a work-group development platform for the future. Because more and more line-of-business applications are likely to be built on this platform in the coming decade, it is imperative that organizations invest in the right workgroup strategy from the beginning.

Given that all these factors can help minimize operating costs and reduce time-to-action for business-critical activities, choosing the right workgroup computing strategy can yield tremendous competitive opportunities.

Customer requirements for workgroup computing

In developing a workgroup computing strategy, Microsoft listened carefully to many corporate customers, application developers, systems integrators, consultants, and others. These people identified three vital requirements of any workgroup computing strategy.

Leverage existing investments

Organizations already have expensive information technology (IT) investments. These investments include minicomputer and host hardware, electronic messaging systems, database management systems, PC hardware and software, user training, and development tools. Organizations don't want to forfeit these investments simply because they want to use their computer systems to help people work together. Adding workgroup capabilities shouldn't require heavy investments in new software and training but should allow customers to build upon what they already have.

Minimize risk

A second key workgroup computing requirement for customers is to minimize risk. How can a vendor reduce risks for its customers? By providing open standards and interfaces that offer security in the midst of an uncertain future; by offering a smooth migration path to new technologies that preserves existing investments and reduces the effects of change; and by providing both strong product support and focused industry leadership.

Freedom of choice

Finally, in considering a workgroup computing strategy, customers identified the ability to choose from a wide variety of computing sources as a critical requirement. No one wants to be locked into a single vendor's solution or limited by a proprietary infrastructure. An effective strategy must provide an open workgroup platform that gives customers the greatest possible freedom in choosing the best applications and development tools from any vendor.

Microsoft's workgroup computing strategy addresses each of these major customer concerns by providing an open architecture and tools that help customers implement successful workgroup solutions. .

Microsoft's Workgroup Computing Strategy

The Microsoft workgroup computing strategy is to provide a solutions-based, open, and evolutionary approach to making it easier for people to work together. The three fundamental objectives of our strategy are to:

- Make it easier for customers to build workgroup solutions that are shaped by real-world activities and business problems.

- Provide an open architecture and work-group development platform for all customers, application developers, and solution providers.

- Evolve the Microsoft Windows operating system and cross-platform applications to include workgroup features so customers can leverage their existing investments.

- Microsoft is delivering both the technology and the services necessary to accomplish these objectives. The key components of our workgroup computing strategy are:

- Extending the Microsoft Windows operating system to provide an open workgroup computing foundation for application developers, solution providers, and all users.

- Evolving key cross-platform desktop applications by incorporating workgroup capabilities to help customers leverage investments in software and user knowledge.

- Delivering leading workgroup-specific applications in important categories such as electronic messaging and group scheduling.

- Providing advanced, relational database technology to ensure data integrity in work-group solutions.

- Providing a broad range of sophisticated development tools that customers, application developers, and solution providers can use to integrate different components as they build solutions.

- Investing in a customer support infrastructure and in third-party partnerships to help customers implement and support their workgroup solutions. These strategic commitments are designed to ensure that workgroup computing becomes a natural part of the way people work, giving organizations the flexibility to adopt the best tools for the group activities they need to support—whether that's simply linking two workers across an office or coordinating a global sales force.

Extending the Microsoft Windows operating system

Workgroup computing is not a single application, but a wide variety of solutions that will help people work together. The tremendous diversity of workgroup activities in different organizations means that workgroup computing needs can't be solved by one application, or even by one vendor. Therefore, customers, application developers, and solution providers (including value-added resellers, consultants, and strategic integrators) need an open development platform on which to build the best workgroup computing solutions using the widest variety of existing tools.

Our strategy is focused on creating such an open architecture in the Microsoft Windows operating system. This is a markedly different approach from that of other computer industry vendors. Rather than create an all-encompassing application that tries to meet every customer's workgroup needs, Microsoft—as an operating system vendor—is committed to providing an open workgroup development platform that allows each organization to create the best solution for its specific needs, using the entire set of available applications and development tools.

The computer's operating system can provide the best such platform for workgroup computing solutions. Platforms such as the Microsoft Windows operating system and the Apple Macintosh will evolve in the 1990s to incorporate fundamental services and application programming interfaces that will make all applications workgroup applications in the same manner that graphical operating environments made printing a natural, easy-to-find and easy-to-understand extension of all applications in the 1980s. There won't be a separate category of proprietary groupware applications—workgroup capabilities will pervade all of the tools that an organization uses in its activities. Extending the operating system is vital to making this possible.

Microsoft Windows and workgroup computing

The Windows system is Microsoft's strategic operating system. The installed base of Windows users has grown to 25 million with more than 1 million new users added each month. Microsoft Windows, with its graphical user interface, improves both personal and group productivity in PC-based LAN environments. Microsoft is committed to embedding fundamental workgroup services in Windows operating systems to provide an open work-group computing foundation. These fundamental services will include information sharing, a common messaging system, standard directory services, a common data access model, and rich security, among others.

The Microsoft Windows for Workgroups operating system with integrated networking is the first Windows-based product to deliver on this commitment. Windows for Workgroups is an enhanced version of the popular Windows operating system version 3.1, which includes built-in file- and printer-sharing capabilities to make it easier for groups of people to share information and resources. In addition, Windows for Workgroups includes electronic mail so users can immediately begin exchanging messages, and organizations can develop messaging-enabled workgroup applications. Windows for Workgroups comes complete with group scheduling and network-enabled dynamic data exchange (DDE) to make working together more efficient and effective.

The Microsoft Windows NT operating system, scheduled to be released in 1993, extends the Windows operating system even farther with additional services for high-end desktop computing. Using the familiar Windows graphical interface, the Windows NT operating system will run powerful 32-bit applications as well as all existing applications for Windows and MS-DOS, preserving investments in software and user training. The Windows NT operating system will also include all of the workgroup features of Windows for Workgroups, combining these with advanced power and scalability on the desktop.

In addition to supporting advanced desktop computing, Windows NT is designed as a powerful server platform to support mission-critical, line-of-business applications for organizations. Windows NT offers sophisticated security and data protection features, multithread and multitasking performance, and support for high volume storage requirements. The Windows NT operating system will run on a wide variety of advanced hardware platforms, providing an effective development platform for workgroup solutions in larger organizations.

Application developers and customers can count on all of the future versions of Microsoft Windows to include workgroup capabilities, as this is a consistent part of our operating system strategy. Microsoft will continue to evolve workgroup capabilities in the Windows operating system and combine those features with significant new technologies in the future. For example, future versions of the Windows operating system will use object-oriented technology to enable users to access and manipulate information regardless of its location or the software application it's in. This approach will embrace a data-centric rather than application-centric model of computing, where the data is the most important object, not the application used to view or manipulate it. This object-based Windows operating system will include sophisticated features for managing and linking objects such as documents, charts, and data files and for replicating these objects across an enterprise. The integration of object-oriented technology into the Windows family will make it even easier to create workgroup solutions that are more intuitive for users.

The Windows operating system provides a strong workgroup development platform for today and tomorrow. Today more than 3000 software vendors are offering more than 6000 applications that can be workgroup-enabled and used immediately as components in customer solutions. This combination of operating system power and application variety gives organizations the ability to pick and choose the elements they need for a specific workgroup computing solution rather than coping with inflexible, monolithic products.

Windows open services architecture

Embedding fundamental workgroup services is one important means of extending the Windows operating system to provide an open workgroup development platform. A second vital means is the support of rich open application programming interfaces (APIs) that enable workgroup solutions to access any electronic messaging or database system in heterogeneous corporate environments.

Microsoft is working to enable outstanding connectivity through the Windows operating system to resources in diverse computing environments. This is an important capability for workgroup solutions that must, for example, run on top of multiple electronic messaging systems or access data stored in different corporate databases. The Windows Open Services Architecture (WOSA) is the operating system architecture that makes this possible today in Microsoft Windows.

WOSA is a set of open APIs in the Windows operating system that allows any desktop application—including electronic mail, word processing, spreadsheets, a database, and more—to work seamlessly with a variety of back-end services from different vendors. Defined with extensive input from other industry vendors through an open process, WOSA provides significant benefits for organizations that are building workgroup solutions. By providing an open architecture, WOSA allows customers to select their client applications and server systems separately, without being tied to one vendor's proprietary package. In addition, WOSA enables users to take advantage of a wide variety of services from their familiar Windows-based desktops without having to worry about the underlying complexities of the back-end systems. WOSA provides the same flexibility to application developers, allowing them to concentrate their limited resources on developing innovative applications rather than duplicating already existing system-level functions such as messaging.

Today, WOSA includes two major sets of APIs that provide customers and application developers with the ability to access different messaging and database services to create flexible workgroup computing solutions. Microsoft's Messaging API (MAPI) will enable customers to use any Windows-based application with different host-based, LAN-based, and public electronic messaging systems. Users or system administrators will simply load, from a Windows desktop, the appropriate MAPI drivers, written as Windows dynamic link library (DLL) files, for the messaging systems they wish to use—an action similar to choosing a printer driver for different printers.

MAPI is the result of a collaboration among Microsoft and more than 100 independent software vendors (ISVs), messaging system providers, corporate developers, and consultants from around the world (see the sidebar "Vendors Who Support MAPI"). It is an open standard that makes it easier for developers to add workgroup features to existing applications and to create entirely new workgroup-specific applications, because they don't have to create different application versions for different messaging systems. MAPI does this by giving developers a common API set to write to that will connect to multiple back-end messaging systems from different vendors.

The open database connectivity (ODBC) APIs provide access to diverse database management systems from Windows-based applications, making it possible to use existing sources of information without having to import and reformat the data for a proprietary database. Based on a call-level interface (CLI) developed by an industry consortium of more than 40 vendors (the SQL Access Group and others), ODBC is an open, vendor-neutral standard that has broad support from both application and database vendors (see sidebar "Vendors Who Support ODBC"). Like MAPI, ODBC provides application developers a common API set and uses drivers, in the form of Windows DLL files, written for particular database systems. From any Windows-based desktop application, users can access information from multiple locations (such as PC servers, mainframes, or minicomputers) and from diverse database systems (such as DB2, ORACLE, dBASE, Microsoft SQL Server database server, and so on).

Why the operating system?

Both Microsoft and Apple are taking important steps to extend their popular operating systems to provide workgroup computing platforms. There are several compelling reasons why the operating system is the only resource that can provide a truly open development platform for workgroup solutions. In addition, there are several related reasons why an application or application development environment (often referred to as middleware) that runs on top of the operating system can't provide customers and application developers with the optimal workgroup development platform.

First, there shouldn't have to be a separate class of applications that enable users to work with other people. We don't have printing and nonprinting applications—it seems equally absurd to force users into a divided world where they use some applications to complete their own work and other applications to collaborate with their colleagues. The only way to ensure that all applications evolve and become workgroup-enabled is to make sure they have access to basic services and APIs built into the operating system.

Second, extending the operating system gives customers greater freedom of choice in their purchasing decisions. Historically, vendors of office automation systems and other workgroup applications have forced users to buy all of their software, including servers, associated client applications, and development tools, from the same vendor. Customers resoundingly rejected that approach when given the choice of selecting the best solutions from multiple vendors after the PC revolution. The operating system provides open APIs that enable customers to separate their client and server decisions and allow them to use any standard development tool. This open architecture allows customers to select or create for their users the best work-group applications—from any vendor—while leveraging their existing investments in messaging systems, database management systems, and other back-end services.

On the other hand, developing solutions on top of a middle-ware application would by definition limit those solutions to the services and programming capabilities provided by that application. Limiting development tools to those provided by that application will hamper the creation of powerful workgroup solutions. In addition, developers and customers will be tied to the infrastructure of one application provided by one vendor, unable to exploit technology advances by other service providers or leverage existing investments in messaging and database management systems.

Third, operating systems establish standard development environments for application developers and customers. Customers and application developers have the security of knowing that any investment they make in writing to standard operating system APIs will be preserved in the future as the operating system continues to evolve and is upgraded.

There are significant differences between writing applications in a middleware environment and developing applications using APIs at the operating system level. A middleware vendor must be able to address the numerous issues managed by operating systems, which is difficult to do. For example, a middleware vendor might focus on document management but ignore SNA connectivity. An operating system vendor cannot be so narrowly focused. The management of such complex issues is the natural role of operating systems, and an extra middleware layer might unnecessarily restrict the power, efficiency, and creativity of application developers and lock customers into the middleware vendor's environment and applications. In addition, there is the risk that solutions will fall out of sync with operating system advances. Customers would be dependent on the middleware vendor's ability to negotiate changes between the application environment and the operating system. As the operating system evolves, the proprietary and redundant nature of application middleware could easily lead to development inefficiencies for ISVs and to software compatibility problems for customers.

Finally, extending operating systems to provide an open workgroup development platform will drive the creation of new, innovative applications and solutions for customers. Because the operating system provides open APIs that allow client applications to be independent of back-end systems, ISVs can focus on developing the best feature-rich applications instead of worrying about duplicating infrastructures, such as messaging and directory systems, which can be provided by other services vendors. Open APIs also benefit the messaging and database service providers because these vendors will gain from the wide variety of innovative applications that take advantage of their services. All of this will, in time, lead to greater freedom of choice for customers, who will be assured of tight integration among the applications and services they choose, thanks to standard APIs and broad industry support of operating system platforms.

In summary, the operating system provides tremendous advantages as a platform for work-group solutions. Consequently, extending the Windows operating system is the most important element of Microsoft's workgroup computing strategy because of its far-reaching impact for customers and the software industry.

Evolving key cross-platform desktop applications

Microsoft applications will take full advantage of the operating system level workgroup services and connectivity standards provided by Microsoft Windows and the Apple Macintosh. We plan to take advantage of these open workgroup platforms to provide work-group capabilities in all of our products, including our existing desktop applications, new workgroup-specific applications, server technology, development tools, and more.

Microsoft has accumulated a great deal of experience in developing and supporting desktop productivity applications. We've consistently applied an activity-based approach to the design of these applications to ensure that we're developing products that actually fit the way people do their work. Adding workgroup capabilities to our applications to facilitate the way people work together is the next logical step.

We will continue to evolve all of our key desktop applications—including the MS Word processing program, Microsoft Excel spreadsheet, Microsoft Project business project planning system, and the Microsoft PowerPoint presentation graphics program—to include workgroup-specific capabilities. In this way, users will interact with their workgroups easily and seamlessly through the everyday desktop applications they are already familiar with.

We have recognized several basic areas for collaborative work and will develop within the next major versions of our applications specific workgroup features that aid these and other processes.

One area for development is *collaboration*, or the dividing of a task so multiple people can work on it and then easily bring together the results. For example, within Microsoft Excel we are investigating what would be a delegation feature for working in a spreadsheet. A user could create a spreadsheet, highlight an area of the spreadsheet, and delegate and send the specified area to another person. All the cells on the spreadsheet would be locked with the exception of the area that the particular user was responsible for. The recipients could fill out their parts of the spreadsheet, return them to the sender, and a special function would merge all the data from the various users into one spreadsheet.

Routing and notification is another important area for workgroup collaboration. Routing is used for a sequential task that requires the attention of many people. For example, someone working on a document or a form may need to route it to several other people for them to add material or note their approval. A routing feature built into an application could use standard MAPI calls to send the document to the appropriate people via the underlying electronic messaging system.

There are other areas for specific product advances that will enable basic tasks—for example, analysis in spreadsheets or document creation in word processors—to be completed more effectively in a workgroup environment. Customers will be able to more easily use Microsoft applications as components or building blocks in their workgroup solutions. In fact, many of our desktop applications are already being used in workgroup solutions today—for example, in enterprise information systems.

Microsoft applications will be at the forefront of exploiting operating system level workgroup services and standards such as WOSA, MAPI, and ODBC in the Windows operating system and the open collaborative environment (OCE) on the Apple Macintosh. We plan to add workgroup-specific capabilities to the next versions of our key desktop applications to further benefit people working together on a network. These core workgroup services will seamlessly tie workgroup-enabled desktop applications into larger organizational processes. As a result, customers will be able to preserve their extensive investments in PC operating systems, application software, and user training and knowledge.

Delivering advanced workgroup-specific applications

In addition to extending the Windows operating system and evolving existing cross-platform desktop applications with workgroup capabilities, Microsoft is committed to developing new and advanced workgroup-specific applications that address the unique needs of multiuser situations.

Electronic messaging: the workgroup foundation

Workgroup computing solutions must be powerful and flexible enough to link people wherever they are working—whether in the same building or in countries around the world. For most organizations, it is their electronic messaging system that provides this network among workers and serves as the foundation for advanced workgroup solutions.

Electronic messaging is the indispensable connection for almost all workgroup solutions. Its store-and-forward architecture provides an effective transport medium for workgroup applications that require the distribution and routing of information across an organization. Reliable transport and directory services are two key requirements for electronic messaging systems. Microsoft is delivering outstanding electronic messaging technology to meet the growing demands of workgroup solutions in larger organizations.

Microsoft Mail for PC Networks is a sophisticated electronic messaging system with the features and power to serve today's workgroup solutions. Microsoft Mail offers support for multiple desktop platforms, including clients running Windows, MS-DOS, the Macintosh, and OS/2. In addition, Microsoft Mail provides remote access support for users of Windows and MS-DOS. Its advanced server features include automatic, fault-tolerant directory synchronization and a global address list to make it easy to connect to people regardless of their location in the enterprise or the type of messaging system they are using.

Almost all large organizations have multiple electronic messaging systems. Providing connectivity to these varied systems from a LAN-based messaging system has often proved to be an impossible task. A complete line of advanced Microsoft gateways provides reliable and sophisticated connectivity between Microsoft Mail for PC Networks and virtually any other electronic mail system within an organization, including X.400, IBM PROFS, SNADS, SMTP, MHS, AT&T Easylink, MCI MAIL, and Fax. In addition, Microsoft gateways support key features such as messaging backboning and message encapsulation. Messaging backboning lets organizations leverage their existing messaging resources by using these systems as high-performance bridges—or messaging backbones—between multiple Microsoft Mail sites. Message encapsulation in Microsoft gateways makes it possible for users to place graphics, charts, sound, and video objects directly in their mail messages for richer communication. Moreover, these complex messages can be sent across messaging backbones between distant sites without any loss of data integrity.

Microsoft is also developing an advanced, Windows NT–based enterprise messaging server (EMS) that will provide an even more powerful client-server messaging platform for workgroup computing solutions. Designed to meet high-end server requirements, EMS is a sophisticated standards-based messaging server that will natively support international and industry messaging standards such as X.400, X.500, MAPI, and XAPI. Its native support for the 1992 X.400 specification includes important features for guaranteed electronic mail delivery time and control, and will ensure that the EMS plugs seamlessly into any organization's X.400 messaging backbone. X.500 support will greatly reduce the overhead associated with managing directories on the system. In addition, EMS is tightly integrated with the security and administration capabilities provided by the Windows NT operating system, so any workgroup solution built on top of the EMS will also benefit from these services.

In addition to its native support for these industry messaging standards, the EMS will offer several features designed specifically for the needs of larger organizations. These include new software clients for the Windows operating system, MS-DOS, and the Macintosh; new Windows NT–based gateways to other messaging systems; an active server agent that allows the system to automatically perform many routine maintenance tasks; and an advanced document-oriented message store for organizing and replicating rich information objects.

Microsoft's advanced messaging technology—including Microsoft Mail and the EMS—provides a vital, reliable foundation for any workgroup solution.

Scheduling, electronic forms, and group conferencing

In addition to electronic messaging, Microsoft is also developing a line of best-of-breed workgroup-specific applications in the following important areas:

- Group scheduling. Microsoft Schedule+ calendaring and scheduling program is already a successful product in the category of applications that can facilitate the process of scheduling meetings and resources among members of a workgroup. Because Schedule+ is a MAPI-based application, customers will be able to integrate it with different electronic messaging systems. In addition, customers with an IBM PROFS messaging system today can maintain full functionality and transparent connectivity—including group scheduling—between their PC LAN and PROFS using Microsoft Mail and Microsoft Schedule+. We will continue to enhance Schedule+ on both the Microsoft Windows operating system and the Apple Macintosh.

- Electronic forms routing. Microsoft is working on technology to make it even easier to create electronic forms (purchase orders, time sheets, employment applications, and so on) that can be intelligently routed via Microsoft Mail and other electronic messaging systems via MAPI. The Microsoft Electronic Forms Designer, which will leverage the Microsoft Visual Basic programming system version 2.0 Professional Edition, will help customers design powerful electronic forms more easily. A component-oriented system such as Visual Basic also gives organizations the ability to design forms that have an easy-to-use graphical interface with standard Windows controls. In addition, because it is an event-driven programming language, Visual Basic makes it possible to create complex forms that provide sequential routing or access to external data, or that trigger other actions and applications.

- Group conferencing. Microsoft is planning to deliver group conferencing technology—also known as group memory or bulletin board systems—to users of Windows, MS-DOS, and the Macintosh. This technology will leverage the document-oriented message store of the enterprise messaging server and will help customers meet their workgroup information-sharing and conferencing needs.

Providing advanced database technology

Databases, along with electronic messaging, provide the core technology for most workgroup computing solutions. Much of the information that organizations want to share, route, and collaboratively manage in their workgroup solutions already exists in databases. As a result, database tools play a key role in making workgroup solutions succeed.

Often, the first challenge is simply getting to an organization's existing data from within workgroup solutions. This data, which is an organization's most vital asset, is typically dispersed among a variety of databases. It's not unusual to find customers who have critical information in DB2 and ORACLE databases on a mainframe, in an Rdb database on a minicomputer, in a SQL Server database on a PC server, or even in a dBASE application on a user's desktop. Customers must be able to seamlessly and dynamically access data from any of their existing databases for use in their workgroup solutions.

The key to Microsoft's workgroup strategy is the architecture we provide for open connectivity, which allows PCs to access diverse databases within an enterprise. As discussed earlier, Microsoft's architecture for making this possible is open database connectivity, or ODBC. ODBC defines a common API for accessing data in an environment containing both relational and nonrelational database management systems. With ODBC, an application can concurrently access, view, and modify data from multiple, varied databases. Apple has also endorsed ODBC as a key enabling technology for accessing data from applications for System 7, and will be integrating ODBC support into System 7 in the future. With growing industry support, ODBC is quickly emerging as an important industry standard for data access for both Windows- and Macintosh-based applications.

Microsoft is also providing a range of advanced relational database tools to help customers use their critical data, with confidence and security, in workgroup solutions. Microsoft now offers a full family of database tools for the desktop and server that allows customers to choose the right Microsoft tool for specific workgroup needs. On the desktop, we offer two new programmable relational database management systems (DBMSs): the Microsoft Access and Microsoft FoxPro databases. For the network server engine in enterprise workgroup solutions we provide the Microsoft SQL Server DBMS. While these products share similar advanced capabilities, each is designed to best address particular business challenges. More importantly, all are designed to help organizations preserve the referential data integrity required for critical line-of-business workgroup solutions.

The Microsoft Access DBMS is a full-featured, multiuser relational database management system that can seamlessly manipulate live data from remote databases. Designed for the Microsoft Windows operating system from its conception, Microsoft Access is extremely visual and easy to use. It makes extensive use of drag-and-drop technology and visual design for queries, forms, and reports. It also provides an integrated development environment together with Access Basic, a full-featured programming language based on the core language of the Microsoft Visual Basic programming system. Corporate MIS and PC developers can create powerful workgroup solutions—for example, sales- and inventory-tracking applications—using Microsoft Access as a front end for large enterprise databases such as Microsoft SQL Server or ORACLE.

The Microsoft FoxPro DBMS is a full-featured, multiuser relational database built on the Xbase language, with fully integrated SQL, rich graphical tools, and our exclusive Rushmore query-optimization technology. Applications created in FoxPro will run on the Microsoft Windows or MS-DOS operating systems and, in the near future, on the Apple Macintosh and SCO UNIX operating systems. FoxPro is a powerful combination of the industry's fastest-performing desktop DBMS with the industry's best Xbase technology for customers who need to build workgroup solutions across multiple PC platforms.

Many large organizations are migrating their departmental and line-of-business workgroup applications from mainframes and minicomputers to local area networks. Microsoft SQL Server provides the database transaction processing power, fault tolerance, comprehensive security features, and high performance necessary to effectively downsize many complex, enterprise-wide applications to a network server. The advanced data integrity mechanisms of SQL Server can enforce complex business rules within the database server, ensuring the consistency and integrity of critical enterprise data. This centralized control reduces both application development time and maintenance costs. SQL Server can also connect to relational and nonrelational data anywhere in an organization via a growing number of gateways based on the open data services (ODS) technology. SQL Server is an outstanding database server for business-critical workgroup applications such as order-entry or inventory management.

With the operating system level ODBC APIs and a comprehensive family of relational database products, Microsoft offers organizations tremendous freedom in choosing the right database tools for their workgroup solutions.

Providing a broad range of sophisticated development tools

Microsoft's workgroup computing strategy rests on a key assumption: Because people work together in so many different ways, organizations need maximum flexibility in building their workgroup computing solutions. Our open workgroup architecture, based on the Windows operating system, lets customers and third parties easily build customized workgroup solutions using familiar development tools from any vendor. There are literally thousands of development tools for the Microsoft Windows operating system from which developers can choose.

In many cases, powerful and programmable everyday applications such as Microsoft Access, FoxPro, Microsoft Excel, and Word can address an organization's workgroup needs. However, when more complex solutions require additional integration, Microsoft has the development tools to successfully implement advanced solutions.

Microsoft offers a full range of development tools that customers, application developers, and solution providers can use to integrate different components as they build their work-group computing solutions. These tools include traditional programming environments such as the Microsoft C/C++ development system and the high-productivity Microsoft Visual Basic programming system, allowing developers to choose the tools that best meet their project needs and skills. In addition, all Microsoft development tools provide free run-time licenses so developers can freely distribute applications built with these tools.

Investing in a customer support infrastructure

Organizations face a variety of challenges as they design, implement, and support their workgroup solutions. These organizations are increasingly looking to vendors to offer a broad range of innovative technology services. Microsoft helps customers achieve their workgroup computing objectives by providing high-quality support services and investing in partnerships with third-party solution providers.

Microsoft consulting, technical support, and training

Microsoft Consulting Services (MCS) works closely with clients to design technical solutions to their business problems. With more than 250 employees worldwide, MCS provides planning, high-quality design and development, and integration of new technology into an organization's evolving information technology environment. This "technology transfer" approach aims to empower corporate developers so they can successfully meet the ongoing information systems challenges within their companies.

While focused on understanding and serving corporate customers, MCS is able to leverage Microsoft's solution strategies such as workgroup computing and messaging. MCS clients see benefits in terms of increased productivity, enhanced communication, faster and easier access to information, and reduced maintenance. MCS is committed to helping clients leverage and protect their investments in information technology.

Microsoft Product Support Services (PSS) is dedicated to helping customers get the most out of their Microsoft products and solutions. PSS is available to any customer (either an individual or organization) who acquires a Microsoft operating system, application, or development tool. Technical support is available through two key channels: electronic services and telephone support. A wide range of options, including CompuServe, toll and 900-number phone support, and FastTips (interactive, automated phone support) are available for those users who prefer the convenience of individually accessed, incremental technical support.

Product Support Services also offers two levels of priority access for large accounts, commercial developers, and OEMs: Professional and Premier. Professional support provides priority technical assistance and unlimited access to support. Premier, the highest level of technical support available from Microsoft, provides organizations with individualized technical consultation on Microsoft products, as well as unlimited access to support.

Microsoft offers technical education and training courses for all phases of technology adoption, to all staff levels in an organization, including information systems managers, MIS managers, corporate developers, support professionals, and users. Microsoft training groups provide the knowledge and skills required to build and support real-world business solutions all of which result in the largest return on an investment in Microsoft technology. Because the training needs of organizations vary greatly, Microsoft is tremendously flexible in its training options, providing regional training locations, the Microsoft training partners, video training, Microsoft Press books, customized training, on-site training at customer locations, and corporate licensing programs.

Microsoft has always invested, and will continue to invest heavily, in consulting services, technical product support, and training resources to help customers build and support their workgroup solutions.

Microsoft Solutions Channels

In addition to these support resources, Microsoft has launched a major initiative, Microsoft Solutions Channels, to meet the unique needs of organizations that apply technology to business. Through this comprehensive program, Microsoft works with selected independent partners such as consultants, integrators, and value-added resellers, and supports their efforts with information, training, and tools.

By taking advantage of the wide range of support offered by the Solutions Channels program, these third-party firms develop significant expertise in ways to use Microsoft products to solve business needs. Customers can turn to these solution providers for strategic planning, custom development, systems integration, consulting, training, technical support services, and more when developing their workgroup solutions.

Summary

Microsoft's workgroup computing strategy is focused on creating an open workgroup development platform in Microsoft Windows and on delivering applications and development tools that can take advantage of the open architectures provided by leading operating systems. Our strategy encompasses technology from all of our product groups because workgroup computing solutions vary greatly, depending on specific customer needs.

Our workgroup computing strategy delivers significant advantages for organizations of all sizes:

Solution-based focus—Workgroup solutions should be defined by real-world workgroup activities. Consequently, Microsoft's strategy is to deliver technology that customers can use to implement solutions that precisely match their needs.

Open architecture—Microsoft is focused on creating an open architecture for all customers, application developers, and solution providers. Our strategy does not restrict an organization to the limited applications, systems infrastructure, database model, or programmability tools of one vendor or middleware application.

Evolutionary approach—Microsoft has an evolutionary strategy, not a revolutionary one. Because we are extending the operating system to provide an open workgroup development platform, customers and application developers will be able to evolve all of their applications and development tools forward to meet their workgroup computing needs.

Selecting a workgroup computing strategy is one of the most important information technology decisions a customer must make. This decision will have a long-term impact on an organization's competitive success. Significantly, Microsoft's strategy meets requirements that are vital to customers seeking effective workgroup computing: freedom of choice in purchasing decisions, ability to leverage existing technology investments, and minimizing of the risk involved.

Microsoft has a clear and persistent vision for workgroup computing: Give people the tools they need—in everyday applications they're familiar with—to create workgroup solutions that fit the way they work. It's another way we're making it easier for individuals, groups, and entire organizations to work together more effectively.

Content

MAPI and Messaging Applications[4]

Messaging-Aware Applications

---

[4] Excerpted from "Microsoft Messaging Application Program Interface (MAPI)." A complete version of this white paper is located on the Microsoft Developer Network Development Library, under Backgrounders and White Papers, Operating System Extensions. Copyright 1993. Used with permission. All rights reserved.

MAPI allows basic messaging capabilities to be easily integrated into virtually any desktop application. Using the Common Messaging Calls or Simple MAPI, developers can add message capabilities to their applications' own user interfaces. A word-processing program could be enhanced to include a Send Message option next to the print selection. Such an option would send the document as a mail message to a recipient.

MAPI also supports application macro languages, such as those in Microsoft Excel and Word. This method of incorporating message capabilities into existing applications is extremely flexible. For example, a spreadsheet macro could be written that automatically sends a monthly budget spreadsheet to a designated recipient when the file is updated with new sales figures.

Applications are called messaging-aware when they do not depend upon messaging for their functions. That is, the basic messaging capabilities provide an additional value to the regular features of that application.

Sales Report Automation Macro

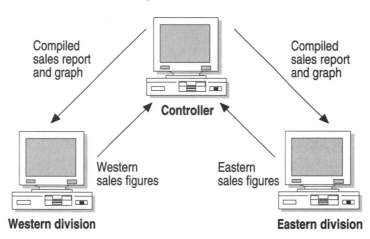

Figure 12.2   Using Microsoft Mail with Microsoft Excel: The Eastern and Western sales divisions create sales reports that are automatically sent to the controller machine at the corporate office. The controller machine automatically consolidates the two reports and sends the combined report back to the sales divisions.

Simple MAPI and CMC are designed for messaging-aware applications.

Messaging-Enabled Applications

Unlike messaging-aware applications, *messaging-enabled* applications require some type of messaging capability in order to function. One example is a scheduling application in which users can view the schedules of their coworkers and send meeting requests to the coworkers' calendars. Another example is a forms-routing application that sends an expense report to a series of recipients and records their approval or disapproval.

Simple MAPI and CMC are designed for messaging-enabled applications.

Messaging-Based Workgroup Applications

The most advanced type of messaging application is the workgroup application, which requires full access to all of the back-end messaging services, including the message-store, address-book or directory, and transport functions. These applications include e-mail clients, workflow automation programs, and bulletin board services. For example, a workflow application might allow a user to inspect a message stored in a certain project folder to see if the appropriate workers have signed off on their tasks. This application could also include a sophisticated search-and-store feature that retrieves relevant files from a bulletin board system and stores them in the folders of certain recipients.

A workgroup application could also be created for an advanced expense-report system in which the application selects the appropriate managers to send the report to based on the type of expense. In addition, this application could search the schedules of the appropriate managers, identify who is available to approve the expense report, and automatically route the report to that manager.

For these advanced workgroup applications, we recommend that developers also use Extended MAPI.

Topic

Describe the other types of communication (besides LAN-based electronic mail) to which MAPI provides access.

Content

The MAPI Spooler[5]

The spooler and the transport provider work together to handle the responsibilities of sending and receiving messages. You can have multiple installed transports installed on the same system, but MAPI supplies the one spooler required.

---

[5] Excerpted from "Understanding and Using Extended MAPI." A complete version of this presentation is available on the Microsoft Developer Network Development Library, under Conferences and Seminars, Tech*Ed March 1994. Workgroup Applications. Copyright 1994. Used with permission. All rights reserved.

Drivers for each transport exist in the form of a Windows DLL to provide the interface between the MAPI messaging subsystem spooler and the underlying back-end messaging systems or services. The message spooler is similar to a print spooler except that it assists with the routing of messages instead of print jobs. The spooler, MAPI, and the transport drivers work together to handle the sending and receiving of messages.

When many different transport drivers are installed on a Windows-based desktop, messages from client applications can be sent to a variety of transport services. When a message is sent from a client application, MAPI responds to the CMC, Simple, or Extended MAPI calls first, routing the message to the appropriate message store and address book service providers. When a message is marked for sending, it is handled by the message spooler where it is delivered to the appropriate transport driver.

The message spooler looks at the message's address to determine which transport to use to send the message. Depending on the recipients, the message spooler may call on more than one transport provider. The spooler performs other message-management functions as well, such as directing inbound messages to a message store and catching messages that are undeliverable because no transport provider can handle them. The spooler also provides an important store and forward function, maintaining a message in a store if the needed messaging service is currently unavailable. When connection to the service is reestablished, the spooler automatically forwards the message to its destination.

Except for dialog boxes at the initial transport logon, the spooler and transport providers operate in the background, transferring messages among various messaging services. The spooler does its work and makes calls to the transport providers when the foreground applications are idle, so users don't have to wait while they are working with the messaging application.

Windows application developers enjoy the benefits of the spooler and other messaging subsystem features without having to write additional code beyond the MAPI calls. MAPI automatically assigns the appropriate tasks to the appropriate service providers.

Content

Slow-Link Services

MAPI supports slow-link providers as well as those that make near-instantaneous access to the messaging system through a LAN connection, for example. Slow-link services are those such as dialup or wireless which have relatively limited data capacity.

Applications should be aware of slow-link services and offer good support, through MAPI, for these types of providers. One example of good slow-link support is to prompt the user before beginning a download of new messages. The application could provide status information (message subject, sender name, date/time, and so on) about waiting messages and then allow the user to choose interactively which messages should be retrieved.

C H A P T E R   1 3

Windows Telephony API (TAPI), License Service API (LSAPI), and Windows SNA

Topic

Describe the services that TAPI provides to the application developer.

Content

What Telephony Is[1]

Telephony is a technology that integrates computers with the telephone network. With telephony, people can use their computers to take advantage of a wide range of sophisticated communications features and services over a telephone line.

The Windows Telephony SDK consists of two main parts:

- **TAPI:** The Windows Telephony Application Programming Interface (TAPI) lets programmers develop applications that provide "personal telephony" to users of the Microsoft Windows environment.

- **TSPI:** The Windows Telephony Service Provider Programming Interface (TSPI) lets programmers develop back-end services that handle requests from applications that conform to the Telephony API..

---

[1] Excerpted from chapter 1 of the *Telephony Service Provider Programmer's Guide* in the Windows 3.1 Telelphony Software Development Kit. Copyright 1992 - 1995. Used with permission. All rights reserved.

Windows Telephony (sometimes referred to as just "Telephony") supports both speech and data transmission, allows for a variety of terminal devices, and supports complex connection types and call-management techniques such as conference calls, call waiting, and voice mail. Telephony allows all elements of telephone usage—from the simple dial-and-speak call to international e-mail—to be controlled with the Windows graphical user interface.

The focus of this guide is on TSPI, although TAPI will be referred to frequently.

Using Telephony in Applications

Telephony capabilities help people get the most from telecommunications systems. Users can not only efficiently manage their voice calls, but also data-transfer operations, which makes telecommuting more productive. These advanced functions will become available to users in the familiar form of Microsoft Windows applications.

The Telephony API and SPI give developers a consistent set of tools for creating these Windows-based telephony applications. Although the sophistication of applications will increase over time, we can already predict some of the functionalities that will soon be incorporated into them. The following examples describe various possibilities, all programmable with TAPI:

- **Personal information managers** that offer features such as automatic dialing, voicemail sorting, and collaborative computing over telephone lines.

- **Strengthened information applications** through the connection of database managers, spreadsheets, and word processors directly into the telephone network.

- **Electronic directory managers** that let users manage complicated telephone functions such as setting up conference calls. It could be possible, for example, to initiate a conference by dragging three or four names from an electronic directory into a "conference box" and clicking "connect." In the future, video as well as audio conference calls will be available at the desktop, supported by TAPI.

- **Icon-driven control of data transmission**. With drag and drop, users can send files from a local disk to that of a remote colleague, specifying first whether to transmit the document as a file, a facsimile, or electronic mail. When ISDN connections become more widespread, users can send data to the recipient simultaneously with a voice call to the same person.

- **Functions making use of caller-ID**. Users can identify an inbound call while on another line without putting anyone on hold. The user could then send the second caller a prerecorded personalized message such as "Hold on, Bill; I'll be right with you," or route the inbound call directly to voicemail.

- **Remote-control applications** let users operate their PCs from a distance over public telephone lines. Developers can use Telephony to write both the host and the caller modules of such remote-control applications.

- **Access to information services** through Telephony applications. Although all of today's information services have their own front ends, developers can write new interfaces, standardized or customized for specific environments.

Although valuable, these applications rely on the existence of service providers that support this functionality. The role of the service provider programmer is therefore to use TSPI to build service providers that execute TAPI functions that are called by applications.

Topics

Describe Assisted Telephony.

Describe the full TAPI.

Content

Telephony API: Three Service Levels[2]

All the functionality of Assisted Telephony exists in the full Telephony API, but Assisted Telephony has its own set of commands. Applications whose telephony functionality goes beyond the most basic call control or are meant to handle inbound calls must be built using Telephony. The Telephony API defines three levels of service:

- The elementary level of service is called Basic Telephony and provides a minimum set of functions that corresponds to "Plain Old Telephone Service" (POTS). TAPI service providers are required to support all Basic Telephony functions.

- The next service level is Supplementary Telephony service, which provides advanced switch features such as hold, transfer, and so on. All Supplementary

---

[2] Excerpted from chapter 2 of the *Telephony Service Provider Programmer's Guide* in the Windows 3.1 Telelphony Software Development Kit. Copyright 1992 - 1995. Used with permission. All rights reserved.

services are optional; that is, the service provider is not required to support them.

- At the Extended Telephony level, the API provides well-defined API extension mechanisms that enable application developers to access service provider-specific functions not directly defined by the Telephony API.

Note The set of TAPI functions do not map one-to-one onto the set of TSPI functions. In particular, functions related to privilege, phone number translation, and inter-application communication are handled by the TAPI.DLL and have no corresponding function in TSPI. Other functions such as those used for service-provider configuration and initialization have no corresponding functions in the TAPI.

Basic Telephony Services

Basic services are a minimal subset of the Windows Telephony specification. Since all service providers must support the functions of Basic services, applications that use only these functions will work with any TAPI service provider. The functionality contained in Basic Telephony roughly corresponds to the features of POTS.

Today, many programmers will use only the services provided by Basic Telephony. But others, such as those writing code for PBX phone systems, will need the functions of Supplementary Telephony. Soon, the demand for ISDN and other network services, along with advancements in telephone equipment, will drive even greater usage of Supplementary Telephony.

Note Because control of phone devices is not assumed to be offered by all service providers, phone-device services are considered to be "optional." That is, they are *not* a part of Basic Telephony. For a list of phone-device services, please read the following section on Supplementary Telephony services, and for more information on phone devices, see the section "Device Classes" earlier in this chapter.

Supplementary Telephony Services

Supplementary Telephony services are the collection of all the services defined by the API other than those included in the Basic Telephony subset. It includes all so-called "supplementary" features found on modern PBXs, such as hold, transfer, conference, park, and so on. All supplementary features are considered optional; that is, the service provider decides which of these services it does or does not provide.

An application can query a line or phone device for the set of supplementary services it provides using functions such as **lineGetDevCaps** or **lineGetAddressCaps**. Note that a single supplementary service may consist of multiple function calls and messages. It is important to point out that the Telephony API, and not the service provider developer, defines the behavior of each of these supplementary features. A service provider should provide a Supplementary Telephony service only if it can implement the exact meaning as defined by the API. If not, the feature should be provided as an Extended Telephony service.

As mentioned under Basic Telephony services above, phone-device services are considered "optional." Therefore, all phone-device services are part of Supplementary Telephony.

Extended Telephony Services

The API contains a mechanism that allows service-provider vendors to extend the Telephony API using device-specific extensions. Extended services (or device-specific services) include all extensions to the API defined by a particular service provider. Since the API defines the extension mechanism only, the definition of the Extended-service behavior must be completely specified by the service provider.

TAPI's extension mechanism allows service-provider vendors to define new values for some enumeration types and bit flags and to add fields to most data structures. The interpretation of extensions is keyed off the service provider's *Extension ID*, an identifier for the specification of the set of extensions supported, which may cross several manufacturers. Special functions and messages such as **lineDevSpecific** and **phoneDevSpecific** are provided in the API to allow an application to directly communicate with a service provider. They are used to allow extending the set of functions (in contrast to enumerations, bit flags, and data structure fields) supported by the service provider. The parameters for each function are also defined by the service provider.

Vendors are not required to register in order to be assigned Extension IDs. Instead, a utility is provided that allows the generation of Extension IDs locally. This unique ID is composed of an Ethernet-adapter address, a random number, and the time of day. An ID is assigned to a set of extensions (before distribution), not to each individual instance of an implementation of those extensions. A tool called EXTIDGEN.EXE is provided within the Windows Telephony SDK that allows service provider authors to generate these IDs.

Extending Data Structures and Types

A range of values is reserved to accommodate future extensions to the Basic and Supplementary function set. There is a range reserved for future definition of structures and types within the Windows Telephony specification, and a separate range reserved for provider-specific extensions. The "Extensibility" section in the data structure entry in the online reference and in the later chapters of this guide tells the amount by which the data structure can be extended.

Topic

Describe the services LSAPI provides to the application developer.

Content

Microsoft Windows[3]

Under the Microsoft Windows environment, each license system service provider is implemented as a Dynamic Link Library (DLL). Applications access the License Service API interface through the license manager DLL (LSAPI.DLL). This DLL, implemented by Microsoft, is responsible for coalescing the installed license service providers. It is not a license provider in and of itself.

Each service provider implements the functions exactly as described in this specification, and contains the same entry points and calling conventions (along with their associated ordinal values) as the LSAPIxx.DLL (where xx = 16 or 32 depending on platform). For the enumeration function, each provider simply responds with a single entry which identifies itself. The License Manager DLL will collate the responses from each of the service providers and present the results to the client application. Configuration information dictates the default ordering of the license systems for the particular client.

The indirection through the License Manager DLL should not have a significant performance hit. Furthermore, applications will be infrequently accessing the DLL. However, if the provider DLLs are located on a network server rather than on the client workstation, a small penalty may result due to the remote access.

License system provider DLLs:

- Must provide the same entry points and parameters as defined for the Windows License Manager DLL.

- Should be small (code and data size) and very efficient (fast). Perform as much work as possible at the server side.

- Should not perform challenge authentication within the provider. Rather, the challenge should always be performed within the license server system. The

---

[3] Excerpted from "License Service Application Programming Interface (LSAPI) Specification 1.1." Complete text of this specification is available on the Microsoft Developer Network Development Library, under Specifications. Copyright 1994. Used with permission. All rights reserved.

challenge serves as an end-to-end authentication that the license server system indeed knows the secret(s) contained on the license itself.

Microsoft Windows 3.x

Applications will access the providers indirectly through the LSAPI16.DLL, which will be supplied with Microsoft Windows, and with license systems. The LSAPI16.DLL is usually placed into the Windows directory (e.g., \WINDOWS), but also may be anywhere as long as it appears in the search path (as defined by the PATH environment variable).

The calling convention used in the License Manager DLL is FAR PASCAL. Refer to the Microsoft Windows 3.x Software Development Kit for further information on writing DLLs.

In the Windows directory (or anywhere along the PATH), there is an initialization file (LSAPI.INI) which contains the following sections and parameters:

Section Name	Parameter	Description
[Settings]	Order=	This defines the default order in which license system providers are queried for a particular license. An order of "2 1 3 4" indicates that Provider2 is to be queried first, Provider1 second, etc. Note that each number is separated by a space.
		If a number appears here that does not match a provider, the number is skipped. Likewise, if any providers are listed which do not appear in this list, they will be queried after the listed providers. These providers will be queried in the order in which they appear in the [Providers] section.
[Providers]	Provider*N*=	One entry for each license system provider installed on the client. Each license system must place a line with a unique value for *N*. The line contains the full pathname to the DLL, a semicolon (;), the interface specification version number provided in the DLL (for now, all are 1.00); another semicolon followed by a brief text description of the particular license system. The entire line must not exceed 255 characters.
[Vendor]	Vendor-specific	Each License system vendor optionally may include limited information in the LSAPI.INI file by placing information under their unique *Vendor* name.

For future compatibility, applications and license system vendors should read and write the LSAPI.INI file using the Windows **GetPrivateProfileString**() and **SetPrivateProfileString**() API calls. In no case should this file be directly accessed. In order to locate the LSAPI.INI file, the installation process should first search the Windows directory, followed by all of the directories specified in the PATH environment variable. :

The following is a sample LSAPI.INI file of a system with four license service providers:

```
[Settings]
Order=2 1 3 4

[Providers]
Provider1=C:\WINDOWS\SITELOCK.DLL;1.00;Brightwork SiteLock
Provider2=C:\DSLA\DSLA.DLL;1.00;Digital Software Licensing System
Provider4=C:\WINDOWS\NETLS.DLL;1.00;HP/Gradient NetLS
Provider3=C:\FLEXLM\FLEXLM.DLL;1.00;Highland Flexible License Mgr
```

Microsoft Windows NT and beyond

Applications will access the providers indirectly through the LSAPI32.DLL, which will be supplied with Microsoft Windows, and with license systems. The LSAPI32.DLL is usually placed into the Windows NT 3.1 directory (e.g., winnt\SYSTEM32), but also may be anywhere as long as it appears in the search path (as defined by the PATH system environment variable).

The license service provider configuration information will be kept in the NT System Registry. The configuration information which applies to the whole system be placed under the \HKEY_LOCAL_MACHINE, while information that is specific to one user should be stored under that user's profile and accessed via \HKEY_CURRENT_USER. The information in the Registry should be structured in the same way as the information in the LSAPI.INI file. There should be a "LSAPI" sub-key under the \HKEY_LOCAL_MACHINE\SOFTWARE and \HKEY_CURRENT_USER\SOFTWARE sub-keys. "LSAPI" should have two default sub-keys called "SETTINGS" and "PROVIDERS" and a sub-key for each license service provider. There should be a value under "SETTINGS" called "ORDER", which should be a string with the order information. There should be values under "PROVIDERS" with names of the form PROVIDERx", where "x" is an integer ID for that provider.

A sample follows:

```
\HKEY_CURRENT_USER\SOFTWARE\LSAPI\SETTINGS\ORDER=2 1 3 4
\HKEY_CURRENT_USER\SOFTWARE\LSAPI\PROVIDERS\Provider1=C:\WINDOWS\...
\HKEY_CURRENT_USER\SOFTWARE\LSAPI\PROVIDERS\Provider2=C:\WINDOWS\...
\HKEY_CURRENT_USER\SOFTWARE\LSAPI\PROVIDERS\Provider3=C:\WINDOWS\...
\HKEY_CURRENT_USER\SOFTWARE\LSAPI\PROVIDERS\Provider4=C:\WINDOWS\...
```

SubKeys of \HKEY_CURRENT_USER\ SOFTWARE\LSAPI	Description
SETTINGS\ORDER	This defines the default order in which license system providers are queried for a particular license. An order of "2 1 3 4" indicates that Provider2 is to be queried first, Provider1 second, etc. Note that each number is separated by a space.
	If any providers are listed which do not appear in this list, they will be queried after the listed providers. These providers will be queried in the order in which they appear in the PROVIDERS\ section.
PROVIDERS\Provider*N*	One entry for each license system provider installed on the client. Each license system must create a key with a unique value for *N*. The value is set to the full pathname to the DLL, a semicolon (;), the interface specification version number provided in the DLL (for now, all are 1.00); another semicolon followed by a brief text description of the particular license system. The entire line must not exceed 512 characters.
Vendor-Name\...	Vendors that wish to use the registration database for private configuration information may create a key: \HKEY_CURRENT_USER\SOFTWARE\ LSAPI*Vendor-Name* where the name is a unique trademark name. Below that, the vendor may create keys of its own choosing. At this time, it is recommended that provider developers limit the amount of private configuration information stored into the registry.

Contact Microsoft's Developer Relations Group at (206) 882-8080 for further information.

Topic

Describe the level of copy protection provided by LSAPI.

Content

Overview[4]

Software Licensing technology is a relative newcomer to the computing industry. A number of software licensing products offering this technology have begun to enter the marketplace. Enough products currently exist to cause software publishers to become cautious about use of these products without the existence of a standard API that is supported by all conforming licensing systems. This caution, along with growing importance of software licensing technology and its ability to support a growing variety of software licensing policies, has produced a demand for the development of an industry standard in this area. Such a standard would describe the interface between the application software and a software licensing product. Standardizing the interface would allow software publishers to make the changes to their product's code only once, and would not lock them into using a specific software licensing product or policy.

This document describes such a standard. It describes an application programming interface, or API, that software publishers can use to include license verification into their products, in a manner independent of specific software licensing systems. Licensing systems provide management of the rights to use software. The API allows vendors to develop a single package that will cooperate with licensing systems across the different licensing systems that support this standard. Software licensing, in general, assists the managers of computer networks in tracking the number of applications in use within their companies—a need identified by the Microcomputer Managers Association[*] and the Netware Masters Group.[*]

---

[4] Excerpted from "License Service Application Programming Interface (LSAPI) Specification 1.1." Complete text of this specification is available on the Microsoft Developer Network Development Library, under Specifications. Copyright 1992 - 1995. Used with permission. All rights reserved.

[*] See *Network Software Licensing* white paper by the Microcomputer Managers Association, dated October 2, 1991. The MMA can be contacted at (908) 580-9091.

[*] The Netware Masters Group can be contacted at [TBD].

The License Service Application Program Interface (LSAPI) provides a simple interface to licensing systems, while hiding the complexities from the software developer. It has been designed to minimize the level of effort required to minimally incorporate licensing into application software, requiring as few as two function calls. By taking advantage of the LSAPI interface, an application does not need to know anything about the type of network in use, the types of computers in the enterprise, the licensing policies, or the types of back-end services available in order to enjoy seamless access to license data. As a result, even if the network, computers, or services should change, the desktop application doesn't need to be rewritten. In other words, LSAPI enables applications to connect to all the licensing services they need across multiple computing environments in a platform-independent manner.

Once the LSAPI calls have been incorporated into the application, the software publisher can choose to use any of the conforming software licensing products that support the LSAPI standard without changes to their program. Applications conforming to the specification may make a conformance statement such as:

"This license system product is compliant with LSAPI 1.10"

The remainder of this document describes the LSAPI standard. First it describes both the goals and non-goals of the API. It then presents the detailed definition of the LSAPI. Next, it discusses the challenge/response mechanism and license policy circumvention protection issues. The document closes with a discussion of the license system service providers.

This API does not involve copy protection, hardware protection devices, or other methods to prevent software copying. These methods are independent of, and are not germane to, this API and this document. Rather, this API provides a standard software development approach to software license management.

Several benefits are obtained by use of the common License Service API as an industry standard:

- Software publishers need to write to only one API to cooperate with conforming licensing systems.
- New distribution methods can emerge. For example, several software packages could be distributed in demo versions on inexpensive CD-ROMs or diskettes. After trying the packages, a buyer could obtain documentation and a "key" that would unlock one of the packages, making it fully-functional.
- Computer managers in companies with a variety of workstations, applications, and networks may eventually use licensing system software that supports this API to administer these various resources under a single front-end.

It is expected that there will be a period of evolution as software publishers incorporate licensing into their applications.

Goals

- Provide a simple standard API which application software can utilize for licensing. The API should be suitable for a wide variety of software publishers, software licensing products, operating systems, and network platforms.

- Provide license system independence (allow a single application source and/or executable to interface to more than one license system).

- Provide an API which *facilitates* the most common software licensing policies (such as concurrent use, personal use, node-locked, etc.)

- Minimize the effort required of software publishers to implement simple use of software licensing within their products.

- Allow software publishers to isolate their product's code from licensing policy. Policy is handled by the licensing system rather than by the application.

- Allow support for the standalone as well as networked environments on machines ranging from the smallest of computers through the largest super computers.

- Offer a reasonable level of protection against license system tampering. Provide the ability to establish, beyond a reasonable doubt, when such tampering has occurred.

- *Help the Honest Person be Honest.*

Non Goals

- It is not a goal to guarantee complete protection against unauthorized use of licensed software.

- It is not a goal to describe a standard License Interchange Format.. This is an independent topic requiring a different group of participants, with a different set of issues to resolve. This topic is considered to be outside the scope of this document.

- It is not a goal to define a standard API for license system management.

- It is not a goal to describe how licensing of passive items (such as font data, etc.) is accomplished.

- It is not a goal to describe or recommend licensing policy.[*]

This specification provides the means for a software vendor to develop an application which is license system independent. At this time, the software publisher will still need to issue licenses on a license system specific basis. However, a single binary executable may be produced (on some operating system platforms) which is license system independent.

---

[*] Such recommendations are available through the Software Publishers Association, the Microcomputer Managers Association, and the Netware Masters Group.

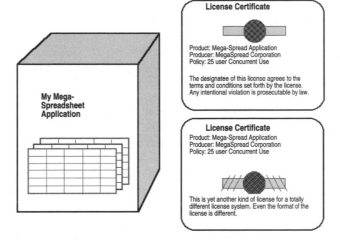

Figure 13.1   License certificates

Topics

Describe the services that the Windows SNA API provides to the application developer.

List and describe the components of the Windows SNA API.

Content

WOSA includes a set of components that address the key issue of connectivity, based on formal or de facto standards for enterprise communications that can be valuable in financial enterprise computing: the Windows SNA APIs, Windows RPC and Windows Sockets.

Windows SNA APIs[5]

The set of Windows SNA APIs were defined and endorsed by a working group consisting of Microsoft, IBM and other leading industry vendors. Since SNA communications are critical to many financial services environments, these are key tools for integrating systems based on the WOSA Extensions for Financial Services into the existing infrastructure in financial institutions. The companies involved in

---

[5] Excerpted from the "Windows Open Services Architecture Specifications." Complete text of this specification is available on the Microsoft Developer Network Development Library, under Specifications. Copyright 1992 - 1995. Used with permission. All rights reserved.

the definition of the SNA API specifications include: Andrew Corporation, Attachmate, Computer Logics, Data Connection, Digital Communications Associates, Easel, Eicon Technology, FutureSoft, IBM, ICOT, International Computers Limited, Microsoft, MultiSoft, AT&T Global Information Solutions, Network Software Associates, Novell, Olivetti, Siemens Nixdorf, Systems Strategies and Wall Data.

This jointly developed set of specifications defines standard interfaces between Windows-based applications and IBM SNA protocols, and is a key connectivity component of the Windows Open Services Architecture (WOSA). An application written to these interfaces will be able to run unchanged over many vendors' SNA connectivity products under Windows. Also, since the APIs are not tied to a particular version of the Windows operating system, programmers can incorporate a common set of SNA code into their applications that will run on Windows, Windows for Workgroups and Windows NT, as well as future versions of Windows.

The Windows SNA API sets are listed below. Please refer to the individual specifications for each of these components for additional details.

- **Windows LUA (enables IBM 4700-compatible communications)** — The Logical Unit Application (LUA; commonly referred to as LU0) API is used to gain access to the lower-level SNA data streams that are common, especially in financial services environments. The specification includes both the basic Request Unit Interface (RUI) API and the higher level Session Level Interface (SLI) API.

- **Windows APPC** — The Advanced Program-to-Program Communication (APPC) API is used to write cooperative applications for the LU6.2 protocol.

- **Windows CPI-C** — The Common Programming Interface for Communications (CPI-C) API also uses the LU6.2 protocol to write cooperative applications for the LU6.2 protocol.

- **Windows HLLAPI (enables 3270/5250 emulation)** — The High Level Language API (HLLAPI) allows application programs to interact with a host using existing 3270 and 5250 emulation products.

- **Windows CSV (enables communication with IBM NetView®)** — The Common Service Verbs (CSV) API provides interfaces for communication with the IBM NetView management system and for character set translations.

Windows RPC (Remote Procedure Call)

The Windows RPC interface provides a standard Windows API for access to the Remote Procedure Call capability for network-independent interprocess communication in heterogenous distributed environments. RPC makes the development of client-server applications easier, and supports interoperability with other OSF/DCE RPC-compliant systems. The Windows RPC interface is supported by the Windows NT operating system, and defined in the Windows NT Software Development Kit (SDK).

Windows Sockets

The Windows Sockets specification defines a Windows API that is useful in many environments, especially for communication between Windows-based clients and UNIX hosts/servers. This specification defines a network programming interface for Windows, based on the "socket" paradigm popularized in the Berkeley Software Distribution from the University of California at Berkeley. The Berkeley Sockets programming model is a de facto standard for TCP/IP networking. The Windows Sockets API is consistent with release 4.3 of the Berkeley Software Distribution (4.3BSD).

The Windows Sockets API includes both the familiar Berkeley socket style routines and a set of Windows-specific extensions designed to allow the programmer to take advantage of the message-driven nature of Windows. It is intended to provide a single API to which application developers can program and multiple network software vendors can conform, and to simplify the task of porting existing sockets-based source code. It has a high degree of familiarity for programmers familiar with programming with sockets in UNIX and other environments.

CHAPTER 14

Windows Sockets API, and WOSA Extensions for Financial Services (XFS) and for Real-Time Data (XRT)

Topics

Describe the services the Windows Sockets API provides to the application developer.

Describe the role of client and server as they relate to sockets.

Content

Plug into Serious Network Programming with the Windows Sockets API[1]

J. Allard
Keith Moore
David Treadwell

In today's heterogeneous networks, closed proprietary standards are unwelcome. As networking has evolved over the last two decades, hardware and software providers have learned that cooperation can yield very rewarding results. The Windows Sockets effort is a useful and efficient open networking standard developed by more than twenty cooperating vendors in the TCP/IP (Transmission Control Protocol/Internet Protocol) networking community.

---

[1] "Plug into Serious Network Programming with the Windows Sockets API," by J. Allard, Keith Moore, and David Treadwell. Reprinted with permission from *Microsoft Systems Journal* (Vol. 8, No. 7) July 1993, copyright 1993 Miller-Freeman Inc. All rights reserved.

The Windows* Sockets API provides applications with an abstraction of the networking software below it. The present Windows Sockets specification, version 1.1, defines this abstraction for TCP/IP. For many, the TCP/IP protocol represents the greatest common denominator between the various systems that make up today's enterprise networks. In fact, the TCP/IP protocols were developed similarly to the Windows Sockets specification: open cooperation between many interested parties with different requirements. Windows Sockets doesn't stop at TCP/IP, however. The level of abstraction is complete enough to support other protocol families as well, such as the Xerox® Network System (XNS) protocols, Digital's DECnet protocol, or Novell's IPX/SPX family. Following the specification, your application can be developed and/or run over any Windows Sockets-compliant TCP/IP implementation.

Windows Sockets is implemented as a DLL provided by the vendor of the given network protocol software. A Windows Sockets developer leverages the APIs from both Windows Sockets as well as the Windows operating system itself to create a network-aware application. Figure 14.1 illustrates the building blocks of a Windows Sockets application. The areas shaded in gray are provided by the network protocol vendor.

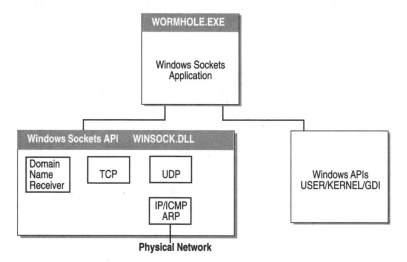

Figure 14.1   Building a Windows Sockets application.

Our goal is to offer developers a taste of this powerful new API. We assume that the reader is familiar with networking basics. To keep things simple, we will focus our discussion on using Windows Sockets to develop network applications over the

---

* For ease of reading, "Windows" refers to the Microsoft Windows operating system. "Windows" is a trademark that refers only to this Microsoft product.

TCP/IP protocol.

Today, more than thirty application vendors have announced the development of commercial applications to Windows Sockets such as X Window servers, terminal emulators, and e-mail systems. Several commercial and public domain versions of Windows Sockets-compliant TCP/IP stacks are available. Many corporate developers are standardizing on Windows Sockets for heterogeneous application development under the Microsoft Windows operating system.

The Birth of Windows Sockets

The charter of the Windows Sockets committee was simple: to design a binary-compatible API for the TCP/IP protocol family under Windows. The effort was kicked off at the Fall 1991 Interop networking conference.

Infuriated by a lack of standardization, TCP/IP application vendors were forced to develop their applications to be aware of several divergent APIs. This allowed their applications to run over multiple TCP/IP implementations, making their products available to the widest possible audience. With more than ten different TCP/IP implementations on the market, many vendors created an abstraction layer to the network interface, a common denominator that could be supported by all of their implementations. Their applications were then developed to this proprietary abstraction layer. Providers, or code that glued the application to a specific vendor's TCP/IP implementation, were developed for each of the TCP/IP implementations the application supported.

This approach was costly and frustrating. Application vendors were continuously updating their provider modules as TCP/IP implementers modified or updated their libraries. Moreover, new implementations were springing up quickly, and it took time before the appropriate provider could be made available to customers. Application vendors found it difficult to maintain, test, and support multiple providers. This caused TCP/IP implementers difficulty as well, especially if a critical third-party application didn't run over their implementation. Customers had to choose a TCP/IP implementation based on their application needs rather than the merit of vendors' transports.

Vendors were so motivated to straighten out the TCP/IP networking API confusion that in just nine months the Windows Sockets committee published the first version of the specification. The first anniversary of the effort was marked with several technology and interoperability demonstrations at Fall Interop 1992. Windows Sockets became a reality.

The Sockets Paradigm

The sockets paradigm was first introduced in Berkeley UNIX (BSD) in the early eighties. Initially designed as a local interprocess communication (IPC) mechanism, sockets evolved into a network IPC mechanism for the built-in TCP/IP. A socket simply defines a bidirectional endpoint for communication between processes. Bidirectional simply means that applications can transmit as well as receive data through these connections.

A socket has three primary components: the interface to which it is bound (specified by an IP address); the port number or ID to which it will send or receive data; and the type of socket, either stream or datagram. Typically, a server application listens on a well-known port over all installed network interfaces. A client generally initiates communication from a specific interface from any available port. The type of the socket (stream or datagram) depends entirely on the needs of the application. Windows Sockets is closely related to the Berkeley sockets model; many of the APIs are identical or very similar. In addition to the Berkeley-style functions, Windows Sockets offers a class of asynchronous extensions that facilitate the development of more Windows-friendly applications.

Stream versus Datagram Sockets

The Windows Sockets model offers service for both connection-oriented and connectionless protocols. In TCP/IP, TCP provides a connection-oriented service, whereas UDP (User Datagram Protocol) offers connectionless service. In the sockets model, connection-oriented service is offered by stream sockets, while connectionless service is provided by datagram sockets.

TCP is a reliable connection-oriented protocol. It is used by applications that exchange large amounts of data at a time, or that require reliability and sequencing. For example, FTP (File Transfer Protocol), which facilitates the ASCII or binary transfer of arbitrarily large files, represents an application written to TCP or stream sockets. In contrast, if an application is willing to manage its own sequencing or reliability, or is using the network for low-bandwidth iterative processing, UDP is often used. For example, an application that keeps system clocks synchronized by periodically broadcasting its system time would probably be written to use UDP. }

Network Byte Order

Since Windows Sockets applications cannot be aware of the type of remote computer system they will be dealing with a priori, it is necessary to define a common data representation model. Sockets use the big-Endian model for "on-the-wire" data representation, also known as the network byte order.

The Windows Sockets interface offers APIs for converting the local system representation (or host byte order) to and from the network byte order. There is no harm in using these routines on systems that store data in the big-Endian model natively; in fact it is encouraged. By religiously using the byte-ordering APIs, your code can be used on systems with different internal representations without inheriting byte-ordering problems, making your code more portable.

The Windows Sockets API

This guided tour of the Windows Sockets API is aimed at giving you a basic understanding of the building blocks of a Windows Sockets application (see Tables 14.1, 14.2, and 14.3). After the walkthrough of the API, we'll discuss the use of Windows Sockets by our WormHole sample application.

Although the Windows Sockets specification contains about a dozen different structures, a few are required by nearly all Windows Sockets applications.

```
struct sockaddr {
      u_short sa_family;
      char    sa_data[14];
};
struct sockaddr_in {
      short   sin_family;
      u_short sin_port;
      struct  in_addr sin_addr;
      char    sin_zero[8];
};
```

Table 14.1   Major Windows Sockets APIs

Function	Action
accept	Acknowledges an incoming connection and associates it with an immediately created socket. The original socket is returned to the listening state.
bind	Assigns a local name to an unnamed socket.
closesocket	Removes a socket descriptor from the per-process object reference table. Only blocks if SO_LINGER is set.
connect	Initiates a connection on the specified socket.
getpeername	Retrieves the name of the peer connected to the specified socket descriptor.
getsockname	Retrieves the current name for the specified socket.
getsockopt	Retrieves options associated with the specified socket descriptor.
htonl	Converts a 32-bit quantity from host byte order to network byte order.
htons	Converts a 16-bit quantity from host byte order to network byte order.
inet_addr	Converts a character string representing a number in the Internet standard "." notation to an Internet address value.
inet_ntoa	Converts an Internet address value to an ASCII string in "." notation, for example, "a.b.c.d".
ioctlsocket	Provides control for descriptors.
listen	Listens for incoming connections on a specified socket.
ntohl	Converts a 32-bit quantity from network byte order to host byte order.
ntohs	Converts a 16-bit quantity from network byte order to host byte order.
recv*	Receives data from a connected socket.
recvfrom*	Receives data from either a connected or unconnected socket.
select*	Performs synchronous I/O multiplexing.
send*	Sends data to a connected socket.
sendto*	Sends data to either a connected or unconnected socket.
setsockopt	Stores options associated with the specified socket descriptor.
shutdown	Shuts down part of a full-duplex connection.
socket	Creates an endpoint for communication and returns a socket descriptor.

*These functions may block if acting on a blocking socket

Table 14.2   Windows Sockets Asynchronous Extensions

WSAAsyncGetHostByAddr	Asynchronous versions of the
WSAAsyncGetHostByName	standard Berkeley getXbyY functions.
WSAAsyncGetProtoByName	For example, the WSAAsyncGet-
WSAAsyncGetProtoByNumber	ProtoByNumber function provides an
WSAAsyncGetServByName	asynchronous message-based WSAAsyncGetServByPort implementation of the standard
	Berkeley gethostbyname function.
WSAAsyncSelect	Performs asynchronous version of select().
WSACancelAsyncRequest	Cancels an outstanding instance of a WSAAsyncGetXByY function.
WSACancelBlockingCall	Cancels an outstanding blocking API call.
WSACleanup	Signs off from the underlying Windows Sockets DLL.
WSAGetLastError	Obtains details of last Windows Sockets API error.
WSAIsBlocking	Determines if the underlying Windows Sockets DLL is already blocking an existing call for this thread.
WSASetBlockingHook	Hooks the blocking method used by the underlying Windows Sockets implementation.
_WSASetLastError	Sets the error to be returned by a subsequent WSAGetLastError.
WSAStartup	Initializes the underlying Windows Sockets DLL.
WSAUnhookBlockingHook	Restores the original blocking function.

Table 14.3   Database Functions

gethostbyaddr*	Retrieves the name(s) and address corresponding to a network address.
gethostname	Retrieves the name of the local host.
gethostbyname*	Retrieves the name(s) and address corresponding to a host name.
getprotobyname*	Retrieves the protocol name and number corresponding to a protocol name.
getprotobynumber*	Retrieves the protocol name and number corresponding to a protocol number.
getservbyname*	Retrieves the service name and port corresponding to a service name.
getservbyport*	Retrieves the service name and port corresponding to a port.
	*These functions may block if acting on a blocking socket

The sockaddr structure specifies a local or remote endpoint address to connect a socket to. An endpoint address contains the appropriate endpoint identification information for the underlying network transport to deliver the data to the application. As the contents of endpoint addresses differ between network protocols, the sockaddr structure accommodates endpoint addresses of variable size. The first field of sockaddr contains the family number identifying the format of the remaining part of the address.

In the Internet address family, the sockaddr_in structure stores the endpoint address information and is cast to type sockaddr for the functions which require it. Other address families must define their own sockaddr_xx structures as appropriate. For TCP/IP, the sockaddr_in structure breaks the endpoint address into two components: port ID (sin_port) and IP address (sin_addr). It pads the remaining eight bytes of the endpoint address with a character string (sin_zero). The port and IP address values are always specified in network byte order. The value for sin_family under TCP/IP is always AF_INET (Address Family Internet).

```
struct hostent {
      char FAR *          h_name;
      char FAR * FAR *    h_aliases;
      short               h_addrtype;
      short               h_length;
      char FAR * FAR *    h_addr_list;
};
```

The hostent structure is generally used by the Windows Sockets database routines to return host, or system, information about a specified system on the network. The host structure contains the primary name for a system including optional aliases for the primary name. It also contains a list of address(es) for the specified system. This information is generally sought for information about remote systems by a Windows Sockets application using the database routines.

```
struct  protoent {
        char FAR *        p_name;
        char FAR * FAR *  p_aliases;
        short             p_proto;
};

struct servent {
        char FAR *        s_name;
        char FAR * FAR *  s_aliases;
        short             s_port;
        char FAR *        s_proto;
};
```

The protoent and servent structures are also filled by the Windows Sockets database routines. These structures contain information about a particular protocol (such as TCP or UDP) or service (such as finger or telnet), respectively. Along with the primary name and an array of aliases for the protocol or service, these structures also contain their corresponding 16-bit IDs, necessary to build a valid TCP/IP endpoint address.

```
typedef struct WSAData {
        WORD          wVersion;
        WORD          wHighVersion;
        char          szDescription[WSADESCRIPTION_LEN+1];
        char          szSystemStatus[WSASYS_STATUS_LEN+1];
        unsigned short  iMaxSockets;
        unsigned short  iMaxUdpDg;
        char FAR    *  lpVendorInfo;
} WSADATA;
```

Finally, the WSAData structure is filled in by a Windows Sockets DLL when an application calls the WSAStartup API. Along with Windows Sockets version information, the structure contains vendor-specific information, such as the maximum number of sockets available and the maximum datagram size. The szDescription and szSystemStatus members can be used by an implementation to identify itself and the current status of the DLL. For example, an implementation may return the text "Joe's ShareWare Windows Sockets implementation v1.2. 7/4/93" in szDescription. The specification of the lpVendorInfo member is completely up to an implementer and is not defined in the Windows Sockets specification.

Setting Up Your Windows Sockets Application

As mentioned, Windows Sockets offers some extensions to the Berkeley sockets paradigm to allow your application to be friendlier in Windows. All such functions are preceded by the characters WSA, short for Windows Sockets API (see Table 14.2). The use of WSA functions is strongly advised and there are two WSA functions that your application can't avoid: WSAStartup and WSACleanup.

WSAStartup "attaches" your application to Windows Sockets and causes the Windows Sockets DLL to initialize any structures it might need for operation. Additionally, WSAStartup performs version negotiation and forces an internal Windows Sockets reference count to be incremented. This reference count allows Windows Sockets to maintain the number of applications on the local system requiring Windows Sockets services and structures. The version negotiation allows an application to determine whether or not the underlying Windows Sockets implementation is able to support the same version of the Windows Sockets specification the application does. A Windows Sockets implementation may or may not support multiple versions of the specification. Other Windows-Sockets-specific information may also be filled in, such as the vendor of the implementation, the maximum datagram size supported, the maximum number of sockets that an application can open, and so on.

The startup code in Sample Code 1 runs only under version 1.1 (the most current version of the Windows Sockets specification), and requires that there are at least six sockets available to the calling application.

Sample Code 1   Windows Sockets Initialization]

```
#define      WS_VERSION_REQD       0x0101
#define      WS_VERSION_MAJOR      HIBYTE(WS_VERSION_REQD)
#define      WS_VERSION_MINOR      LOBYTE(WS_VERSION_REQD)
#define      MIN_SOCKETS_REQD      6

WSADATA      wsaData;
char         buf[MAX_BUF_LEN];
int          error;


  .
  .
  .
```

```
error=WSAStartup(WS_VERSION_REQUIRED,&wsaData);
if (error !=0 ) {
      /* Report that Windows Sockets did not respond to the WSAStartup()
call */
      sprintf(buf,"winsock.dll not responding.");
      MessageBox (hWnd, buf. "Windows Sockets Error",MB_OK);
      shutdown_app();
}

if (( LOBYTE (wsaData.wVersion) < WS_VERSION_MAJOR) ||
      ( LOBYTE (wsaData.wVersion) = - WS_VERSION_MAJOR &&
        HIBYTE (wsaData.wVersion) < WS_VERSION_MINOR)) {

      /* Report that app requires Windows Sockets version
WS_VERSION_REQD   */
      /* compliance and that the WINSOCK.DLL on system doesn't support
it. */

      sprintf(buf,"Windows Sockets version %d.%d not supported by
winsock.dll",
             LOBYTE (wsaData.wVersion), HIBYTE (wsaData.wVersion));
      MessageBox (hWnd, buf. "Windows Sockets Error",MB_OK);
      shutdown_app();
}

if (wsaData.iMaxSockets < MIN_SOCKETS_REQUIRED ) {

      /* Report that winsock.dll was unable to support the minimum
number of   */
      /* sockets (MIN_SOCKETS_REQD) for the application
*/

sprintf(buf,"This application requires a minimum of %d supported
sockets.",
        MIN_SOCKETS_REQUIRED);
      MessageBox (hWnd, buf. "Windows Sockets Error",MB_OK);
      shutdown_app();
}
```

A Windows Sockets application generally calls WSACleanup during its own cleanup, decrementing the internal reference count and letting Windows Sockets know that it's no longer needed by the calling application. Whatever cleanup this function forces is implementation-specific and shielded from the application. The application author should be sure to check for any of the possible error conditions from WSACleanup and report them before exiting, as this information might indicate a network layer problem in the system.

Error Handling

To provide a consistent mechanism for reporting errors and to ensure the safety of Windows Sockets applications in the multithreaded Windows NT (New Technology) operating system, the WSAGetLastError API was Introductionduced as a means to get the code for the last network error on a particular thread. Under Windows 3.x, thread safety is not an issue, although WSAGetLastError is still the appropriate way to check for extended error codes. Many Windows Sockets APIs return an error code in the event that there was a problem, and rely on the application to call WSAGetLastError to get more detailed information on the failure. The code in Sample Code 2 illustrates how an application might report an error to a user.

Sample Code 2   Reporting an Error

```
LPHOSTENT    host_info;
char     user_buf[MAX_BUF],        appl_buf[MAX_BUF];
    .
    .
    .
/* Attempt to resolve hostname specified by user_buf ,return meaningful */
/* message to the use in the event of an error , */

host_info=gethostbyname (user_buf);
if(host_info==NULL){
    sprint(buf , "Windows Sockets error %d:  Hostname:  %s couldn't be resolved.",
        WSAGetLastError(),user_buf);
    MessageBox (hWnd,buf,"Windows Sockets Error" ,MB_OK);}
    .
    .
    .
```

In addition to WSAGetLastError, an application may choose to use WSASetLastError to set a network error condition that will be returned by a subsequent WSAGetLastError call. Obviously, any Windows Sockets calls made between a WSASetLastError and WSAGetLastError pair will override the code set by the WSASetLastError call.

Database Routines

The TCP/IP protocol relies on binary representations for addresses and various other identifiers. However, end users and programmers prefer to use easy-to-remember names (such as FTP or rhino.microsoft.com). It is therefore necessary to provide a common method to resolve both services and hostnames into their respective binary equivalents. To solve this, the Windows Sockets specification offers a set of APIs known as the database routines (see Table 14.3).

The database routines fall into three categories. The host resolution routines return the IP address for a host based on system or hostname. The protocol resolution routines return the protocol ID of a specific member of a protocol family (such as TCP), and the service resolution routines return the port ID of a service based on a service name/protocol pair. All of the database routines return information in the structures described earlier.

Applications use the gethostbyname and gethostbyaddr functions to learn about the names and IP address(es) of a particular system knowing only the name or the address of the system. Both calls return a pointer to a hostent structure as defined earlier. The gethostbyname call simply accepts a pointer to a null-terminated string representing the name of the system to resolve. The gethostbyaddr accepts three parameters: a pointer to the address (in network byte order), the length of the address, and the type of address.

Generally the hostname or IP address is offered to the application by the user to specify a remote system to connect to and the IP address is resolved by Windows Sockets by either parsing a local host's file, or querying a domain name system (DNS) server. The details of the resolution are implementation-specific, abstracted from the application by these APIs.

The getservbyname and getservbyport functions return information about well-known Windows Sockets services or applications. Each of these system calls returns a pointer to the servent structure described earlier. Typically, an application will use these calls to determine the port ID for a well-known service (such as FTP) to create an endpoint address.

The code fragment in Sample Code 3 shows how getservbyname fills in the sockaddr_in structure, which will be used to connect a socket to a well-known port (the ftp protocol port over TCP).

Sample Code 3   Filling the sockaddr_in Struct

```
char                 buf [MAX_BUF_LEN];
struct sockaddr_in   srv_addr;
LPSERVENT            srv_info;
LPHOSTENT            host_info;
SOCKET               s;


    .
    .
    .


/* Get FTP service port information */

srv_info=getservbyname("ftp","tcp");
```

```
if (srv_info= = NULL) {
    /* Couldn't find an entry for "ftp" over "tcp" */

    sprintf(buf,"Windows Sockets error %d: Couldn't resolve FTP service
port.",
            WSAGetLastError());
    MessageBox (hWnd,buf,"Windows Sockets Error",MB_OK);
    shutdown_app();
}

/* Set up socket */

srv_addr.sin_family = AF_INET;
srv_addr.sin_addr.s_addr = INADDR_ANY;
srv_addr.sin_port=srv_info->s_port;

    .
    .
    .
```

The getservbyname function resolves the port number of the ftp service over TCP. The port ID contains the sockaddr_in structure (endpoint address) for future use by the application. As we mentioned before, the address family for TCP/IP is always assigned as AF_INET. We use the INADDR_ANY macro to specify any local IP interface to accept incoming connections (more on this later).

To round out the database routines, getprotobyname and getprotobynumber fill in a protoent structure, sometimes used by applications to create a socket over a particular protocol such as UDP or TCP. More often than not, however, an application will use the SOCK_DGRAM and SOCK_STREAM macros to create either datagram or stream sockets.

Data Manipulation Routines

Several routines convert values between network byte order and host (or local system) byte order. Windows Sockets offers byte-ordering routines for 16-bit and 32-bit values from both host byte order and network byte order. The htons function takes a 16-bit value (a short), and converts it from host byte order to network byte order—hence the name htons (host to network short). The other byte-ordering functions available are htonl, ntohs, and ntohl.

Two other useful routines, inet_ntoa and inet_addr, convert IP addresses between dotted-decimal strings and network byte-ordered 32-bit values. These routines are useful to convert the IP address of an endpoint user input. In the example listed in Sample Code 4, a TCP-based server application uses the inet_ntoa function to log incoming connection attempts.

Sample Code 4   Accepting Incoming Connections

```
SOCKET          cli_sock,    srv_sock;
LPSOCKADDR_IN   cli_addr;
char            *cli_ip,     buf[MAX_BUF];
int             len;

  .
  .
  .

/* Accept incoming connection, create new local socket cli_sock */

cli_sock=accept(srv_sock,(LPSOCKADDR)&cli_addr,&len);

if (cli_sock= =INVALID_SOCKET){
     return(ERROR);
}

/* Convert endpoint IP address from network byte order to ASCII */

cli_ip=inet_ntoa(cli_addr.sin_addr);
sprintf(buf,"Incoming connection request from: %s.\n",cli_ip);
log_event(buf);
```

Setting Up Client and Server Sockets

Most Windows Sockets applications are asymmetric; that is, there are generally two components to the network application—a client and a server. Frequently these components are isolated into separate programs. Sometimes these components are integrated into a single application (as is the case in our sample application, WormHole). When both the client and server components of a networking application are integrated, the application is generally referred to as a peer application. Both the client and the server components go through different procedures to ready themselves for networking by making a number of Windows Sockets API calls. The state diagrams in Figures 14.2 and 14.3 illustrate the state transitions for setting up client- and server-side socket applications.

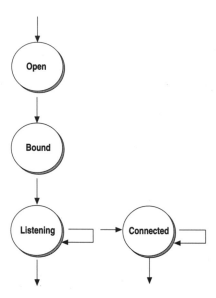

Figure 14.2   Setting up a stream-based server.

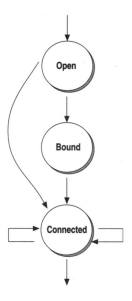

Figure 14.3   Setting up a stream-based client.

Setting Up a Stream-based Client

The socket call creates an endpoint for both client- and server-side application communication. When calling socket(), the application specifies the protocol family and either the socket type (stream or datagram), or the protocol it expects to use. Both the client- and server-sides of a network application use the socket call to define their respective endpoints. The socket function returns a socket descriptor, an integer that uniquely identifies the socket.

Once the socket is created, the server-side associates the freshly created socket descriptor and a local endpoint address via the bind API. The local endpoint address is comprised of two pieces of data, the IP address and the port ID for the socket. The local IP address determines which interface(s) the server application will accept connection requests on, and the port ID identifies the TCP or UDP port from which connections will be accepted. It is for these two values that the network byte-ordering routines (htonl, htons, and so on) were created. These values must always be represented in network byte order.

Alternatively, an application may substitute the value INADDR_ANY in place of a valid local IP address, and the system will accept incoming requests on any local interface, and will send requests on the most appropriate local interface. Most server applications do exactly this. To associate a socket with any valid system port, provide a value of 0 for the sin_port member of the sockaddr_in structure. This will select an unused system port between 1025 and 5000. As mentioned before, most server applications listen on a specified port, and client applications use this mechanism to obtain an unused local port. Once an application uses this mechanism to obtain a valid local port, it may call getsockname to determine the port the system selected.

The listen API sets up a connection queue. It accepts only two parameters, the socket descriptor and the queue length. The queue length identifies the number of outstanding connection requests that will be allowed to queue up on a particular port/address pair before denying service to incoming connections.

The accept API completes a stream-based server-side connection by accepting an incoming connection request, assigning a new socket to the connection, and returning the original socket to the listening state. The new socket is returned to the application, and the server can begin interacting with the client over the network.

From the client's perspective, the application also creates a socket using the socket call. The bind API is used to bind the socket to a locally specified endpoint address that the server will use to transmit data back to the client. Once a local endpoint association is made, the connect API establishes a connection with a remote endpoint. This routine initiates the network connection between the two systems. Once the connection is made, the client can begin interaction with the server on the network.

Although the client may choose to call bind, it is not necessary. Calling connect with an unbound socket will simply force the system to choose an IP interface and unique port ID and mark the socket as bound. Most client-side applications neglect the bind call as there are rarely specific requirements for a particular local interface/port ID pair.

The code in Sample Code 5 creates and connects a pair of stream-based sockets using the API flow outlined above. Although the code in Sample Code 5 makes use of the bind API, it would be just as effective to skip over this call as there are no specific local port ID requirements for this client. The only advantage that bind offers is the accessibility of the port, which the system chose via the sin_port member of the cli_addr structure that is set upon success of the bind call.

Sample Code 5   Creating and Connecting a Stream Client and Server
Server-side (connection-oriented)

```
#define              SERVICE_PORT         5001

SOCKET               srv_sock,            cli_sock;
struct sockaddr_in   srv_addr,            cli_addr;
char                 buf[MAX_BUF_LEN];


    .
    .
    .


/* Create the server-side socket */

srv_sock=socket(AF_INET,SOCK_STREAM,0);
if (srv_sock= =INVALID_SOCKET){
     sprintf(buf,"Windows Sockets error %d: Couldn't create socket.",
          WSAGetLastError());
     MessageBox (hWnd,buf,"Windows Sockets Error",MB_OK);
     shutdown_app();
}

srv_addr.sin_family=AF_INET;
srv_addr.sin_addr.s_addr=INADDR_ANY;
srv_addr.sin_port=SERVICE_PORT;        /* specific port for server to
listen on */

/* Bind socket to the appropriate port and interface (INADDR_ANY) */

if (bind(srv_sock,(LPSOCKADDR)&srv_addr,sizeof(srv_addr))=
=SOCKET_ERROR){
     sprintf(buf,"Windows  Sockets error  %d: Couldn't bind socket.",
          WSAGetLastError());
     MessageBox (hWnd,buf,"Windows Sockets Error",MB_OK);
     shutdown_app();
}
```

```
if (listen(srv_sock,1)= =SOCKET_ERROR){ /* Listen for incoming
connections */
     sprintf(buf,"Windows Sockets error %d: Couldn't set up listen on
socket.",
                WSAGetLastError());
     MessageBox (hWnd,buf,"Windows Sockets Error",MB_OK);
     shutdown_app();
}

/* Accept and service incoming connection requests indefinitely */
for ( ; ; ) {
     cli_sock=accept(srv_sock,(LPSOCKADDR)&cli_addr,&addr_len);
     if (cli_sock= =INVALID SOCKET){
        sprintf(buf,"Windows Sockets error %d: Couldn't accept incoming
\
                connection on socket.",WSAGetLastError());
        MessageBox (hWnd,buf,"Windows Sockets Error",MB_OK);
        shutdown_app();
     }

.
. /* Client-server network interaction takes place here */
.

     closesocket(cli_sock);
}

.
.
.


—


Client-side (connection-oriented)
/* Static IP address for remote server, for example. In reality, this
would be
   specified as a hostname or IP address by the user */

#define     SERVER            "131.107.1.121"

struct      sockaddr_in       srv_addr,cli_addr;
LPSERVENT   srv_info;
LPHOSTENT   host_info;
SOCKET      cli_sock;


.
. /* Set up client socket */
.
```

```
cli_sock=socket(PF_INET,SOCK_STREAM,0);

if (cli_sock= =INVALID_SOCKET){
    sprintf(buf,"Windows Sockets error %d: Couldn't create socket.",
            WSAGetLastError());
    MessageBox (hWnd,buf,"Windows Sockets Error",MB_OK);
    shutdown_app();
}
cli_addr.sin_addr.s_addr=INADDR_ANY;
cli_addr.sin_port=0;                        /* no specific port req'd */

/* Bind client socket to any local interface and port */
if (bind(cli_sock,(LPSOCKADDR)&cli_addr,sizeof(cli_addr))=
=SOCKET_ERROR){

    sprintf(buf,"Windows Sockets error %d: Couldn't bind socket.",
            WSAGetLastError());
    MessageBox (hWnd,buf,"Windows Sockets Error",MB_OK);
    shutdown_app();
}

/* Get the remote port ID to connect to for FTP service */
srv_info=getservbyname("ftp","tcp");
if (srv_info= = NULL) {
    sprintf(buf,"Windows Sockets error %d: Couldn't resolve FTP service
port.",
            WSAGetLastError());
    MessageBox (hWnd,buf,"Windows Sockets Error",MB_OK);
    shutdown_app();
}
srv_addr.sin_family = AF_INET;
srv_addr.sin_addr.s_addr = inet_addr(SERVER);
srv_addr.sin_port=srv_info->s_port;

/* Connect to FTP server at address SERVER */
if (connect(cli_sock,(LPSOCKADDR)&srv_addr,sizeof(srv_addr))=
=SOCKET_ERROR){
    sprintf(buf,"Windows Sockets error %d: Couldn't connect socket.",
            WSAGetLastError());
    MessageBox (hWnd,buf,"Windows Sockets Error",MB_OK);
    shutdown_app();
}
.
. /* Client-server network interaction takes place here */
.
```

For connectionless, or "datagram" sockets, Windows Sockets usage is a little simpler. Since the communication in datagram sockets is connectionless, it is not necessary to use the APIs needed for creating a connection: connect, listen, and accept. The flow of Windows Sockets APIs that a typical connectionless client-server pair will generally traverse is shown in Figures 14.4 and 14.5. A client may choose to connect the datagram socket for the convenience of multiple sends to the remote endpoint. Connecting a datagram socket will cause all sends to go to the connected address, and any datagrams received from a remote address different than the connected address are discarded by the system. Generally, connectionless clients use the sendto API to transmit application data. The sendto call requires that the destination's endpoint address be specified with every call to the API.

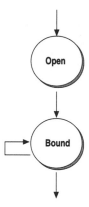

Figure 14.4   Setting up a datagram-based server.

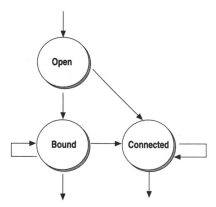

Figure 14.5   Setting up a datagram-based client.

By connecting a datagram socket, a client sending a large amount of data to the same destination can simply use the send API to transmit without having to specify a remote endpoint with every call, and the client need not concern itself with the possibility of receiving unwanted data from other hosts. Depending on the type of application you are developing and the Windows Sockets implementation, connecting datagram sockets may improve application performance.

The sample code in Sample Code 6 illustrates how the TFTP protocol (a connectionless protocol for file transfer) client and server might be implemented over Windows Sockets.

Sample Code 6   Implementing a TFTP Client and Server
Server-side (connectionless)

```
SOCKET                srv_sock;
struct sockaddr_in    srv_addr;

.
.
.

/* Create server socket for connectionless service */

srv_sock=socket(PF_INET,SOCK_DGRAM,0);

if (srv_sock= -INVALID_SOCKET){

    sprintf(buf,"Windows Sockets error %d: Couldn't create socket.",
            WSAGetLastError());
    MessageBox (hWnd,buf,"Windows Sockets Error",MB_OK);
    shutdown_app();
}

/* Resolve TFTP service port to listen on */

srv_info=getservbyname("tftpd","udp");

if (srv_info= = NULL) {
    sprintf(buf,"Windows Sockets error %d: Couldn't resolve TFTPd
service port.",
            WSAGetLastError());
    MessageBox (hWnd,buf,"Windows Sockets Error",MB_OK);
    shutdown_app();
}

srv_addr.sin_family = AF_INET;
srv_addr.sin_addr.s_addr = INADDR_ANY;   /* Allow the server to accept
*/
                                          /* connections over any
interface */
srv_addr.sin_port=srv_info->s_port;
```

```
/* Bind remote server's address and port */

if (bind(srv_sock,(LPSOCKADDR)&srv_addr,sizeof(srv_addr))=
=SOCKET_ERROR){

    sprintf(buf,"Windows Sockets error %d: Couldn't bind socket.",
        WSAGetLastError());
    MessageBox (hWnd,buf,"Windows Sockets Error",MB_OK);
    shutdown_app();
}

/* Client-server network interaction takes place here */

    .
    .
    .


/* Static IP address for remote server, for example. In reality, this
would be
    specified as a hostname or IP address by the user */

#define      SERVER            "131.107.1.121"
_
struct sockaddr_in           srv_addr,cli_addr;
LPSERVENT                    srv_info;
LPHOSTENT                    host_info;
SOCKET                       cli_sock;

    .
    .
    .


/* Create client-side datagram socket */

cli_sock=socket(PF_INET,SOCK_DGRAM);
if (cli_sock= =INVALID_SOCKET){

    sprintf(buf,"Windows Sockets error %d: Couldn't create socket.",
        WSAGetLastError());
    MessageBox (hWnd,buf,"Windows Sockets Error",MB_OK);
    shutdown_app();
}

cli_addr.sin_family=AF_INET;
cli_addr.sin_addr.s_addr=INADDR_ANY;
cli_addr.sin_port=0;                        /* no specific local port
req'd */
```

```
/* Bind local socket */
if (bind(cli_sock,(LPSOCKADDR)&cli_addr,sizeof(cli_addr))=
=SOCKET_ERROR){

     sprintf(buf,"Windows Sockets error %d: Couldn't bind socket.",
          WSAGetLastError());
     MessageBox (hWnd,buf,"Windows Sockets Error",MB_OK);
     shutdown_app();
}

/* Resolve port information for TFTP service */

srv_info=getservbyname("tftp","udp");
if (srv_info= = NULL) {

     sprintf(buf,"Windows Sockets error %d: Couldn't resolve TFTP
service port.",
          WSAGetLastError());
     MessageBox (hWnd,buf,"Windows Sockets Error",MB_OK);
     shutdown_app();
}

srv_addr.sin_family = AF_INET;
srv_addr.sin_addr.s_addr = inet_addr(SERVER);
srv_addr.sin_port=srv_info->s_port;

if (connect(cli_sock,(LPSOCKADDR)&srv_addr,sizeof(srv_addr))=
=SOCKET_ERROR){
     sprintf(buf,"Windows Sockets error %d: Couldn't connect socket.",
          WSAGetLastError());
     MessageBox (hWnd,buf,"Windows Sockets Error",MB_OK);
     shutdown_app();
}
/* Client-server network interaction takes place here */
```

Since a connectionless client such as TFTP will undoubtedly be doing successive transmissions with the server (especially during long transfers), we have chosen to connect the socket, allowing the use of the send and recv APIs rather than sendto and recvfrom. The use of connect with datagram sockets is purely optional.

Sending and Receiving Data

Once an application successfully establishes a socket connection, it is ready to start transferring data over the connection. With stream (TCP) sockets, data transfer is said to be reliable, meaning that the application may assume that the underlying transport will ensure that the data gets to the remote host without duplication or corruption. When a connection is established on a stream socket, the TCP transport creates a virtual circuit between the two machines. This circuit remains open until both applications decide that they're finished sending data on the circuit (typically a graceful close), or until a network error occurs that causes the circuit to be terminated abnormally.

An application sends data using the send API. This API takes a socket descriptor, a pointer to a buffer to send, the length of the buffer, and an integer that specifies flags that can modify the behavior of send. To receive data, an application uses the recv API, which takes a pointer to a buffer to fill with data, the length of the specified buffer, and a flags integer. The recv function returns the number of bytes actually received, and send returns the number of bytes actually sent. Applications should always check the return codes of send and recv for the number of bytes actually transferred, since it may be different from the number requested. Because of the stream-oriented nature of TCP sockets, there is not necessarily a one-to-one correspondence between send and recv calls. For example, a client application may perform ten calls to send, each for 100 bytes. The system may combine, or coalesce, these sends into a single network packet, so that if the server application did a recv with a buffer of 1000 bytes, it would get all the data at once.

Therefore, an application must not make any assumptions about how data will arrive. A server that expects to receive 1000 bytes should call recv in a loop until it has received all of the data (see Sample Code 7). Likewise, an application that wants to send 1000 bytes should send in a loop until all of the data has been sent (see Sample Code 8).

Sample Code 7   Looping While Receiving Data

```
SOCKET      s;
int         bytes_received;
char        buffer[1000];
char        *buffer_ptr;
int         buffer_length;
.
.
.

buffer_ptr = buffer;
buffer_length = sizeof(buffer);

/* Receive all outstanding data on socket s */

do {
    bytes_received = recv(s, buffer_ptr, buffer_length, 0);
    if (bytes_received = = SOCKET_ERROR) {
            sprintf(buf,"Windows Sockets error %d: Error while receiving
data.",
```

```
                        WSAGetLastError());
            MessageBox (hWnd,buf,"Windows Sockets Error",MB_OK);
            shutdown_app();
        }
    buffer_ptr += bytes_received;
    buffer_length -= bytes_received;
} while (buffer_length > 0);
.
.
.
```

Sample Code 8   Looping While Sending Data

```
SOCKET          s;
int             bytes_sent;
char            buffer[1000];
char            *buffer_ptr;
int             buffer_length;
.
.
.


buffer_ptr = buffer;
buffer_length = sizeof(buffer);

/* Enter send loop until all data in buffer is sent */

do {
    bytes_sent = send(s, buffer_ptr, buffer_length, 0);
    if (bytes_sent = = SOCKET_ERROR) {
            sprintf(buf,"Windows Sockets error %d: Error while sending
data.",
                    WSAGetLastError());
            MessageBox (hWnd,buf,"Windows Sockets Error",MB_OK);
            shutdown_app();
        }
    buffer_ptr += bytes_sent;
    buffer_length -= bytes_sent;
} while (buffer_length > 0);
_.
.
.
```

Data transmission on datagram sockets is significantly different from stream sockets. The most important difference is that transmission is "not reliable" on datagram sockets. This means that if an application attempts to send data to another application, the system does nothing to guarantee that the data will actually be delivered to the remote application. Reliability will tend to be good on LANs, but can be very poor on WANs such as the Internet.

The next important difference in datagram sockets is that they are connectionless, which means there is no default remote address assigned to them. For this reason, an application that wants to send data must specify the address to which the data is targeted with the sendto API. An application that needs to know where data came from receives data with the recvfrom API, which returns the address of the sender of the data.

The final significant difference in data transmission for datagram sockets is that it is message-oriented. This means that there is a one-to-one correspondence between sendto and recvfrom calls, and that the system does not coalesce data when sending it. For example, if an application makes ten calls to sendto with a buffer of two bytes, the remote application will need to perform ten calls to recvfrom with a buffer of at least two bytes to receive all the data.

Sample Code 9 shows a code fragment from a datagram sockets application that echoes datagrams back to the sender. As mentioned earlier, it is possible to connect() a datagram socket. Once a datagram socket is connected, all data is sent and received from the remote address to which the datagram is connected, so it is possible to use the send and recv APIs on connected datagram sockets.

Sample Code 9   Echoing Datagrams Back to the Sender

```
SOCKET          s;
SOCKADDR_IN     remoteAddr;
int             remoteAddrLength = sizeof(remoteAddr);
BYTE            buffer[1024];
int             bytesReceived;

for ( ; ; ) {
      /* Receive a datagram on socket s */

   bytesReceived = recvfrom( s, buffer, sizeof(buffer),0,
                             (PSOCKADDR)&remoteAddr, &remoteAddrLength );

      /* Echo back to the server as long as bytes were received */

   if ( bytesReceived != SOCKET_ERROR ||
       sendto( s, buffer, bytesRecieved, 0,
               (PSOCKADDR)&remoteAddr, remoteAddrLength ) = =
       SOCKET_ERROR ){
           sprintf(buf,"Windows Sockets error %d: Error while sending
data.",
                    WSAGetLastError());
           MessageBox (hWnd,buf,"Windows Sockets Error",MB_OK);
           shutdown_appl();
       }
   }
```

Terminating a Connection

An application has several options for terminating a connection. The simplest is to call the closesocket API, which takes only a socket descriptor as input. This API frees resources associated with a socket and initiates the graceful close sequence. This sequence is complete when the remote application also closes its socket.

If an application determines that it is finished sending data, but may want to receive more data, it can call the shutdown API. This API notifies the remote end that the local application will not be sending any more data, but may continue to receive data. (The shutdown API may also be used to indicate to the system that the application does not desire to receive more data, or that the application will neither send nor receive more data. These uses of shutdown are less common and not particularly useful.)

Finally, an application may cause an abortive or hard close on a connection with the SO_LINGER socket option in conjunction with closesocket. Setting the linger timeout to 0 causes the circuit to be terminated immediately, whether the remote end has completed its data transfer or not, and any unreceived or unsent data is dropped. This option should be used with caution, and only if the results are understood and intended. The following code fragment demonstrates how to perform a hard close on a connection:

```
LINGER      lingerInfo;
INT         err;
SOCKET      s;

 .
 .
 .

/* First set the linger timeout on the socket to 0. */
/* This will cause the connection to be reset. */

lingerInfo.l_onoff = 1;
lingerInfo.l_linger = 0;

setsockopt( s, SOL_SOCKET, SO_LINGER,
            (char *)&lingerInfo,
            sizeof(lingerInfo) );
closesocket(s);
```

How can an application know that the remote end has terminated the connection? The answer depends on whether the remote end terminated the connection gracefully or abortively. If the termination was abortive, then send and recv calls will fail with the error WSAECONNRESET. This indicates to an application that data may have been lost, and the error condition should be reported to the user.

If the termination was graceful, then any recv calls made after all data has been received will return zero as the number of bytes received. This indicates that the remote end has gracefully terminated its end of the connection and the local end may close the socket without fear of data loss. The code fragment in Sample Code 10 illustrates how an application initiates a graceful close and then waits for the remote end to close gracefully before closing the socket.

Sample Code 10   Closing Gracefully

```
SOCKET        s;
INT           err;
BYTE          buffer[1024];

err = shutdown( s , 1 );
if ( err = = SOCKET_ERROR ) {
    sprintf(buf,"Windows Sockets error %d: Error during shutdown.",
            WSAGetLastError());
    MessageBox (hWnd,buf,"Windows Sockets Error",MB_OK);
    shutdown_appl();
}

/* Receive the rest of the pending data */

while ( (err = recv( s, buffer, sizeof(buffer), 0 ) != 0 ) {

   if ( err = = SOCKET_ERROR ) {
        sprintf(buf,"Windows Sockets error %d: Error while receiving
data.",
                WSAGetLastError());
        MessageBox (hWnd,buf,"Windows Sockets Error",MB_OK);
        shutdown_appl();
    }

.
.
.
    /* do something with the data we received. */

}

/* The other side has also terminated.  we can safely close now */

closesocket( s );
```

In Sample Code 10, the application keeps calling recv until it returns zero bytes received. If an application closes a socket and there is data available to be received, or data arrives later, the system will abort the connection and throw out the data, since there's nobody to give it to. Well-behaved applications should ensure that they receive all data before closing a socket.

Asynchronous Windows Sockets Calls

By default, an application's socket calls will block until the requested operation can be completed. For example, if an application wishes to receive data from another application, its call to the recv API will not complete until the other application has sent data that can be returned to the calling application.

This model is sufficient for simple programs, but more sophisticated applications may not wish to block for an arbitrarily long period for a network event. In fact, in Windows 3.1, blocking operations are considered poor programming practice. Applications are expected to call PeekMessage or GetMessage regularly to allow other applications to run and receive input. The Windows Sockets interface uses a concept called a blocking hook to prevent Windows from locking up when an application makes a blocking call. However, blocking calls are discouraged, and beyond the scope of this article. See the Windows Sockets specification for more information.

To support sophisticated applications, Windows Sockets supports nonblocking sockets. If an application sets a socket to nonblocking, then any operation that may block for an extended period will fail with the error code WSAEWOULDBLOCK. This error indicates to the application that the system was unable to perform the requested operation immediately.

How, then, does an application know when it can successfully perform certain operations? Polling would be one (poor) solution. A better mechanism is to use the asynchronous notification mechanism provided by the WSAAsyncSelect API. This routine allows an application to notify a Windows Sockets implementation of certain events of interest, and to receive a Windows message when the events occur. For example, an application may indicate interest in data arrival with the FD_READ message, and when data arrives the Windows Sockets DLL posts a message to the application's window handle. The application receives this message in a GetMessage or PeekMessage call and can then perform the corresponding operation.

The code fragment in Sample Code 11 demonstrates how an application opens and connects a TCP socket and indicates that it is interested in being notified when one of three network events occurs:

- Data arrives on the socket.
- It is possible to send data on the socket.
- The remote end has closed the socket.

Sample Code 11   Calling WSAAsyncSelect

```
/* Static IP address for remote server, for example. In reality,
this would be specified as a hostname or IP address by the user
*/

#define    SERVER            "131.107.1.121"

#define    SOCKET_MESSAGE    WM_USER+1
#define    SERVER_PORT       4000

struct sockaddr_in          srv_addr;
SOCKET                      cli_sock;

.
.
.

/* Create client-side socket */

cli_sock=socket(PF_INET,SOCK_STREAM,0);

if (cli_sock= =INVALID_SOCKET){
    sprintf(buf, "Windows Sockets error %d: couldn't open socket.",
            WSAGetLastError());
    MessageBox(hWnd,buf,"Windows Sockets Error",MB_OK);
    shutdown_appl();
}

srv_addr.sin_family = AF_INET;
srv_addr.sin_addr.s_addr = inet_addr(SERVER);
srv_addr.sin_port=SERVER_PORT;

/* Connect to server */

if (connect(cli_sock,(LPSOCKADDR)&srv_addr,sizeof(srv_addr))=
=SOCKET_ERROR){

    sprintf(buf,"Windows Sockets error %d: Couldn't connect socket.",
            WSAGetLastError());
    MessageBox (hWnd,buf,"Windows Sockets Error",MB_OK);
    shutdown_appl();
}

/* Set up async select on FD_READ, FD_WRITE, and FD_CLOSE events */
```

```
err = WSAAsyncSelect(cli_sock, hWnd, SOCKET_MESSAGE,
FD_READ|FD_WRITE|FD_CLOSE);
if (err = = SOCKET_ERROR) {
    sprintf(buf,"Windows Sockets error %d: WSAAsyncSelect failure.",
            WSAGetLastError());
    MessageBox (hWnd,buf,"Windows Sockets Error",MB_OK);
    shutdown_appl();
}
```

When one of the specified network events occurs, the specified window handle
hWnd receives a message containing a wMsg of SOCKET_MESSAGE. The
wParam field of the message will have the socket handle, and lParam contains two
pieces of information: the low word contains the event that occurred (FD_READ,
FD_WRITE, or FD_CLOSE) and the high word contains an error code, or 0 if
there was no error. Code similar to the fragment in Sample Code 12, which would
belong in an application's main window procedure, may be used to interpret a
message from WSAAsyncSelect.

Sample Code 12   Interpreting WSAAsyncSelect Messages

```
long FAR PASCAL _export WndProc(HWND hWnd, UINT message, UINT wParam,
                                LONG lParam)
{
    INT err;

_    switch (message) {

.
.   /* handle Windows messages */
.

    case SOCKET_MESSAGE:
    /* A network event has occurred on our socket. Determine which
network
    /* event occurred.*/

            switch (WSAGETSELECTEVENT(lParam)) {
            case FD_READ:
                /* Data arrived.  Receive it. */
                err = recv(cli_sock, Buffer, BufferLength, 0);
                if (WSAGetLastError() = = WSAEWOULDBLOCK) {
                    /* We have already received the data. */
                    break;
                }
```

```
                             if (err = = SOCKET_ERROR) {
                                   sprintf(buf, "Windows Sockets error %d: receive
error.",
                                        WSAGetLastError());
                                 MessageBox(hWnd,buf,"Windows Sockets
Error",MB_OK);
                                   shutdown_appl();
                             }

    .
    .  /* Do something useful with the data. */
    .

                             break;

                   case FD_WRITE:
                         /* We can send data. */

                             err = send(cli_sock, Buffer, BufferLength, 0);
                             if (err = = SOCKET_ERROR) {
                                   if (WSAGetLastError() = = WSAEWOULDBLOCK) {
                                         /* Send buffers overflowed. */
                                         break;
                                   }
                                   sprintf(buf, "Windows Sockets error %d: send
failed.",
                                           SAGetLastError());
                                   MessageBox(hWnd,buf,"Windows Sockets
Error",MB_OK);
                                   shutdown_appl();
                             }
                             break;

                   case FD_CLOSE:
                         /* The remote closed the socket. */

                             closesocket(cli_sock);
                             break;
                   }

                   break;
          }
```

After the Windows Sockets DLL has posted a message for a particular network
event, the DLL refrains from posting another message for that event until the
application has called the reenabling function for that event. For example, once an
FD_READ has been posted, no more FD_READ messages will be posted until the
application calls recv. This prevents an application's message queue from
overflowing with messages for a single network event.

WSAAsyncSelect can simplify and improve organization in Windows-based applications by allowing them to be fully event-driven. Such an application responds to network events in much the same way it responds to user events such as mouse clicks. In addition, applications that use WSAAsyncSelect are better behaved since they must frequently call PeekMessage or GetMessage to receive the network messages.

Getting the Spec

The current version of the Windows Sockets specification, 1.1, is distributed electronically on Internet and CompuServe. If you're not able to obtain the specification electronically, ask a Windows Sockets vendor—most will give you a copy on disk. The most recent versions of the specification are available via anonymous FTP on rhino.microsoft.com, microdyne.com, or vax.ftp.com. On CompuServe, check the Microsoft Software Library forum (GO MSL). A variety of different file formats are readily available. (For developers familiar with the 1.0 specification, the Microsoft Word and PostScript versions of the 1.1 specification offer change-bars in the left-hand margin to denote changes made to the 1.0 specification.) In addition to the specification, you will also find Joel Goldberger's extremely useful Windows Sockets online help file (WINSOCK.HLP), sample applications, and other nifty stuff.

If you're interested in Windows Sockets, your comments, experience, and feedback are welcome on the Windows Sockets electronic discussion list. Currently, there is an electronic mailing list of several hundred Windows Sockets developers, users, and wizards who offer technical support and discussion of the API. To subscribe, e-mail winsock-request@microdyne.com. If you're a Usenet user, the mailing list is cross-posted to the alt.winsock newsgroup. In addition, you also might want to peruse the comp.os.ms-programmer.win32 and comp.protocols.tcp-ip.ibmpc groups, which frequently see Windows Sockets-related traffic. The Windows SNMP effort maintains a similar mailing list. To subscribe, e-mail winsnmp-request@microdyne.com.

Asynchronous Database Routines

Just as simple network operations like recv can block for extended periods of time, so can the database routines like gethostbyname. This is especially true if they go through DNS, which can require considerable time due to the network activity involved. To allow well-behaved applications to use the database routines, the Windows Sockets API supplies asynchronous versions of these database routines. Their use is similar to the synchronous database routines, with two important exceptions. First, completion of the operation is indicated via a Windows message, as with WSAAsyncSelect. Also, the application is required to include a buffer to be filled in by the Windows Sockets DLL with the information requested by the application. This is in contrast to the synchronous database routines, which return a pointer to space owned by the Windows Sockets DLL.

To make an asynchronous database call, an application passes information about the call, a window handle to receive the completion message, a message code, and a buffer for the output information. The Windows Sockets API defines a constant, MAXGETHOSTSTRUCT, which is the maximum size of a hostent structure. An application should use a buffer of this size to pass to the asynchronous database routines to guarantee that all the output information will fit in its buffer. A sample call to WSAAsyncGetHostByName is shown in Sample Code 13.

Sample Code 13   Calling WSAAsyncGetHostByName

```
#define GETHOST_MESSAGE   WM_USER+2

BYTE    HostBuffer[MAXGETHOSTSTUCT];
HANDLE TaskHandle;

/* Resolve hostname "hostname" asynchronously */

TaskHandle = WSAAsyncGetHostByName(hWnd, GETHOST_MESSAGE, "hostname",
                                   HostBuffer, MAXGETHOSTSTUCT);

if (TaskHandle = = SOCKET_ERROR) {

    sprintf(buf,
            "Windows Sockets error %d: Hostname couldn't be resolved.",
            WSAGetLastError());
    MessageBox(hWnd,buf,"Windows Sockets Error",MB_OK);
    shutdown_appl();
}
```

WSAAsyncGetHostByName and the other asynchronous database routines return a task handle that identifies the operation in progress. This handle allows an application that may have multiple outstanding asynchronous database routines to associate completion messages with the request, since the task handle is returned in the completion message as wParam. To receive and process the completion message, an application uses the code found in Sample Code 14.

Sample Code 14   Processing the Completion Message

```
long FAR PASCAL _export WndProc(HWND hWnd, UINT message,
                                UINT wParam, LONG lParam)

{
    INT err;
```

```
        switch (message) {

        .
        .  /* handle other Windows messages */
        .

        case GETHOST_MESSAGE:

          /* An asynchronous database routine completed. */
          if (WSAGETASYNCERROR(lParam) != 0) {
          sprintf(buf, "Windows Sockets error %d: Hostname couldn't be
resolved.",
                WSAGetLastError());
            MessageBox(hWnd,buf,"Windows Sockets Error",MB_OK);
            shutdown_appl();
            }


        .
        .  /* HostBuffer now contains a host buffer, Use info from it. */
        .


}
```

Windows Sockets on Windows NT

Although the initial focus of Windows Sockets was on 16-bit Windows 3.1-based applications, Windows NT supports Windows Sockets as well. To run existing 16-bit Windows Sockets applications, Windows NT supplies WINSOCK.DLL. 32-bit Windows Sockets are supported with the DLL called WSOCK32.DLL (clever name, huh?). In general, all of the Windows Sockets routines in the 32-bit DLL are identical to their 16-bit counterparts, although their parameters are of course widened to 32 bits.

The most significant difference in writing Windows Sockets applications for Windows NT is that it is a fully preemptive, multithreaded operating system. Therefore, if an application blocks on a Windows Sockets call, system performance does not suffer. In addition, it is feasible to write a multithreaded application that uses one thread to process user input and another to block on sockets calls. Such an application could still be responsive to user input.

The asynchronous Windows Sockets calls are still useful in Windows NT. Their biggest advantage is that they allow an application to be fully event-driven, fitting better within the Windows-based programming paradigm. In addition, there are 32-bit versions of Windows Sockets in the works for the Win32s® API. A 16-bit application written to use the asynchronous routines can be easily ported to Win32s without the negative system impact of blocking calls.

WormHole—A Sample Application

To demonstrate Windows Sockets, we developed WormHole. WormHole is a peer Windows Sockets application that allows users to establish network "wormholes" between systems and then drag-and-drop files to one another (OK, so we've watched too much Deep Space 9). A simple 16-bit MDI application, WormHole runs on Windows 3.1 systems equipped with a Windows Sockets-compliant TCP/IP implementation. WormHole can be conditionally compiled as a 32-bit Windows NT-based application that will run over the Windows NT 32-bit TCP/IP transport and 32-bit Windows Sockets interfaces. The makefile explains how to compile this application for Windows NT. (Full source code for WormHole can be found on any MSJ bulletin board and via anonymous FTP from rhino.microsoft.com—Ed.)

To demonstrate as many Windows Sockets concepts as possible, WormHole utilizes both stream and datagram sockets, and is completely event-driven (asynchronous). This allows a WormHole to simultaneously service multiple client connections and act as a WormHole client. Host windows are created when a user specifies a destination system (either by IP address or hostname) to connect with. Specifying a remote system does not establish a network connection; it simply creates a host window on the client to provide feedback during file transfers.

Wormholes (connections) are established every time a user initiates a file transfer by dragging a file from the File Manager into a host window. We refer to the system on which this happens as the WormHole client. The WormHole application implements a very simple protocol, which would not be entirely uncommon in a production environment. The wormhole setup takes place over a simple pair of datagram frame transactions, followed by stream connection establishment that facilitates the file transfer. Figure 14.6 illustrates the transactions for connection establishment. Remember that since WormHole is a peer application, every instance of WormHole on the network is capable of acting as a WormHole client and a WormHole server simultaneously.

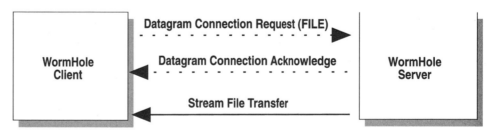

Figure 14.6   The WormHole protocol.

The WormHole Protocol

The wormhole establishment begins on the client side by sending a FILE frame datagram that specifies to the server the name of the file to transfer, the length of the file, and a unique transaction identifier (xid). The xid allows the server to "disambiguate" between multiple outstanding FILE requests. The server acknowledges the FILE request with either a PORT frame or a NACK frame (see Table 14.4). A PORT frame informs the client that the server will accept an incoming file, returning a specified stream socket port for the client to connect to as well as the xid specified in the original request. If the server wishes to refuse the FILE request, it may respond with a NACK (negative acknowledgment) frame that contains the xid it is refusing and optionally an error code (such as "insufficient disk space," or "duplicate filename").

Table 14.4   Datagram Connection Frames and Contents

Request	Acknowledge	Refuse
FILE	PORT	NACK
Transaction ID	Transaction ID	Transaction ID
File length	Port Number	Error code (optional)
Filename		

Upon receipt of a PORT frame, the client establishes a stream socket connection to the specified port and begins to transfer the file. Since the server is listening on a port it created in association with a particular transaction, and it knows the filename and length, it is not necessary to transfer anything aside from the actual file data. Once the entire file has been received by the server, the stream connection is shut down gracefully.

Because the connection request (FILE), acknowledgment (PORT), and refuse (NACK) frames are all transmitted on the network using an unreliable datagram protocol, it is quite possible for these frames to be lost in the shuffle of network activity. The WormHole protocol also implements some retry timers to allow a client to retry a failed connection request. A WormHole client will retry a connection request by retransmitting up to four FILE frames to the server. To keep things simple, the server does not implement a retry timer on possible lost PORT or NACK frames. We instead rely on the client to resend a FILE request if a PORT frame gets lost.

Since the server creates a local window, transaction association, and the like upon receipt of a FILE frame, it does maintain a timer-per-file transaction to allow for the cleanup of acknowledgment (PORT) frames that go unanswered. Finally, since the file transfer itself takes place over reliable stream sockets, it isn't necessary to implement these types of precautions for the actual file transfer. WormHole simply relies on the failure of the send and recv APIs in the event of network or connection problems.

Where is Windows Sockets Headed?

Although Windows Sockets is a new technology, much evolution has already taken place in the TCP/IP community. Microsoft is encouraging third-parties and corporate developers to use Windows Sockets as the client-server and distributed application API by including the API as part of WOSA, the Windows Open Services Architecture.

Several PC-based TCP/IP implementations are offering Windows Sockets support, and over twenty application vendors are shipping Windows Sockets-compatible applications.

The Windows Sockets waters may remain calm for a short while, probably only long enough to allow application vendors and TCP/IP implementers to produce 1.1-compatible offerings. There are already a number of ideas for features that future revisions may incorporate: transparent transport independence, access to raw sockets for lower-level network functions, and the ability to share a connected socket between different applications are a few.

The success of the Windows Sockets effort has spawned two similar undertakings: Windows SNMP (Simple Network Management Protocol) and ONC/RPC (Open Network Computing/Remote Procedure Call) for Windows. Both strive to provide application vendors with a common API across divergent implementations under Windows. Many of the participants of these efforts come from the Windows Sockets group, but more interested parties are joining every day.

If Windows Sockets is a sign of things to come in networking with Windows, application development under Windows will continue to become easier, more flexible, and more powerful.

Topic

Describe the services that WOSA XFS provides to the application developer.

Content

WOSA Extensions for Financial Services[2]

Background

The Banking Systems Vendor Council, an organization of leading vendors of information technology to the financial services industry, was formally announced at the American Bankers Association National Operations and Automation Conference (NOAC) in Denver on May 18, 1992. Revision 1.0 of this specification was released at NOAC in New Orleans on May 24, 1993.

The charter members of the Banking Systems Vendor Council are:

Andersen Consulting	Microsoft Corporation
AT&T Global Information Solutions	Ing. C. Olivetti & C. S.p.A.
Digital Equipment Corporation	Siemens Nixdorf Informationssysteme AG
EDS Corporation	Tandem Computers
International Computers Limited	Unisys Corporation

The Banking Systems Vendor Council has held many multi-vendor development meetings, in addition to numerous additional hours invested in defining this specification for the WOSA Extensions for Financial Services.

Objectives

The charter of the Banking Systems Vendor Council is to develop an approach to financial enterprise computing that will allow financial institutions to develop

---

[2] Excerpted from "Windows Open Services Architecture Specification." Complete text for this specification is available on the Microsoft Developer Network Development Library, under Specifications. Copyright 1992 - 1995. Used with permission. All rights reserved.

complete, consistent sets of solutions that meet these objectives:

- Reduce the costs of software development and maintenance by:
  - improving the efficiency and productivity of development organizations,
  - reducing the costs of developer training, and
  - allowing the use of a much larger set of existing applications.
- Improve the "time to market" of new applications via easier development and rapid deployment.
- Allow institutions the flexibility to build systems modularly, using the largest possible range of hardware and software products from multiple vendors, and to upgrade these systems incrementally while maximizing the value of the original investment.
- Define an architecture that allows scalability of solutions across a broad range of hardware platforms.
- Encourage the development of more and better applications by promoting widespread adoption of standard interfaces and platforms.
- Reduce the costs of training users.

Strategies

The following key strategies have been adopted by the Banking Systems Vendor Council to implement the objectives defined above:

- Use the Microsoft Windows operating systems family as the strategic platform for client-server computing.
- Adopt the Windows Open Service Architecture (WOSA) family of open interfaces and associated services for the integration of Windows and Windows-based applications into enterprise computing solutions.
- Utilize existing WOSA elements wherever possible, defining new elements, or extensions to existing elements, only when no suitable candidate(s) exist in the evolving WOSA family that meet the needs of financial services computing. In all cases, existing formal or de facto standards will be utilized to the maximum degree possible.
- Enhance WOSA with the Extensions for Financial Services to meet the special requirements of financial applications for access to services and devices.
- Maintain the highest possible level of compatibility of both the API and SPI specifications as the Extensions for Financial Services evolve to include new and enhanced capabilities.

  WOSA comprises a family of stable, open-ended interfaces for enterprise computing environments that hides system complexities from users and application developers. WOSA allows the integration of Windows and

Windows-based applications seamlessly with all the services and enterprise capabilities that application developers and users need. It includes such interfaces as:

- Open Database Connectivity (ODBC) for standard access to databases,
- Messaging Application Programming Interface (MAPI) for standard access to messaging services, and communications support, including Windows SNA, RPC, and Sockets.

Each of the elements of WOSA includes a set of Application Program Interfaces (APIs) and Service Provider Interfaces (SPIs), with associated supporting software. The architecture of WOSA is shown below:

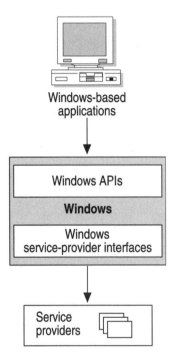

Figure 14.7   **WOSA: Windows Open Services Architecture**

For additional information on WOSA, see the *WOSA Backgrounder* (Microsoft part number 098-34801).

The Extensions for Financial Services extend WOSA by defining a Windows-based client-server architecture for financial applications. The extensions (as with the other elements of WOSA) include a set of APIs and SPIs common to multiple financial applications.

The WOSA Extensions for Financial Services are planned to include specifications for access to financial peripherals (such as passbook/journal/receipt printers, magnetic card readers/writers, PIN pads, etc.), financial transaction messaging and management, as well as related services for financial networks such as network and systems management and security. All these capabilities are specified for access from the familiar, consistent Microsoft Windows user interface and programming environments. Whenever possible, the capabilities will be incorporated into the family of standard WOSA elements, and will utilize existing formal and de facto standards.

Benefits

Adoption of the Windows platforms, the WOSA architecture and the Extensions for Financial Services will deliver a wide range of benefits to banks and other financial services institutions, satisfying the objectives stated above by allowing them to:

- Access financial services and devices using standard Windows user and programming interfaces, with the resultant savings in user and developer training.

- Utilize the large, growing range of Windows-based applications and development tools.

- Exploit the variety of products that will be developed by the multiple vendors that will support this initiative.

- Develop applications which will be able to run with few or no changes on the full range of Windows operating systems (and associated range of hardware platforms). The Windows family consists of the Windows version 3.1, Windows for Workgroups and Windows NT operating systems. Future versions of the Windows operating systems family will also be supported.

- Deploy modular and adaptable line of business solutions (financial services delivery systems, relationship banking, etc.) to address the changing conditions experienced in today's markets.

Note that since the interfaces specified in WOSA are open and utilize many industry standards, vendors and users have many options to develop solutions that involve interoperatibility with other operating system platforms.

WOSA Extensions for Financial Services Overview

A key element of the Extensions for Financial Services is the definition of a set of APIs, a corresponding set of SPIs, and supporting services, providing access to financial services for Windows-based applications. The definition of the functionality of the services, of the architecture, and of the API and SPI sets, is outlined in this section, and described in detail in Sections 5 through 10.

The specification defines a standard set of interfaces such that, for example, an application that uses the API set to communicate with a particular service provider can work with a service provider of another conformant vendor, without any changes.

The specification is intended to be usable within all implementations and versions of the Windows operating systems, from Windows version 3.1, Windows for Workgroups version 3.1 and the initial versions of Windows NT, and onwards. It thus provides for both 16 and 32 bit operating environments (operating under the Win32s subsystem in 16 bit environments).

Although the WOSA Extensions for Financial Services define a general architecture for access to service providers from Windows-based applications, the initial focus of the Banking Systems Vendor Council has been on providing access to peripheral devices that are unique to financial institutions. Since these devices are often complex, difficult to manage and proprietary, the development of a standardized interface to them from Windows-based applications and Windows operating systems can offer financial institutions and their solution providers immediate enhancements to productivity and flexibility.

Other issues critical to financial enterprise computing will also be addressed in the future by the Banking Systems Vendor Council, and similar definitions for these areas will be added to the Extensions for Financial Services (or as basic WOSA elements). These are expected to include:

- Financial transaction messaging and management
- Network and system management
- Security
- Emerging technologies such as object-oriented development, multimedia capabilities and pen computing

See Section 4 for more detail.

Architecture

The architecture of the WOSA Extensions for Financial Services (WOSA/XFS) system is shown below.

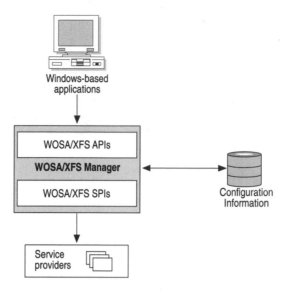

Figure 14.8   WOSA Extensions for Financial Services Architecture.

The applications communicate with service providers, via the WOSA Extensions for Financial Services Manager, using the API set. Most of these APIs can be invoked either "synchronously" (the Manager causes the application to wait until the API's function is completed) or "asynchronously" (the application regains control immediately, while the function is performed in parallel).

The common deliverable in all implementations of this WOSA Extensions for Financial Services specification is the WOSA Extensions for Financial Services Manager, which maps the specified API to the corresponding SPI, then routes this request to the appropriate service provider. The Manager uses the configuration information to route the API call (made to a "logical service" or a "logical device") to the proper service provider entry point (which is always local, even though the device or service that is the final target may be remote). Note that even though the API calls may be either synchronous or asynchronous, the SPI calls are always asynchronous.

The developers of financial services to be used via XFS and the manufacturers of financial peripherals will be responsible for the development and distribution of service providers for their services and devices. A setup routine for each device or service will also be necessary to define the appropriate configuration information. This information will allow an application to request capability and status information about the devices and services available at any point in time.

The primary functions of the service providers are to:

- Translate generic (e.g., forms-based) service requests to service-specific commands.

- Route the requests to either a local service or device, or to one on a remote system, effectively defining a peer-to-peer interface among service providers.

- Arbitrate access by multiple applications to a single service or device, providing exclusive access when requested.

- Manage the hardware interfaces to services or devices.

- Manage the asynchronous nature of the services and devices in an appropriate manner, always presenting this capability to the XFS Manager and the applications via Windows messages.

The system design supports solution of complex problems, often not addressed by current systems, by providing for maximum flexibility in all its capabilities:

- Multiple service providers, developed by multiple vendors, can coexist in a single system and in a network.

- The service class definition is based on the logical functionalities of the service, with no assumption being made as to the physical configuration. A physical device that includes multiple distinct physical capabilities (referred to as a "compound device" in this specification) is treated as several logical services; the service provider resolves any conflicts. Note also that a logical service may include multiple physical devices (for example, a cash dispenser consisting of a note dispenser and coin dispenser).

- Similarly, a physical device may be shared between two or more users (e.g., tellers), and the physical device synchronization is managed at the service provider level.

- The API definition and associated services provide time-out functionality to allow applications to avoid deadlock of the type that can occur if two applications try to get exclusive access to multiple services at the same time.

- The architecture is designed to provide a framework for future development of network and system monitoring, measurement, and management.

Note that Figure 14.8 is a high level view of the architecture and, in particular, it makes no distinction between service providers and the services they manage. This specification focuses on service providers rather than on services, because the way a service provider communicates with a service is a vendor-specific internal design issue that applications and the XFS Manager are unaware of. In fact, there are many different ways that service providers can make services available to applications. Hence, this specification refers primarily to the service providers, since these are the modules with which the XFS Manager communicates. There are occasional references to 'service' where this is appropriate.

Example

Figure 14.9 below shows a WOSA/XFS system supporting a set of financial peripherals. Note that in this framework the XFS Manager interfaces directly with a set of service providers that interface directly with the physical devices. Thus, the service providers are shown as implementing the service provider, service, and device driver functions, although these are more likely to be two or more separate layers. Many other configurations are possible.

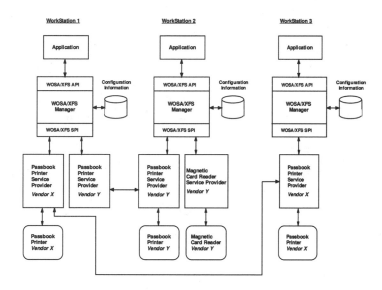

Figure 14.9   A WOSA/XFS architecture example for a branch office banking system.

It should also be noted that one vendor's service providers are not necessarily compatible with another vendor's, as shown in Figure 14.9. If one application has to access the same service class as implemented by different vendors, a service provider is installed for each vendor.

API and SPI Summary

Sections 5 through 7 of this document present the interfaces that allow a financial application to communicate in a standard fashion with financial services and devices. The functions are at a sufficiently high level to allow for seamless redirection to other parts of the underlying operating system. A printer, for example, might rely on a set of services provided by the operating system, but in order to handle the unique characteristics of a financial printer and application, the service provider would preprocess the command, then redirect the derived commands to the operating system's printing services. In other implementations, the printer might be supported entirely by WOSA/XFS service mechanisms, and not use the operating system printing services in any way.

The API is structured as sets of:

- **Basic functions**, such as **StartUp/CleanUp**, **Open/Close**, **Lock/Unlock**, and **Execute**, that are common to all the WOSA Extensions for Financial Services device/service classes,
- **Administration functions**, such as device initialization, reset, suspend or resume, used for managing devices and services, and
- **Specific commands**, used to request device/service-specific functions, and sent to devices and services as a parameter of the **Execute** basic function.

To the maximum extent possible, the syntax of specific commands that are used with multiple device/service classes is kept consistent across all devices. A primary objective is to standardize function codes and structures for the widest possible variety of devices.

The SPI is kept as similar as possible to the API. Some commands are processed exclusively by the XFS Manager, and so are not in the SPI, and there are minor differences in the specific parameters passed at the two interface levels.

A typical scenario showing the usage of the APIs is shown below. This example illustrates the functions used to print a form.

- **StartUp** (connects the application to the XFS Manager, including version negotiation)
- **Open** (establishes a session between the application and the service provider)
- **Register** (specifies the messages that the application should receive from the service provider)
- **Lock** (obtains exclusive access to the service by the application)

  multiple **Execute** functions, passing one or more specific commands:

  Print_Form

  etc.
- **Unlock** (releases exclusive access to the service by the application)
- **Deregister** (specifies that the application should no longer receive messages from the service provider)
- **Close** (ends the session between the application and the service provider)
- **CleanUp** (disconnects the application from the XFS Manager)

Note that within a session (defined by **Open** and **Close**), an application may at any time change the classes of messages it wishes to receive from the service provider (using **Register**), and may either **Lock** the service only for specified periods (typically for each transaction), or for the entire session. Also, note that several of the commands are optional, depending on how the device is being managed and shared (i.e., **Lock/Unlock**, **Register/Deregister**).

Device Classes

The following classes of devices are being implemented for the first version of the WOSA Extensions for Financial Services:

- Printers
  Receipt
  Journal
  Passbook
  Document

- Magnetic stripe readers / writers
  Swipe
  Dip
  Motorized
  Writeable

- Cash dispensers (note, coin and check)
  ATMs
  Teller cash dispensers

- PIN pads
  with and without display
  with and without encryption

- Check readers
  MICR
  OCR
  image scan

The following classes of devices or services, and others that customers and vendors request, will be evaluated for inclusion in future versions of this specification:

- Smart cards

- Depositories

- Signature capture devices

- Bar code readers

- Card embossers

- Hologram readers

Other WOSA Components

This section briefly describes the current components of the Window Open Services Architecture. For more information on any of the components, refer to the individual specifications (see Appendix F for details on how to get more information on WOSA and its components). WOSA is an extensible and growing environment; additional components will be added in areas such as directory services, distributed security, and systems management, as well as vertical market extensions such as the Extension for Financial Services.

Enterprise Communications

WOSA includes a set of components that address the key issue of connectivity, based on formal or de facto standards for enterprise communications that can be valuable in financial enterprise computing: the Windows SNA APIs, Windows RPC and Windows Sockets.

Windows SNA APIs

The set of Windows SNA APIs were defined and endorsed by a working group consisting of Microsoft, IBM and other leading industry vendors. Since SNA communications are critical to many financial services environments, these are key tools for integrating systems based on the WOSA Extensions for Financial Services into the existing infrastructure in financial institutions. The companies involved in the definition of the SNA API specifications include: Andrew Corporation, Attachmate, Computer Logics, Data Connection, Digital Communications Associates, Easel, Eicon Technology, FutureSoft, IBM, ICOT, International Computers Limited, Microsoft, MultiSoft, AT&T Global Information Solutions, Network Software Associates, Novell, Olivetti, Siemens Nixdorf, Systems Strategies and Wall Data.

This jointly developed set of specifications defines standard interfaces between Windows-based applications and IBM SNA protocols, and is a key connectivity component of the Windows Open Services Architecture (WOSA). An application written to these interfaces will be able to run unchanged over many vendors' SNA connectivity products under Windows. Also, since the APIs are not tied to a particular version of the Windows operating system, programmers can incorporate a common set of SNA code into their applications that will run on Windows, Windows for Workgroups and Windows NT, as well as future versions of Windows.

The Windows SNA API sets are listed below. Please refer to the individual specifications for each of these components for additional details.

- **Windows LUA (enables IBM 4700-compatible communications)** The Logical Unit Application (LUA; commonly referred to as LU0) API is used to gain access to the lower-level SNA data streams that are common, especially in financial services environments. The specification includes both the basic Request Unit Interface (RUI) API and the higher level Session Level Interface (SLI) API.

- **Windows APPC** The Advanced Program-to-Program Communication (APPC) API is used to write cooperative applications for the LU6.2 protocol.

- **Windows CPI-C** The Common Programming Interface for Communications (CPI-C) API also uses the LU6.2 protocol to write cooperative applications for the LU6.2 protocol.

- **Windows HLLAPI (enables 3270/5250 emulation)** The High Level Language API (HLLAPI) allows application programs to interact with a host using existing 3270 and 5250 emulation products.

- **Windows CSV (enables communication with IBM NetView)** The Common Service Verbs (CSV) API provides interfaces for communication with the IBM NetView management system and for character set translations.

Windows RPC (Remote Procedure Call)

The Windows RPC interface provides a standard Windows API for access to the Remote Procedure Call capability for network-independent interprocess communication in heterogenous distributed environments. RPC makes the development of client-server applications easier, and supports interoperability with other OSF/DCE RPC-compliant systems. The Windows RPC interface is supported by the Windows NT operating system, and defined in the Windows NT Software Development Kit (SDK).

Windows Sockets

The Windows Sockets specification defines a Windows API that is useful in many environments, especially for communication between Windows-based clients and UNIX hosts/servers. This specification defines a network programming interface for Windows, based on the "socket" paradigm popularized in the Berkeley Software Distribution from the University of California at Berkeley. The Berkeley Sockets programming model is a de facto standard for TCP/IP networking. The Windows Sockets API is consistent with release 4.3 of the Berkeley Software Distribution (4.3BSD).

The Windows Sockets API includes both the familiar Berkeley socket style routines and a set of Windows-specific extensions designed to allow the programmer to take advantage of the message-driven nature of Windows. It is intended to provide a single API to which application developers can program and multiple network software vendors can conform, and to simplify the task of porting existing sockets-based source code. It has a high degree of familiarity for programmers familiar with programming with sockets in UNIX and other environments.

MAPI (Messaging API)

The MAPI specification, developed in consultation with independent software developers and industry consultants, defines an application interface and a service provider interface that help ensure complete system independence for messaging applications and services. This allows mixing and matching of mail front ends (and other message-enabled applications) with service providers, giving organizations the freedom to choose messaging systems and applications according to what best fits their needs, rather than being limited to the few that happen to be compatible.

These capabilities have enormous impact on enterprise messaging systems: adding messaging features to any Windows-based application is easy for developers, making basic workgroup activities, such as sharing documents, reports and charts, easy for end users. MAPI also encourages the development of advanced workgroup applications that give workers better ways to work cooperatively, sharing and exchanging information in a corporate setting.

ODBC (Open Database Connectivity)

ODBC is an open, vendor-neutral interface for database connectivity that provides access to a variety of PC, minicomputer and mainframe systems – including Windows-based systems and the Apple Macintosh – in an easy, consistent manner. It has wide support from the leading database vendors, allowing access to virtually all databases, as well as many other vendors pledging ODBC support of their tools. An emerging industry standard for client-server database access, ODBC is an implementation of the Call Level Interface specification developed by the SQL Access Group, a group of more than 40 vendors committed to database interoperability. ODBC has also been endorsed by the SQL Access Group.

ODBC provides a universal method for accessing both SQL and non-SQL data. Implementing ODBC speeds the development of applications that support multiple database management systems, reduces application complexity and minimizes support requirements for both solutions providers and DBMS vendors.

License Service API

The License Service API is a specification that will provide one consistent way for application developers to incorporate software licensing into their applications. This, in turn, will help companies ensure compliance with licensing agreements when using developers' software. The License Service API was jointly developed and announced by more than twenty industry leaders, including independent software vendors, the Software Publishers Association and the Microcomputer Managers Association.

The API enables software publishers to develop applications that cooperate with the different licensing systems that will support the standard. The application program is isolated from the details of license management. A License Service API-compliant application simply requests permission to run. The underlying licensing system, in turn, grants or denies permission based on the availability of a license for the requesting application.

The specification, which embodies five functions, standardizes one aspect of software licensing: the API used by applications software to access licensing services. There are further areas that can be defined, including standardization of license policies and the license format. License Service API is designed to facilitate the most common policies such as concurrent use, personal use and others.

Windows Telephony API

The Windows Telephony API defines a standard, open set of interfaces to give Windows-based applications access to circuit-switched telephone networks, providing call establishment and control, including advanced functions such as hold, transfer, conference call and call park. The API provides maximum flexibility for transparently connecting PCs to all types of telephone systems, while isolating applications from the complexity of the wide variety of these systems (analog, key system, PBX, ISDN, cellular, etc.). These capabilities allow computing devices running Windows to be full participants in the global telephone network.

WOSA Extensions for Real-Time Market Data

The WOSA Extensions for Real-Time Market Data have been defined by a multi-vendor group, the Open Market Data Council for Windows. The goal is to provide a standard mechanism for applications to exchange live market data and news, based on the Object Linking and Embedding 2.0 (OLE 2.0) technology. The WOSA Extensions for Real-Time Market Data define a standardized use of OLE 2.0, which allow applications to receive and exchange the market data and news that are the lifeblood of the banking and securities industries, in a common, open format, no matter what the source.

The Future of WOSA and the Extensions for Financial Services

The members of the Banking Systems Vendor Council recognize that a variety of other issues are important to the success of financial services computing systems. Although the current version of the WOSA Extensions for Financial Services does not address these issues, it is the intention of the Banking Systems Vendor Council to address them in later versions of the Extensions. This will involve standardized APIs, through the adoption of existing formal or de facto standards, through the extension of existing standards as appropriate, or through the creation of new interfaces where necessary. Many of these APIs may be included as standard elements of WOSA, with general applicability to enterprise computing. The following areas will be addressed:

Financial Transaction Messaging and Management

The initial version of the WOSA Extensions for Financial Services does not define standard interfaces for financial transaction messaging. It is the intention of the Banking Systems Vendor Council to ensure access to this functionality in later versions of the Extensions. Existing examples that are candidates for adoption include the X/Open DTP specifications.

Network and System Management

The members of the Banking Systems Vendor Council recognize that powerful, flexible centralized control of a network of branch offices is critical to the success of financial services institutions. Although the current version of the WOSA

Extensions for Financial Services does not consider or support the management of networks in financial enterprises, it is the intention of the Banking Systems Vendor Council to address these needs in later versions of the Extensions. The areas to be addressed include:

- Remote system control
- Alarm generation
- Fault and problem management
- Performance measurement, analysis and management
- Resource utilization tracking ("accounting" issues)
- Configuration management (hardware and software)
- License management
- Software distribution, including automatic notification, optional rollback, etc.

Security

The wide range of issues related to system security is also critical to the success of financial services computing systems. Although the current version of the WOSA Extensions for Financial Services does not define access to security mechanisms, it is the intention of the Banking Systems Vendor Council to address these needs in later versions of the Extensions. The areas to be addressed include:

- Access control
- User authentication
- Encryption/decryption
- Key management

As in other areas, interfaces to existing standards (such as DES, Kerberos, etc.) will be evaluated and adopted wherever possible.

Emerging technologies

The members of the Banking Systems Vendor Council will evaluate a variety of other technologies as they evolve, to understand their impact on the financial services computing environment. These will include object-oriented development and system paradigms, multimedia hardware and software capabilities, and pen-based systems.

Topic

Describe the services that WOSA XRT provides to the application developer.

Content

WOSA Extensions for Real-Time Market Data[3]

Objective

The WOSA/XRT Design Specification serves one main purpose: Define a binary standard for accessing real-time market data from Windows applications There are two groups of individuals that will benefit from defining this standard—developers and customers.

Developers will receive the following benefits:

- There will be a common interface for accessing real time data.
- Application development will become tool independent.

Customers will receive the following benefits:

- The applications will be easier to use.
- It will give the customer the choice of off the shelf OLE 2.0 compliant applications to use for their solutions, which will allow these solutions to be developed and implemented faster.

---

[3] Excerpted from "Windows Open Services Architecture Specification." Complete text for this specification is available on the Microsoft Developer Network Development Library, under Specifications. Copyright 1992 - 1995. Used with permission. All rights reserved.

- The technology that WOSA/XRT provides allows real-time data users to focus on business problems rather than data access problems.

For example, if a Solution Provider (Independent Software Developers, Independent Consultants, etc.) decides to use Microsoft Office to create an application which accesses real-time market data, the OLE 2.0 interface of WOSA/XRT would allow the application to be created in a high level language such as Visual Basic for Applications or Visual Basic 3.0. The application could be seamlessly integrated with the Microsoft Office giving, ease of use, flexibility, and customizability.

The above noted customer and developer benefits will have a positive impact on the use of real-time market data. Better, easier, and more frequent use of real-time market data will lead to increased numbers of users. This in turn will eventually lower the cost each user is charged in reaction to the forces of supply and demand.

It is important to note this specification is not intended to solve all problems relating to real-time market data access. The following list of topics is intended to clearly delineate those areas not initially addressed by Version 1.0 of WOSA/XRT. Because WOSA/XRT is based on OLE 2.0 technology, and because a basic premise of OLE 2.0 is that an object user can 'Query' an object for its capabilities, there is no reason why future versions of WOSA/XRT cannot address the issues noted below and still maintain complete backwards compatibility.

- **Over The Wire Formats**. WOSA/XRT Version 1.0 defines a standard way in which Windows applications can access market data. It assumes that there are already existing mechanisms for getting that data from the server or data feed onto the users machine. WOSA/XRT Version 1.0 does not define a networking model, protocol stacks, or "over the wire data formats."

- **Cross Platform Interoperability**. WOSA/XRT Version 1.0 targets Windows desktop applications only. There are no specific provisions in WOSA/XRT Version 1.0 for Interoperability with other operating systems beyond those provided by OLE 2.0. However, Microsoft is committed to providing OLE Interoperability with other operating systems such as UNIX; when those systems become available WOSA/XRT will interoperate seemlessly.

- **Ticker Plants / Feed Servers**. WOSA/XRT Version 1.0 is focused on solving the very real problem of getting market data into off-the-shelf Windows applications. This specification does not attempt to directly address the issues of creating object oriented "ticker plants" or data feed servers. However, much of the technology described here and in the OLE 2.0 Specification could be used to implement these components.

- **Normalize Symbology**. It is beyond the scope of this version of WOSA/XRT to try to 'normalize' the Symbology used by the vendors in the market data industry.

WOSA/XRT Design Overview

The following diagram illustrates WOSA/XRT's role in the larger scope of Real-Time Market data access. This diagram should make it clear that Version 1.0 of WOSA/XRT is concerned only with providing access to real-time market data from desktop applications.

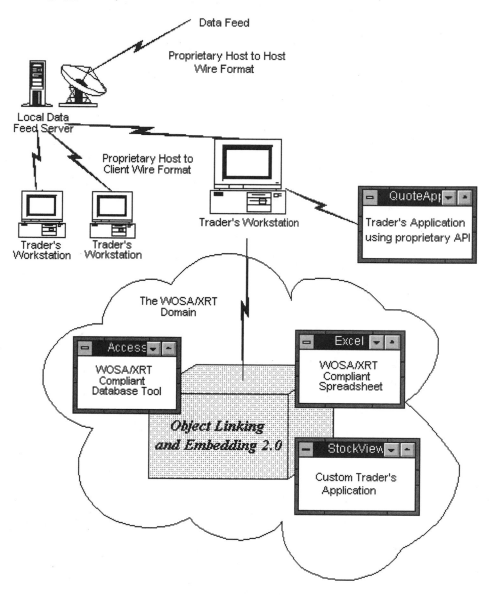

Figure 14.10   Design overview

Requirements

This specification must define a standard that meets the following requirements:

- Applicability to 'desktop-app.' based solutions. The key requirement for WOSA/XRT is to simplify access to real-time and semi-real-time market data from desktop Windows applications. Users and integrators should be able to easily integrate real-time market data from multiple vendors using commercial Windows applications:

    - Interoperability with Commercial OLE 2.0 Enabled Windows Applications.

    - Any application that serves as an OLE 2.0 container and OLE Automation controller should be able to utilize WOSA/XRT Data Objects.

    - OLE Automation as a development tool.

    - WOSA/XRT data objects must be able to be controlled and accessed through OLE Automation.

    - Advanced User Interface.

    - While the WOSA/XRT specification does not specify any user interface guidelines, it is essential that the specification allow for any of the advanced user interface features made possible by OLE 2.0.

- Normalize access to multiple data sources. It is a requirement of this specification that a common interface be presented by all Data Objects.

- Permissioning. WOSA/XRT must provide a standard mechanism for vendors to ensure that only those users who have the rights to the data can access it from their desktop applications.

- Interactive and Broadcast Feeds. The WOSA/XRT architecture must be able to handle market data from both interactive and broadcast feeds.

- High-performance data transfer. It is required that the system be capable of maintaining a transaction rate of at least 400 data changes a second.

- The OMDC has specified that 300–400 messages a second are possible during peak market periods on a 486/25 with 16 MB RAM.

Architecture Overview

Step 1: Data User creates instance of Data Object and obtains IUnknown*

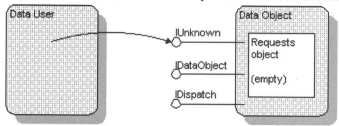

Step 2: Data User obtains IDispatch* and requests items and properties (OLE Automation)

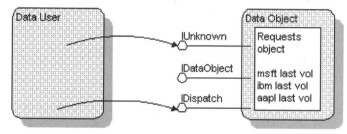

Step 3: Data User obtains IDataObject* and begins Uniform Data Transfer

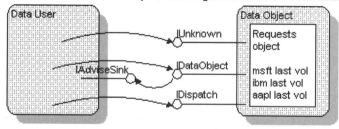

Figure 14.11   Architecture overview

The WOSA/XRT architecture is based on two components of OLE 2.0: OLE
Automation and Uniform Data Transfer (UDT). Automation is used by the client
application to make requests of the data source. Data is then transferred from the
data source to the client through UDT.*

---

* See the OLE 2.0 Software Development Kit for details of OLE Automation
and Uniform Data Transfer.

In this specification the term Data User is used to indicate the client application, while the OLE object that provides the standard interface to the data source is called the Data Object. A Data Object supports IDispatch (Automation) and IDataObject (UDT), while the Data User supports IAdviseSink (UDT).

As with any OLE 2.0 object, a WOSA/XRT Data Object supports the necessary OLE interfaces and supports the creation of an OLE 2.0 class object (i.e. supports IClassFactory::CreateInstance). This is called the Object Server, which can instantiate a specific instance of the Data Object. A data feed vendor or integrator may implement any number of Object Servers which can support more than one Data Object class. Each WOSA/XRT Data Object must have Class ID associated with it and must be correctly registered in the Registration Database. Therefore, developing a WOSA/XRT Data Object is essentially the same as developing any other OLE 2.0 object; the only possible difference is the interfaces the object supports.

The overall architecture of WOSA/XRT is a request-advise–based system. This works by doing the following:

1. A Data User obtains a pointer to a Data Object.
2. The Data User requests the items (and properties) it is interested in (this is done through OLE Automation (IDispatch)).
3. (optional) the Data User sets up an advise sink (which is similar to a call back function) where it will receive notifications from the Data Object that some or all of the items it has requested have changed property values.

Steps 1 and 2 typically involve concepts revolving around OLE Automation and the WOSA/XRT Programmability Interface and step 3 involves Uniform Data Transfer and the WOSA/XRT Data Formats.

There are essentially three techniques that can be used by the Data User to receive the data:

- Implement an IAdviseSink
- OLE 2.0 Linking
- Poll through OLE Automation

Implement an IAdviseSink

An OLE 2.0 Container application which serves as a WOSA/XRT Data User should implement an IAdviseSink interface that understands the WOSA/XRT clipboard format (see section 6.2 The WOSA/XRT Clipboard Format).

The following Visual Basic for Applications (VBA) example illustrates how a Data User would create an instance of a Data Object, make requests of the object, and setup the advise sink:

Code	Purpose

`Dim xrtobj As DataObject`
 	
`Dim props As Properties`
	Declare a VBA variables.. Since the add-in provides a typelibrary, DataObject can be declared as a WOSA/XRT object. xrtobj must be declared at the module or project level since it will be referenced in at least two separate functions.

`Set xrtobj =`
`Realtime.Extension.DataObjects.CreateObject(`
`"QuoteMaster.Quotes", "Lisa's Data")`
	Call the add-ins CreateObject method, telling the add-in to create an instance of 'QuoteMaster.Quotes', and to return the object's IDispatch pointer. The name is required by the add-in to keep track of multiple data objects.

`Set xrtobj = CreateObje`
`Call the VBA function CreateObject, telling`
`itct("QuoteMaster.Quotes")`
	Call the VBA function CreateObject, telling it to create a pointer.n instance of 'QuoteMaster.Quotes', and to return the object's IDispatch pointer.

`xrtobj.Requests.Add("USD:*", "German` `Mark","British Pound", "Japanese Yen")`	Request to be updated on the exchange rates for the US Dollar vs. the Mark, Pound, and Yen.
`xrtobj.Requests.Add("MSFT", "Last",` `"Volume")`	Request to be update whenever the Last or Volume properties of the MSFT security change.
`xrtobj.OnDataChange = "VBDataChangeCallback"`	Specify a VBA subroutine for the add-in to call each time the add-in receives a data update from the WOSA/XRT object.
`xrtobj.GetData "workbook.xls", "sheet1", B2"`	Initialize spreadsheet with data.
`xrtobj.Actve = True`	Tell the DataObject to start sending notifications to the IAdviseSink.

`Sub VBDataChangeCallback()`
`xrtobj.GetData "workbook.xls", "sheet1", B2"`
`End Sub`
	Implement callback subroutine. The subroutine can contain any VBA code. In this example, we want the spreadsheet to be updated with the latest data.

When the Data Object passes Excel new data through IAdviseSink, Excel makes that data available to worksheets via an Automation interface and/or worksheet callable functions. Refer to the WOSA/XRT Excel Real-time Add-in User's Guide for more information.

In the above example, the fictional data feed vendor "QuoteMaster" has defined properties (fields) such as "German Mark", "Last", and "Volume". WOSA/XRT does not define a standard set of these property names. It is recognized that in the Market Data Industry, each vendor treats the meaning of properties differently, and it is beyond the scope of this standard to rectify this situation. [*]

OLE 2.0 Linking

While it is not a requirement of WOSA/XRT objects to support all of the OLE 2.0 linking interfaces, it is anticipated that many objects will.[*] In the case where a WOSA/XRT object does support the linking interfaces, the user will simply be able to use standard clipboard operations to paste a linked WOSA/XRT object into their document.

Polling through OLE Automation

In many cases it is not necessary to access market data in true real-time. Many users simply need to have the latest data available at any time. These solutions can use polling to request the latest data from the Data Object at predefined intervals using only OLE Automation.[*]

If getting true real-time updates is not a priority, there are several advantages to a polling based solution:

- **Ease of implementation**. The Data User, in order to receive update notifications must implement the IAdviseSink interface. However, this interface is not natively implemented (or not easily accessible) in some common

---

[*] It is possible that future versions of WOSA/XRT will provide a mechanism for programmatically requesting a list of the properties a Data object supports.

[*] Objects built using the Microsoft Foundation Classes (MFC) 2.5 get OLE 2.0 Linking support "free."

[*] This type of solution could also use notifications. The Data Objects are required to support a method that allows the Data User to specify how often update notifications are made. The Data User could essentially say, "Update me very *n* seconds."

programming environments, such as Visual Basic 3.0 and Visual Basic for Applications. These applications require a DLL or a VBX to use the advise sink. This additional complexity can cause confusion for end users.

- **Less load on system resources**. Each IAdviseSink::OnDataChange notification requires some CPU cycles to process the changed data. By only asking for data when it is needed, a polling system can result in more responsive applications.

The sample VBA code below illustrates how a polling only solution would be implemented:

Code	Purpose
`xrtobj.Username = UserName`	WOSA/XRT supports user level permissioning[*]
`xrtobj.Password = Password`	Finish logging in by setting the password property
`Set p = xrtobj.Requests.CreateProperties("High","Low", "Last", "Volume")`	Create a Properties object that contains "High", "Low", "Last", "Volume" properties.
`xrtobj.Requests.Add("MSFT", p)`	Add a request for the "High", "Low", "Last", and "Volume" on "MSFT" to the Requests object.
`xrtobj.Requests.Add("AAPL", p)`	Add a request for the "High", "Low", "Last", and "Volume" on "AAPL" to the Reqeusts object.
`xrtobj.Requests.Add("NOVL", p)`	Add a request for the "High", "Low", "Last", and "Volume" on "NOVL" to the Reqeusts object.
`For Each o In p`	Output column headings by iterating over the Properties object p.
`    Debug.Print o.Name + Chr$(8)`	Print the name property of the current Property, followed by a tab character.
`Next`	
`Debug.Print Chr$(13)`	Print a new line.
`Set all = xrtobj.Items`	Set the variable 'all' to the Data Object's Items object

---

[*] User, application, and machine-level permissioning is supported.

Code	Purpose
`For Each i In all`	Iterate through the Items collection, which represents a snapshot of the data feed.
`For Each prop In i`	Iterate through all the properties of the current Item object (i).
`Debug.Print prop.Value + Chr$(8)`	Print the value property of the current Property.
`Next`	
`Debug.Print Chr$(13)`	Print a new line.
`Next`	

The Debug window in Visual Basic for Applications in Excel 5.0 would show the following output after the above code was executed:

Name	High	Low	Last	Volume
MSFT	95.75	94.25	95	39023
AAPL	23.875	22	23	31211
NOVL	47.5	42.25	43.5	12123

As this sample shows a Data Object's Properties, Requests, and Items properties are implemented and exposed as OLE Automation collections.[*]

---

[*] See the OLE 2.0 SDK documentation and the document COLLECT.DOC for more information on collections and properties.

Index

X

WELCOME TO THE WORLD OF WINDOWS® 95

The MICROSOFT®
WINDOWS 95
RESOURCE KIT
provides you with all of
the information necessary
to plan for and implement
Windows 95 in your
organization.

ISBN 1-55615-678-2
1376 pages, $49.95 ($67.95 Canada)
One CD-ROM

Details on how to install, configure, and support Windows 95 will save you hours of time and help ensure that you get the most from your computing investment. This exclusive Microsoft publication, written in cooperation with the Windows 95 development team, is the perfect technical companion for network administrators, support professionals, systems integrators, and computer professionals.

The MICROSOFT WINDOWS 95 RESOURCE KIT contains important information that will help you get the most out of Windows 95. Whether you support Windows 95 in your company or just want to know more about it, the MICROSOFT WINDOWS 95 RESOURCE KIT is a valuable addition to your reference library.

The Information You Need to Become an Expert on Windows NT!

A One-Stop Comprehensive Resource
Microsoft® Windows NT™ Resource Kit, version 3.51

Support for Windows NT Workstations and Windows NT Advanced Server is crucial to those installing and administering this powerful operating system. There's simply no better source of support than the MICROSOFT WINDOWS NT RESOURCE KIT. This third edition covers the recently released Windows NT version 3.51 by including a new volume, *Microsoft Windows NT version 3.51 Update*, that covers the changes in version 3.51. The MICROSOFT WINDOWS NT RESOURCE KIT shows you how to install, configure, troubleshoot, and optimize Windows NT Workstation and Windows NT Advanced Server on the following hardware platforms: Intel®, MIPS®, and Digital Alpha AXP™. At more than 3000 pages in five volumes, with one CD, this is the most complete source of information on Windows NT available anywhere. The CD includes many new utilities, technical updates of the main utilities, and support for the PowerPC.

Windows NT Resource Kit Utilities on CD-ROM

The CD-ROM contains an indispensable collection of utilities and accessory programs for supporting, troubleshooting, and optimizing Windows NT. Utilities are compiled for both Intel and Windows NT–compatible RISC-based systems.

Pick up yours today!
$199.95 ($269.95 Canada)
ISBN 1-55615-926-9

Exclusively for Owners of the Microsoft Windows NT Resource Kit version 3.5

Microsoft® Windows NT™ version 3.51 Update
This book-and-CD package provides owners of the *Windows NT Resource Kit version 3.5* with an inexpensive way to update their Kits to version 3.51. This all-new volume provides extensive coverage of the features that are new to Windows NT version 3.51 and updates and corrects the four main volumes in the resource kit. It also contains the Resource Kit Update CD, which includes many new utilities, technical updates of the main utilities, and support for the PowerPC. To use this update effectively, you must have the four-volume *Windows NT Resource Kit version 3.5*.

$39.95 ($53.95 Canada)
ISBN 1-55615-928-5
